AUSTRALIAN LIVES

AUSTRALIAN LIVES

An Intimate History

ANISA PURI AND ALISTAIR THOMSON

MONASH University Publishing

Monash University Publishing
Matheson Library and Information Services Building
40 Exhibition Walk
Monash University
Clayton, Victoria 3800, Australia
www.publishing.monash.edu

Monash University Publishing brings to the world publications which advance the best traditions of humane and enlightened thought.

Monash University Publishing titles pass through a rigorous process of independent peer review.

www.publishing.monash.edu/books/al-9781922235787.html

Series: Australian History
Series Editor: Sean Scalmer

Design: Les Thomas

Cover image: Charles Blackman (b. 1960), *Suite I* 1960.
Oil on composition board, 120.7 x 182.2cm.
Purchased 1988 with funds from the Russell Cuppaidge Bequest as a memorial to Russell Cuppaidge, CBE. Queensland Art Gallery Collection. Image courtesy QAGOMA.
© Charles Blackman. Licensed by Viscopy, 2017.

National Library of Australia Cataloguing-in-Publication entry:

Creator:	Puri, Anisa, author.
Title:	Australian lives : an intimate history / Anisa Puri and Alistair Thomson
ISBN:	9781922235787 (paperback)
Series:	Australian history.
Subjects:	Australians--Interviews.
	Australians--Social life and customs--20th century.
	Australia--Social conditions--20th century.
	Australia--Social conditions--21st century.
	Australia--History--20th century.
	Australia--History--21st century.
Other Creators/Contributors:	
	Thomson, Alistair, author.
Dewey number:	994

Printed in Australia by Griffin Press an Accredited ISO AS/NZS 14001:2004 Environmental Management System printer.

MIX
Paper from responsible sources
FSC www.fsc.org FSC® C009448

The paper this book is printed on is certified against the Forest Stewardship Council ® Standards. Griffin Press holds FSC chain of custody certification SGS-COC-005088. FSC promotes environmentally responsible, socially beneficial and economically viable management of the world's forests.

CONTENTS

We dedicate this book to our brothers,
Andrew Thomson and Nikhil Puri,
with affection and admiration.

INTRODUCTION

Intimate History

Intimate histories illuminate everyday life as it changes across time. Big picture histories often focus on pivotal events of politics, war or industry that are well-chronicled and widely reported. The lives of so-called 'ordinary people', and how they are affected by social, economic and political forces, are less well-documented and require novel historical sources.

Oral history preserves the memories of people who may not have written about their lives in diaries, letters or memoirs, or whose personal records have not survived. It widens the scope of history and increases the range of historical characters. Oral history is especially effective in capturing the more intimate aspects of everyday lives—love and loss, moving home or country, sustaining or questioning faith—that are too easily left out of history's big picture. In interviews people recount romance, migration or religion, and in doing so they convey the meanings and feelings of experience: what it felt like to arrive in a new country or start at school; what it meant to join a church or leave your marriage; and why you opted for one career and not another.

Of course, none of us live in a vacuum and none of these life decisions and events are solely individual or truly independent. To paraphrase Karl Marx, we make our own lives but not in circumstances of our own choosing. Intimate history shows how individuals live with, and sometimes against, the compelling forces of economy, society and politics and, at times, the natural world. Take, for example, Patricia (Trish) Barrkman's account of divorce in Brisbane in the 1970s, which is detailed in the chapters on Midlife and Activism. Trish had been married for two decades, had followed her husband's career across several states and was raising their three children when she learnt her husband was having an affair. To attain a divorce in 1974, Trish had to embark on a painful and embarrassing process of finding witnesses who could attest in court to his adultery. One year later, the Family Law Act introduced no fault divorce and 'that was a whole new ball game. So, suddenly, everybody was separating'. Trish explains that divorce was still frowned upon in Brisbane suburban society, and describes how she fought outdated school rules that discriminated against single mothers like her, who needed to work full-time, and their so-called 'latchkey children'. Trish read Germaine Greer's path-breaking feminist text *The Female Eunuch* (published in 1970) and became 'a bit of a women's libber'. In Trish's account we can see the interaction of family dynamics, social attitudes, economic pressures, political activism and legal reform. We can also see how such interactions between individuals and society change across time, and how people might effect change in small or large ways.

People's ability to determine or resist the circumstances that impact on their lives depends to a great extent on resources and power. Throughout this book people describe lives buffeted by circumstance and explain how they were more or less successful in managing events and determining their future. Yet people can also be activists, seeking to transform the world beyond their immediate family. In the chapter on Activism, Australians of all ages and backgrounds describe involvement in politics and protest, community campaigning or voluntary work. They explain how and why they tried to make a difference, to ameliorate or alter the circumstances that shape their own and other people's lives.

Intimate histories are engaging and accessible. In each person's life there are poignant, insightful and often very funny stories, about birth and death, growing up and growing old, working life and simple pleasures. At the end of her interview, Melbourne woman Kim Bear explains that 'stories are a great way to inform people about what it is to be human'. Of her life history, which started in Canberra in 1965, Rhonda King reflects that 'it's got elements of comedy and there are elements of heartache and drama and thriller—it's got so many things in it'. In *Australian Lives* Rhonda recounts losing her father, and a sister with cerebral palsy, becoming a teenage mum, and having a turbulent life with the Mormons. You'll read that Kim Bear left home at sixteen, terminated a teenage pregnancy and decided in her thirties not to become a mother. You'll discover that Trish Barrkman survived kidney disease and became an advocate for renal patients and organ donation. Each story in *Australian Lives* is intimate and unique, yet together they speak of larger themes in Australian history and contemporary Australian society.

Creating *Australian Lives*

The life stories in this book were recorded for the Australian Generations Oral History Project, a collaboration between historians at Monash and La Trobe universities, the National Library of Australia, and ABC Radio National.[1] Between 2011 and 2014 we recorded 300 life history interviews—averaging four hours each—across Australia. We chose the 300 participants from just under 700 people who volunteered to be interviewed. Our selection aimed to ensure the interview archive would comprise a diverse range of Australians in terms of age (about fifty born each decade from the 1930s to the 1980s, with a sprinkling born in the 1920s), social class and educational background, gender, sexuality, disability, region (roughly proportionate to the spread of people between metropolitan, regional and remote Australia and to the population of each state and territory), indigeneity and ethnicity (just over a quarter of interviewees were born overseas, from many different countries). In total, 1221 hours of Australian Generations audio recordings are archived at the National Library, where they are available for research and public use, subject to conditions stipulated by each interviewee.

For this book we've chosen a smaller, but still diverse, set of fifty interviews. We selected a small enough group so readers can get to know each narrator, and a large enough group so the interviews represent a range of Australian lives and histories. We only use interviews that are available online with permission from each interviewee, because we want readers to

---

1 The Australian Generations Oral History Project was funded by an Australian Research Council Linkage grant, LP100200270. The two authors were project team members: Anisa as Project Officer, Alistair as Project Director. The project website at http://artsonline.monash.edu.au/australian-generations/ includes links to the interviews and to written publications and ABC radio programs using the interviews. For more details about the project and its technologies, see: Kevin Bradley and Anisa Puri, 'Creating an Oral History Archive: Digital Opportunities and Ethical Issues', *Australian Historical Studies* 47, no. 1 (2016), pp. 75–91; Alistair Thomson, 'Digital Aural History: an Australian case study', *Oral History Review*, 43, 2, 2016, 292–314; Kevin Bradley, 'Built on Sound Principles: Audio Management and Delivery at the National Library of Australia', *IFLA Journal* 40, no. 3 (2014), pp. 186–94; Katie Holmes and Alistair Thomson, 'Oral History and Australian Generations', *Australian Historical Studies* 47, no. 1 (2016), pp. 1–7 (that issue of *Australian Historical Studies* includes seven articles by members of the Australian Generations research team, each of which uses the interviews to examine a theme in Australian history or methodological issues in oral history).

also be listeners with an option to hear each spoken extract, as we explain below.

Extracts from the interviews are arranged within two types of chapters. One set of chapters traverses the life course, starting with Ancestry and then charting Childhood, Youth, Midlife and Later Life, and exploring change and continuity in each life stage from the 1930s to the 2010s. Interspersed between these life stage chapters are thematic chapters about Faith, Migrants, Activism and, in conclusion, Telling My Story. Some chapters have sub-sections that focus on particular topics. For example, Youth canvasses high school, teen family life, youth culture, first loves, from school to work, and military service.

Within each section the interview extracts are usually arranged chronologically so readers can follow change across time and consider the factors that may have influenced significant transformations. For instance, 'First loves' starts with the glory boxes that young women in the first half of the twentieth century used to gather household items for their prospective marriage, and it concludes with dating in the Kimberley in the 2000s.

From thousands of pages of transcripts we selected extracts that illuminate change and continuity and how individuals lived with and against the economic forces, cultural expectations and legal constraints of their times. We also chose extracts that highlight how different types of Australians—male or female, city or country, poor or prosperous—have managed their lives and faced distinctive challenges and opportunities. And, of course, we picked stories that evoke the humour, drama and pathos of human life.

Reading and Listening: An Aural History

Stories are told through voice as well as word. The texture and sound of speech convey meaning. Speakers emphasise significant words and phrases with increased volume or a well-timed pause. We speed up with excitement or emotion, or slow down for a difficult, unrehearsed story. Silence can indicate pain or embarrassment, or the struggle to relate a memory that has no easy story. The voice can suggest warmth and pleasure, anger and disappointment, sarcasm or disapproval. Laughter can be joyous, anxious or ironic. We have tried to capture some of this aurality in our editing and presentation of interview extracts: emphasised words are *italicised*, laughter and sighs are noted in (parentheses), lengthy pauses are indicated by three dashes (---), while a single long dash (—) indicates an aside or afterthought.

But there is a limit to how much of this aural nuance can be captured in text. The patterns of the spoken word are different to those of written prose. Speech is 'ragged at the edges; it twists and turns, gnaws away at meaning and coils itself up'.[2] Narrators zig-zag from one topic to another, as each memory triggers a connected story or feeling. There are false starts as we fumble towards the story we want to tell, and most of us pepper our speech with 'um' and 'ah', 'kind of', 'like' or 'sort of'. For a linguist these might be invaluable clues, but for the reader they can be confusing and irritating.

We have edited each extract, seeking to capture the nuance of the spoken word while also ensuring a readable and coherent text.[3] We removed redundant words that did not add to the meaning of an extract, deleted passages that were not directly relevant to a story's primary focus, and merged passages from different parts of an interview which relate to the same topic. We did not add words, except in [square brackets] to ensure coherence, and we did not alter words except where the repetition of a vernacular usage (such as 'yeah' or 'gotta') was distracting rather than meaningful and, in very few cases, where it was clear that the narrator had mistakenly used the wrong word. We occasionally fixed grammar to enhance readability, though we also sought to maintain the style and flow of speech. We retained interviewer questions where they made a significant impact on the narrator's story, as a reminder that these stories were created within an interview relationship. Your experience of reading the interview extracts will not be the same as that of reading written prose. We hope you will 'hear' and appreciate the rhythms and textures of the spoken word.

---

2 Samuel, 'Perils of the Transcript', in Robert Perks and Alistair Thomson (eds), *The Oral History Reader* (London and New York: Routledge, first edition, 1998), p. 391 (first published in 1971).

3 Our approach to editing is discussed in Thomson, 'Digital Aural History'. See also Linda Shopes, 'Editing Oral History for Publication', *Oral History Forum d'Histoire Orale* 31 (2011), at www.oralhistoryforum.ca/index.php/ohf/article/view/385, accessed 29 April 2014.

The wonders of digital technology allows you to simultaneously be reader *and* listener, and to enjoy both written and spoken versions of each interview extract. In the electronic version of this book the introduction to each extract is visibly hyperlinked so that a reader can click on the link and have a new window open showing the interview on the National Library online listening system (in extracts where we brought together passages from two different parts of the interview, there is another hyperlink to access the second passage; in the paperback these links are formatted with **BOLD CAPITAL LETTERS**). Click once more to accept the Library's conditions for use and the selected extract will start playing after several seconds (longer if your internet connection is slow). The links to the National Library interviews work most reliably with a Chrome browser. While you listen to the extract you can read the Library's verbatim transcript or you can continue to read the edited transcript in the book. The audio will continue playing beyond the selected extract so you can listen to more of that person's story, or you can close the Library window and continue reading, and listening, to other extracts in the e-book.[4] We provide details of each catalogue record in the narrator index.

As you read and listen to each extract you will see how the edited text in the book is not the same as the Library transcript, and that neither replicates the spoken word. The book's edited text offers a clear, focused and readable version of the narrator's story; the audio track offers additional meanings conveyed in sound and by the way each person tells their story. For the listener, oral history becomes aural history with enriched access to the interviews.[5]

Additional resources enhance your reading and listening. Each extract has a short introduction with contextual information (the narrator's year of birth is always included so you can gauge their age at the time of the

---

4 For more detail about how this works, see Thomson, 'Digital Aural History'. If you want to delve deeper into an interview, you can download the mp3 files and an unedited transcript by clicking on 'Download Files' in the Library's online listening system. Note that it is possible that down the track an interviewee may decide to restrict access to an interview that is currently online.

5 On oral history as aural history, see Douglas Lambert and Michael Frisch, 'Digital Curation through Information Cartography: A Commentary on Oral History in the Digital Age from a Content Management Point of View', *Oral History Review* 40, no. 1 (2013), pp. 135-153; Simon Bradley, "History to Go: Oral History, Audiowalks and Mobile Media," *Oral History* 40, no. 1 (2012), pp. 99-110; Siobhán McHugh, 'The Affective Power of Sound: Oral History on Radio', *Oral History Review* 39, no. 2 (2012), pp. 187-206.

narrated event). The introduction to each chapter provides background historical information about the topic or life stage, including details of social, cultural, political or economic milestones. Each chapter concludes with a list of further reading on the topic, and includes links to further listening. These listening links will take you to related extracts in other Australian Generations interviews so you can access a wealth of additional interview material. Finally, you can use our Narrator Index to follow one narrator throughout the book, and the General Index to find extracts related to a place or subject.

For some readers and listeners the book may be a starting point for further enquiry using the extraordinarily rich, diverse and accessible Australian Generations oral history archive. But for now, relish the stories in this book and join our narrators as they relate the joys and tribulations of Australian lives and traverse the history of contemporary Australia.

Further Reading on Oral History

Abrams, Lynn, *Oral History Theory* (Abingdon: Routledge, second edition, 2016).

Boyd, Douglas A., and Larson, Mary A. (eds), *Oral History and the Digital Humanities: Voice, Access, and Engagement* (New York: Palgrave Macmillan, 2014).

Darian-Smith, Kate and Hamilton, Paula, 'Memory and history in twenty-first century Australia: A survey of the field', *Memory Studies* 6, no. 3 (2013), pp. 370–383.

Gammage, Bill and Spearitt, Peter (eds), *Australians 1938* (Sydney: Fairfax, Syme & Weldon Associates, 1987).

Gothard, Jan, *Greater Expectations: Living with Downs Syndrome in the 21st Century* (Fremantle: Fremantle Press, 2011).

Hamilton, Paula and Shopes, Linda (eds), *Oral History and Public Memories* (Philadelphia: Temple University Press, 2008).

Perks, Robert and Thomson, Alistair (eds), *The Oral History Reader* (London and New York: Routledge, third edition, 2016).

Portelli, Alessandro, *The Death of Luigi Trastulli and Other Stories: Form and Meaning in Oral History* (Albany: State University of New York Press, 1991).

Ritchie, Donald A. (ed.), *The Oxford Handbook of Oral History* (New York: Oxford University Press, 2011).

Thomson, Alistair, 'Oral History', in Anna Clark and Paul Ashton (eds), *Australian History Now* (Sydney: University of New South Wales Press, 2013), pp. 73–89.

Raleigh Yow, Valerie, *Recording Oral History. A Guide for the Humanities and Social Sciences* (Lanham, Maryland: Rowman & Littlefield Publishers, third edition, 2014).

CHAPTER 1

ANCESTRY

All of the Australian Generations interviewees were asked about family background, and most relished the opportunity to relate what they knew of their ancestry. For some, this knowledge is the fruit of diligent work with online technologies and databases that have revolutionised genealogical research, whether about nineteenth century convicts or free settlers, Indigenous Australians, postwar migrants or war service. The quest for ancestral knowledge is influenced by the boom in family history and autobiography; by the widespread desire to uncover origins and explain family paths and family character. As Anna Clark explains in a recent book about Australian historical consciousness, family history is one of the main ways we know about the past. The search for historical inheritance and its transmission to subsequent generations is 'a quest for identity and belonging'.[1] Thus Ginette Matalon's family history, as related in this chapter, begins with a 'meaningful story' that has 'long range consequences', and Lisa Jackson explains that she has 'definitely inherited' stubbornness and advocacy from her Aboriginal grandmother and her mum.

While some of the ancestry stories in this chapter are the outcomes of painstaking research and documented evidence, others rely on oral traditions that have crossed several generations and become family legends with potent resonance and uncertain veracity. Some are narrated with a language and flow akin to classical mythology or folktale. In nineteenth century Palestine, Ginette Matalon's 'very beautiful' great-grandmother—also Ginette—has been deserted by her husband and is about to have her children removed by the authorities—'Thieves! Robbers! Thieves! Robbers!'—when they are rescued by a 'handsome fellow' who has heard

---

1 Anna Clark, *Private Lives Public History* (South Carlton: Melbourne University Press, 2016), p. 60.

the screams and offers to marry Ginette, adopt the children and take them all to Australia!

The oral traditions of family history often draw upon narrative structures and themes that are familiar from the wider culture. For example, descendants of migrants frequently relate the story of their bold ancestors who found refuge and made a better life against the odds in Australia. Lynne Sanders-Braithwaite's English west-country peasant forbears became successful farmers in north-coast New South Wales; Douglas Fong's Chinese great-great grandparents survived racism on the nineteenth-century Victorian goldfields and established a business dynasty in Western Australia; Ouranita Karadimas' Greek mother and Milijana Stojadinovic's Yugoslav grandmother were adventurous women who grasped migration as an opportunity to escape the limited opportunities for poor women in mid-twentieth-century Europe. Such stories tell us much about migrant travails and successes, about the complex personal and family dynamics of migration, and about the nature and importance of oral tradition within migrant families (which, after all, comprise all but Indigenous Australians).

Sometimes, too, family traditions smooth out the jagged edges of a forbear's history or conceal factors that might complicate the story. As Sam Neill's character remarks in the 2016 Australian film, *The Daughter*, referring to the invented parenthood of the eponymous daughter in a struggling New South Wales timber town, 'Everyone's got a story like this. It's as old as the hills.' Our narrators are often alert to the faults of family history and the secrets and lies of family legend.

Sometimes family stories are too sharp to research, too difficult to broach, too shameful to share. Sometimes a later generation is determined to uncover a messy truth and deal with the painful consequences. In so doing they widen understanding not just of that family history, but also of the histories of all Australian families. In this chapter we hear Michelle Cripps' curiosity about the divorces that were never talked about among her early twentieth-century forbears; Les Robinson places his birth-father on the family tree against the wishes of a much-loved stepfather; David Cooper recalls an earlier generation who would not admit to their convict ancestry.

This curiosity and revelation is possible because the stigma of family shame shifts across time as social attitudes change. The old fear of the 'convict stain' that David Cooper describes has now been replaced by celebration of convict ancestry (underpinned by a belief that convicts were more likely hard-done-by victims than hard-core criminals). We'll meet Ruth Apps' Irish ancestor Bridget and hear Ruth's pride that Bridget was transported for hitting a policeman during a demonstration.

In later chapters we'll see how powerful taboos about domestic violence and child sexual abuse are also slowly lifting, and that survivors and descendants are finding it easier—though never easy—to tell such stories. It will also be clear that for many Australians in the twenty-first century it is no longer shameful to talk about homosexuality in the family or to tell one's own gay or lesbian life story.

Indigenous narrators are especially alert to the forces that have torn their families apart, the wounds that still scar family memories, and the secrets and lies that have haunted Aboriginal history. Yet these indigenous storytellers share a wider commitment with their families and communities to research and explain Aboriginal family history. Lisa Jackson, of east and west coast Aboriginal descent, and with British ancestry too, reminds us that her white settler forbears were actually colonisers, and that her paternal grandparents required official permission to marry under legislation that controlled so many aspects of Aboriginal life, not just who you could marry but also where you could live and how you might work and play. Arthur Hunter in the Kimberley recalls the twentieth-century assimilation policies that assumed mixed-race and light-skinned children would be better off if they were removed from their Aboriginal families and placed in white foster families or government institutions.

Yet while Indigenous men and women like Arthur Hunter and Lisa Jackson share their family histories of discrimination and loss, they also celebrate their forbears' resilience. They highlight survival and success, not least in sustaining or recreating family and community. They recount this tradition of resilience as a legacy they have inherited which shapes their own character and action. For these Indigenous Australians, as much as for any Australians, ancestry is important and family history matters.

***RUTH APPS** (born 1926) from Parramatta in Sydney's west relishes this family story about her Irish convict ancestor.*

Most of my ancestors are Irish. My favourite ancestor is my five-greats grandmother, called Bridget. She was an Irish girl and apparently got mixed up in a demonstration in Ireland. Her records state that she put a rock in a sock and she swung it around and hit a policeman. She was promptly sent out here. She married another convict, and so it goes down. On my father's side, his parents came to Australia in about 1850. They came free and he was born here not long after they arrived.

Frank Heimans: So that's where you get your red hair from is it, the Irish?

That's right (laughs). I've got a lot of Irish in me. I went back there for a visit and immediately we landed, I had that feeling, 'I'm home.' It was an almost uncanny feeling. We went back to where Bridget was born and whilst we couldn't find any houses or anything like that, I looked at the hills and I thought 'They're the same hills that Bridget saw' and I really felt comfortable.

She's actually buried in Parramatta which is one suburb from here. She married in the same church that I go to now, in St John's, a church in Parramatta.

***GINETTE MATALON** (1936) relates a family history that traverses Cairo and Sydney across three centuries.*

I'll tell you one meaningful story—'cause obviously we haven't got time to tell you about each member of the family. This is why my family came to Egypt and why we eventually came to Australia. It's the same story. It has two long range consequences.

So, I would like you to go back in time to the century before last and there is my maternal great-grandmother living in what was then Palestine. Her husband had left her with two children and gone off to seek fortune in Argentina, or South America—so he said. Never wrote, never came back. She was there with a boy aged ten and a girl aged eight. She was doing a bit of dressmaking—nothing much. Some well-meaning neighbours said she has no visible means of support and they reported her to the British, to the Salvation Army, and they came and they said, 'You really can't bring up your children adequately, we'll have to take these children away from you and look at foster parenting.'

So she's there standing—very beautiful woman and she was called also Ginette by the way, I'm named after her—she was standing on the verandah and yelling, 'Thieves! They want to steal my children! Thieves! Robbers! Thieves! Robbers!' A very handsome fellow passes and he says, 'Can I come up and have a chat with you?' So he comes up and he says, 'I heard the story. I have a contract to go'—he was in ship-handling—'I have a contract to go and work in Melbourne, Australia. I can marry you, adopt your children and we go and live in Australia.' She accepted because she didn't want to be separated from her children.

But her son had hoped that his biological father would still come back. Now I don't know whether she ever divorced from this man, but we'll let it be at this, she left Palestine with this man and her daughter on a ship and they went to live in Melbourne. Eventually the boy joined them, Leopold. My grandmother was called Emma.

Now they went to live in Melbourne and my grandmother had a fabulous childhood in Melbourne. She became really, really immersed in the Australian culture. When she finished school, which I think was at the age of fifteen, sixteen, she became an apprentice milliner and she was very good at this trade. The ladies would travel apparently miles to come to her to have hats done by her and they paid her well. They paid her so well that she managed to economise towards her dowry 200 gold guineas.

But she started dating non-Jewish fellows because this is whom she was surrounded by. So she dated McDougals and McDowalls and Browns and Blacks and her mother was very concerned. She started writing all over the world to relatives and distant relatives to see if somebody would want to come to Australia or want to marry her daughter who was beautiful, clever, skilled and had 200 gold guineas.

So, a fellow in Egypt wrote to her, 'I've got five sons. Come with your daughter. Bring the 200 gold guineas and she can have her pick of my sons.' So off they went—my great-grandmother and my grandmother—to Egypt. She left her husband and her son in Melbourne and they didn't have the money for the full trip—they only had money from Sydney to Colombo. So they stopped in Colombo and they went to work in a pub, in a bar. They worked as waitresses and they served drinks to fellows. The owner would serve them tea—coloured water of some sort—and they drink with the clients, to make enough money to have money for the next part of the trip.

Finally, they went to Egypt and my grandmother selected the most handsome of the boys and they got married. Unfortunately my great-grandmother never had enough money to come back to Australia. My grandmother was brought up with this love of this mythical country—Australia. She had a fold-out, which she would sit me next to her and show me the bush and the kangaroos and the wildlife.

During the war, we had a lot of Australian soldiers with their hats popped up on the side. We'd go out—my grandmother and I—and her whole body was very thrilled when she saw these Australian soldiers. We'd sit and she'd say to me, 'Go to this man and ask him in English, "What time is it?"' I'd say to her, 'But you have a watch.' She said, 'Go and ask him, "What time"—in English—" What time is it?"' So I'd go and see what time is it and the fellow would come and sit with her. This was the nicest thing in her life.

Also she brought to Cairo some of the Australian cultures. She did not want to have servants. She said, 'We're not using slaves.' So she worked herself. She didn't have nails. She washed, she sewed, she cooked. She didn't want to live in the high-rise building that we used to live—oh it wasn't a really high-rise, it was three or four stories high—she wanted a villa which was the closest to the cottages where she had lived in Melbourne. My grandfather, who loved her dearly, built a villa for her in the Heliopolis, which was a more exclusive area where the rich Egyptians would live. She had maybe a dozen—my mother was telling me—cats. She had cats, she had birds, she had pets, things that were not the usual in Egypt. But she had brought with her, her young person tradition.

Later on when things were not as good as it should be for the Jewish people in Egypt, and they had to look at other countries to move to, obviously her children had—she had three children—had been convinced by her that the nicest place to live in the world was obviously Australia. So they started working towards Australia, although she had already died in the meantime.

DOUGLAS (DOUG) FONG *(1938) explains how his Chinese-Australian family ended up in Broome in the early twentieth century.*

Perhaps I can go back a little bit further to the days of the Victorian Goldfields. My great, great grandfathers both came to the Bendigo and Ballarat goldfields. They stayed there for a short while and realised that they weren't going to make much money digging for gold, and also having to deal with assault by other miners. So they moved to Melbourne. On my mother's side of the family their name was Lee, and so they became quite influential in the Victorian and the Melbourne Chinese community. My great-great-grandfather on my father's side was actually awarded a life governorship of the Melbourne General Hospital in 1887, so he must have also done a lot of work in the community over there.

He eventually came across to Perth and set up a business there. He was also the first chairman of the Chung Wah Association which is the first organised ethnic association in

WA. So he was the first president in 1910, and his son who was my grandfather was also on those committees.

Grandfather worked in Geraldton for a while and helped set up a business there—the Sydney Fong Company which is quite influential for many years in Geraldton. Then he eventually came to Broome in about we think 1917 or 1918 because we have a copy of what we think is his first pearl dealer's licence dated 1919. We think he would have had to been here at least twelve months beforehand to go through the bureaucratic process of being given his pearl dealer's licence.

LESLIE (LES) ROBINSON *(1947) recalls some of the personal challenges of tracing family history.*

Trying to do the family tree, it's been awkward because my present father, who died a few years ago now—he was a good man and he adopted us and he was quite willing to adopt us—and if he'd known if I was doing the family tree and he saw me concentrating on the Davis side—I'm Davis blood, there's nothing I can do about that—he would have been a bit upset, to think I'm associating with the Davis and not with him, Robinson.

I remember when I started work, I was a spray painter. I did spray painting in Sydney and I was doing that for about six years. I paid my way through college and all the rest of it and that was really good. Then when we moved up to Bundarra years later, I became a teacher. I did mature age study as a teacher and he went cold on me for a few years because—and I think the only thing I can think of was, being a spray painter, I was basically blue collar like him. He was a street sweeper, and then I changed to teaching and I was a white collar like my original father.

***LYNNE SANDERS-BRAITHWAITE** (1949) recalls the impact of the First World War upon her north-coast New South Wales family.*

Jo Kijas: What sort of background did your dad come from?

His father ran a ham and beef shop and he was a six foot tall man. Dad said he used to wear a corset because he was very proper, extremely proper. His wife was the same height as mum. She was four foot ten, my grandmother. But she died while the boys were away at war, so there was a lot of grief and sorrow in there too and I found that out later in letters.

I now know a lot more about them 'cause I looked at family history. They came out from Devon—my dad's father's side of the family—in the mid-1800s. They were peasants and farmers over there. So they came out to here and come to live on the mid-north coast, but they lost the farms during the war to the ones who stayed behind, and ended up in the city too. The last person in my line, the last person to come here from anywhere else, was 1850. My brother's very proud of that. It makes some sense to us because we've just never had anyone since then that hasn't been born here. So we go back a long way. I think I'm eighth generation Australian here, which matters to me now. I didn't know that at the time.

So yeah, he came back, he left as a young boy of nineteen and came back as a sergeant major in his mid-twenties and his mum had died, they virtually said from grief. She got a shock. He'd been shot and she's had a heart attack and died, and the doctor said she'd just given up hope. Two of her boys were overseas. So he came back to just his dad.

***OURANITA KARADIMAS** (1958) explains how her parents, both from the Greek island of Ithaka, agreed to marry before they first met in Sydney in 1957.*

My father had been living in Australia since 1928. He came out here at the age of ten and that was before my mother was born. The way my parents met was through a proxy. My father in the 1950s decided that it might be time he got married but he'd been here for a long time—he'd been here since 1928—and he didn't see himself marrying a girl from Australia—not even a Greek girl from Australia.

So he wrote back home to his niece in Ithaka and said, 'Do you know any nice girls that I could perhaps approach, that might be interested in coming over and living here, and da, da, da.' So they suggested that there was a lovely girl in the Pilikas family and her name was Louisa and she might be interested and, 'Why don't you send a letter of introduction?' So they did the introductions and my father—as a way of introduction—sent over a photo to my mother that we still have. It's amazing that she said yes after seeing this photo, because he looks like a thug in the 1950s or something (laughs). He's got this five o'clock shadow and he looks terribly stern and serious. I thought, 'Ah!' My mother always kept that photo and we've still got it because it's like, '*Why* would you accept this man? (laughs)'

Anyway she figured that he was very genuine. But the important thing was that the families knew of each other because reputation and respectability, you know, middle-class respectability is a very important value in Ithaka. The families knew each other and my father had no doubt that any girl that was introduced from the Pilikas family would be wonderful. My mother's parents also knew of my [paternal] grandmother and her family and they had an incredibly wonderful name. So my mother had no issues with that at all.

Plus my mother I think was quite an adventurous woman and did not want to marry a merchant seaman, because she was not the kind of woman who would put up with having her husband away on various sea adventures for long periods of time. So she thought, alright, the opportunity to travel, the opportunity to do something different. I think she was quite an adventurous and very bright woman. I think she saw the limitations of life as a wife on Ithaka, so she took the plunge.

*While tracing his family tree from convict Van Diemen's Land to modern Melbourne, **DAVID COOPER** (1959) began to suspect that he had Aboriginal ancestry.*

I still don't know 100 per cent for certain. What I do know is that my grandmother, her generation of children were disciplined and told off if they asked questions about her mother's father. You know, children should be seen and not heard and all that sort of stuff. They'd literally get told off and learnt not to ask. At the same time as that, they were getting told that they had a Spanish gypsy princess in the family and that was to explain why some people had a little bit of colour in their skin. The colour was more in the cousin's skin than in our direct family. That was the explanation. I've always been suspicious about that because that just doesn't sound right, and being [having] an interest in family tree, I'm desperate to trace all my family lines and try and figure it out.

Was she an orphaned Aboriginal child? Or was the father—which is what I think happened—I think that the father was part Aboriginal. I think there's something going on there. It's been the big family secret. I just want to try and find out. I don't know that I will.

See they all say, those people, that generation, they kept the fact they had convicts a secret as well. It's just it was easy for us to prove that, because the records were there. So they can try as hard as they want to keep their convict past a secret, and probably for good reason. You don't want your kids growing up thinking that your grandad was a thief, 'cause you think it might make them a thief.

Well, why did they want to keep it a secret that they've got Aboriginal people in the family? Well it could be racism, but if they bred with them, maybe it's not their racism towards the Aboriginals, maybe it's just they don't want their kids being treated badly because of that colour.

***MICHELLE CRIPPS** (1960) recalls another reason for secrets in* her *Tasmanian family history.*

My grandmother migrated from Wales when she was six with her parents and her brother, and married my grandfather. These are my paternal grandparents. My grandfather had a stroke very early on and I only ever knew him not being able to speak properly and not working, but he had worked prior to that as a younger man.

My maternal grandparents, my grandfather was a dockie on the docks of Burnie wharf and my grandmother was a stay-at-home mother as you tended to be in those days. My husband's grandparents were from the mainland. But what's interesting is both of us have got a divorce back in the family and of course that was *never* ever talked about so both our family histories stopped very short. Now we could do some digging and find out, but my great-grandmother separated and that was just not talked about and my husband's grandmother separated as well.

Karen George: When did you become aware that that was in the family?

I knew fairly early on, but I didn't really understand what it meant. I just knew I had this fantastic great-grandmother who I knew really well and spent quite a bit of time with. But it wasn't till a bit later on that I really understood why I just had the great-grandmother.

***LISA JACKSON** (1972) traces a European and Aboriginal family history that has impacted upon her character and values.*

My dad's mum, my grandmother is non-Aboriginal—she's white—and my dad's father is an Aboriginal man. He comes from I think they call it Carrs Creek up there in northern New South Wales. We've actually been able to trace his family further towards Bourke, Brewarrina and to a Donnelley family. We're still trying to get confirmation about that but that's what they reckon.

Whereas my grandmother on my dad's side, her family has been traced back to 1788 when the settlers first came over—colonisers, sorry—first came over. She was a Perkins and up in Grafton they had a brewery. It was the Perkins Brewery and so Castlemaine bought the Perkins Brewery. The Castlemaine Perkins Brewery now—which is what it's now known as—makes the XXXX beer in Queensland.

Frank Heimans: That's pretty successful.

Well that's the *non*-Aboriginal part of the family. So we still have a great uncle, he's still alive and we met him once. It was amazing. They've got all these Aboriginal people and then *he* pops in, he goes, 'Yeah, I'm your great uncle'. We just looked at him and we're like, this just spins us all out (laughs).

What about the family on your mother's side from Western Australia. What do you know about them?

My grandmother is in Nannup, and the Nannup family is a very large family in the southwest of WA. My grandmother grew up in the Moore River Native Settlement which is like a 100k, 150k's from Perth—northwest of Perth. It was a very oppressive place. It was a very *horrible* place and her and her two siblings grew up there. I do know that one of her siblings was moved over to Victoria but we've never been able to contact or find any trace of that woman at all.

With my grandfather his family are Badimaya which is from northwest, so they're technically what they call—not Nyoongars—they're called Yamatjis because that's what they call them up in the northwest. He too, his family is a mix of Aboriginal and non-Aboriginal. His great grandmother was an old tribal woman from up that way—the wheatbelt area. She had all her kids in a riverbank.

So that's what I've been able to find out from my cousins who've researched into all this. My grandfather met my grandmother at the Moore River Native Settlement and back in the day, especially in Western Australia under the 1905 Act—the Aborigines Act of 1905[2]—they actually had to get permission from the Chief Protector of Aborigines to get married. So they did. They wrote the letter and asked to get married and so he granted them permission to get married.

My grandmother on my mum's side, because she had that history of growing up in Moore River, she was very guarded. That's passed on from her to my mum. But my grandmother was a bit of a fighter as well. She wouldn't accept things. If someone told her something and she didn't like it then she advocated for herself in terms of what she wanted, the outcomes that she wanted. I think too, I think that's been inherited. I think it is, the stubbornness on both sides of the family have kind of merged together. I think the fact is that my mum had also—I don't think she believes it but I do—she has inherited that advocacy from her and I think I've definitely inherited it from my mum. So there is things that have been seen, observed and learnt.

What sort of values do you think that your grandmother had that she held dearest? What was most important to her?

Family. Because of her growing up within that environment at the mission she held fast that family were important. You stick together. That I think was the biggest value.

Milijana Stojadinovic *(1985) shares the family story of coming to Australia from Yugoslavia in 1970.*

---

2 The Aborigines Act 1905 was 'An Act to make provision for the better protection and care of the Aboriginal inhabitants of Western Australia'. The Act created the position of Chief Protector of Aborigines who became the legal guardian of every Aboriginal child to the age of sixteen, and was not repealed until 1964. See www.findandconnect.gov.au/guide/wa/WE00406, accessed 11 July 2016.

Both my grandparents were children of the war. My grandma was born in '39 and my grandfather was born in, I think '41. Yeah, I'm pretty sure. My grandmother in particular had been really poor, all the time, and never having enough money to do anything, wearing like scraps for clothes but always being really happy and always having a good life and fun. She always talks about how she used to sing and dance and blah, blah, blah.

But she always tells me she never wanted to be poor, because of that. I think for her that was a big part of coming to Australia, is that it was a way for her to not be poor. She said to me, 'Milijana, I knew I would never be poor because I knew I could always work to make money for myself. But I never wanted to go through that.' She laughs at it now, she will tell me things like, 'Oh, you know, I had to make a dress from the material that I had from the last dress that I made', and the shoes would be like made out of rubber from something that was in the barn. She laughs at it now. I just think to myself, 'Oh God, that's such a sad, hard thing'. But she just laughs and she goes, 'It was fine' (laughs). So that was the reason why they came.

ARTHUR HUNTER *(1989) recounts what he has learnt about his Aboriginal family history in the Kimberley.*

My nanna was from the Stolen Generation—she is. Her name is Marjorie Hunter, but—Marjorie Daisy. She was from Margaret River, that's between Fitzroy and Halls Creek up in the Kimberley here. She got taken to Beagle Bay Mission, I don't know, back in the '50s or '60s. She was a very young girl when she was taken away from her mum.

My nanna was put in the mission because she's half-caste. The white Australian law back then was to get all the half-caste kids, or light-skinned kids, away from their parents and to give them better life—well *try* to give them better life—and better education and learn the white way. Trying to get them away from their roots you know—like cultural sites and everything, which they kind of destroyed, and they be losing very quickly and very rapidly. We have old people dying without telling their stories. They didn't get it on TV or video or filmed or interviewed or anything. So yeah—pretty sad what happened.

But from what I gathered and what she told me she said that she loved it. Beagle Bay has a lot of memories of her childhood. Just the childhood she had there, and with her having her parents, and she had friends that became long families now. So she still has a connection with people in Broome. She's with the Stolen Generation here in Broome. She travels up and down all the time for meetings and gatherings and everything. So that's from what I gathered so far.

The Kimberley Stolen Generation—I think its purpose is to ask people if—well Indigenous people—they got stolen or their parents, kids or grandkids, just ask questions like who they are and where they really from and if they got a connection up here. So they ask around and Kimberley Stolen Generation I think—well I'm pretty sure—it does the research, finds the people and brings them together for the first time in *years* you know. Like maybe since childhood.

Further Listening on Ancestry

Trish Barrkman, TRC 16, 1933, http://www.nla.gov.au/amad/nla.oh-vn5972545/1-8641
John Murphy, TRC 275, 1940, http://www.nla.gov.au/amad/nla.oh-vn6504268/0-540
Ronnie Gauci, TRC 140, 1947, http://www.nla.gov.au/amad/nla.oh-vn6290910/0-903
Geraldine Box, TRC 36, 1949, http://www.nla.gov.au/amad/nla.oh-vn6190857/0-142
Alison Fettell, TRC 300, 1952, http://nla.gov.au/nla.obj-220185705/listen/4-1423
Gina Polito, TRC 231, 1954, http://www.nla.gov.au/amad/nla.oh-vn6421369/2-284
Ian Reid, TRC 208, 1961, http://nla.gov.au/nla.obj-220066743/listen/0-1858
Jodie Bell, TRC 114, 1970, http://www.nla.gov.au/amad/nla.oh-vn6290885/0-182
James Mayol, TRC 213, 1974, http://www.nla.gov.au/amad/nla.oh-vn6449993/0-393

Christian Bow, TRC 72, 1978, http://nla.gov.au/nla.obj-219896923/listen/0-40
Jason Johnson, TRC 245, 1981, http://nla.gov.au/nla.obj-220115636/listen/0-93
Kirsty Wallett, TRC 170, 1982, http://www.nla.gov.au/amad/nla.oh-vn6290935/0-470
Gemma Nourse, TRC 193, 1989, http://nla.gov.au/nla.obj-220049717/listen/0-260

Further Reading on Ancestry

Ashton, Paul and Hamilton, Paula, *History at the Crossroads: Australians and the Past* (Ultimo, NSW: Halstead Press, 2010).

Clark, Anna, 'Inheritance', *Private Lives Public History* (South Carlton: Melbourne University Press, 2016), pp. 48–71.

Clark, Anna, 'Inheriting the Past: Exploring Historical Conscious Across Generations', *Historical Encounters* 1, no. 1 (2014), pp. 88–102.

Cohen, Deborah, *Family Secrets: Living with Shame from the Victorians to the Present Day* (London: Viking, 2013).

Cuthbert, Denise, Swain, Shurlee and Quartly, Marian, *The Market in Babies: Stories of Australian Adoption* (Clayton: Monash University Publishing, 2013).

Davison, Graeme, *Lost Relations: Fortunes of My Family in Australia's Golden Age* (Crows Nest: Allen & Unwin, 2015).

Davison, Graeme, 'Speed-relating: Family History in a Digital Age', *History Australia* 6, no. 2 (2009), pp. 43.1–43.10.

Green, Anna, 'Intergenerational Family Stories: Private, Parochial, Pathological?', *Journal of Family History* 38, no. 4 (2013), pp. 387–402.

Haebich, Anna, *Broken Circles: Fragmenting Indigenous Families 1800–2000* (Fremantle: Fremantle Arts Centre Press, 2000).

Haebich, Anna, 'Forgetting Indigenous Histories: Cases from the History of Australia's Stolen Generations', *Journal of Social History* 44, no. 4 (2011), pp. 1033–46.

Huggins, Rita and Huggins, Jackie, *Auntie Rita* (Canberra: Aboriginal Studies Press, 1994).

Morgan, Sally, *My Place* (Fremantle: Fremantle Arts Centre Press, 1987).

Nugent, Marie, 'Aboriginal Family History: Some Reflections', *Australian Cultural History*, no. 22 (2003), pp. 143–53.

Thomson, Alistair, 'Searching for Hector Thomson', *Anzac Memories: Living with the Legend* (Melbourne: Monash University Publishing, new edition 2013), pp. 257–82.

CHAPTER 2

CHILDHOOD

Childhood is often missing from history. Children are rarely the movers and shakers of historical change. Indeed, children are often at the mercy of forces beyond their control, as parents and other adults make decisions on their behalf, wars destroy homes and fragment families, politicians legislate for child welfare and control, and adult economics buffet family budgets and dependent lives. The impacts of such forces have changed over the past century with transformations in family structures, shifting intersections between state and family and the increasing commercialisation of childhood. Yet between the pressures and expectations of the adult world children have made their own lives, if not in circumstances of their choosing, and have fashioned and refashioned Australian childhood.

Children are perhaps most vulnerable in times of war and conflict, as illustrated in the opening section of this chapter. During World War II families in far-north Australia were evacuated to escape Japanese air raids and the imagined invasion, and families of German, Italian and Japanese descent were torn apart by the internment of so-called enemy 'aliens'. In 1942 Doug Fong was evacuated from Broome to Perth with his Chinese-Australian family. Doug was a small child but he recalls the wartime abuse from Anglo-Australians who thought he was Japanese, and that when they returned to Broome after the war the town had been devastated by bombing and looting. Southern Australian children were only mildly inconvenienced by wartime restrictions and rationing—certainly by comparison with their counterparts in overseas zones of war and occupation—though they shared their parents' anxieties about family members who had joined the armed forces, and they did what they could by knitting home comforts for the troops and fund-raising for the war effort.

If most young Australians were protected by physical distance from the war, many of the migrants who came to Australia after it ended had suffered childhoods at war. Ginette Matalon recalls the terror of Cairo air raids and the fear of German conquest which was especially acute for her Egyptian Jewish family. Connie Shaw's Dutch family risked their lives helping Allied pilots and Jewish refugees escape from occupied Holland, and Connie barely survived starvation in the war's closing months. Fred Henskens lived on his teenage wits in Japanese-occupied Batavia until he was captured and interned, and then witnessed the postwar beginning of the Indonesian uprising against the Dutch colonial state. Refugee children often bear the scars of violence and loss. In south Sudan in the 1980s, James Mayol was captured and sold as a child slave. When he escaped and reunited with his brother he could no longer cry: 'there's no any water coming from my tears anymore'. James' adult life, like that of other migrant and refugee Australians, was shaped profoundly by a war-torn childhood and by efforts to overcome a terrible start in life.

Children of war veterans can also suffer battles of the peace waged by physically and mentally-damaged ex-service parents. Ruth Apps' World War I Anzac dad lost the use of an arm when he was blown up near Ypres in 1917, and the war's long-term effects erupted in Sydney in 1939 when renewed anxieties about bombing took him 'mentally back to war'. Surrounded by her father's damaged World War II veteran mates, Lynne Sanders-Braithwaite's home life was 'tainted' by fears that there might be another war. Lisa Jackson was proud of her Aboriginal father's war service but knew that Vietnam had 'really impacted' on his mental health.

Children have little say in their family's fortunes, yet those fortunes impact every childhood, as we see in this chapter's second section about childhood family economy. Our oldest narrators recall childhoods blighted, in Australia or abroad, by interwar poverty and the Great Depression of the 1930s. One of Kathleen Golder's first memories is eviction from the family home in the north of England and then sleeping on a single bed with three brothers in their grandparents' tiny cottage. In rural Tasmania in the 1930s Leo Cripps' widowed mother raised five boys on her father's tenant farm and depended on the rabbits they trapped. By the time Leo was twelve he was earning his keep splitting posts with a bullock team. In 'Depression times' Ruth Apps' mother made 'every stitch of clothing' for her three Wagga Wagga children. By contrast, in Cairo Ginette Matalon grew up with servants in a wealthy household, until Egyptian nationalist persecution in the 1950s forced her Jewish family to flee to Paris and then Sydney, where they shared a tiny inner-city flat with relatives.

Children of the postwar years often benefitted from the improving but variable economy of the 1950s and '60s. Parents who remembered interwar hardship and wartime insecurity determined to create stable homes in the suburbs. Migrant parents worked long hours to ensure their Australian dream. Gradually some, though not all, families began to enjoy the fruits of a consumer boom in housing, cars and domestic appliances. Success was hard-won yet insecure, for adults and children alike. In the early 1980s, after her father died and his business was bankrupted, Rhonda King's family was forced out of their home and into housing commission accommodation furnished from Opportunity Shops. Kirsty Wallett's parents' Riverina farm teetered on the edge of rising interest rates and falling commodity prices in the early 1990s. Lisa Jackson lived much of her early life in the 1970s and early '80s in 'Department Housing', and like other Aboriginal and poor white children she grew up with an 'in-built fear of welfare' and a determination to assert respectability and avoid state interference in family life. By contrast, in the mid-1990s the Ngunjiwirri people of Arthur Hunter's mother's family had achieved rights to land in East Kimberley and, in a dramatic example of positive social and economic change, young Arthur grew up on country at their cattle station.

The patterns of childhood family life, illustrated in the third section of this chapter, have altered dramatically across the past century. While economic hardship and war undoubtedly impacted family relationships in the first half of the twentieth century, some of our narrators recall more stable, 'close-knit' families living the postwar Australian domestic dream. In the early 1960s, before she started school in Burnie on Tasmania's north coast, Michelle Cripps' father would 'touch base' with mum and kids at home every lunchtime. 'Blue Hills was on the radio and then dad would ring to say, "How's things? How's the day?"' Ten years earlier, in 1950s suburban Sydney, Lynne Sanders-Braithwaite's childhood felt like the American television series, *The Wonder Years*. Dad came home from the war to set up a carpentry business, mum cooked, sewed and took the three kids to school, and one of their 'big achievements in life' was to live in a 'full brick only' street in the western-suburbs house that dad built.

This domestic idyll depended on a parental division of labour that was reinforced—until the beginnings of change in the 1970s—by social expectations about men's and women's work, lower women's wages and workforce discrimination against married women, and the lack of affordable childcare for mothers who had moved away from the support of extended families. In the early 1970s, while her father was alive and the family was comfortably off, Rhonda King's parents split their roles in the usual way. 'She's doing the housework, she's doing the kids, she's doing the cooking, she's doing the shopping. He's doing the bloke work.' But her young mother (born in 1941) and older father (born in 1921) had different ideas about parenting, and when dad was away in the week new freedoms blossomed in the home.

For some Australians the ideal family has been an impossible dream. Though adults lived longer as the twentieth century progressed and were less likely to die a premature death through illness or childbirth, parental death could still rock family foundations, as it did for several of our narrators. The loss of a parent, through death, desertion or separation, devastated family fortunes. Commonwealth widows' pensions were not introduced until 1942 (this pension replaced a New South Wales provision dating from 1926; eligibility included deserted wives, divorced women, and women whose husbands were in prison or a mental hospital). There was also a terrible emotional cost. Children lived with grieving parents but often had little understanding or support for their own confused bereavement. After the death of her father in 1945 Ginette Matalon was told not to make any noise and not to attend the funeral. Her widowed mother sobbed every night but Ginette didn't cry for her beloved father because 'I thought this would add to her sadness which it would'.

Single parents had it tough throughout most of the twentieth century. Unless they were entitled to a widow's pension they did not receive state support until the supporting mother's benefit was introduced in 1973. Indeed, the prospect of single-parent hardship, and the stigma of illegitimacy, caused the widespread institutionalisation and adoption of illegitimate babies well into the 1970s. Adoption was sometimes voluntary, sometimes forced, as with Suzie Quartermain, born in Melbourne in 1975 to unmarried teenage parents whose maternal grandmother refused to allow the baby to be raised by her paternal grandparents. Single mothers (and occasional single fathers) who kept their children might marry again or rely on their extended family to help raise the children. While stories about nasty step-parents fuelled Ginette Matalon's anxiety, Veronica

Schwarz's 'lovely' stepfather Charles was 'one of the best things that ever happened to her and to me'.

Families in all their varieties—fractured or otherwise—provided love and care yet could also incubate cruelty and neglect. In the 1950s Les Robinson's deserted mother farmed out the 'feral' Les to 'horrid' relatives in south Sydney; in 1960s rural Queensland Kim Bear's 'fearsome' widowed mother belted her two daughters with 'anything from the lower branches of the willow tree' to fly swats, shoes and 'dad's old belts'. In the 1990s ten-year-old Jay Logan considered shooting his violent stepfather.

Parental mental ill-health exacerbated children's suffering. Alison Fettell's mother was depressed after the loss of an infant child in the mid-1950s, and stayed in bed in the mornings while Alison and her older siblings took responsibility for the younger children. Donat Santowiak's Polish parents' fragile marriage got worse when his migrant father's qualifications were not recognised in 1960s Victoria. Sickened by the humiliation of labouring work and the loss of his Polish family, Donat's dad became paranoid, unpredictable and violent. In the darkest moments Donat's pet dog provided solace, and in his teens his anxiety was 'washed away' by alcohol.

Violence or abuse was also perpetrated outside the family. In recent years Australians have learnt the worst of abuse—and concealment of abuse—within institutions that were intended to care for children. It has become easier—if of course never easy—to tell stories of child sexual abuse. In her interview Alison Fettell was determined to describe the sexual abuse in a neighbour's home that so impacted her Sydney childhood, but at the time of the abuse in the 1950s she could not articulate the experience and her parents 'didn't put it together or chose not to'.

Young Australians in the twenty-first century are mostly protected by vaccination and public hygiene from the infectious diseases that killed or disabled children until the second half of the twentieth century. Veronica Schwarz, for example, recalls the terrifying ordeal of polio in the early 1950s. Medical science has found cures for many disabling childhood complaints, and understanding and support for disability has improved markedly in recent decades, yet chronic illness and disability have been potent features of some children's family life. Rhonda King recalls a close relationship with her older sister born with cerebral palsy in the 1960s, but she also recalls the filthy conditions and neglect in a Newcastle hostel for disabled children. From north Queensland in the 1980s, Jason Johnson describes the games his mother created so that he and his brothers could learn about being blind and thus better support their sister.

Families teach culture, and sometimes they negotiate the tensions and opportunities of different cultures. Lisa Jackson and Arthur Hunter recall learning Aboriginal culture—in suburban Perth and in the Kimberley—from parents and grandparents. James Mayol explains how South Sudanese family structures are very different to those in Australia, and Rachel Brown, born to an Australian father and Filipino mother in 1985, describes the linguistic and cultural challenges of understanding her Filipino family and society. Migration and multiculturalism have enriched and complicated the experience of Australian family and childhood.

In the section on childhood pleasures we see some of the most dramatic transformations in Australian children's lives. Across the ages, outdoor play has been central to both the mythology and the experience of Australian childhood. In the 1930s Ruth Apps' playground included the Murrumbidgee Lagoon and the beaches of Sydney, and Donald Grey-Smith was 'free to explore (almost) anywhere' along the cliffs and beaches of Victoria's Mornington Peninsula. In John Murphy's 1940s Melbourne suburban boyhood 'everything was outside', including footy, cricket, tennis and bike-riding, and the eastern roads out to the Dandenong Ranges were not yet clogged by motor traffic. Russell Elliott's central-Victorian farm 'was my playground' in the 1950s and '60s, and in north Queensland in the 1980s and '90s Jason Johnson played Aussie Rules and rugby 'till the sun went down'.

Boys and girls played differently and sometimes separately, though gender roles might be resented and resisted and would only slowly change over time. Ruth Apps was not allowed to join her brothers as they swung on willow branches across the Lagoon in the 1930s, but Alison Fettell refused to play with her sisters and their dolls in the late 1950s and was delighted when her father went against type and bought her a 'wonderful' green toy Cadillac friction car. Still, by the 1980s in Perth, Lisa Jackson was the only girl 'game enough' to take on the boys in the cricket nets.

Electrical and digital entertainment has provided rapidly-changing childhood pleasures across the past century. Ruth Apps saw Shirley Temple on screen when the first 'talkies' came to Wagga Wagga in the 1930s, and then relished the 'Saturday Arvo Flicks' in wartime Sydney. Australian families began to enjoy television during the Melbourne Olympics in 1956. In 1969 schoolkids gathered in classrooms around the country to watch the televised moon-landing, and in 1977 Ian Reid and his Adelaide siblings successfully 'wrangled' their mother to upgrade the black and white valve television because 'we *really* need a colour TV' for the Centenary Test between Australian and English cricketers. In the early 1990s young Adam Farrow-Palmer in Sydney interspersed backyard tree-climbing and trampolining with backroom Super Nintendo video games, and by the time he hit high school in the 2000s increasingly-sophisticated, online multiplayer games were becoming 'more of a focus and there was less running around and exploring'. For a young man born in 1988, 'throughout my whole life basically video games have been a part of it'.

The take-up of electronic and digital play developed over time but always depended on money and attitudes. Russell Elliott was more or less bound to his farm playground (and his transistor radio) because his parents didn't want to go out to the pictures or other community events. In the late 1950s Les Robinson's battling south-Sydney parents could not at first afford a television so Les and his siblings each paid sixpence a time to watch *Rin Tin Tin* and *The Mickey Mouse Club* at a house up the road. Ouranita Karadimas only ever saw television in the 1960s on Friday and Saturday nights when she was sent to the neighbours because her Greek parents' Albury fish and chip shop was especially busy. Without regular access to television, she fell in love with books and reading. Though the culture of commercial entertainment framed and changed childhood pleasures across the century, children adopted and adapted play in their own fashion, whether outdoors or indoors, individual or social, for boys or girls.

Changes in early years schooling, illustrated in the final section of this chapter, are perhaps less obvious than changes in popular culture or in the experience of teenagers at high school. From the 1870s all Australian children were expected to attend primary or 'elementary' school. Teaching and learning styles have changed across time (with bitter debates in policy and politics), as exemplified by Russell Elliott's memory of rote learning in his initial years at Natte Yallock primary in the 1950s, and the inspiration of a new teacher who encouraged his pupils to engage in active, participatory learning. In the 1960s, learning difficulties like David Cooper's undiagnosed dyslexia were poorly-understood and ill-supported, and kids on the autism spectrum like Phil May were lucky if they found other 'nerds' who preferred electronics to footy (in the 2010s, Phil's autistic son still found it difficult to fit into a 'normal' school). Migrant and refugee children, whose education may have been interrupted by circumstances in their countries of origin, often struggled with the language of instruction and the racism of fellow-pupils, and even the ignorance of teachers who could not pronounce names like 'Ourania' (she became 'Ouranita'). Aboriginal children, like Arthur Hunter in the Kimberley who loved learning in the bush with relatives but felt 'shamed' by his ignorance in the school classroom, might also battle to fit in mainstream schooling. Classrooms and playgrounds could be rough and scary places: authoritarian teachers might be violent, though, as we will see in the next chapter on Youth, corporal punishment was more pervasive and ferocious in high schools up till the latter part of the twentieth century.

War and Childhood

***RUTH APPS**' (1926) father served with the First AIF (Australian Imperial Force) at Gallipoli and on the Western Front until he was wounded in 1917.*

> He was loading ammunition ready for the battle of Messines which was to take place the next day. An artillery shell came from the German line, landed on the ammunition that he was standing on and he was blown up. Now his left arm was just shattered, and till the day he died he had shrapnel in his body. And we kids used to love to feel daddy's shrapnel and you could feel it under his skin in various parts—his legs, his torso—and that remained in his body until he died.

IN 1937 RUTH'S FAMILY OF FIVE, *including an older brother and younger sister, moved from Wagga Wagga in rural New South Wales to the Sydney suburb of Hurstville.*

Once war broke out in 1939, my father *mentally* went back to war. It was *very* difficult for my mother. We had a nice house there. He wouldn't sleep in it. He got a stretcher and he slept under a tree in the backyard because he said, 'I can get away from the bombs that way.' Course there were no bombs in Sydney but he could hear them. And he liked being out in the open air. It was difficult for the family because all the neighbours knew. One of my school friends said, 'Your mother makes your father sleep in the backyard.' It wasn't true, he didn't want to, didn't want to come inside. He became *extremely* unreasonably bad-tempered. Now I'm not being critical, there was a reason behind it. Medical people were not interested, you know, they said 'Oh he's just melancholy.' Nowadays of course they would've treated him better.

Because my father was physically injured my mother was the strength behind the family. She organised everything. She organised the finances. She saw to it that we were well educated, and my father was somewhat in the background.

RUTH RECALLS WARTIME SCHOOLING *in Sydney.*

Well in 1939 I was thirteen and in 1st Form in high school and I spent '39 to '43 in high school. We were not badly affected. There were food shortages but we were never hungry. You could never buy *chocolate* for instance because that always went to the troops and there were little things like that. At the school I was at we had regular first-aid practice and the certain bell signal went and we all had to run and there are 850 girls in navy blue uniforms running across an open park two by two and into an air-raid shelter which was a—they were going to build extra water storage, and they were great big pipes, and they had fitted them out with seats and that was going to be the air-raid shelter. Had a Japanese flight come along they would've just strafed the lot of us in a straight navy blue line but nobody thought of that. And we always had to wear an identification card and a rubber teething ring which we were to put between our teeth to stop the bomb blast. All sounds pretty primitive now but we did those things.

There were restrictions. For instance, speech-day prizes, we *never* got books because our prize money was sent off for the war effort. So I've got multiple bits and pieces of certificates saying that I had won this prize but very kindly had donated it to the war effort, which I hadn't. I wanted the book but there was no choice (laughs). There were brownouts, not blackouts. And cars were restricted of course, and so once again you took to your legs and you walked.

And there was the constant worry that my brother was away and we used to write to him but, you know, sometimes you wouldn't get a letter for three months or so and I think that affected my mother more than it affected us. We knitted scarves and balaclavas and that kind of thing and made donations. But my mother lived in a constant state of fear. That took me up to the end of 1943. I was still too young to join anything and I was going to go to teachers college but my mother really turned on a tantrum. She said, 'Your brother is away and I'm worrying about him. You go away to college I'll have to worry about you.' So I gave up the idea and I went to the Metropolitan Secretarial College for a year and spent one of the happiest years I think of my life.

DONALD GREY-SMITH*'s (1931) father served with the Australian forces during World War II. Young Donald lived with his mother and brother in Rye on the Mornington Peninsula south of Melbourne.*

When Australia entered the Pacific War, our part of Victoria was vulnerable and it became a military zone. We had troops there and suddenly a big influx of American troops, Marines coming back from various battles and actions in the Pacific and they swamped our little town, really. And most of the townspeople were quite hostile to their presence. But my mother, working on the principle that she hoped that when my father was in foreign places that people were being kind to him, offered hospitality. And I still get angry when I realise that some of the townspeople suspected her of immoral motives. It was never really said, but I just know the coldness and the coolness that was directed towards her, that was behind us. She shouldn't have been fraternising with these people.

Some of the townspeople arranged dances to entertain the young Marines. Most of the Marines were only eighteen or nineteen anyway. There was a shortage of partners and what partners were available were mostly middle-aged women and I knew from my own dancing experience that they tended to wear corsets in those days with something like Georgette fabric on their dress. When you were dancing with them, your hand would slip around them. Well, because of the shortage of partners and because I like dancing, my aunt had taught me to dance—she was a great dancer—I offered myself as a partner. And this caused a certain amount of humour and humorous exchange between the young men. But they accepted the offer. So I found myself dancing with young men, and that was when I really became aware of the fact that I was sexually attracted to men. These beautiful, young male bodies were so different from the bodies that I was used to dancing with. It was a kind of an awakening. Nothing happened about it but it was just an awareness in my mind. And with that came the awareness that I wasn't supposed to have such feelings, that this was totally unacceptable in the world that I lived in.

VERONICA SCHWARZ *(1939) came to Sydney as a young child during the war.*

My very *first* memory was the Japanese bombing, the submarines in Sydney Harbour. I was born in Darwin and my father was a member of the AIF and my mother was a nurse.

And when the Japanese entered the war in 1941 he of course was to be sent overseas and we went to Sydney and he sailed off. My mother and I stayed in Sydney and I must have been about, well, two going on three. My memory, the very first memory is of all this noise and light and panic and people running around and us going down into some sort of enclosed space. I later found out that that would have been the time that the Japanese submarines—miniature subs—were in Sydney Harbour, and all panic broke loose in Sydney.

DOUG FONG *(1938) grew up in Broome on the north coast of Western Australia. Broome was bombed by the Japanese in 1942 and the Fongs, along with many others, were evacuated to Perth. After the war the family returned to Broome by sea.*

I think it took us a week or something like that. I remember being quite sea sick. There was a Japanese family came back with us. They'd been released from Cowra—the Japanese prison camp over in New South Wales. And so they came back with us. Those poor people had to travel steerage—they were on the front in the uncomfortable part. I remember them copping a little bit of abuse from non-Asians. It was one of the problems for the Chinese during the war years too. I remember growing up in Perth and being called Japanese quite often. So it's one of the things that we had to put up with. You just turn the other cheek or you learn to fight—one or the other. But coming back to Broome, just a completely different attitude here in Broome. All the different ethnic groups were pretty well accepted and got on pretty well together.

GINETTE MATALON *(1936) grew up an only child in Cairo, where her father was a manager in a French bank and led a jazz band in the evening, and her mother ran a large household with servants.*

So, when Second World War started I was quite young and we had a shelter in the building. So the raids would start, my mother would pull over my head a huge blanket—so that I wouldn't catch cold—and we'd go down to the shelter while the sirens were on, the noise. We had spotlights going up in the sky which I would watch. But what would frighten me, there was a lady coming down to the shelter and she was petrified of the whole experience that she used to yell. If you ask me then, what was war, it was this lady shouting in the dark. It really petrified me to hear her yelling.

During the war my whole family was whispering, whispering. The Germans were not very far from Cairo and we were Jewish and my father was also a staunch supporter of de Gaulle. We were protégé français—under French protection. And he was very much of an activist in the de Gaulle movement. So although I was a toddler and I did not understand all this, I knew there was danger. At night my mother and my father would whisper. And in those very early years of my life, I think I was sharing the bedroom with them. I'm not so sure now but I can hear them in the dark whispering and talking about danger—which I understood that there was danger and the person in danger was my father who was very young.

Unbelievable as it may seem, the Germans were stopped. My father didn't die under the Germans, he died of natural death, on the first of January 1945, which was my personal, my own holocaust—was the death of my father on the first. He didn't die from the war at all.

*At the outbreak of World War II, **CONNIE SHAW** (1937) and her older brother Henk lived in a town in the Dutch province of Utrecht, where their parents both worked as nurses in a mental hospital.*

My father was called up for service because it looked like there was a war situation. A few weeks later, the Germans overran Holland, and my father was taken prisoner-of-war. He was marched up to Belgium and a lot of people tried to escape there, get into boats. They were all trying to get to England apparently. But as most of the boats were being fired on, he didn't like the odds, so he dropped himself in a creek and stayed there until it was safe to get away and finally made his way back home after a few weeks. By that time, we'd had a very large aerial fight over the airport, which I actually remember quite well. I remember the wings and planes coming down and wings coming down. The wings were just circling down. They didn't just drop. They just tipped the circle down and there was parachutes. I asked my mother just before she died, and she said, 'Oh I didn't think you'd be able to remember that because that was right at the start of the war.'

After that, well, when dad came home they decided it was a little bit dangerous to live there, it was in a few hundred metres of the airport. So we changed and moved into the village of Zeist. Well the first thing was that my father was in hiding at the mental hospital. He was dressed as a patient and worked there like that. I believe the Germans were rather frightened of mental patients so they didn't look too close down there. Us kids were told we weren't allowed to tell the Germans anything and if they ask about family members, well they weren't there.

Then we started getting people coming to the house and it was impressed on us that we weren't allowed to tell anybody that they were there. When people came to the house, they all disappeared upstairs. When the Germans came to the house they disappeared behind the walls in the top floor. Then all of a sudden, they'd disappear. Then later on we found that mum or dad were taking them somewhere. Then we started getting other men around which spoke different languages, which turned out to be either Canadian or Australian pilots or airmen they were taking at night time, to apparently prearranged areas a lot further away, I think in the beginning, because dad used to be away a long time when they took them somewhere. Later on sometimes Henk or I or both of us used to take them to some lakes which were some kilometres away, but, you know, you could walk it. We were always told to leave them there and then go home, but one day we decided we hide and take a look (laughs). A plane came and picked them up and landed on the water and took off. So we got an idea what was happening then.

Apart from the airmen, they were all Jewish. I actually never thought about it until somebody said something about it a while ago and they said, well, 'Why did you parents do that?' I thought well apart from the fact that they were just like that, my grandmother was Jewish. Dad's mother. Her family was all Jewish. I didn't know at the time.

There was almost no food. The last food that we had that looked like food I suppose you could say was my dad's and my sister's birthday in 1945, twenty-first of March. We used up the last can of condensed milk and the last bunch of grapes and there would have been at least six people there. And that was it (laughs). Dad came. After that, we had some vouchers. You could go to the soup kitchen and we went to the soup kitchen with these vouchers with two billies. And we got one billy of, I think it was cold soup (laughs). All I know, there was something floating in it and there was a bit of grease floating on the top of it. And in the other one it was custard cooked in water without sugar. When we came home with it, dad said somebody put the socks in it. That's the last time we went there (laughs). It didn't resemble anything in a way of food to be quite honest.

The V1s and the V2s [German long range guided rocket missiles] had been going up, not too far away from us, 'cause we could always hear them go up. And they had this eerie noise when they went over and a lot of them came down. And I think it must have been days where we were just sitting there. We couldn't go out. There was just gunfire over us. And Willy [a camp guard who had warned them when the Germans were planning to search the house] came and he said the Germans were all fleeing, so mum gave him a change of clothes and her bike and that's the last we saw of him. Then a few days later the Canadians, with their tanks, came through. They had all sorts of food. That night, there was a bit of an open area in the town there, in the village and they had bonfires there and music and dancing all night.

***FRED HENSKENS'** (1929) father served in the Dutch merchant navy and his mother was born in the Dutch East Indies. Together with two sisters and a brother, they were living in Batavia when the Japanese invaded Java in 1942. At first, only Fred's father was interned, but when he was fourteen Fred was rounded up by the Japanese and placed in an internment camp.*

It was a brand new camp, all big bamboo huts with wooden platforms inside and we all had to stay there inside. We got seventy centimetres—two and a half foot—room each person and we slept on that. So we had to stay there. We didn't know what was going on. The next day they got us together and they counted us up and they told us we have to work. So, I had to cut grass the first day for cows—dairy cows. There was a dairy farm there but the milk only went to the Japanese officers, or the Japanese hotels or whatever it was. Lucky I was used to that sort of work, and it was very hot. I could carry the stuff easy on my back on this yoke—the grass I mean—to the dairy, and after a day or so I was --- I got very weak because our food was no good. We used to get starch for breakfast, just like starch it was, and only a spoonful of rice with soup for lunch and a bit the same for tea time at night.

I wasn't there that long, I can't remember how long exactly but all of a sudden one day they just opened the gates and never said a word and said, 'Do as you like. You can go home if you want to.' We didn't know what's going on. So all we went out of the gate (laughs), and we didn't have to work, and I went home. I didn't see any Allied troops, oh, for the first three, four weeks nearly. Didn't see anything and the Indonesians were starting to play up. They wanted freedom and they wanted—

Matthew Higgins: Independence?

—independence or something and I didn't know what was going on and they would get *nasty* with everyone and they had guns and they were trying to kill you sometimes and the Japs were supposed to keep law and order but they didn't do it too well.

LYNNE SANDERS-BRAITHWAITE*'s (1949) father served in the Second AIF.*

I lived in fear of a third world war all the time, you know. And now looking back, well that would be the stories I heard. Dad remained secretary of his army battalion till he was in his late sixties or seventies. So we had a lot of the men, the more damaged men, in the home, and the families, so we were all, well I was definitely afraid of war. And probably of the nuclear bomb, but I think mine was more specifically the sort of war that I was hearing described amongst the people that I knew, my uncles and my father and his friends. So I would say, even though we were living in what looked like and did turn out to be a peaceful and stable home life but *always* tainted for me by the sense that there would be a war.

LISA JACKSON*'s (1972) father was a Vietnam War veteran.*

He didn't tell me much. I think the Vietnam War really impacted on him in terms of his mental health. So he didn't tell me much but he was proud to be a soldier and he was proud to be an Aboriginal soldier. When he died, Department of Veteran Affairs put up a headstone for him but they also organised for the Vietnam Veterans Association out there in the wheat fields in WA. They organised a guard of honour for him because he was part of the Vietnam Veterans Association. They helped organise the funeral for him which I think was a great honour for him.

He didn't talk much about it but he would mention 'Oh I've been there' or 'I've done that' or 'I've seen that.' We saw some of his old war photos. He took photos of Vietnam and with the trucks and that. So I have seen some photos but he wouldn't go into much detail.

I think him and some of my cousins and my uncle were a bit unique in that. They served the Australian armed forces and they defended the country that didn't recognise them as citizens and that would've been, I think that for them --- it also gave them stability in terms of their work life and their life in general, steady income and that. But also the fact is that they defended the country that didn't recognise them as people.

In 1986 combatants from north Sudan destroyed ***JAMES MAYOL****'s (1974) village in southern Sudan. James was captured and enslaved for several years.*

I went to school actually in 1985 to 1986. Then the *whole* town was put in fire by the militias. The militias were being organised by the government. We call them *muram*[1] in our language. But the reality—there were soldiers, well-organised troops but they have to put on civilian's uniform and carry guns, get on camels and horses. Then they have the idea to riot all Dinka's properties, kill the eldest people and kidnap the childrens. So unfortunately I was one of the kids that been kidnapped during 1986. And they took in us as their hostages.

Atem Atem: So when they took you, where did they find you?

They find me in Aweil. Yeah, because people has to run and then they have to do an ambush, they captured you and they taken us. When we come along the way we found a train, we came just near to Aweil and then didn't reach Aweil. Train was empty. So they had to put all these people on the train. That's how I found it to myself. This is not a militias, is not *muram*. It's a well-organised --- The train, it was organised—waiting.

---

1 Dinka refer to the nomadic Arab tribes, the Murahaleen, as 'muram' or 'maraam'. The Murahaleen traditionally fought the Dinka over cattle-grazing grounds. During the war some were armed by the Sudan government to fight against the Dinka.

Well, they were telling me first, we kill all your people. No one is alive. Secondly, we need to change your name. Thirdly, you need to become Muslim. You see? And you're being beaten every day for refusing to go to Quranic school. You see. I was one of them, one of the childrens who actually didn't want to learn what it call Quranic school. You see? What I learned I end up saying just a few words with Quran because I wasn't able to accept that challenge. I was just choosing either to die or not, or not to stay with them. They try to beat me, to threaten me and this wasn't change. It didn't change my life, my concept, until I escaped.

The way I escaped was very strange. I escaped at night because there's a market where all Arab people can go. And that's also where the slaves are sold. You see? The slaves from south Sudan, the slaves from Chad. But mostly they bring in Dinka. They go to that market is very far away. It would take like, the two days to come back. And I planned this for many years that this will be my day to escape. To escape at night when they started going to the market—that will be my first time to escape. My time chosen. I choose that time when they started going, all right, and I started also to go away. Because I knew they were going to come three days later. But I walked on my feet three days to come to the town. They're going opposite side. And I went opposite side. So I walk that 200 kilometres in two and half days. See, partly running, running, running at night. Have to go up to this tree and sleep on the tree. In the morning I have to come down and run again, until I found myself in a big city. At the daytime just running, running. If I heard any sounds of people or sounds of horses or sounds of any car, I have just to hide, and they will come pass by.

This is about 1988—something like that. So situation was very bad. So I end up going to the military garrison and recruited myself—become a soldier.

Atem Atem: So why did you choose to go the garrison?

Because there's no other option. There's no school. In the life there's nowhere to sleep. There's nowhere to accommodate myself. And becoming a soldier, you have a sense of powerful there. You see, that's the only jobs was being there. So and I went on training—for two years on training. Then after graduations they asked me, our troops, immediately they want to take us back to South sudan so that we can go and have a war. Then I escape again. I couldn't able to go to south Sudan. So I escape in 1990s.

I WENT LOOKING FOR MY BROTHER. When I met him, I actually ask him few questions about my parents. He said to me he doesn't have an idea. We'd been left, both of us, we left like fifteen years apart. He doesn't even know what is going on there. If they're alive, and they're dead. He have information that his mother pass away. But still he got some sisters somewhere, he doesn't know whether they are alive or not. He doesn't have information about my mum. And of course our father is already dead. He doesn't have information about my mum or my sisters.

So that was the information he released. He was happy that we can met, we can be reminder of the family. He didn't know even that I was alive. He was just crying and crying and crying. But for me I can't make any cry again 'cause whatever I see, you know, there's no any water coming from my tears anymore.

I was having a plan but I didn't want to tell him my plan. I kept at my plan in secret. I supported him and then I escape even from him again.

Further Listening on War and Childhood

Donald Grey-Smith, 1931, http://nla.gov.au/nla.obj-220110052/listen/0-2326
Trish Barrkman, 1933, http://nla.gov.au/nla.obj-219822018/listen/0-139
Michael Bicanic, 1937, http://nla.gov.au/nla.obj-220089713/listen/0-603
Donat Santowiak, 1950, http://nla.gov.au/nla.obj-220175608/listen/0-383
Barbara Krickl, 1962, http://www.nla.gov.au/amad/nla.oh-vn6252047/0-2569
Bronwyn Macdonald, 1964, http://www.nla.gov.au/amad/nla.oh-vn6390885/0-1026
Adam Farrow-Palmer, 1988, http://nla.gov.au/nla.obj-219982656/listen/0-253

Making Do: Childhood Family Economy

***KATHLEEN GOLDER** (1920) grew up in Cheshire in north-west England.*

Actually one of my very first memories was being evicted. My parents were evicted from this house, it was called Carlton House. It was near Wrexham. I'll think of the name afterwards. In those days my father was a grocer and baker. He became a grocer and a baker after going through the war. But bad times came and he couldn't pay his bills so he went bankrupt. They just put you out in the street in those days. I remember that. I'd be about seven. The *strange* thing was I came back from school, in Queensferry—that's the name of the place—Queensferry. We came back from the school and I said to my mother, 'I told the teacher we're going to Australia.' My mother said, 'We're not going to Australia. Go back with your brother and tell the teacher you're not going to Australia, you're going to Sutton Weaver, in Cheshire.'

I HAD THREE BROTHERS—one a year younger and two older than me—and we left Carlton House and went to live in this house of grace [a tied cottage on an estate] that was my grandparents' on my father's side. They had really *nothing* except what they needed for themselves—these old people. They were well into their seventies, and my mother arrives with these four children. I remember being put in a bed—an iron bed—and with my three brothers. Two to top, two to bottom with only the thing she could find to put on us which were old coats. Ah, that I remember. That was my first memory of going back, going with them to this cottage that was built in 1550. There was no running water. That was my first memory.

***LEO CRIPPS**' (1923) father died in 1930 from a lung disease caused by his work as a miner in Victoria, and his mother then moved with her five sons to her father's small tenant farm in the central highlands of Tasmania.*

Look, my mother was on a widow's pension. Thirty shillings a fortnight to bring up five boys (laughs). I think had it not been for the rabbits and things like that, a lot of people during that Depression would've starved. We got pretty hungry at times. Once we was there on our own, mum wasn't there but one of the uncles was there, Jack was there, and he decided to cook some scones. 'Course those days you didn't have self-raising flour, you had to use cream of tartar and soda, you see, to get 'em to rise. So he cooks these scones and he said, 'Tommy, you're the youngest, you have first taste.' Tommy got hold of his scone and he put it in his mouth and he chewed it. Said, 'What are they like, Tom?' He said, 'They're not bad, but they're bloody nasty.' He'd put cream of tartar and tartaric acid. But we were pretty hungry, we ate 'em (laughs).

IT WAS BACK WHEN I WAS ABOUT, between eleven- and twelve-year-old, the old bloke that was next door, he was a shepherd next door, he had a contract for splitting posts and he asked if he could take me with him to help him. We'd camped out in a tent for the whole of the winter while we was doing this and we used the bullocks for dragging the logs out of the bush and sledging them up to the road and all this sort of thing. But the old bloke had—what we know now, I think is a hip—and he couldn't handle the bullocks in the bush. So I had to do the bullock driving with the bullocks, particularly in the bush, and I had to of course yoke them all up and everything. I only used to use two in the bush for dragging because it's too long a thing, you see, but to yoke them up in the winter, in the frost, the chains and the bows used to get *freezing* and they'd stick to your hands. What I used to do to warm me hands up, I used to put them up in the flanks of the bullocks and that used to warm me up enough that I could get 'em yoked up, you see. Spent that winter in the tent and we lived on bread and meat and stuff like that, and when I finished he give me two pair of working trousers, and these were long trousers, and by gee they was nice (laughs). That was me pay, two pair of working trousers for the whole of the process. Oh, no, I didn't get paid, oh, no, no.

***RUTH APPS** (1926) spent her early years in the New South Wales country town Wagga Wagga.*

I remember a lot of the Depression. In those days men who were out of work and on the dole could only collect the dole each week in a separate town. So they used to walk into Wagga and we were the first large house that they would encounter coming in off the road. I can clearly remember they used to come *always* through the back door and ask my mother for something to eat. Now it was Depression time so obviously everyone was a bit hard up. My mother used to make her own bread. I can clearly see that she used to cut off a large slab of homemade bread, spread it with homemade dripping, salt and pepper, and then boil their billy. They provided the tea. They would sit on the back step and talk, and they were often men, sometimes professional men, very interesting to talk to but they were out of work and it was somewhere for them to get a meal. They would then go into the township itself where they would collect their—I think it was about five shillings a week, it was all they got. But they would go in they'd say, 'Well Mrs, you have given me something to eat.' That's all clearly in my mind.

My father was generally at home because he'd been badly injured in the war and he would sit there and talk to them. And even though times were tough we always had *The Sydney Morning Herald* every morning, and they would sit there and read *The Sydney Morning Herald*. Now even today I still get the

The Herald every day. It's a habit that's well entrenched. But the men, generally speaking they'd be a bit grubby, but they'd be carrying their swag—if anyone knows what a swag is, it's a rolled up blanket in which they had what little clothing they had—and they would carry that over their shoulder and they would simply walk. My father was a bit handy and if their soles were off their shoes he would get thick cardboard and put it on a shoe last and make their shoes last a little bit longer. Only his right arm worked. His left arm was there but it had been shot away and it just hung limply by his side. But he used his right hand.

In those days because it was Depression times my mother made every stitch of clothing that went onto we three children. She had a Singer sewing machine, a treadle, and she can be machining away frantically and furiously while she made clothes for us. And to supplement their income she would make clothes for other women and they would pay her for it.

What had happened, they had been developing houses. When the Depression struck people could no longer pay any rent and if they couldn't pay any rent there was no income for my family—my mother and father. So they would leave the tenants in the house because it stopped vandals getting in, but the income just wasn't there. But those women of the Depression days were *incredibly* good at spinning out money, what little they got. My father had a military pension, obviously, and that provided money.

***GINETTE MATALON** (1936) recalls a well-to-do childhood in Cairo.*

I was born in Cairo in Egypt, at home. It was a very primitive birth. We had a midwife. Everybody was probably present—my grandmother, my aunty, my mother. And I was born at home as I said, in Egypt, in a humungous apartment—it had seven bedrooms. We all lived together. Immediate family and extended family—everybody lived together, with servants—being Egypt, we had lots of servants. We had a male servant for the hard work, female servants and later on I had my personal companion servant. I still called her a servant but at that time I did not consider her as a servant at all. What happened when I was eight, I lost my father. And maybe a few months before I also lost a prematurely-born little sister girl. And because my father died and my mother thought she wouldn't have immediately any other children, they thought they would get me a companion from the village.

This girl came and she actually slept in my room, in a bed, which was there for the servants in Egypt because they had sleeping quarters on the top floor of the buildings but she slept in my room with me. She was three years older than I, and she was my closest friend. Her name was Rachea and we had a relationship as if she were my sister, *but* I must confess I had no social conscience whatsoever in her respect. I went to school. Never entered my mind what is Rachea doing while I'm at school. She was probably helping with the cleaning of the house. I never even asked her, 'How did you spend the morning?' I would come home at two o'clock and she was there to listen to all the gossip of my class, the teachers, everything. She would teach me the latest dancing steps and so on. But I never worried about her. 'Is she learning? Can she read? What is she doing?' Absolutely no conscience, no social conscience.

Three years later, my mother said, 'Rachea's going back to the village', and I said, 'Why?' She said, 'She's getting married.' By that time she would have been thirteen. She was getting married at the village and that was the last time I had a personal companion.

The youngest of six children, ***TRISH BARRKMAN*** *(1933) grew up on a sixty acre (twenty-four hectare) dairy farm at Loch in south Gippsland, Victoria.*

I wanted to recap on two or three mainly social issues over those years. Number one that I think was in 1947, I was still living in Gippsland and electricity was introduced to the area and that was a *huge* step forward in society on many, many levels. Then it was only a few short years after that that the Holden motorcar came into being. Well, the electricity issue, up until then we lived with kerosene lights and candles. So you can well imagine reading and things like that. We milked cows by hand. Once electricity came into being, we had electric machines for milking the cows and of course you had instant hot water in your home.

Hamish Sewell: And was that an instantaneous thing or did that take quite some time?

From my memory, it took quite some time. It was something that was discussed and talked about for quite some time, and I think for a lot of people it was a big financial issue also, 'cause if my memory is correct, you had to pay. The electricity came to your property but then the owner of the property would have to pay x amount for each pole that had to be erected to your house and cowshed. I'm almost sure. So I think for many families it was a big financial issue, but I also think that there was probably some form of government help. It certainly made life for people living on dairy farms, and certainly in the little village, much, much easier. You could see where you were going (laughs).

***ALISON FETTELL** (1952) was the fourth of six siblings (one of whom died at two days) in the south-western Sydney suburb of Bankstown.*

Growing up in the '50s and '60s, we didn't have a car and we didn't have a phone and my father worked in [a] foundry and my mother didn't work. Very blue-collar. I don't know how mum managed to feed us but she always did.

MY FATHER WAS—although, as I said, we were, oh I suppose poor—if ever he was going out, he would ensure that his clothes were perfect. His pants were ironed within an inch of their lives. He would use a wet rag on his trousers and a hot iron to make sure that the crease down the front was fine and there was never two creases. You don't have two creases. In my family, it's not two creases. I can remember it was incredibly important for me that my shoes were shiny and that my clothes were clean, and that they were ironed. Like, my shirts were ironed. Even from a young age. To the point where, I think I mentioned earlier that when my youngest brother started school—I may not have mentioned it on tape—I would make sure his hair was done, his teeth were cleaned and his shoes were shined and his clothes were ironed.

I don't remember thinking *why* that was important for me but as an adult now, I think it had something to do with not wanting to look poor possibly. Not sure, but I think it was important for me to look clean and well-presented even as a child, and making sure that my younger siblings were the same. Not so the older ones, but the younger ones.

***OURANITA KARADIMAS** (1958) was born to parents from Ithaka in Greece who owned a fish and chips shop in Albury, New South Wales.*

Our life revolved around the fish and chips shop. I remember my father and mother working in the kitchen together with my uncle who arrived in 1964, with my aunt who had arrived in 1958. My grandmother was there for a while. So we had an extended family living there and various members working in the fish shop. My brother and sister were born at that time. I have fantastic memories of my brother making a bow and arrow and chasing a cat over the wood pile that we had at the back of the shop because we had a big wooden stove for all the cooking.

WE NEVER ATE FISH SHOP FOOD at family time. That was food that they ate—the customers ate—that was *never ever* on the family dinner table. On the family dinner table was the food that my mother cooked in the back part of the house and that was the Greek food. The kind of cooking that she and her family did on Ithaka. Lots of meals cooked in one pot. Lots of vegetarian kind of food, legumes, lots of soups with different types of legumes, lentils, chickpeas, chicken soups, baked chicken and baked leg of lamb, that sort of thing. Also some lovely unique Greek snacks like thick slices of bread soaked with water and then the water squeezed out, with olive oil and oregano on top and topped with feta cheese, very simple food like that.

DAVID COOPER*'s (1959) dad was a printer at* The Herald and Weekly Times *and mum cleaned rooms and waitressed at a local pub. In 1958 they bought their first home on a new housing estate in Bonbeach on the Mornington Peninsula south-east of Melbourne.*

My dad was born and bred in Richmond, in rented accommodation. Never had any money. So to get a war service loan and own the home, was like, that was their whole ambition in life if you know what I mean. That was their most important thing ever. They never had much money to do very much. My dad was a cautious sort of person and wouldn't want to buy anything unless he had the money. My mum in lots of ways was the risk taker and you could probably say wore the pants in the family. She was the sort of person that, very determined, very determined to get her own way and wouldn't let anything stop her.

SHE JUGGLED THINGS quite well and she'd make things work for her. We never went without anything. Might have taken a few shortcuts. The Scouts used to have a stall once a year to raise money, and she would always work full-time but a lot of the other mothers, they weren't working. So they'd be there with the homemade cakes and all that sort of stuff. But she wouldn't want to miss out. She'd want to contribute. What she used to do, during the year she would save empty jam jars and she'd wash them out, put them in the bottom of the cupboard, and then she would buy a giant tin of plum jam from the Chelsea pub, she'd buy it off the boss. So it would be an industrial size thing. The night before the stall, she'd come home and she'd open up the can and she'd shovel it with a spoon and fill up these other things and she wouldn't lie, she wouldn't write 'homemade plum jam'. She'd just write 'plum jam', but because it's in the glass with a bit of material over the top and it's got plum jam, everyone just thought that she'd made this plum jam. So she used to get praised, 'Oh Marge, I don't know how you do it', you know, 'You work full time and you make this beautiful plum jam.' 'Oh, you'll have to buy.' Half the people on the stall used to buy her plum jam before the people in Chelsea would get a chance. It would all be sold out.

*After **RHONDA KING**'s (1965) father died in 1981, his Canberra crane business went bust and Rhonda's mother was forced to file for bankruptcy.*

So then we had to sell everything. We had to sell our house in Canberra. We had to sell the house on the farm. We had to sell all of our possessions. Everything that we had. We kept a few, you know, precious items and then we had nowhere to live all of a sudden. No house at all, so we went and stayed with our aunty, she's not our real aunty but went and stayed with her for a little while and we had no house to live in so mum went to the local MP and said, 'I need somewhere to live' and thankfully they did something and within a few days we had a house to live in in Narrabundah.

But then that changed our lives completely again because we were in Narrabundah (laughs), next to the Griffith shops so we were kind of in the good suburb, almost, but it meant that my brother and sister being the age they were—which was, I think they were under ten at the time—they were growing up in this area where it was pretty rough and the kids were pretty rough and so they got exposed to drugs and lots of stuff that you don't want your kids to get exposed to. I don't know to what degree but I could tell that it wasn't having a beneficial effect on their lives, living in that area.

Then I remember we had to go—because we had nothing, it was coming up to winter—we had to go to St Vincent de Paul. They have an actual—if you didn't know this (laughs)—have an actual place that you can go to that isn't the shops, so it's like the centre where you can go and get pots and pans and clothes and coats and whatever else that you need. So we went there and, it kind of felt exciting, 'Oh we can take anything we like', you know, 'I'm going to get this coat' and we're going to have this and we're going to have that frypan. But the reality of it was that that was the best we could do. We couldn't go to the local store. We couldn't go anyway because we had absolutely no money. We had nothing. We just went from a fairly affluent lifestyle to zero. So that was quite a shock to the system.

***LISA JACKSON** (1972) grew up in an Aboriginal family in New South Wales (her father's state of origin) and moved to Western Australia (her mother's state of origin) after her parents separated.*

I lived most of my life in Housing, Department of Housing. Here in New South Wales we lived in Department of Housing and in Perth we lived in Department of Housing. When we moved to Perth we had a four-bedroom home first with my nan. My mum with two kids and my nan with, you know, five kids. And you fluctuate anywhere between five and eight kids and we were sleeping everywhere.

Then my mum got married and we moved into private rental. That was the first time I think we've ever done private rental. Then what we did was we as a family took a conscious decision to help my brother in terms of saving money and as a way of stabilising him in terms of his alcoholism and drug use. We decided that we'd all buy a house together, and so we bought a house. And the real estate agent then said to us, 'Congratulations, you now own your own piece of Australia.' And I thought, how ironic (laughs) he telling me I'm buying it back bit by bit. It's our land to begin with. But I never said that to him. I said, 'Oh, well, thanks for that' (laughs).

I KNOW AS A YOUNG PERSON we weren't allowed to talk to Welfare. We had this in-built fear of Welfare, 'Oh Welfare's coming to get you' and we didn't understand what that meant. I didn't understand 'Welfare'. Then my cousins were, 'Oh, oh, they're coming' and I'm like, 'What's coming, who's coming?' 'Welfare.' So you know after a while when you hear the word 'Welfare' then you go, 'Oh yeah, okay.'

It was a threat. Your houses had to be cleaned. I grew up in spotless homes. Our bedrooms had to be cleaned and you had to present really, you know, well. Wash and hygiene and clothes, everything. So the implications of that generation have moved on and you've had to make yourself presentable. You get told, 'You're an Aboriginal person but you *have* to be better than a white person in terms of your education, your work standards, your personal standards, your own personal ethics.'

***JASON JOHNSON** (1981) grew up with his brother and sister, and a large extended family, at Bramston Beach near the north Queensland town of Babinda, where his father worked in the sugar mill.*

Growing up at Bramston Beach, we had it worked out when we were kids. We all had different sort of roles and we often lived, off the land is the easiest way to put it. So fishing, me and my brother and my sister and my cousins, we would go and catch live bait, which we would then use to catch barramundi at different times of the year when they were on the move. And the dragging of the net, often as kids we would drag in the shallow water, often catching bait to go fishing. Would have been five, six. We'd be out in the water up to our necks dragging the net through the water with either our grandad or our dad walking along the beach keeping an eye on us. At times we would go by ourselves if the water was good. We'd sometimes get in trouble 'cause there wasn't an adult around that knew where we were going or what we were up to. Obviously for the threat of jellyfish and crocodiles and sharks and the like. But we would often come back with what we needed and everyone had their arms and legs so everyone'd be happy. Then if we were going for the larger fish, like we were actually going to fill their freezers up with everybody with some fish, the adults would drag the larger nets along the beach and we'd all run along the beach with the hessian sacks and we'd have to collect all the fish out of the nets, and the crabs and everything. It would be spread amongst everybody that lived down at Bramston Beach essentially.

***KIRSTY WALLETT** (1982) was raised on a third generation dryland farm near Leeton in the New South Wales Riverina.*

In the early '90s when interest rates were at an all-time high and commodities were at an all-time low, we came pretty close to losing the farm. My father worked the farm with my grandfather. And my grandparents lived at the other end of the property which was a fantastic way to grow up. So I always had them there. Early '90s the bank said you can either walk off the farm—they said this to my grandfather—or you can sign it over to your son because he's got more years left in him and he might have more chance of paying back the huge amount of debt that you've got. That was common for a lot of families in the area. My aunty and uncle had a farm about forty minutes from where we were and they walked off their farm and moved to Queensland. So I was probably ten, twelve at the time but I knew what was going on. It was really sad for the family because there was a lot of emotional attachment to a farm. It's not just a business and it's not just a family business. There is a lot of attachment to what is essentially just a chunk of land. There's a lot of history involved in the property that we lived on. So it was a big thing but my dad did an amazing thing and turned out to be a bit of a businessman. Because we were only ten minutes from Leeton, he subdivided it and sold it off as hobby farms. So that's basically how the family survived that bump in the road.

As a boy ***ARTHUR HUNTER*** *(1989) moved between his father, who lived in Wyndham, and his mother, who lived at Lamboo Station, an East Kimberley pastoral property purchased in 1994 by the (then) Aboriginal and Torres Strait Islander Commission through the WA Aboriginal Lands Trust, and handed over to the local Ngunjiwirri people in the same year.*

My mum's side—like we have a cattle station in the family. That's been in the family since I was very, very young or since I was born. That's between Halls Creek and Fitzroy, about thirty, forty k's out of Halls Creek and on Fitzroy Road, Fitzroy Crossing. It's about 10 k's dirt road into the bush, which is pretty good, spectacular. Since I was young I spent times in Wyndham and at our station called Lamboo Station.

My mum and dad split when I was very young, well I think when I was a baby. They split and so I've just been going back and forward to Lamboo, Lamboo and Wyndham. Zoom back and forward and when I'm out in the bush like with my mum, on the station is like mustering, getting cattle, waking up in the morning, all that stuff. Like I miss it now you know. I wish that I could have stayed back there and worked on the land with the family and my grandparents. The bush life, for me growing up, I knew my food and I knew my bush fruits. I know what time to leave for hunting and where to go and how to track down certain food source or animals to get. And I just had fun as I was growing up there. You just walk down to the bush. We went hunting for goannas. It was the best times.

Miss it. Just coming into town, I got disconnected from country and that lifestyle. For me, from being a little country boy with my family that I really love and I will always love, for me to leave them is pretty hard. But now and then—maybe once every two years or a year—I go back home hunting, enjoying the station life. Fixing fences, fixing bores, mustering—when I can, or when I'm not working or travelling. I really love the bush. When I'm back home I feel more alive. I feel a spirit inside that's really happy. And I feel that my country is happy too, that I'm back home. So I think that's one thing that I've missed and that the country missed me—that I've been away for that long.

My uncles taught me a lot and my mum and aunties and, especially my grandparents. They try to teach me stuff about you know—well they do, and they did—teach me stuff about skin groups and my language and where I'm from, which country that they are from. They taught me a *lot*, my juja and jabbi—that's from down Halls Creek side—we call our grandparents, juja is nanna and jabbi, that's grandpa. That's Djaru side I think. Or Kija—one of them two. But I've learnt a lot from my grandparents. They took me out bush when I was very young. They practically was my second parents. They taught me stuff, they took me places that I've never been to.

Further Listening on Making Do: Childhood Family Economy

Bert Castellari, 1923, http://www.nla.gov.au/amad/nla.oh-vn6252044/0-1630
Michael Bicanic, 1937, http://www.nla.gov.au/amad/nla.oh-vn6421364/0-1018
Greer Bland, 1944, http://www.nla.gov.au/amad/nla.oh-vn5972533/0-1956
Ronnie Gauci, 1947, http://www.nla.gov.au/amad/nla.oh-vn6290910/0-2451
Les Robinson, 1947, http://www.nla.gov.au/amad/nla.oh-vn6504265/0-1409
Geraldine Box, 1949, http://www.nla.gov.au/amad/nla.oh-vn6190857/0-717~0-786
Donat Santowiak, 1950, http://nla.gov.au/nla.obj-220175608/listen/1-681
Russell Elliott, 1950, http://www.nla.gov.au/amad/nla.oh-vn6223258/0-130
Richard Galea, 1958, http://www.nla.gov.au/amad/nla.oh-vn6535733/0-2825

Michelle Cripps, 1960, http://www.nla.gov.au/amad/nla.oh-vn6252075/0-3415
Ian Reid, 1961, http://nla.gov.au/nla.obj-220066743/listen/0-4363
Phil May, 1962, http://www.nla.gov.au/amad/nla.oh-vn6569680/0-2176
Suzie Quartermain, 1975, http://nla.gov.au/nla.obj-220022403/listen/0-785
Jay Logan, 1981, http://www.nla.gov.au/amad/nla.oh-vn6569699/0-2084

Childhood Family Life

GINETTE MATALON*'s (1936) father died in Cairo in 1945.*

Nobody when my father died sat with me for two minutes to find out whether I was grieving for my father, how I felt about it, to *tell* me that my father had died. The only thing I remember was thirty-first of December, New Year's Eve, my father was going out to play at a big function for New Year's Eve, and my mother had the touch of the flu—she was in bed—and she says, 'Go and wave to dad at the window'. So I go out and blow him a kiss and he's dressed handsome as can be in a black dinner suit—very shiny material—and he went.

And the next morning I wake up and all the mirrors are covered and the washing lady—Oma—comes to me and she said, 'Don't make any noise, your father has died.' I said, 'What?' She said, 'Your father is dead. Don't make any noise, they're all busy.' So I didn't go to the funeral. The only difference—immediate difference—they took my bed from my room and they wheeled it into my mother's bedroom. I heard her every night crying and I didn't dare cry because I thought this would add to her sadness which it would. But she *never* talked about my father to me, neither did anybody else.

The only thing I remember is a cousin of my father one day was sitting in mourning for the days of mourning, she came to visit and she had a daughter my age. And she realised I didn't have books at home. So she said to my mother, 'Doesn't your daughter read?' My mother at the time must have said, 'No, we have no books' or something, or 'We get books from the library.' The next day she came with a pile of books from her daughter and this is the beginning of my love for books. I would say when I start it was escapist for me not to deal with the sadness of my father, the people crying around me, the prayers, whatever.

So I take this book and start reading and I would immerse myself in the stories. Unfortunately, a lot of the stories had bad stepparents. Stepfather—nasty—stepmother, and secretly I developed this anxiety that my mother would remarry and the stepfather would not like me at all and he would have other children. And whether my mother sensed it, whether I voiced it to her, she never remarried.

After a young childhood at Victoria Downs cattle station in the Northern Territory, ***VERONICA SCHWARZ*** *(1939) moved with her single mother to Brisbane. Her mother worked as a barmaid and had no alternative childcare, so from the age of eight Veronica was sent to a boarding school, which she hated, until her mother and grandparents bought a café and milk bar with a residence at the back.*

I think I was twelve and I had come out of boarding school when my mother was able to bring me to a place where *she* was living and working at the shop. And she married my stepfather, Charles. That was one of the best things that ever happened to her and to me because he was a lovely man, and he and I had similar interests. We loved history, we loved physics, we loved metaphysics, we loved philosophy and we'd read much the same books and talk to each other over breakfast while my mother'd just watch us over the top of her black coffee while she smoked a cigarette (laughs).

We were living in a house in St Lucia at the time—before they were married I think. I came home from school on a Friday afternoon after a big sports afternoon—we always had sports on Friday afternoon. While I was nerdy academically I could get away with it 'cause I was good at sport so it was always an exciting day for me and I always ran flat out. I got home and I was very tired, and the next morning I woke up and I had a pain in my knee and a sort of a numbness. And my mother was immediately alert to it and called the doctor—they came to the house in those days. And he diagnosed it as the onset of polio. Which in those days meant going to hospital—there was no cure, no treatment—they just put you in hospital and looked after you. Or if it got really worse, put you in an iron lung so you could still breathe.

But my mother had a good friend she had gone to school with and who was a nurse also with her in Darwin. They have always kept in touch. When she phoned her friend and told her what was happening, the friend knew about Sister Elizabeth Kenny, who had discovered, used a treatment for polio with children in outback Queensland and had cured them. The treatment consisted of hot packs and a physiotherapy-style exercise regime. My mother decided she would do that rather than just letting me be taken to hospital. She got the doctor to agree to the diagnosis of 'abortive polio'—whatever that might mean. And she kept me home and on her own single-handedly—because my stepfather was a travelling repairman round the state of Queensland, he was never home during the week—so on her own, day after day, she applied these hot, wet towels to my legs.

The paralysis got up as far as my waist—which as you can imagine had some complications as well. But she kept on with the hot packs, and the doctor kept an eye on how I was going. Gradually the feeling and movement came back into my legs. Then she got a physiotherapist to come to the house and put me through a series of exercises so I first learnt to crawl, and then to walk, and very slowly, finally was able to walk at a normal rate again. I think I mentioned to you, off the record earlier—off the microphone—that I had a race with my grandmother up the hall—who was crippled with arthritis—and she beat me hands down at the time. Which puts it in perspective as to how far I finally came to return to normal. Yep.

LES ROBINSON *(1947) grew up in Sutherland Shire, south Sydney, around the Georges River.*

Hamish Sewell: So when your father left, you were put out for adoption at that point?

No, mum kept us. She went and lived with her sister at Marylands and took us, traipsed us with her. We lived at Marylands with her sister and her husband. I'm not sure what period of time, I'd say about twelve months, and we caused a lot of friction between the husband and, you know, the aunty and uncle. We had to more or less leave. So I went to Oyster Bay School first off and then I went to Picnic Point School. Then we shifted back to the grandparents' place and we stayed with them. While we were there, I was put out with another aunt, another sister of my mother's, and they lived at Marylands. I lived there for a while, which is a horrid, not particularly nice time of my life.

They didn't care for you?

Not properly. I'd eat my lunch even before I'd get to school, I was that hungry. I remember sitting in a bath with two of her kids and there'd be faeces floating in the bath. I was the washer wiper, washer upper wiper, everything kid. When my mother visited once, they're out the front saying goodbyes and everything else and I'm at the sink, washing, wiping up, you know. I remember getting the Sunday paper once to have a look at the comics. Everyone else was asleep and I got a hiding for it, for opening the paper first. He was a sergeant in the army but, you know, just terrible time for me as far as it goes. So I ended up back with mum. Years later I said to mum, I said, 'How come I was the one always shipped out and not Neil or Wayne?' And she said I was a feral and a mongrel and nobody could handle me.

I went to Jannali West Public School, where I was, I suppose [it] would be under twelve months, and that's where mum met Neville Robinson, my future father. And after a while we shifted out to Como West, to live with him. Well they weren't married at the time and they always, remember them saying that—like we're all more or less, not *set up* but knew—if we had someone come to the door like child welfare, mum wasn't sleeping with dad, she always slept in the other room and we knew where people were supposed to be sleeping.

Though Les could not recall new migrants in 1950s Sutherland Shire, he did recall battles with the housing commission kids.

I CAN'T REMEMBER ANY MIGRANTS, anything like that. It was just housos, housing commission, always remember housos. Oh yeah, didn't have anything to do with the housos. I married one in the end (laughs).

They used to live over towards Jannali more from us. There was a bit of a ridge that separated Como West from Jannali and that's where the housing commission started over there and, oh we had many a brick fight and everything else, or rock fight with the housos. Including [future pop star] Normie Rowe. He was one of the housos in that area at the time. We were the other mob, wasn't much difference between us, I don't think. But if you weren't housing commission, you didn't have anything to do with housing commission kids, you know, it wasn't a choice.

***LYNNE SANDERS-BRAITHWAITE** (1949) grew up in Sydney in the 1950s.*

I was born in 1949, towards the end, the firstborn child to a former soldier from World War II. He's twenty-nine, my father, Bruce Sanders and he'd married my mum, Joyce Bell. He said he met her at her sister's engagement party and they were engaged within three weeks and married within three months. They stayed in love for fifty-three years till she passed away. Even then, when we made the decision to turn life support off, he said, 'Isn't she the most beautiful girl in the world?' So it was a long, long love affair. And I was their curly-headed little girl. Nine pound baby which for some reason, they were *enormously* proud that they had this nine and a half pound baby girl with curls (laughs).

Dad had built our house. He'd been back from the war then, for probably about four years. He was a builder. He actually studied for carpentry while he was in the army still and I met some of his old soldier friends in later years and they said that as they were going into battle at El Alamein, everybody else was shaking with fear and smoking cigarettes and, by the light of a candle, Bruce was studying his carpentry workshops ready for after the war. So he was an optimist as well. And it paid off, strangely enough, because he built us a house in the western suburbs of Sydney. And we went to live there when I was nine months old. And we were enormously proud of that too. It was like *The Wonder Years*, from that American television show, a little bit, my childhood. For me anyway, I don't imagine it was all round.

Jo Kijas: What do you mean by that?

Well we lived in a suburban street and our street was designated 'full brick only'. That was another one of our big achievements in life, nine and a half pounds and lived in a full brick only house. Dad had come from a ham and beef shop in Hurlstone Park and mum had come from Redfern and then Rosebery and my poppa was a tram driver, so very much working-class people. And I think carpenter, with his own business, was the next step up, and then they'd gone out into the suburbs as Belmore was then. All the streets around, you could build a fibro house in some of the streets and you could build single brick veneer, I think they used to call it, in some. But ours had to be double brick.

The reason I call it the 'wonder years' was, then I had a younger sister two years later and then a younger brother two years after that, and mum cooked for us and sewed for us and took us to school, and dad went off to work so there was a real wonder year element. Our street was safe and our schools were safe. And cousins everywhere. They were in the next suburb.

DONAT SANTOWIAK *(1950) migrated from Poland as a thirteen-year-old only child with his parents in 1964, to join members of his mother's family who had come to Australia in 1950 as Displaced Persons and were now living in industrial La Trobe Valley in eastern Victoria.*

My mum virtually had no one left in Poland. My dad's family, I wasn't conscious or aware of it at the time, but I know and I can understand that they would have been really broken-hearted about him coming here—particularly his mum—'cause they never reconnected. Dad's family would have been really sad about dad going. I don't know how more deeply that whole dynamic kind of --- 'cause mum and dad really didn't get on, you know. That's the plain truth.

It was only when we came here that I think everybody realised, 'Shit. What did we leave behind?' In terms of relationships, in terms of jobs, in terms of—my dad was very highly regarded in terms of his work. He was actually *managing* a cooperative. He had about ten blokes working for him. So we came here and he got a pair of gumboots and a shovel and told to dig a hole in the bottom of a mine. Dad ended up having a nervous breakdown.

OH HE BECAME VERY ANGRY. He became, almost like he was really having some severe mental illness. He would not sleep very much. It would have been when we came to Morwell. So it would have been probably I'd say [after] about a year or something like that. Just terribly unpredictable. Dad was—and I don't know whether it was his genetic predisposition or whether it was partly the war experience or what—but he was quite paranoid. He was quite untrusting. He'd set up listening devices in the house. Really bizarre. To a point where he was gonna kill us one night. And, you know, chased us with a knife. The coppers were called by the neighbours and they took him away and he spent a few weeks at Larundel [asylum] in Melbourne. That's what happened.

He came back and none of that sort of extreme ever occurred again. But I suppose it's not hard to imagine the --- how do you readjust to some sense of normality in terms of living together after you've been threatened with your life? So, for me, around about seventeen, eighteen—when the booze came along—it kind of really, all that stuff just sort of washed away.

Donat's lifelong love of dogs and cats began with his first dog Bobby.

I DID HAVE A DOG and that's rather a sad story because it even sometimes, you know, emotionally gags me a bit today, thinking about it. His name was Bobby and he was a bit of a moggie kind of Fox Terrier style of dog. And mum and dad were having a big altercation and the police was called. I can't remember who called the police. And bugger me, when the copper turned up, Bobby bit the copper. The copper pulled out a revolver and he was gonna shoot him there in the backyard. But we were ordered to pay for his uniform being torn and we were ordered to have the dog destroyed. So --- that's where I get still a bit heavy today, you know. I had to walk the dog to the pound to get him gassed. Shit, it was about a four k walk, and every step I took I was so bloody distressed. 'Cause Bobby was my mate, you know. M'mm. So I've tried to have animals with me most of the journey. Yeah. So Bobby was probably responsible for keeping my wellbeing.

ALISON FETTELL *(1952) from Bankstown in Sydney had five siblings, one of whom died at two-days-old, and she recalls the impact of that death on her mother.*

I had an awful lot to do with my two younger siblings. There's only about sixteen months between myself and my youngest sister but then there's five years between me and the youngest brother. We kind of—my younger sister and I—really brought him up in a sense. Like we would make sure he was dressed and polished to go off to school. Hair done, teeth done, shoes polished—that sort of thing. 'Cause mum wasn't terrifically well. I think she was still suffering from the loss of her second child that we never understood as children. I looked into all that later in life for myself, to try to understand mum's --- mum's personality in a sense—what had changed in her life, which clearly had changed dramatically over the years. She was often a sad woman when I was a child. Quite depressed.

Roslyn Burge: Was your brother not cared for that you needed to step up to the plate and dress him?

I don't know. I think he was okay but mum stayed in bed, in the mornings. So the school mornings were get yourself out, that kind of thing. But no, he was cared for. I think my elder brother though—the child that was born after the child that died—I think personally there was a little bit of a lack there. Not on purpose. Mum just wasn't well.

Alison also recalls the impact of childhood abuse.

I STRUGGLED WITH HIGH SCHOOL. Because I—this may or may not be the right time—but because I had abuse in my background, I reflect on my schooling. I was impacted by that and I don't think I was really able to concentrate as well at school. I did struggle. I honestly thought I was quite dumb.

Alison, are you happy to talk about that abuse?

Yes, yes. There were two lots of abuse from the same family but different members. The first abuse—and I didn't remember this until I was in my early thirties --- when they talk about repressed memory I am one of those people. I was having a gynaecological examination and this particular man, doctor, was the spitting image of this older man, and I freaked out. I had this instant memory. I could recollect it immediately but I hadn't processed it as a growing adult at all. I had other abuse that had happened when I was probably six, seven and eight but that wasn't the older man. The older man was only once, and I clearly kept myself very separate from him. I never ever was alone with him again that I can remember. I think I told my mother but I don't think I could verbalise it properly. When I told her after I'd had the memory, she said, 'You know, I remember you used to hide behind my legs whenever he ---' But she didn't put it together or chose not to. I don't know what.

I have a vivid memory of that. I was four and he was an old man—a white-haired old man. It happened, and I know which year it happened and I know how old I was because the neighbours had just gotten the TV and they were rich compared to us. And it was '56. They got the TV the year that TVs came out because they were the only people in the street that had got a TV. And I remember being little and I wandered in to the, or I must have got told to go down the back rumpus room and he was there. I hadn't felt unsafe with him but clearly I was. Everybody else must have been in the front of the house when it happened. As I said, I recalled it when I was in my thirties and, yeah, I'm still revolted by it.

The other abuse that occurred over a longer period of time was a different kind of abuse I suppose. Well, still sexual but it was, I don't know how to really explain it --- It was wrong, incredibly wrong. In my thirties when I realised the abuse of when I was four, I decided to address it in my life, because it had been impacting me. And I actually went and fronted the abuser. Not the old man but the younger, the younger. I tracked him down and went and saw him at his workplace—he owns the business. 'Cause I'd written to him twice, trying to explain to him how badly this had impacted me. I still didn't feel right about it and I thought I've got to front this. So I went and saw him.

I remember the look on his face when he saw me walk into the foundry. I had a discussion with him, and just said, 'Look, I just want an apology. And I want to make sure that you're not doing this with anybody else. I know you've got children. It was wrong, it was not okay and it damaged me.' So I needed to express that to him. He was incredibly apologetic, and didn't think that he'd done anything wrong. I walked in shaking and I left shaking but I was pleased that I'd done it and I have had no contact with him since. He was a teenager and I was a little one. I think we might have been six or seven years difference but when you're seven or eight or nine—it's hard for me to remember exact ages ---

KIM BEAR*'s (1959) father died in a trucking accident in 1960, when she was a toddler and just before her sister was born. The family of three lived in Loftus, south Sydney, until they moved to Dalby on the Queensland Darling Downs when Kim was seven.*

There was a hearing and I think coronial inquest into dad's death because the person who'd caused the accident was a drunk driver and he actually survived the accident but my father didn't. I think it was pretty tough for mum right from that moment. She did used to do housekeeper type jobs. And my sister was born in December 1960. Yes it was just the three of us really. Mum did keep us fairly separate from our relatives. I think she'd had more than enough of relatives around the time I was about three or four and she always felt like people were trying to tell her how to do everything. She wasn't stupid. Even though she hadn't had a lot of education, she had a lot of common sense and she was a very proud person. Very good-looking woman, extremely tall, almost six foot tall, very slim and stood very tall and erect as well, and I think she probably frightened a lot of people (laughs).

She could be quite fearsome. She was very hard on my sister and I, and I think that partly came from possibly her frustration at how *her* life had panned out and probably wasn't anything like what she thought would happen. She did used to be very handy with the stick, and we had a *range* of hitting implements at our house actually. Anything from the lower branches of the willow tree to—what else do we have—dad's old belts, few old pairs of shoes.

I'll never forget once we had a chook shed in our yard and mum used to—what she used to do, she'd have the chooks in a certain position for a while and then after about six months would move the chook shed and then we'd grow our veggies underneath where they'd been. One day she took us out for the digging up under the new chook shed and of course she's digging away and my sister and I were watching where she was digging and the two of us just waiting and waiting and sure enough, out came a red fly swat and an old belt. This is where we'd hidden all the smacking things in the garden (laughs). So she'd found us out and luckily on that particular occasion she saw the funny side of it and we didn't get a smack with them, but boy oh boy, she was pretty scary.

We were quite afraid of her as children and I put that down partly to what must've been her upbringing as well, which from all accounts was pretty ferocious as well. She did used to lose her temper really, really quickly. In fact we learned when we were small that if we came home or if we were aware of her washing her hair that would mean that she was about to put them into rollers, which always gave her a headache and her fuse would be even shorter. So if you heard her washing her hair you just stayed outside and kept away from her and stayed quiet because the minute those rollers went in you're done for. One noise or anything wrong and you would cop it. So, we spent a lot of time in the chook shed, as kids.

***MICHELLE CRIPPS** (1960) was born in Hobart, but when she was small the family moved to Burnie, where her parents came from, on the north coast of Tasmania.*

My dad originally was a banker and worked for the Hobart Savings Bank—which doesn't exist anymore—and then after banking moved into insurance for the rest of his life. Mum had begun working with Holman's Airlines—reception work—then stopped to have children, and then went back to work eventually as a teacher's aide, and did that for the rest of our lives at school. My father died two years ago. We were always a fairly close-knit family. I've got a brother and two sisters. I guess I've inherited qualities from both my mum and dad. One of the key things is, mum was involved in theatre and musicals and I'm *very* involved in theatre and drama. Dad was involved in Lions and Jaycees and then mum has been involved in community groups for years and so I guess my sense of community and the fact that *I'm* involved now, on boards and work in the community, has very much come from them.

Karen George: Can you tell me a bit about them as people, what kind of things stick out?

With dad, it was the fact that he would come home at lunchtime and then, when he wasn't coming home from lunchtime, he would ring mum every day at lunchtime and just touch base and I will *always* remember that. It was almost like a routine. If mum was home, *Blue Hills* was on the radio and then dad would ring to say, you know, 'How's things? How's the day?' and they would touch base before he came home of an evening. So I've *always* remembered that sense of communication that they always had. Mum too sings and plays the piano and so again I remember us gathering around, and that sense of community, of being together. And of them always being there for us. Once we were leaving primary for high school, we always got the 'talk' about sex and life and it was always prefaced with, 'You can come to us any time. It doesn't matter how bad, what the problem is, come and talk to us.' And I've used that with my own kids, that you don't judge, you just talk and deal with them. Yes, so that's been really important.

RHONDA KING*'s (1965) father was born in 1921 and her mother in 1941. Rhonda recalls their different roles and attitudes in parenting.*

I don't really remember him being involved in caring for the kids at all. I can remember on occasion he'd muck around with us and play. But he usually was at work and then he would come home and—I could be telling a lie here but my memory is—he would come home and expect dinner to be ready. He'd expect it to be meat and three veg. If it was anything else, I can remember him having fits if my mum would put a salad on the table. He would just, he would really—I'm not joking—hit the roof. He went so cranky one night because of this salad she put there. He was not happy. And I'm looking at the salad thinking, 'What's wrong with the salad?' But I probably don't like salads now because of that (laughs).

She's doing the housework, she's doing the kids, she's doing the cooking, she's doing the shopping. He's doing the bloke work.

Mary Hutchison: But then she also played quite a role in the business ---

She did. Yes, later on. You know as we got older, watching them trying to discipline us as kids and take care of that side of things was, I guess you didn't look at it from an outside perspective when you're in it. You're just like, 'Why can't they decide what's going on?' But dad had a real, you know, kids should be seen and not heard. Kids will do as they're told. Kids will, you know, '*I* make the rules. I'm the father. You'll do it this way and that's all there is to it. There is no discussion.' And then mum being born in the '40s probably was just in the later or the beginning edge—I don't know—of the baby boomers where things were more about, 'Yeah, free, love, ooh yeah.' You know, 'Feel good, be good, everything's great' (laughs).

When we lived on the farm he would come to Canberra for the week to work and she would be with us on the farm during the week and it was wonderful. It was fantastic and dad would come out on the weekends. Soon as we knew dad was coming it was all like, 'Ooh' (laughs). Which is awful. We should be like, 'Yeah, dad's coming.' But we were all like, 'Oh no, here he comes. Here comes all the clamping down. We won't have freedom. Boyfriends can't come over. Ooh.' Anyway.

Rhonda also recalls growing up with a sister with cerebral palsy who died at the age of seven.

I THINK THE EFFECT—for *me* as the child in that family having a sister with cerebral palsy and then two youngest, a brother and sister—was that I became introverted. Because I could see that mum was busy. 'Cause back in the '60s and '70s there wasn't the kind of support there is now for parents that have a child with a disability, and a severe disability. Most people would just turn away. I would see it. I'd be walking through the shopping centre with mum, and my sister Julie would be in the pram and I'd be holding the side of the pram walking with her. I had a relationship with Julie that I can't explain. I knew what she was thinking. I used to interpret to mum what she needed and I can't even go, oh, it was because she did this that that's why I knew. I just would say, 'Her foot's hurting.' Or, 'She's hungry.' Or, Mum would be like, 'Oh thank goodness you're here.' But I would see people and I'm like, 'Why are they looking away? What's wrong with them? Why are they --- ?' You could sense it. I didn't understand why because I didn't see her that way.

Because I knew that Mum was really occupied with having to take care of her, I became obsessed with reading. I just would read and read and walk round with a book in my face and fall down holes because I wasn't watching where I was walking. I think I was quite introverted. Probably quite shy.

Closer to when she died, she got taken to a hostel place up in Newcastle because my mum was really stressed. She went through a nervous breakdown. The key phrase for the day was to have a nervous breakdown, back in those times. Seemed to be quite common. They call it other things now. I don't know why it happened. So the doctors recommended that Julie should be put into a home because it was really difficult for my mum to take care of her and all the kids and the business and all the rest of it. So mum—against her better judgment—took her up there and put her in there. I don't know how long she was in there. It was only a few weeks I think.

We went up for a visit and mum said, 'Oh well, we'll go in first and go check where she is so we can all come in to say hi.' And they just came out *with* her. They wouldn't leave her in there. She said when they went in there, the kids were just all lying around on the floor and in their own waste. She said it was just awful and she was absolutely horrified because she thought she was doing the right thing because this is what the doctor said they should do to make sure she'd get the best care. Anyway it wasn't very long after that she passed away. It was from a brain tumour which obviously is not as a result of being in this place. But of course mum felt incredibly guilty because she had put her there when she was in pain. Because before she went there she'd been screaming all the time. She just was screaming constantly, non-stop screaming. I remember thinking to myself—it sounds awful—but I remember thinking, 'I hope that she dies soon.' Not because I thought, 'Oh get rid of this bloody screaming.' It was because I just knew that it was better for her to die because she was in pain.

I just remember the time before the screaming and the pain started. That we could just be there and it was like—it sounds weird—like a vibrational kind of a thing that we just would be there and mum would put her into this special chair. She had a really big table in front—there's a photo somewhere and we've put a princess hat on Julie and she's sitting there. She's got cerebral palsy right? So she can hardly even hold her own body up straight, so the chair's helping her to sit up. And she's sitting there and she looks kind of like, 'Whatever' (laughs). Her facial expression's like, 'Whatever', and I'm like, 'Yes we're princesses. We're playing princesses.' I'm running around too with my crown and waving a wand or whatever and she's just sitting there. I always thought it was great because I had this playmate. Always there. Always willing to play whatever game what I want. She never argued. 'Sure, I'll be a princess. Whatever.'

But she couldn't speak so she couldn't, you know, make words. She couldn't go to the toilet, couldn't stand up, couldn't sit up, couldn't --- there was nothing that she could do for herself. So, yes, it would've been really hard for my mum I think. For me, not so much maybe because I felt like I kind of connected with her but then, yeah, when that screaming started, that was when mum got really stressed out obviously. But I just remember thinking, 'I hope that she dies soon.' And not even really knowing what death was at that time because I was still quite young.

LISA JACKSON *(1972) recalls an extended Aboriginal family in Perth.*

When we got a bit older we had cousins who went out shooting and they used to go roo shooting. So mum used to make up some *beautiful* kangaroo stews and dampers. My mum used to make beautiful dampers—absolutely beautiful dampers, and chocolate cake. We almost had a damper factory in our house, and stew. When my mum started working with the frail aged and disabled people, she used to make 'em up a big stew at least once a week and they used to put them in the container and send them home with stew. And every now and again you get the kangaroo stew. Only on special occasions but they used to love it and we used to be able to eat it because mum use to have some left over. But when it came to bush tucker, not much, it was just meat and three veg.

My mum used to take us to some Aboriginal meetings in Perth. I couldn't understand *why* we were all here but then mum said, 'Well, look we are Aboriginal and this is part of our heritage. This is what we do'. I thought, 'Oh okay, whatever.' And then we saw in Perth—across one of the train lines there used to be an old rubbish dump—I used to see some Aboriginal people living there and I used to ask, 'Why are they living in there and I'm living in a house?' and mum says, 'Well, that's where they live, that's their home.' I didn't get it. I honestly didn't get it. Like I said, it wasn't until I was in high school that I started seeing things a bit different. Seeing things and realising being an Aboriginal person is not just a unique thing, it's also a culturally unique thing. And our culture is a little bit, you know, is *different* from mainstream and I am different from everyone else. My life experiences will be different and cultural experiences will be different. So *that* for me was more of a watershed moment and it was a changing moment because I then started to become aware of what was happening in terms of culture.

***JAMES MAYOL** (1974) recalls family life within a southern Sudan Dinka community in the 1970s and 1980s.*

My father married three wives. From the first wife, he got only one child and that's the one I told you now he's eighty-five years old. He's still alive. We don't know what happened because they have a family break off after he [James' father] had one child. Then his wife left and he remained. The second wife is also pass away. And my mother, the third wife, also pass away in 2006. So together now we have from my family side, I've got four sisters and I'm only the man alive because all my other brothers got killed during the war. From the second wife I still got two brothers and three sisters, from the second wife.

Atem Atem: Just going into the little bit of the tradition, that was three wives. Were they living in the same place or they had different houses?

During that time we had to have different houses but not too far away each other's. My father occupied *big* land. He put all these three houses in different areas. It was very accessible for us to move around. You can go anywhere. You can go to there or you go in there. It's just like one family, but put them in different places.

***SUZIE QUARTERMAIN** (1975) describes her adoption story.*

My earliest memory is my second birthday. We'd just moved to Sale—my dad was a teacher—so all my memory started in Sale. But I was actually born in Melbourne to unmarried parents. When my mother's parents found out that she was pregnant she was seven months along. She got locked in her room till I was born. She wasn't allowed to see my father. So I was forcefully adopted out—against my parents' wishes—by my grandparents.

Katie Holmes: How old was your mother?

Seventeen. My father was eighteen. My grandparents on my *father's* side offered to raise me as their youngest was six. But being the mother's parents they had all the say. So I was taken from my mother at birth and put in foster care for six weeks. Then I went to my parents that brought me up.

MY OLDER BROTHER AND I always had a really strong connection because we were adopted. We both knew how it felt to be --- (sighs) I don't think there's a word for it. It's not different because, like our parents, you would never have known we were adopted. They never favoured any of us but we just knew what it was like to be rejected. That was the thing. It was rejection. Sorry, I'm getting a bit teary.

That's okay.

Yes. So, oh he was a menace. He was horrible. He'd typewriter us, Chinese burn us, torment us. But if anyone so much as looked sideways he would do it to them. So as we got older, he left school and then he went back. So we did Year 10 together. And that's when we kind of clicked. He was always a bit immature so we were on the same social level, and all of that stuff.

At what age did you become aware that you were adopted?

I knew I was right from the beginning because I remember them reading me a book about an adoption. But it never bothered me till I was about fifteen. Till I started meeting friends who looked exactly like their parents—and I've got two particular girlfriends that look exactly like their mothers—and thinking, you know, 'Where did *I* come from? Who do I look like?'

JAY LOGAN*'s (1981) mother was nineteen when Jay was born. She left his father, who was violent, when Jay was very young. Jay spent some of his early childhood living with his grandparents on their farm in Tenterfield, and some with his mother who moved around Queensland until settling at a sales representative job in Rockhampton where she partnered with a second violent man.*

I loved my mum. I loved her, you know, as a little kid—as little kids do. I don't think I had any real issues with mum at all. I had more, probably a similar relationship with my grandparents in the sense of they were sort of a surrogate family. I think mum struggled a bit with her youth dealing with a child and yes, I did end up with my grandparents for a bit.

When a new man came along, he convinced her to move away and oh yes, you don't need to work, I'm working. And he was driving trucks. And we moved to Hervey Bay. My grandparents were living in Rockhampton as well—on the island, Keppel Island—and he managed to separate that family unit, or us from the rest of the family and after that, things got bad. He had control of the money. He had control of, basically all of us, when my sister was coming along. He was in charge and he was, yes, he was violent. So not a nice guy.

Matthew Higgins: So did he hit your mother?

Yes. I come out one night—I was terrified to be honest, I'd go and hide in my room—I come out one night and my mother was, oh probably seven, eight months pregnant. Same as my wife is. And he kicked her legs out from underneath her in the kitchen and I didn't know what to do. You know I contemplated—it's not a thought that a ten-year-old has—but he was a gun nut so he had firearms in the house at all times. Under the bed and whatever. There was only one pistol in the house that *I* could think of using, that was small enough for me. But I actually considered using it. But I was too scared to do that. I mean, what if it didn't work or something? I remember thinking those possibilities. But yeah, it was a scary time for me anyway.

So how did she and you and your sister get away from him?

Well, as much as I know, she rang my aunt and my aunt transferred some funds to her and then we got on a plane and we came to Canberra. She was an escape. So we came down and lived with my Uncle Gerry and Aunty Julie.

At Bramston Beach on the north Queensland coast, ***JASON JOHNSON*** *(1981) and his brother learnt about living blind from their sister.*

It was difficult for us when we were kids at first because obviously our sister was blind and there was a lot that we had to do to assist her with everything. I suppose the challenge which has helped me greatly in life as I've grown older is my mother always turned everything into almost like a game, but it was a test for us. It was a challenge for us as older brothers to be able to communicate effectively, so that she could understand how to do things. We used to play games out in the back yard where we would get blindfolded and then my sister would have to guide us around and we'd play different games where one of the kids would be blindfolded and we'd have to articulate a certain obstacle course that the kids had to move through. That's how my mum came up with ideas for us to develop so that we could actually help our sister out through things. We could clearly explain things to her so that she could do it.

***KIRSTY WALLETT** (1982) was eleven when her mother was diagnosed with multiple sclerosis.*

I didn't realise what I didn't have until I met other people. I don't particularly feel sorry for myself about it but I didn't have a mother who made my lunches every morning. And I didn't always have my mother cook dinner for me every night. And you know I was—I mean mum made us fairly independent before she got sick anyway. I know why she did that because her and I were very close and we've talked about it, and she did that because she lost her parents. She thought, 'If anything ever happens to me, my kids are going to be able to go to other people, be independent.' That was why she worked part-time so that she would raise us as being independent. But I kind of feel like sometimes—maybe because I was the eldest—and I did shelter my brother and sister from a lot of it because it was stressful, so I took on the mum role even though I didn't necessarily need to a lot of the time. I think that I grew up, before my time. But then also when I was *actually* an adult I found accepting responsibility, commitment and stability—I didn't want it, because I kind of had it, I'd had enough of it.

***Rachel Brown** (1985) was born in Cebu City in the Philippines, where her mother was a school teacher and her father an expatriate Australian Vietnam War veteran. They moved to Australia when Rachel was eight months, and every five years they visited relatives in the Philippines.*

I only met my grandmother. I think my grandfather died before I was born. She was quite old when I was young. I just remember her being the matriarch of the family—and she'd had a *big* family. My mum comes from thirteen. She'd [her grandmother] had all her children around her and her grandchildren and it was always such a lively house where she lived. And she still kept up with the day to day running of the house and ordered everybody around doing things and that kind of thing.

The language barrier was, and is, still a big problem for me because it stops me from really understanding their life. When I'm there, unless they are speaking to me, they are speaking Cebuano. They'll stop the conversation. They can speak in English actually a lot of them, but they prefer to speak in Cebuano. It's only when they're talking to me or when I'm directly involved in the conversation that it will be in English (laughs). Well, my mum never taught me. She said that her philosophy was, 'Well, we're in Australia now so what's the point, you don't need it. You'll just have to speak English. I'm learning English. I don't want to speak Cebuano with you.' She didn't see the relevance of it.

Further Listening on Childhood Family Life

Ruth Apps, 1926, http://www.nla.gov.au/amad/nla.oh-vn6252043/0-140
Donald Grey-Smith, 1931, http://nla.gov.au/nla.obj-220110052/listen/0-393
John Murphy, 1940, http://www.nla.gov.au/amad/nla.oh-vn6504268/0-3746
Russell Elliott, 1950, http://www.nla.gov.au/amad/nla.oh-vn6223258/1-1545
Gina Polito, 1954, http://www.nla.gov.au/amad/nla.oh-vn6421369/2-28
David Cooper, 1959, http://nla.gov.au/nla.obj-220009702/listen/0-3801
Ian Reid, 1961, http://nla.gov.au/nla.obj-220066743/listen/0-3508
Bronwyn Macdonald, 1964, http://www.nla.gov.au/amad/nla.oh-vn6390885/0-2145
Jodie Bell, 1970, http://www.nla.gov.au/amad/nla.oh-vn6290885/0-797
Lisa Jackson, 1972, http://www.nla.gov.au/amad/nla.oh-vn6252067/0-1101
James Finnegan, 1981, http://nla.gov.au/nla.obj-220176798/listen/0-1380

Childhood Pleasures

The collapse of ***RUTH APPS****' (1926) parents' Wagga Wagga property development business during the 1930s Depression restricted the use of the family car to three months in the year. That was not the only constraint on a young girl's pleasures.*

Living in Wagga we were not far from the Murrumbidgee River and the Murrumbidgee Lagoon and we used to play there. They had willow trees on the banks and my brother would swing across hanging onto a willow branch, but I wasn't allowed to do it because I was a girl and things were very different in those days.

There were virtually no cars. My parents had a 1923 Buick, that they'd had, but every January it would be registered for three months and we would come to Sydney for a holiday. Now we brought all our food with us. It was put on a tucker box on the side—the running board of the car—and our clothes had been packed in. My mother drove because my father was not able to. But she was a lady I think before her time. A garage in Wagga Wagga, they used to put her on a train. She would come to Sydney—cars were all imported from America in those days—and she would pick up a car and drive it back to Wagga for the dealers.

WE'D COME TO NARRABEEN and put up a tent there. You probably couldn't do it nowadays, but we would put up a tent and we would have about three weeks here in the city. *Always* one trip. We would take the tram into Manly and then the ferry across to Circular Quay where we'd then *always* go to Anthony Hordern's—which doesn't exist any longer—where our school uniforms were bought for the following year and we *always* had that treat of having morning tea in Anthony Hordern's Restaurant and it was a highlight. We were country kids. We would go to the beach—and it wasn't known in those days—my mother would cover us in coconut oil which meant we promptly fried and we would come out in blisters, but we would happily swim there in the surf. And my father was a good swimmer and he would take us out and it was very enjoyable. My parents must've had to make sacrifices to do that for us, but it was such a happy time.

WHEN WE WERE IN THE COUNTRY, I think the first talkies started when I would've been about seven or eight or thereabouts. Shirley Temple was a great run. You'd *flock* to the—it would cost threepence, I suppose three cents, and for that you enter, and you're always given a penny to buy a bag of lollies. We would go there and absolutely enchanted by Shirley Temple. I've seen her movies later as I've grown up and as an actress she is pretty poor but we thought it's absolutely wonderful. Once we came to Sydney, to live, again there were the movies of a Saturday afternoon. All through the war years we'd go to the Saturday afternoon movies, or the 'Saturday Arvo Flicks' as they were called. You could sit down the front stalls for threepence, back stalls for sixpence. And for ninepence you could go up into the dress circle and that was the ultimate. Of course once I had a boyfriend he always took me to the nine-penny seats and we watched movies, a great deal. They were very, very important in our life.

***DONALD GREY-SMITH** (1931) recalls an outdoor childhood around Rye on Victoria's Mornington Peninsula.*

My brother and I both had bicycles. We sometimes walked to school, sometimes we rode our bikes. We were free to explore, to climb trees. There were just a couple of restrictions. We were never allowed to swim from the pier because my mother had experienced a shark attack off the pier in her youth and that was out of bounds. And we weren't allowed to go to the white cliffs, which was a cliff formation which was hazardous. But apart from that, we were free to explore, everywhere.

When I look at my grandchildren and see how controlled their lives are, I realise what a great blessing it was to have that freedom. My particular attachment was to the beach, and to the beach in all seasons. It's a very protected beach, just inside Port Phillip Bay. So in summer, during the summer holidays, my brother and I would spend the whole day on the beach and my mother would bring lunch down to us and have lunch with us in the form of sandwiches, and we'd be there really all day. Kicked my shoes off when school finished and didn't put them on again until we went back to school after the school holidays. In winter, when the storms came and the tide was right up and washing against—the trees were being undermined and falling—I loved that wild wintry stormy weather on the beach as much as the calm summer weather.

Growing up after the war in Melbourne's south-eastern suburb of South Camberwell, ***JOHN MURPHY*** *(1940) also enjoyed an outdoor childhood.*

The fireplace in the lounge room—outside there was this big brick kind of construction which, you know, with the chimney, so that was where you'd hit the tennis ball or that kind of thing. Or kick the footy. So I spent a lot of time outside and my friends would come and we'd spend a lot of time outside. Everything was outside in those days, as a younger child growing up.

Down the corner about fifty yards—we would have said—fifty metres away, cricket and footy and there'd be about five, six, eight of us. We'd have teams and we'd do that probably most days after school. During the holidays we'd go down to the park and play footy or cricket or whatever, tennis. So it was plenty of activity, sporting activity, but mainly games, not so much running. Although we used to ride. When I was from say twelve to fourteen or fifteen, we'd ride our bikes, for instance to

Ferntree Gully, which is a fair way. And other places like that, on our bikes. But of course traffic wasn't then --- but we were still on Toorak Road going down Burwood Highway, going out bush.

***LES ROBINSON** (1947) recalls the arrival of television in the late 1950s in Como West, south Sydney.*

One night sticks in my mind. All hanging around, laying around the back lawn in summer. Just fooling around, fooling around with the old man and everything else down there. We had a guava tree, and eating fruit straight off the guava tree and all. One reason that sticks in the mind so much is that we picked a lot to go back up inside and then we went back up inside and we found out it was all full of worms. Grubs. So we've been eating these things all night and they're full of grubs.

But other than that, like sitting and watching telly. We had our own spots. We used to sit on the floor in our own particular spot, and no one sat in your spot. Dad, since he worked next door with a fish pond place, had made a fish pond stand specially for our television to go on. It wasn't a cabinet or anything else for it, it was one of those steel angle iron fish pond stands that he made specially for the TV. And the TV, actually, we didn't get until later. We used to go up the road to Pratts, people up the road, they used to run the soccer club. We were members of the soccer team, and we used to pay sixpence each a night to watch television up there and we used to watch *Rin Tin Tin* and *The Mickey Mouse Club*. A few of us used to go, it wasn't all of us, but I know definitely four or five of us used to go up there a couple of nights a week and pay our sixpence and watch their TV, along with a few other kids.

***RUSSELL ELLIOTT**'s (1950) playground was the family farm in central Victoria.*

I guess the whole farm was my playground because as an only child and with limited capacity to go to functions—we had a car, but my parents weren't of the ilk of going to the pictures every Saturday night or going, you know, to a lot of events and things. So at a pretty early age I guess I realised that I had to make my own fun, and the rural aspect of our property became literally my playground. Especially the famous creek at the back of the house which dad started to plant trees on. I would hate to think how many hours I spent traversing that creek up and down, through it, looking at its various moods, looking at the things going on there, the bottle swallows [Fairy Martins] that were building in under the crevices. Pardalotes that were drilling little holes in through old root stump things into the bank to make a nest. Seasonal Rainbow Birds that came there every year and did the same thing—burrowed their way in. It just became a blank canvass for me really. There was something different there all the time. Whenever you went down—whether it was in the middle of summer, when it was hot and everything was dry—there was still something to look at, to marvel at, insects, ants or something moving around. In the winter when it started to flow there was obviously water puddles and holes in it. As the water receded some of the ponds disappeared, they lost the water but they were really quicksand and it was always a challenge to see if you could make your way through one of the quicksand areas in the creek and it was no small feat to do it.

Like Ruth Apps, but almost thirty years later, ***ALISON FETTELL*** *(1952) remembers the gender expectations about play, that she challenged.*

I was very much a tomboy, and my elder sister and my younger sister weren't. So I didn't play with my sisters very often, because they did different things. My younger sister liked to play with dolls and stay inside and—as she got a little bit older—helped mum with the housework which I loathed.

The closest thing I had to a doll was a monkey that had symbols that clapped, that I quite liked. But my father bought me that and this *wonderful* Cadillac car—friction car—that was this beautiful green. You'd pull it back and because it was friction it would then take off on its own. I'd been sick, my brother and I had every disease known to man, in a row. So we had measles, mumps and chickenpox, all three weeks in a row. So my mother had us home for nine weeks. And dad for some reason took pity on me. I don't know what he bought my brother but these are the things he bought me. I don't know how he found the money to do that but he did, and those sorts of toys. My dad had me picked. He really did. He knew the sorts of things that I would be delighted in. That car and the monkey with the symbols. He would never dream to buy me a doll—which I loved that about him (laughs).

Many Australians of ***RICHARD (RICK) GALEA****'s (1958) generation remember watching the first moon landing on television at school.*

That's the thing I just recall so clearly. It was so much excitement about it. It was due to land just after our recess time—what we used to call 'little lunch'. It was about 'round ten am. The school was like, it was like everybody had been beamed up into, away. There was not a sign of anybody, except at the tuckshop. These poor ladies looked like they were going to miss out on it, but there was *nobody* around. Everybody was just crammed into what they used to call a 'TV room'—it couldn't have fit another person in there, it was that full.

I just recall so much, grabbing my lunch—sorry, my recess—and running full speed across the yard and open up the door as the light came on. Everybody just looked at me and gasped. And I closed the door as quickly as I could behind me and the guys were, the astronauts were actually on the ladder. Everybody's jaw was just sort of, eyes were just bulging and, and he said those famous words, you know, 'One step for --- ',

'One small step, one big step for mankind' I think it was. Every time I ever see a replay of that, it feels like I'm in that room, it's just a huge visual. I think the fact that I got there just, actually photographed it, you know, forever in my head. I was in Fifth Class, probably I'd say, ten, ten-ish. It was 1969.

OURANITA KARADIMAS *(1958) recalls a life with no family television in the 1960s.*

In my growing up years which were in Albury we did not have television. There were two things that dominated my leisure time, well actually three. Number one was spending time in the shop. At times being very useful to my father in terms of serving customers. At other times just generally faffing about the place. Number two was my reading. I loved reading from a very early age and used to love lying on my bed and reading. And I remember reading *Gone With the Wind* in I think my early high school years. That's one book I remember very well. I read lots—oh I loved, oh I collected all of the Enid Blyton series *The Famous Five* and *The Secret Seven.* I had the *whole set* because I used to make my mother take me down to Blake's Book Shop and News Agency on the main street—Dean Street—and gradually I collected the whole lot.

The other part of my leisure time was spent in the backyard behind the shop where we lived and I loved practicing my athletics in a very amateur way. My parents were very preoccupied with the shop so I preoccupied myself with practicing athletics, running up and down the backyard and also practicing my shot put by heaving bricks instead of shot puts across the yard. Those were the three areas, that's where I spent my leisure time.

The only time we ever watched television was when a neighbour of ours—several doors down—used to take us on a Friday or a Saturday night when the shop was really busy and we used to watch television at her place. I remember it very clearly, it was black and white. We used to watch the news, then we used to watch something else and then we used to watch *Bandstand*, and I'm sure that was Saturday night. That was our television viewing.

__IAN REID__ (1961) and his older brother lived with their widowed mother in Black Forest, an inner southern suburb of Adelaide.

I have a vivid memory that we'd nagged her and nagged her and nagged her—once the Centenary Test was coming on in '77—and said, 'We *really* need a colour TV for the Centenary.' You couldn't watch the Centenary Test with a black and white TV, you know. We were successful in wangling this. That was quite a big event for us to get a colour TV, for that event. Before that we had an old black and white valve TV. A valve would go every month or so it would seem. There was this old guy down on Goodwood Road who'd come—Mr Watkins I think his name was—he'd come and, and fix your TV which basically, well he'd look, pull the back off the TV, work out which valve had blown, pull it out, put another valve in, and off you'd go (laughs). Another couple of months later he'd be back again to fix the TV. But we did have that. And we had, mum of course with her music, she had a very nice big radiogram. Was a big piece of furniture. It would have been probably, oh one and a half metres wide. Had two big drawers. One drawer coming down was the AM radio—with all the stations on the glass—and the other side was I think a triple-decker LP player.

Now living in Sydney, __LISA JACKSON__ (1972) recalls a sporting childhood and the beach in south Perth.

I liked netball. That was one of the things I was good at. When I got older I got banned from playing much sport because apparently I was too dangerous. But yeah, it's just one of those things, but I enjoyed it. Actually because my brother was in a cricket team I used to help the bowlers opening up, practice with them in the nets. I was the only girl game enough to do that and none of the other girls would. 'Oh yeah, I'll take it on'. So I like cricket too. I could bat. I can't bowl but I could bat and I could field. They were two of the other things I could do, and netball.

I still like netball. And swimming, but not swimming in a pool, swimming out in the beach. We always used to swim, go out the beach. Even now as an adult for me my connection to home, from Sydney to Perth, is the sea water, because it smells the same. The beach it doesn't look the same but it smells the same. It's about the smell. It still smells the same and the sun goes down on different sides so you get used to that. So that's what I used to do, from walking around Kwinana, you know, visiting friends, because you couldn't afford the bus fare you might as well walk.

JASON JOHNSON *(1981) recalls a sporting childhood in north Queensland.*

I started my younger years playing AFL. All my coaches and everything loved me playing AFL. I remember as a young boy being about six or seven and my mother would drive us from Bramston Beach to Babinda, and all the kids would load into the back of the utes and we would drive from Babinda to Cairns in the back of the ute. We would play AFL all day till the sun went down and then we'd get driven back to Babinda where we'd meet up with our parents again and then we'd all head off to all four corners of the globe. Back to all our different little places where we lived.

Moved to Cairns, I was about eleven. I had a friend, Shelton Murphy. He was a Aboriginal guy. I come home from school with him one day and I walked in and said, 'Mum, I'm going down to play rugby league. I'm going with Shelton. I'll be back later.' I had never played rugby league, didn't even really know what it was. Started playing at the age of eleven and kept going right through my teenage years, till I started working and joined the military.

ADAM FARROW-PALMER *(1988) from Sydney recalls early computers and the transformation of childhood play in the 1990s and 2000s.*

There was a boy up the road who I was friends with from a young age. We'd often play in each other's backyard on his trampoline. We had the old type of trampoline that didn't have a wall around it. Now all the trampolines don't have any springs and they have the nets. That was a real trampoline that you could fall off and frequently crack your head on to the side or fall through the springs. We would look at his fish and his tadpoles in his backyard. Play in his cubby house. There's a shed out the back and we'd jump off the top of the shed on to the grass or on to the trampoline. We'd climb trees. Often this was interspersed with playing his Super Nintendo. We'd play games together in his back room. Sometimes on my house we'd play computer games like *Tony Hawk*—a good skateboarding game.

That was through primary school, pretty common. Later the computer games became more of a focus and there was less running around and exploring. During high school you'd go round someone's house and you'd have a four-player game going and you'd take turns all looking at the little screen. At birthday parties, well people had sometimes bowling or other activities like that. But for leisure between male friends, video games was often an anchor, that was a standard. Otherwise you'd go to the movies, too.

I think the first computer, the only thing you could 'play'—if you call it that—was Microsoft Paint. So you'd draw on the computer. But then all my computers after that you could load games and play. Like 2D platformers with big blocky graphics or that kind of thing. But yeah, throughout my whole life basically video games have been a part of it.

Further Listening on Childhood Pleasures

Ginette Matalon, 1936, http://nla.gov.au/nla.obj-219968733/listen/0-515
Doug Fong, 1938, http://nla.gov.au/nla.obj-219960559/listen/0-1950
Greer Bland, 1944, http://www.nla.gov.au/amad/nla.oh-vn5972533/0-4499
James Box, 1946, http://www.nla.gov.au/amad/nla.oh-vn6252081/1-2544
Geraldine Box, 1949, http://www.nla.gov.au/amad/nla.oh-vn6190857/0-572~0-612
Lynne Sanders-Braithwaite, 1949, http://www.nla.gov.au/amad/nla.oh-vn6290876/0-1218
Rick Galea, 1958, http://www.nla.gov.au/amad/nla.oh-vn6535733/1-2683
Kim Bear, 1959, http://www.nla.gov.au/amad/nla.oh-vn6190847/0-938
David Cooper, 1959, http://www.nla.gov.au/amad/nla.oh-vn6290926/0-2818
Michelle Cripps,1960, http://www.nla.gov.au/amad/nla.oh-vn6252075/0-761
Phil May, 1962, http://www.nla.gov.au/amad/nla.oh-vn6569680/0-2268
Christian Bow, 1978, http://nla.gov.au/nla.obj-219896923/listen/0-227
James Finnegan, 1981, http://nla.gov.au/nla.obj-220176798/listen/1-179

Early Schooling

***GREER BLAND** (1944) was the eldest of three children growing up about ten kilometres north-west of Traralgon in the Gippsland bush, where her parents cut pulpwood for paper mills.*

Of course you started in Grade 1 those days and at four and a half that's a bit young. Didn't wanna go. It was middle of winter. There was, I reckon, six inches of frost on the ground. I was cold. Mum said, 'You're going and that's all there is about it.' So she put me outta the gate and over the fence, and told me to go and meet this lady. I saw this lady not far away. To me she was a lady, but I guess she was only about five or six, seven years older than me, was going to the same place, or into

Traralgon or somewhere. She said go and see her. She'll help you on and off the bus and tell you when to get off. So that was pretty scary. Four and a half put over the fence and told to get going and to go with a stranger.

Well this wasn't like a bus you know today, it was completely void of all lining, and the corrugated road was absolutely atrocious. You couldn't talk, you couldn't hear yourself talk. I was scared to death, you got no idea. I got home after the first day and I said, 'Well that's it mum, that's it. I am not going back on that bus no matter what.' Well we didn't bargain on mum being pretty heavy-handed, and I went back.

***RUSSELL ELLIOTT** (1950) started his education at a rural primary school with about thirty students in the central Victorian country town of Natte Yallock.*

Grade 3 and Grade 4 were pretty much barren years I would think in reflection. The teacher was an absolute traditionalist. I don't think he would hold the job these days for the way he went about things. He sat at his table and smoked, and every afternoon we had to sing the times table from start to finish. Least I know what seven sixes are but probably not much else. We basically worked out of books on his direction and if we didn't do what we were supposed to do, he yelled and carried on.

Thankfully he left. Going into Grade 5, for the next two years at school we had a new schoolteacher—a chap called Brian Sword—who came from Melbourne as a teacher and, wow, that was like a breath of fresh air. Under his stewardship for two years it was, yeah quite amazing, and I still look back on what he did with us as a group of children and marvel at it. I suppose he had a captive audience to a degree that we'd all been stifled for the two years undoubtedly, and suddenly this guy came in with so many new ideas, so much enthusiasm, that we just lapped it up and went along for a fairly joyous ride with him.

We never had any reading material—our library was sterile in the nth degree, books that you would never even bother to open, let alone be interested in. He saw that. He came up with the idea, 'The Mothers' Club have given the school an amount of money and we're going to buy some library books.' 'Oh that'll be wonderful.' 'But, you as students are going to be in the selection process. Next Saturday, a bus will be going to Bendigo to the booksellers. You are all going to be part of it because when you get over there the bookseller—if you haven't seen one—he's got all the books out on display, all the story books and stuff there. You go over there and we will select'—however much The Mothers' Club gave us, few hundred dollars—'and we will buy books that you feel you would like to read.' So we went over there. Amazing, and we must have gone into probably just a storeroom and all these books. We came back with a series of—and it might be looked on a bit sadly now—*The Secret Seven, The Famous Five*. Enid Blyton. But they were good fodder to start people reading.

Nicole Curby:* I *started reading Enid Blyton.

Yes, so did I and, you know, they brought back the full sets of them, multiple sets of them and immediately said, 'Right, they're to take them home at night and read them.' So as quick as we could get them, we took them home read, read, read, read, read, read, backwards and forwards we went. He increased in subsequent buys the level of books and their complexity et cetera, et cetera, but it was a very, very interesting thing. Again, involvement, he involved us in it. We suddenly saw a reason why we should read. So that was a quantum leap.

***OURANITA KARADIMAS** (1958) spoke Greek but no English when she started primary school in Albury.*

When I first was enrolled at school, the principal I don't think knew what to do with my name. Because in Greek my name is Ourania, and I don't think they knew how to write it, to Anglicise it. And so they tried out various little options, and it was Ourania and then my mother would say Ouranitsa, Ouranitha. And somehow or other we got to Ouranita and it sounded like Juanita or something that someone was familiar with and so we ended up with my spelling. I'm not going to change it now. I'm stuck with it and that's the little story I have to tell with my name.

With my *identity*, I didn't realise until we moved to Sydney how much of a bit of an outsider I felt when I was younger. These things happen to you and you don't realise why they're happening to you in the moment but on reflection you go, 'Oh okay.' I always felt a little bit different to the other kids at school. I'm sure it's because I was in a Greek-only speaking household and a fairly sheltered household at that. Whereas the other kids at school a) had television, so they were all talking about things like the *The Man From U.N.C.L.E.* and *20,000 Leagues Under the Sea*, and *Doctor Who*, and I had no idea what these things were. So I'm sure that's why I was a little bit on the outer. I didn't know. The other thing is it never occurred to any of us to badger my parents for a television. So whenever we went to someone's place who had a television, oh that was fantastic, oh it was great.

So I did feel a little bit odd and it was only when our family moved to Sydney in 1972 and we settled in Dulwich Hill and I went to Canterbury Girls, where *every* second girl was Greek, Italian, Spanish, Portuguese, Korean, Vietnamese, something else. I thought, oh I feel much more normal here, oh, right, because I was with lots of other kids who had the same migrant experience. That's when I felt, 'Oh I feel much more at home, why is that?'

***KIM BEAR** (1959) recalls the racism of a rural Queensland school in the mid-60s.*

I can remember an incident when I was small—when we'd gone to Dalby—and it was the first time we ever had Aboriginal children in our class—we didn't have any in Sydney. On about day three, I think, after we'd started at school, my sister piped up at dinner and said to my mum, 'What's an Abo?' My mother nearly died, she said, 'Who said that word to you? Who's been talking like that?' My sister said, 'Oh some of the kids are calling my friend Esther an Abo.' Esther *was* full blood Aboriginal. Mum said to my sister, 'Do you notice any difference between you and Esther?' My sister said, 'Well, she runs faster than me and she's got a better tan', and that was it. That was the difference, for my sister. I remember mum explaining where the word came from and what it meant. I can remember her saying to my sister and I 'All you ever need to know is that if you cut people they bleed red.'

*Though it was not diagnosed during his 1960s Victorian primary schooling, **DAVID COOPER** (1959) now thinks he may have been dyslexic.*

It took a long time for me to learn to read. What I remember about that is how frustrated I would be able to make people when they were trying to teach me to read. You'd have, you know, 'This is John, this is Betty.' And then you turn the page over and they'd go, 'This is?' and I wouldn't remember John's name. And they'd go, 'It's the same word on the other page.' How could it be the same word on the other page, 'cause it's on a different page.

My mum would end up getting so frustrated. She'd yell at me. People were thinking I was taking the mickey out of them, that I wouldn't remember these words. So I remember getting yelled at a lot, and I remember being frustrated and I didn't like school because of that. And I can remember with the times table, I still don't know my times table. Still can't do it, which is a bit embarrassing. I just used to keep my head low and thought, this will be over. And I thought I was getting away with it, because eventually they stopped teaching you the three times table. And they don't teach it anymore. But that doesn't mean you don't need it when you get older, if you know what I mean. So I learnt what verbs and nouns were, I never understood what an adjective was, and all that sort of stuff. You pay the price for that later.

I gave up and became determined not to learn it, a little bit, I think. You know, I'll teach you that I don't need it. That determination's come in handy later. But it did stop me. Like if I'd had my choice, when I was getting ready to leave school, I would have probably chose to become a police cadet and join the police force. But I knew that it was pointless because I knew that I'd never be able to take a statement off anybody and I wouldn't be able to spell the words, and all that sort of stuff. So it affected me that way.

PHIL MAY*'s (1962) father was ex-British army, and after living in several different countries, in 1970 the family migrated to Australia and lived in Brisbane where Phil started at a state school. When that didn't work out he moved to a private school where he was picked upon because he had a 'pommy accent' but then found company with the other 'nerdy' kids.*

We lived in an immigration—Wacol Hostel—for weeks but it wasn't tough. I don't have bad memories of the place. The adults probably have a very different perception, particularly with your comings and goings being more constrained. But children are used to their comings and goings being constrained so, no.

I did actually do a year in primary school in Queensland. I hated that year. The primary school system in Queensland at that stage was not suitable for somebody like me. It was a very rough classroom. The teachers were very authoritarian, there was a lot of yelling, there was cuffing of children or hitting of children. Fortunately not me, I stayed under the radar for that. I was quiet enough and well enough behaved that I never came to attention. I do have a very strong memory of one of the larger children who'd been held back—I think it was two years—he was very large. He threw the desk out the window and when the teacher objected he tried to throw the teacher out the window. We were on the second storey. It was a rough school. My parents noted the rapid decline in my academic progress and put me back in the private school. There was actually some money they could have done with saving at the time but I did not function well in the Queensland public education system as it was in the early seventies. It wasn't for me.

I WAS NOT INTERESTED IN RUGBY. I was not interested in cricket. I was a nerdy person. I was actually doing things like I had an electronics kit my parents had bought me—one of those ones with little springs that you attach the wires to and make various circuits. I was much more happy doing that and I found a few friends who were just as happy doing that, and so that's what we did. We were definitely on the outer. We were not mainstream children at all. Looking back on it now—being charitable—you'd say that we were all on the spectrum. These days you'd just call us nerds, but I am actually on the spectrum. I have an autism spectrum diagnosis. I suspect that a lot of the people that I interacted with back then were similar because they behaved the same way I did. They were not highly sociable children but they could become adept at reasonably intricately technical things because they would interest them more than playing football or cricket.

JAMES MAYOL *(1974) started school in 1986 in Aweil, south Sudan.*

When we come to education, you know, my father pass away. Nobody can put me to school. So I have to force myself to go to the church. That Sister Amandit, she's the one who running this project. To put kids into a school. Teach them how to prays and teach them their letters. What we call *Our Man in the Pan*. That was a small book. I remember that book contains only letter and then a man, a man and pan. There's nothing more than that.

By the time you come there, first they teach you how to pray. And if they teach you to how to pray, then now you become part of the Catholics. Or whatever church you go. Then they'll go on, on the process to baptise you. You don't have any option. It wasn't really something that you choose. This is what you do.

ARTHUR HUNTER*'s (1989) early education was split between Wyndham where his father lived and the Aboriginal cattle station where his mother's family lived.*

Oh my schooling, Jesus. I tell you from the start now. Chapter one of my life—jokes! As I was a kid growing up, I was going Wyndham and Halls Creek back and forward. But at a very young age my family, we did the schooling thing back at home, back in our station. They taught us stuff. It was a family school where we went. We had journals, we had, you know, we tell what we did on the weekend or on the station. We helped out. Like we learnt a lot.

Elaine Rabbitt: But by 'family school' do you mean your mum was teaching you or was it by radio?

My mum and aunty was teaching us. At first I was kind of shocked that they do, they're doing that. But it was fun you know. School is really good but having it with your family, and you're learning too because like you know them properly. So it was really fun. And then we went into town and went to school there.

In Wyndham?

Wyndham and Halls Creek—I was going back and forward because you know, my mum in Halls Creek, my dad was in Wyndham, so I was back and forward. And I was a really, really quiet boy, really shy. I didn't really get along with people. I'm not a people's person. But maybe when I want to be I can be. Back in the days where you couldn't get a good conversation out of me like what I'm doing now with you. So it was really—for me back then—it was really, I think I was shame. And I don't know what the meaning 'shame' is, I think is just being ignorant I reckon. I reckon when I was back then I was being ignorant.

Further Listening on Early Schooling

Brian Carter, 1931, http://www.nla.gov.au/amad/nla.oh-vn6290887/0-1066
Connie Shaw, 1937, http://nla.gov.au/nla.obj-219992795/listen/1-142
Veronica Schwarz, 1939, http://www.nla.gov.au/amad/nla.oh-vn6290927/0-1389
John Murphy, 1940, http://www.nla.gov.au/amad/nla.oh-vn6504268/0-4390
James Box, 1946, http://www.nla.gov.au/amad/nla.oh-vn6252081/2-3874
Les Robinson, 1947, http://www.nla.gov.au/amad/nla.oh-vn6504265/0-3249
Geraldine Box, 1949, http://www.nla.gov.au/amad/nla.oh-vn6190857/0-2592
Lynne Sanders-Braithwaite, 1949, http://www.nla.gov.au/amad/nla.oh-vn6290876/1-494~1-557
Gina Polito, 1954, http://www.nla.gov.au/amad/nla.oh-vn6421369/0-1635
Kim Bear, 1959, http://www.nla.gov.au/amad/nla.oh-vn6190847/0-2894
Michelle Cripps, 1960, http://www.nla.gov.au/amad/nla.oh-vn6252075/0-3134
Ian Reid, 1961, http://nla.gov.au/nla.obj-220066743/listen/0-3126
Barbara Krickl, 1962, http://www.nla.gov.au/amad/nla.oh-vn6252047/0-1815~0-1876
Bronwyn Macdonald, 1964, http://www.nla.gov.au/amad/nla.oh-vn6390885/0-1849
Rhonda King, 1965, http://www.nla.gov.au/amad/nla.oh-vn6390877/0-3557
Lisa Jackson, 1972, http://nla.gov.au/nla.obj-219901040/listen/2-976
James Finnegan, 1981, http://nla.gov.au/nla.obj-220176798/listen/1-803
Adam Farrow-Palmer, 1988, http://nla.gov.au/nla.obj-219982656/listen/1-2217

Further Reading on Childhood

Ashton, Paul and Wilson, Jacqueline (eds), *Silent System: Forgotten Australians and the Institutionalisation of Women and Children* (North Melbourne: Australian Scholarly Publishing, 2014).

Campbell, Craig and Proctor, Helen, *A History of Australian Schooling* (Sydney: Allen & Unwin, 2014).

Connell, Bill and Spaull, Andrew, 'School', in Bill Gammage and Peter Spearritt (eds), *Australians 1938* (Sydney: Fairfax, Syme & Weldon Associates, 1987), pp. 175–86.

Darian-Smith, Kate and Pascoe, Carla (eds), *Children, Childhood and Cultural Heritage* (London & New York: Routledge, 2013).

Darian-Smith, Kate, *On the Home Front: Melbourne in Wartime, 1939–1945*, (Carlton: Melbourne University Press, second edition, 2009).

Holmes, Katie, 'Talking about Mental Illness: Life Histories and Mental Health in Modern Australia', *Australian Historical Studies* 47, no. 1 (2016), pp. 25–40.

Johnson, Lesley, *The Modern Girl: Girlhood and Growing Up* (Sydney: Allen & Unwin, 1993).

Kent, Jacqueline, *In the Half-light: Life as a Child in Australia, 1900–1970* (North Ryde, NSW: Angus & Robertson, 1988).

Kociumbas, Jan, *Australian Childhood: A History* (St Leonards: Allen & Unwin, 1997).

Larsson, Marina, *Shattered Anzacs: Living with the Scars of War* (Sydney: University of New South Wales Press, 2009).

McCalman, Janet, *Journeyings: The Biography of a Middle-Class Generation 1920–1990* (Carlton: Melbourne University Press, 1993).

McCalman, Janet, *Struggletown: Public and Private Life in Richmond, 1900–1965* (Carlton: Melbourne University Press, 1984).

McLeod, Julie and Yates, Lyn, *Making Modern Lives: Subjectivity, Schooling and Social Change* (Albany: SUNY Press, 2006).

Musgrove, Nell, *The Scars Remain: A Long History of Forgotten Australians and Children's Institutions* (Melbourne: Australian Scholarly Publishing, 2013).

Pascoe, Carla, 'Be Home by Dark: Childhood Freedoms and Adult Fears in 1950s Victoria', *Australian Historical Studies* 40, no 2 (June 2009), pp. 215–231.

Scott, Dorothy and Swain, Shurlee, *Confronting Cruelty: Historical Perspectives on Child Abuse* (Carlton: Melbourne University Publishing, 2002).

Thompson, Ruth, 'Boys and Girls', in Bill Gammage and Peter Spearritt (eds), *Australians 1938* (Sydney: Fairfax, Syme & Weldon Associates, 1987), pp. 161–74.

Van Krieken, Robert, *Children and the State: Social Control and the Formation of Australian Child Welfare* (North Sydney: Allen & Unwin, 1991).

CHAPTER 3

FAITH

When asked about faith, many Australian Generations interviewees described how their beliefs morphed across their lives. Neither dogmatic nor unbending, views on religion and spirituality might change as life experiences deepen. Parents, grandparents and schools were pivotal in moulding children's initial interactions with religion, and these early encounters are often recalled most vividly. In Wagga Wagga in the 1930s, young Catholic Ruth Apps recalls sectarian tensions: 'the nuns *always* exhorted us, "Don't walk on that side of the road, there are Protestants over there."' When Ruth moved away from Catholicism and became involved with a Congregational Church in Sydney later in that decade, her Catholic friends 'dumped' her. As a child in the 1940s, John Murphy (who grew up to become a Catholic priest) and his family prayed the Rosary every night in his Melbourne home. Jason Johnson, whose three children attend Catholic school in Canberra, recalls the wisdom his Catholic grandmother imparted in the 1980s when he was growing up in Far North Queensland about how to tell right from wrong.

Across the world, in Cairo, Ginette Matalon attended her synagogue on Friday nights 'not for praying, but for socialising with my friends' in an age before telephones became commonplace. Geraldine Box and Ronnie Gauci—both born in the late 1940s—recall not being able to understand Latin services when they attended Sunday church services as children (the Catholic Church did not allow Mass to be spoken in languages other than Latin until Second Vatican Council reforms took place in the 1960s). The proportion of Australians who attended church varied through the twentieth century: numbers rose slightly at times, including during the 1950s, but the practice has steadily declined during recent decades.

South Australian Anglican priest, Donald Grey-Smith, recalls the 'scandal' of 'our Christian disunity' during the 1960s and illuminates how religion and politics intersected and often generated tensions within families and communities. Just over eighty-eight per cent of Australians who participated in the 1961 census identified with a Christian faith, and about one of five marriages was interfaith. In the 1950s Geraldine Box grew up in a mixed-faith household, closely exposed to more than one form of belief: her father was a devout Catholic, her mother, a non-practicing Protestant. In the 1970s and '80s, although Ian Reid's Christian father 'wasn't a great church-goer he was very accepting of mum's [Baha'i] faith'. Growing up, Ian attended both Sunday School and Baha'i classes in his hometown of Adelaide, and chose the Baha'i faith of his own volition at fifteen. In contrast, Bronwyn Macdonald, raised by her Church of England mum and atheist dad in Canberra, declares 'by the time I was *ten* I decided that I was an atheist.' Fresh attitudes towards feminism, divorce and sex, and landmark events such as Gough Whitlam's election in 1972 and the introduction of the Family Law Act in 1975, prompted John Murphy (who resigned from his role as a Catholic priest to marry in the mid-1970s) to conclude 'that the church was too authoritarian.' Over the following years, John found new ways to practice his faith outside of the church.

As younger interviewees became teenagers and young adults, and asserted their independence, some redefined their faith. When Lisa Jackson turned sixteen in the late 1980s, her 'awareness of my culture and my identity in who I was as an Aboriginal person kind of came out'. While she still believed in God, the Pentecostal Church of her upbringing no longer appealed. Lisa reflects on how she reconciles her Aboriginal beliefs and spirituality with the Catholic faith she had started practicing: 'It's not been easy but I've made it work.' Lisa believes that the Dreaming—Australia's first belief system—is 'a different form of the *Seven Days of Creation*' and describes how the Dreaming 'helps define who I am as a person'. In south-west Sydney in the 1990s, a teenage James Finnegan stumbled into paganism ('We just discovered it one day') when he and his cousin walked into a New Age shop. In southern Queensland in the late '90s, Rachel Brown—who had spent '*every single* Sunday' in Church—asked her mother if she could stop attending: 'she said yes'.

The transformation of personal beliefs took place in a changing religious landscape. By 2011, twenty-two per cent of Australians selected 'no religion' in the national census, making it the second most ticked box—sandwiched between the Catholics (twenty-five per cent) and Anglicans (seventeen per cent). While levels of engagement with the most popular non-Christian faiths were significantly lower by comparison—Buddhism, Islam and Hinduism came in at 2.5, 2.2 and 1.3 per cent, respectively—more Australians subscribed to these religions in 2011 than they had in 2006. In fact, the number of Hindus in Australia shot up by eighty-six per cent over that five-year period.

James Mayol, who came to Australia in 2003, is one of many recent migrants and refugees expanding Australia's traditional religious makeup. He explains how 'People worship God through their elders' in his community in northwest South Sudan. Migrants have a long history of diversifying Australia's cultural composition and religious adherence, as Doug Fong's great-great grandparents did when they arrived at the Victorian goldfields in the nineteenth century. The cultural practices of Doug's Broome-based family demonstrate how traditions might be adapted in a new country and climate. The Qingming Festival—a day when observers pay respect to their ancestors—is based on the Chinese lunar calendar and in China is held in April on the fifteenth day of spring. In Australia April is in Autumn, so Doug's family observes the spring festival in August or September instead.

Older interviewees reexamined their faith at various stages in their lives. Ensuring her children learnt about Judaism at their public school in Sydney led Ginette Matalon to fall in love with the Jewish religion. Canberran Rhonda King was a member of The Church of Jesus Christ of Latter-day Saints, but when she divorced in 2003 the church was not supportive and she struggled with the changing shape and status of her family unit. As she poignantly explains: 'we're not taking up the pew' any more. In North Queensland, Ronnie Gauci and his wife stopped attending church 'probably thirty, forty years ago' because of gossiping among the congregation and the moral crises of the Catholic Church, but they did not let this impact their personal relationship with God.

Contemporary faith may not involve a God of any variety. At the time of her interview in 2013, Rachel Brown found comfort in Buddhist philosophy when she felt 'quite down'. 'I might go as far as saying I am an atheist but I try to take the *best* bits of religion and apply it to my life.' Born in 1982, three years before Rachel, Kirsty Wallett was baptised a Catholic but is eclectic and undecided about her faith: 'I'm not an atheist and I'm not agnostic', 'I'm open to science but I'm also open to spirituality', 'I guess I'm a humanist'. She concludes, 'I haven't quite made up my mind --- But I think whatever way you can get out of bed every morning and be comforted when things are tough is, is fine for you.' While religion may be moving in new directions and levels of disbelief rise, faith, in its various forms, continues to provide meaning for many Australians.

***RUTH APPS** (1926) was born into a Catholic family in Wagga Wagga. As a child, she attended the local convent school.*

In Wagga—I'm talking about the 1930s—I think I was telling you on the phone, when we walked home from the convent after school we had to pass the public school and the nuns *always* exhorted us, 'Don't walk on that side of the road, there are Protestants over there'. You did not walk on the same side of the road as the Protestants. You just simply didn't do it. My school friends that were there—we were only children—suddenly didn't come to the birthday parties.

Frank Heimans: So how significant was religion within the community that you lived in, in Wagga?

It was very significant but *very* much in different camps. The Catholics were there, the Church of England as it was called were there, there was a Presbyterian church, there was a Methodist church and never the twain shall meet. They probably met in the streets socially and that kind of thing but there was no interdenominational *effort* whereas nowadays the churches in Parramatta all have an interdenominational service. And it's moved from --- like the Catholics do it one year and the Anglicans do it another year but back in those days there was *very* little mixing.

THERE WERE ELEMENTS of the Catholic faith at that time that I resented as a child. But I accepted the fact that I was a Catholic. I had my first communion when I was six-and-a-half and then confirmed and whenever the nuns said, 'Who's going to be a nun?' I'd put my hand up. But there was a deep-seated feeling that I didn't like it. So not long before we left Wagga I expressed these fears to my mother. The nuns absolutely terrified me and they were cruel in those days. If you didn't write properly it was a strap around the legs kind of thing.

We were having scripture there and the nuns were always wagging their finger, 'God will get you Ruth. You're a naughty girl, God will descend his wrath on you.' I got into this Church of England Grammar School and they're talking about how God loves you. God is love, and I thought this is a different God to the one I knew up the road.

So we came to Hurstville [a Sydney suburb] to live in the end of 1937. I dropped out of church there. We weren't involved in anything. I went to St George Girls High and came in contact with one of my friends whose father was the Congregational minister in, just close handy. And she said, 'Why don't you come along to fellowship one day?' So I said to my mother, 'What do you think?' And she said, 'Yes, that's alright, off you go.' And I loved it. They were loving and they were friendly and I thought this is altogether different. So I stayed with the Congregational Church there in Bexley until I went to work actually, until I left school, very happy there.

Now what was the reaction of your Catholic friends when you'd gone over to the other camp—to the Anglican?

They dumped me (laughs).

GINETTE MATALON *(1936) recalls attending synagogue as a child when living in Cairo in the 1940s.*

I attended synagogue every Friday night. Not for praying but for socialising with my friends and finding out what we would be doing on Saturday night. If I didn't go to synagogue, I wouldn't be in the loop of things. We didn't have phones, we didn't have a mobile phone, we didn't have the net (laughs), we didn't have emails. We had to go to synagogue to decide and know what was going on. So very often I stayed outside—sometimes in the courtyard of the synagogue. I also went to a Sephardi shul [synagogue] because most of my friends were Sephardi and I knew that they would be at this shul on Friday night. Otherwise I wouldn't know what was happening on Saturday night if I didn't go there to see them.

JOHN MURPHY *(1940) describes the religious practices of his Catholic family at home in Melbourne during the late 1940s. John later became a priest.*

Sarah Rood: And would anyone say Grace or any sort of formal---?

Yes, always. Before and after meals. 'Bless us Oh Lord and these Thy gifts which are Thy bounty we are about to receive through Christ our Lord, Amen.' That was the standard formula for saying Grace. I think all the Catholic people around would have done the same thing. It was very common.

And after the meal, was it the same?

Yes—'We give Thee thanks Almighty God for all Thy benefits which we have received through Christ our Lord, Amen.' Kind of knew it off pat (laughs).

The bookends of the meal. Would all of you say it together? How would it go?

Yes. I think dad started off but we all said it. But that leads into another thing because at some stage after the meal—this is during the week now, well every night really, but during the week's more memorable—we'd have the family rosary, which is another formulaic repetitive prayers of Hail Mary and the Lord's Prayer and Glory Be. They were Catholic except for the Lord's Prayer of course which was a bit more common to other Christians. So we'd have this family rosary which is a repetitive prayer. Took about quarter of an hour and every night. And we'd kneel. So we'd kneel, I'd be kneeling near mum. Mum would sit and dad and Morrie and I would be kneeling around the couch or you know. So there'd be a couch and two armchairs. Well we'd be kneeling near those, leaning on them. We'd have our rosary beads, which is like our prayer beads and we'd say that every night. We weren't rare, that was the done thing for Catholics to say the rosary every night.

Was it all praying together but individually or was it a group?

There were what they'd call five decades. So a decade—obviously ten—so you'd have ten Hail Marys followed by --- You'd take it in turns to lead a decade and then you'd finish that decade and then --- It was very repetitive. I mean in some ways it's kind of crazy but it was, I think it was supposed to be a meditative you know, there were little themes. The mysteries of the rosary—joyful, sorrowful, glorious. It was a Jesus, Mary construct really. The rosary's a big thing.

RONNIE GAUCI *(1947) grew up in a Maltese migrant family in inner-city Sydney and moved to North Queensland as an adult. He reflects on his connection to God and his changing relationship with the Church.*

Look, I don't go to church. I did go for a long time every Sunday with mum and dad. Never listened to it much 'cause back then it was in Latin. Look, a lot of the stories coming out now with this child molestation—stuff like that—I've lost interest in the church probably thirty, forty years ago. That's not to say I don't believe there's a God. But I just don't believe in the church. I think it's lost its way. It's business-orientated. It's all money now, it's got nothing to do with God or any.

When anybody asks me, 'Do you go to church?' I said, 'No, I don't. I'm not a practicing Catholic.' I said, 'but if I need to talk to God,' I said, 'I go out the back, sit down peacefully and talk.' I said, 'I don't need to go to church.' They looked at me and said, 'Yeah, you know you're right.' I said, 'Yeah.'

What really turned me against the church other than what I know now is back then when we first come up here we'd go to church. And we knew a lot of the farmers. Church had finished, we'd all go outside and we all gather in little groups. And what did they do? They backstab each other. Me and my wife at that time we could see this happening and after a couple of weeks I said, 'Look, I'm not going anymore.' She said, 'You're right.' She said, 'I don't understand that.' I said, 'They just come out of church, now they get out there and they say, "He's this and he's that and she's that."' I said, 'I don't need that, I don't like that. If someone can't tell you to your face what you are then I don't want no part of it.' I said, 'Now, this is what the church produces then I'm not going anywhere.' She says, 'Well, I'm with you.' She says, 'I agree with you.' We never went back to church. Like I said, it's not that I don't believe in God but I don't believe in the church as what it is today.

I DON'T KNOW IF I SAID IT to you earlier where I, not long after I got married I sat down and spoke to what I think is God and told him what I wanted in life. All I wanted was happy, friendly family. And I did mention the fact that I'm not after riches, I'm not after wealth, I'm not after being famous—that's all I wanted. And I got it. I actually got it. That's why I believe there's a God.

GERALDINE BOX *(1949) started life in a mixed-faith household on the New South Wales Riverina. Her mother was 'notionally' from a Protestant background but was not religious.*

My father was a very firm Catholic. He believed all the teachings. I went to church with him regularly. Every second Sunday the minister would come, the priest would come, to the local church which was on a property somewhere. My brother and I went for a bit and my brother dropped out much earlier than I. I kept on going mainly because I wanted to be with my dad and he and I got on very well. So I'd be dressed up in a frock which I hated, and a hat and gloves and pushed off in the car with mum—with dad, not mum. We would go to the local church which the Catholic men in the district had all built themselves. And the priest would come out and speak in another language that I didn't understand.

By the time I got to be ten I thought no. I asked dad a couple of questions. I said 'Can you explain there, why is he saying that? What's this about?' And dad said, 'No, it's just there, you believe it, it's what is, that's what you do.' And I thought no. So, neither of us went, we didn't go to communion. We were sent to lessons with the nuns in town and both of us said, 'No, we're not going to do this, it doesn't make sense to us.' I think that was probably the worst thing I ever, ever, ever did to dad, was stop going to church. And I said, 'No, I can't do this. It doesn't', in my ten-year-old language, 'it doesn't make sense to me'. They were still using the Latin liturgy at that point. When the priest did speak in English it was just a *haranguing* of all this, what women were doing.

DONALD GREY-SMITH *(1931) recalls the life of an Anglican priest in country South Australia during a heated political climate in the 1960s.*

A lot of travelling. Vast area and I related to the country people well, I think. I got on well, probably better with the pastoral communities rather than the farming communities. The farming communities at that stage were very much influenced by Eric Butler and the Australian League of Rights and had adopted his attitude towards a lot of political, social issues and I was opposing the things he was saying. He didn't go over too well in the pastoral communities at all. But it meant a lot of travelling, being with people, very resourceful people, and I enjoyed that experience.

The other thing which impressed me of course was the scandal of our disunity, our Christian disunity. On the Sunday when I would go to Lock—which was east of Ceduna—I would set off and after I'd gone about twenty miles, I'd see a cloud of dust approaching and that would be Father Kenneally coming to say Mass with a handful of people in Elliston and I was on my way to say Mass with a handful of people in Lock. Soon after that another cloud of dust would come in my direction and that would be the Methodist minister also going to the coast for a service with a few people. And the waste of resources just seemed scandalous. There was nothing we could do about it except be friendly with each other but ---

Did you see much of each other?

Not a great deal, no. Actually I did see quite a bit of Lindsay Faulkner, the Methodist minister because he lived in Lock and the League of Rights had a very strong hold on the community in Lock. They made life very difficult for Lindsay and his wife. So I tried to be supportive of them. It was the time of the Vietnam War. The community was divided over the extent of our involvement and this became a very personal issue where, you know, you had one family from that area had triplets and all three sons were conscripted. And they felt that that was their duty but there were others who were quite opposed so it was a divisive issue in the community anyway and the League of Rights didn't help in that situation.

GINETTE MATALON *(1936) and her mother left Cairo to avoid religious persecution by Egyptian nationalists. They came via Paris and arrived in Sydney in 1958. Ginette married a year later and had two children by 1962. Her boys attended a public school in a suburb near their Beacon Hill home in Sydney's north.*

They went to a school down the hill, which was Brookvale. And there was exposure with non-Australians, a few, a sprinkling of Italian families living in the area. There was two other Jewish families in that school. How did we discover this? Is that Pesach [Passover] came? We moved in January and then March, April the children came home and they said, 'Danny Jagers is eating matzah.' I said, 'Who?' 'Danny Jagers is eating matzah.' So I contacted Mrs Jagers and she became very friendly with me. And there was another little boy also at that school. So Mrs Jagers contacted me and she said, 'I hear from the'—here is again my theory of one thing leading on to another—'the Board of Jewish Education are sending teachers to teach Jewish Scripture in the schools but they only send a teacher if we have six children in the school.' I said, 'We'll go into production (laughs) and create another baby.' Because amongst all of us, the Jagers had two boys, I had two boys and there was the other boy, David. We didn't have this. We didn't quite make the six. So she said, 'What they can do is give us material and you can come one Thursday and I'll come the other Thursday. We'll take the children instead of them be sent like little orphans to the library while the other dominations have their scripture.' I said, 'All right.' So she came maybe once or twice. And then she came to me and she said, 'I hate it. I really hate the material I have to tell the children. I don't want it. If you don't want to come every week we'll discontinue it.' I started going every week and this was the beginning of the biggest love affair in my life. It was a love affair between *me* and the Jewish religion.

I started learning things I had never been exposed to and then eventually the board sent me to a course and eventually the board sent me to university to study Hebrew and, *and, and, and, and* it was the beginning of a whole career in Jewish education.

***JOHN MURPHY** (1940) left the Catholic priesthood to get married in the mid-1970s. His wife-to-be was a nun who also left the order.*

It's a lot different now but in those times it was—Vatican II had happened in '62 to '65 so the whole thing of freedom and rituals changing and language from Latin to English and *all* of that. Then you followed up with Whitlam and the Family Law Act and divorce. So there'd been a big social change in twenty years or so and I was living through that and trying to adjust as well as reconcile what I thought was important and right and what I'd been brought up to think was important and right.

So I ended up—in the '70s and '80s—coming to the conclusion that the church was too authoritarian. It didn't encourage freedom and therefore you've got to create your own freedom and your own experiences, if you like, of what it's like to live the life of the gospel. So we started up a group with some other friends called *oikia* which is like a Greek word for the household, as in economy. So we'd have families going away for weekends and we'd sometimes have a priest, sometimes just do it ourselves. We'd try and *learn* from each other and we had a couple of bright guys there who were lecturers and probably about half a dozen ex-priests and a few ex-nuns and anyone else who wanted to be part of it really. So that kept us going for about fifteen years but then the children grew up and they became teenagers and it was long weekends or footy season or whatever. So it became a bit impractical after a while but we've still got a lot of those friendships. So we're a little bit kind of bolshie I suppose, from the church's point of view. But we're still practicing Catholics and we still are, just not every week but most weeks. We've learned to accept the things that you can't change and create things that you can, basically. It's a little bit of a tension but it's not an innovating one like it would have been, you know, twenty years or thirty years ago. By that stage I'd done enough agonising (laughs), I was beyond agonising.

***IAN REID** (1961) remembers how religious differences were reconciled in his childhood home in the 1960s and 1970s, and in his marital home from the mid-1980s onwards.*

> Although *he* [his father] wasn't a great church-goer he was very accepting of mum's faith. She was a Baha'i and her two brothers were Baha'is and her parents were Baha'is.[1] And in fact she was the first Baha'i in her family. So they I think did have quite a spiritual connection with each other as a husband and wife even though it was of a different religion. Stories are told that when my dad was alive mum would have meetings at her home, you know, Baha'is don't have churches and they have meetings in homes normally. When people would come to home he'd welcome them and make the cup of tea and that sort of thing but leave them to themselves. So he was happy to support others' involvement. Wasn't really into it himself.
>
> My mother and father had this agreement. Because in the Baha'i faith you can't become a Baha'i—you can't accept the Baha'i faith until you're fifteen of your own volition you can't just do whatever your parents do—my mother and father had an agreement that with all of us three children, that we would go to Sunday School—the Christian Sunday School—and go to Baha'i meetings and children's classes. And then at fifteen we could make our own decision. So it was a fairly enlightened attitude I think, open and balanced is how I'd describe it. And we did that pretty well. Both my brother and sister were very involved in the local Sunday School and so on. I guess, after dad died we still did that but it gradually diminished a little bit. And I was probably the one who had less of the Sunday School and probably dropped off when I was about ten or eleven.

Peter Donovan: Did you make a decision on your fifteenth birthday?

---

1 The Bahai faith is one of the world's youngest major religions. It was founded by *Bahá'u'lláh,* (a Persian living in exile in Baghdad, and a follower of the Bab) in the mid-nineteenth century and was established in Australia in the 1920s.

Yes, I did. In fact myself and my brother and sister all at fifteen became Baha'is. So we did that and we've all been active in the Baha'i faith ever since. My mother was very, very active. When my father died in a sense, I think it filled a bit of a gap for her.

I THINK BOTH PARENTS had a few misgivings initially. But I think Annmarie [Ian's wife] is such a lovely person that she won my mother over pretty readily. But of course we did have to get written consent for a Baha'i marriage and we had to have both a Catholic ceremony and a Baha'i ceremony when we got married. We had some difficulties with some recalcitrant priests who didn't like the idea of that so we just moved on and got a different priest. So there were a few things like that to sort through.

There was never a difference between us about what we wanted to achieve. And I guess because I had the experience in my childhood of my father not being a Baha'i—my mother was—where we would, we'd be taught both ideas and make a decision at fifteen, I said, well that's how I saw children being brought up in that sort of environment and she was happy with that as well. I think because she actually taught English and history and also RE—and she'd actually been quite involved in Catholic Youth Groups. She was one of the first young people to set up the Antioch Youth Group in Catholic churches in South Australia so she actually understood some of the meanings behind the rituals and symbols in the church. So for example she understood that in the early church people often weren't baptised until they were quite a bit older. So the idea of not making that decision wasn't such a concern. When our children were born rather than having them baptised we had a blessing ceremony for each of them, with both Catholic and Baha'i readings and relatives from both sides present and so on.

***BRONWYN MACDONALD** (1964) recalls how her views on faith took shape in Canberra in the 1970s.*

What's it called? Church of England? Yes. We all went to Sunday School when we were little. Dad used to take us there and just wait outside and then mum went to church. That lasted for a few years. None of us liked it. She sort of gave up and she didn't really go then either but later on, before dad died, she started going to church again. One of her friends would pick her up and take her and bring her home. Then after dad died she got really involved with the church.

Elena Volkova: Did they go together at some stage?

No. Dad was a *very* strong atheist.

How did that impact on your views on spirituality?

It gave me the knowledge that there were different opinions rather than one thing is a fact. I think a lot of children grow up thinking this is a *fact*. I didn't have that. I got to know that it's opinions. It's people's understanding and it's not necessarily this way or that way. Or in fact any way. Let me be very open-minded about it and by the time I was *ten* I decided that I was an atheist.

I mean, I didn't relate it back to dad at all. Just because I think the stories that I heard from the Bible actually confused me with fairy stories. I'd say, 'Oh, you know, *Jonah and the Whale* really mixed me up with *Pinocchio*. Someone in *Pinocchio* got swallowed by a whale. How can you tell me one's real and one's not?' So at about the age of ten I thought that it was just not true.

I didn't really tell mum about that until I was twenty-four, twenty-five. Must've been older actually. By the time I had three children I was telling her that. And she was very gently reminding me of things (laughs) that proved me wrong. She would just tell me interesting stories from the Bible. For a while there I started to think well maybe, maybe there is a God because wouldn't that be lovely? But in truth that's not what I believe (laughs).

We never argued about it. We let each other be. She was very understanding of me and I'm very understanding of her and we nursed her while she died. I was so pleased that she had God in her life because it made it so much easier for her and it gave her strength. She was an amazingly strong person.

JAMES MAYOL *(1974) describes the traditional belief systems within the Dinka community in south Sudan.*

It wasn't called to be religion but it is traditional way of knowing God. People worship God through their elders. So the elders have to be—somebody is appointed by, the certain group, certain community, to look at that person [who] is very close to the God. He can say word of God. The way you can say the word of God might be very different than the way we look at Christianity and all of that.

Atem Atem: Let's just put it in terms of the Dinka, the way they think of it. So in your family or your clan what was your Jok? Which is like divinity, which is like a smaller God.

In my small community we used actually to worship God through these elders' practices of calling God in traditional way. For example, an older man is considered to be a *wise*, a wise man who actually has a spirit. And very faithful. We used to believe on that wise man and respect him, give him a very high respect.

LISA JACKSON *(1972) reflects on the challenges of maintaining both Christian and Aboriginal beliefs.*

I have a strong Christian faith. I don't practice in the Pentecostal as much. I don't regularly attend church especially Pentecostal church because I don't like the way that they're going in terms of their theology and in terms of some of their practices. I think, I reached the point when I was about sixteen, seventeen, I realised that God was for me—not a problem. But the practices within the church really wasn't for me. I found they people-labelled, there was discriminatory practices and being an Aboriginal person really then my awareness of my culture and my identity in who I was as an Aboriginal person kind of came out. I just thought maybe that's not for me at this point in time. But I never lost my faith. I never stopped believing in God.

Moved to Sydney. I got a job with the National Council of Churches, which then exposed me to an ecumenical movement—meaning all different churches coming together for a common cause and work together. So I got to meet other people from different faiths and see how they put their faith into perspective. I sat back and thought I like this, this is alright. I actually mixed mostly with—the section I was working with was an Indigenous section so we worked with Aboriginal people who had strong faiths and belief in their faiths but they came together to work collaboratively for their own people. And I thought, you know what? I like this. I can actually work this. Then I moved into Catholic Ed and then my faith system changed a little bit in terms to reflect the Catholic stuff. So while I grew up in a Pentecostal household, I'm now more, not Catholic yet, but I kind of practice that Catholic faith. I've been on two World Youth Days and I'm involved with the National Aboriginal Catholic Council and involved with Catholic young people so it's been a really big *part* of my life in terms of that.

Frank Heimans: Was religion a significant factor in the community where you were living?

Not in Perth but my grandparents grew up as Anglicans, Church of England back in the day. My dad grew up—Baryulgil was a Baptist mission so he had more of a Baptist outlook. And when my mum found God through the Pentecostal movement then they all moved over to the Pentecostal movement. I've got cousins who are Mormons. So yes, we're all through the Christian spectrum I guess. Then there's me bringing up the rear with the Catholics. One thing I do really have firm beliefs in as well is in terms of my Aboriginal beliefs and spirituality and how that fits into my sense of religion and my sense of faith.

And how does it fit in?

I've made it work. It's not been easy but I've made it work. I still believe in terms of the Dreaming and I still believe, you know, rock and land formations. I think the Dreaming was a different form of the *Seven Days of Creation*, well that's *my* belief. And the old Dreaming stories like the *Tiddalik the Frog* is my best—I love that story—but the *Tiddalik Frog* story and the *Three Sisters* up there, that's a Dreaming story. And there was another Dreaming story back home. In [the] national park my dad used to work in—it was called The Pinnacles, Cervantes—and they've got little sand moulds but when you look at it from the sea it looks like there's a bunch of people, like an army of people. And the Dreaming story behind that—because I grew up a little bit there—so that too is also significant for me. When I went to Uluru, they've got snake Dreaming tracks on the rock and when I actually saw I'm like, yeah I can see that. So, my Dreaming and my belief in the Dreaming is important to me because that helps, as well as my culture, it helps define who I am as a person.

***JASON JOHNSON** (1981) considers his grandmother's influence when he was growing up in Far North Queensland in the 1980s.*

She was Roman Catholic. She used to sit down with us kids when we were younger and talk to us about a number of different things. We wouldn't go to church at all really when we were younger. Living where we were, you'd have to drive quite a distance to go to church. We didn't go to church often but we would sit down and say prayers and talk about different things and it's something that I remember from my grandmother on my father's side, so Susan Johnson. She would often say to us when you're growing up, you *know* the difference between right or wrong. And when you're *doing* something that's wrong, that little *voice* that you can hear inside of you saying what you're doing now is wrong, that's actually God talking to you letting you know that you shouldn't be doing what you're doing and you need to go and talk to somebody about it. That's something that I definitely remember my grandmother talking to us about when we were very young actually.

When he was in his early twenties, Jason and his wife started a family. At the time of his interview in Canberra in 2013, they had three children under age ten.

***Matthew Higgins:* DO YOU GO TO CHURCH AS A FAMILY?**

Not overly, not as much just at the moment. The kids are still young, learning, going through it all. They've attended Christian schooling since they've been young. So they have a good understanding of the Christian faith. I want to *give* them that opportunity—knowing from the parts of the world that I've been in, regardless of the faith that you follow—it's a good thing to have some form of faith.

It's a question of faith in having an understanding that there's more to it all than what we're just doing on this earth. Otherwise, what's the point in it all? I've had my children. If I was to die tomorrow, it wouldn't matter. There's nothing. It doesn't matter. I view that I need to bring my kids up to understand that kind of understanding. I touch on that point that my grandmother had brought up with us—you know when you're doing something wrong. That little voice that's inside your head that's telling you what you're doing right now is probably not right. You need to listen to that voice and act on it, I suppose. Your parents and your grandparents and family and society in general are there to help guide you through understanding that little voice in your head when it says what you're doing right now is wrong.

After her parents decided to leave the Philippines when she was eight months old, ***Rachel Brown*** *(1985) grew up in a southern Queensland coastal town. She remembers how her faith changed as she got older.*

It definitely played a significant role in my life because my mum is Catholic and she has quite a strong faith. Growing up in the Philippines it's quite common for a lot of—well, most people are Catholic there. So when I was young I would go to Sunday School every week. Actually in the town where we lived, my mother was one of the very few people who knew how to play the piano so she used to play at the Catholic church and the Anglican church. So I used to have to go to *both* the Catholic and Anglican. Like Sunday was *church day* for me because the Anglican had their service in the morning, the Catholic church had their service in the afternoon because the priest had to drive in from out of town. So I had *every single* Sunday was spent in church (laughs).

I used to dread the days as well because none of my friends went. They would all be going off doing something and I knew that and I would always have to go to church. My father didn't go either, he stayed at home. He wasn't religious at all. So I felt like it was a bit of a burden to go. I always felt that from a really young age. The church never really resonated with me. I never found a connection with it. By the time I was maybe thirteen or fourteen, I think, I asked my mum if I could stop going and she said yes. So I just --- didn't go.

I think having two polar opposites of parents in terms of their religious outlook, I wondered, 'Well what's going on here? Why does this one believe in *this* and then they're saying something completely different?' I guess I always thought it was maybe a preference, an opinion, rather than a faith that you have a calling for or something like this. So I just chose something that I could understand and believe in. I chose to, I guess, follow my father's philosophy on it a bit more.

Nowadays, I think I wouldn't call myself religious. I might go as far as saying I am an atheist but I try to take the *best* bits of religion and apply it to my life. I really like the Buddhist philosophy and the idea of the four noble truths and the eightfold path. I just try to think of it as the philosophy that you can use in your life that will bring value to your life, because that's really what religion is at the end of the day. There are good points and bad points that I like to sort of pick and choose.

Elena Volkova: How do you apply the Buddhist philosophy in your life?

It's been recent actually, just in the last few years. I think it came to me when I was just feeling quite depressed, quite down. A good friend of the family's—Janet—she said, 'You know you really should take a look at this. It's helped me.' I finally did and just the *idea* that everything changes and that life is suffering, that's just how it is, and the cause of suffering is attachment to things and you need to be aware of this and if you can remove that attachment or that desire then you get rid of the suffering. That idea just really freed me. It just --- it makes me feel better. Whenever I do feel depressed or down I try to remember this.

Paganism captured ***JAMES FINNEGAN****'s (1981) interest as a teenager hanging out in a south-western Sydney suburb in the mid-1990s.*

I guess that developed when I was probably about fourteen. Me and my cousin were very, very close so I actually kind of split my time between her house and mine so her parents ended up becoming like my second parents. We just discovered it one day. We hung around in Campbelltown a lot and we went into one of the New Age shops and we just discovered it and decided that looks pretty cool and started getting really into it. Obviously I've got a very strong connection to nature and I think that experience with Paganism and Wicca and the affinity with the *moon* and all these things that we can see. It was like having a religion where it was explained because I can *see* this God. The moon is this goddess but I can actually see it and there's a physical energy there. As far as the connection to that, I mean it's scientifically explained, that connection on us so it was able to answer my curiosity but also give me some kind of faith as well. So pretty much whenever I --- particularly when I was scared of things, I would pray to the moon and because I could see it and I guess I could *feel* it, it made me feel safe. Yeah. Even to this day, it's still there. I don't practice any ceremonies or anything but I still definitely feel that affinity to nature and particularly space. I've got a keen interest in our universe.

*After **RHONDA KING**'s (1965) father died, her mother joined The Church of Jesus Christ of Latter-day Saints. In 1992, Rhonda and her husband joined the church too. They divorced after twenty years of marriage when Rhonda was in her late thirties in 2003.*

It was really important to me that I had a *good* marriage because one of the things that they talk about is having a *good, solid* marriage and an active relationship in the church with your partner and that all your kids come to church too and that *they'll all* go get married in the temple too and that *they'll all* serve a mission and that *they'll all* do all these things. So at that point in time this was still really important to me, this really mattered to me. I was really worried now because I'd decided to take the path of going for a divorce, that now my kids weren't going to have a family. They weren't going to have their mum and their dad anymore. So I was really desperately concerned about finding a *dad* for my children and in hindsight it was the worst thing I could've done. I don't know what I (laughs) was thinking. So at all costs I had to find a father for my children. And I did everything I could to find somebody.

But the problem was as a member of the church if you're still technically married you're not allowed to date. You're not allowed to, even if your divorce is in the process and you're not with them anymore, you're not living with them, you're not allowed to date anybody else. They have a program for single adults in the church but I wasn't allowed to attend any of these things because I wasn't technically divorced yet. So I was in this weird sort of no-man's-land of an island. I'd left my awesome job so I didn't have my awesome job anymore. I'd decided I couldn't be married anymore so I didn't have the husband anymore. One of my kids has already left home by now. So there I am, single mother with three kids, no husband, not knowing where I fit in anymore. Where do I fit? We used to go to church and take up the whole pew with all of our kids. Now I go and there's no husband, there's one kid missing, there's one who hardly ever wants to come to church anymore. We're not taking up the pew. We don't fit in with this whole ideal anymore. What do I do? So yes, I was really hell-bent on finding a father (laughs) which sounds just terrible and it really, really was.

DOUG FONG *(1938) recalls how his Broome family have engaged in Chinese cultural practices throughout his life.*

Look, we celebrate Chinese New Year every year, even when our children were small we would give them the little red packets with money inside and—*every* year. Never missed. My mother did the same for us and she also did for her grandchildren and we're hoping that our children will do it for their children when we're no longer around to do that. We'll also go out for a meal [at] Chinese New Year. We also observe Hang Seng, Hang Ting, which is a festival or an event which happens here in Broome in August, early September, depending on the phases of the moon. Where we go to the Chinese cemetery and acknowledge the spirits of those who've passed on. We have a luncheon organised, and we also—on every headstone, there is put paper money, food and maybe some drink to help their spirits on their journey in the afterlife. Also there is a legend that anyone that's passed away in the previous twelve months—the Chinese version of the pearly gates are opened and this person can then go through the pearly gates to the afterlife. And that's anyone who has passed on in the last twelve months. And I jokingly tell guests that even if they miss out they float—it's a bit like Cinderella—they float around for another twelve months waiting for the gates to open again. But seriously though, people sit around either in the shelter or a lot of families sit around the headstone of their grandfather or grandmother or ancestor. Particularly see that with the Yews, the Cais, the Tang Weis, some of the Fongs. It's just a lovely little tradition.

It used to be one time very—in the *very, very* early days—included as part of the Shinju Matsuri Festival. But it's *really* not a tourist, it's not a tourist event, it's a serious event. I think it was only done once. Now it's just kept to connection with the Chinese or invited guests. I remember back in the early, early days when my father was involved in the Chinese community as an office bearer, we'd spend days cooking pork and chicken and sides of beef and so on for the luncheon. Yeah, that was enjoyable 'cause we could always have samples.

KIRSTY WALLETT *(1982) was raised a Catholic in the New South Wales Riverina town of Leeton. Her mother comes from an Irish Catholic background, and her father's family were Anglican although they 'weren't particularly religious at all'.*

No I don't identify as Catholic. I don't tick the box on the census anymore. I was baptised a Catholic but—no. I don't, and I don't, I'm not an atheist and I'm not agnostic but I'm, I'm not --- (laughs) I don't know that I can define myself, you know. I've discussed it with my mum and she often wonders that if tragedy befalls me what faith will I have? And this was a conversation we had a long time ago and I said to her, 'well my faith is in people.' So I guess I'm a humanist. And I think that,

that nobody is essentially all bad—in theory. And that some of the most wonderful things that can happen in your life are because of other people. So, and that, that not everything is explainable. I mean, I'm open to science but I'm also open to spirituality in the sense of I don't know what happens after we die. I'm open to, you know, other forms of spirituality. I'm open to people being able to sense things from other people and I even, I have a friend who's a psychic and I'm quite *open* to that. Like I'd like to think I'm open-minded to it. I haven't quite made up my mind and I don't necessarily have a firm belief on anything. I'm not anti-religion either because I know it works for some people. But I think whatever way you can get out of bed every morning and be comforted when things are tough is, is fine for you.

Further Listening on Faith

Brian Carter, 1931, http://www.nla.gov.au/amad/nla.oh-vn6290887/3-4264
Trish Barrkman, 1933, http://www.nla.gov.au/amad/nla.oh-vn5972545/1-4799
Peter Galvin, 1951, http://www.nla.gov.au/amad/nla.oh-vn6252046/2-1517
Rick Galea, 1958, http://nla.gov.au/nla.obj-220158847/listen/0-664
David Cooper, 1959, http://www.nla.gov.au/amad/nla.oh-vn6290926/1-940
Michelle Cripps, 1960, http://nla.gov.au/nla.obj-219910905/listen/0-2168
Barbara Krickl, 1962, http://www.nla.gov.au/amad/nla.oh-vn6252047/1-2574
Phil May, 1962, http://www.nla.gov.au/amad/nla.oh-vn6569680/0-2015
Jodie Bell, 1970, http://www.nla.gov.au/amad/nla.oh-vn6290885/1-4099
Christian Bow, 1978, http://nla.gov.au/nla.obj-219896923/listen/0-2236
Arthur Hunter, 1989, http://nla.gov.au/nla.obj-219957349/listen/0-5129

Further Reading on Faith

Askew, Marc, 'Praying, Paying and Obeying', in Verity Burgmann and Jenny Lee (eds), *Constructing a Culture: A People's History of Australia since 1788* (Melbourne: McPhee Gribble/Penguin, 1988), pp. 170–89.

Carey, Hilary, *Believing in Australia: A Cultural History of Religions* (Sydney: Allen & Unwin, 1996).

Davison, Graeme, 'Religion', in Alison Bashford and Stuart Macintyre (eds), *The Cambridge History of Australia, Volume 2, The Commonwealth of Australia* (Port Melbourne: Cambridge University Press, 2013), pp. 215–236.

Edwards, Benjamin, *Wasps, Tykes and Ecumaniacs: Aspects of Australian Sectarianism, 1945–1981* (Brunswick East, Vic: Acorn Press, 2008).

Fletcher, Brian, *The Place of Anglicanism in Australia: Church, Society and Nation* (Melbourne: Broughton Publishing, 2008).

Hilliard, David, 'Church, Family and Sexuality in the 1950s', *Australian Historical Studies*, 28 (109), (1997), pp. 133–146.

Hudson, Wayne, *Australian Religious Thought: Six Explorations* (Clayton: Monash University Press, 2015).

Jupp, James (ed.), *The Encyclopedia of Religion in Australia*, (Port Melbourne: Cambridge University Press, 2009).

Manley, Ken R., *From Woolloomooloo to 'Eternity': A History of Australian Baptists*, volumes 1 and 2 (Bletchley, Milton Keynes, UK: Paternoster, 2006).

Mol, Hans, 'Mixed Marriages in Australia', *Journal of Marriage and the Family* 32, no. 2, (1970), pp. 293–300.

McHugh, Siobhan, 'Not in Front of the Altar: Mixed Marriages and Sectarian Tensions between Catholics and Protestants in Pre-Multicultural Australia', *History Australia* 6, no. 2, (2009), pp. 42.1–42.22.

O'Brien, Anne, *God's Willing Workers: Women and Religion in Australia*, (Sydney: UNSW Press, 2005).

Thompson, Roger C., *Religion in Australia: A History* (Melbourne: Oxford University Press, 1994).

CHAPTER 4

YOUTH

Older Australians often recall their youth with vivid anecdotes and a mix of infectious enthusiasm and embarrassment. Youth is a memorable time of turbulent physical and emotional change, as teenage bodies alter and teens assert their independence from parents and other adults while developing new and intimate relations. It is also a formative period, as young adults develop skills and attitudes, fashion their place in youth sub-cultures and in the world of work, and begin to forge distinctive identities.

The experience of youth varies across time and culture. Indeed the notion of a distinct phase of adolescence only emerged in the Western world in the late nineteenth and early twentieth centuries, and was popularised through the 'teenage' label after World War II as young people stayed longer in education, earnt and spent more disposable income and developed lifestyles that often sparked concern amongst their elders. Here we focus on the teens to mid-twenties, from high school to early employment, exploring family relationships and first loves, the shifting pleasures and risks of youth culture, and the military service of young men and women.

'High school', the focus of our first section, was not an option for most Australians until the introduction of universal secondary education after World War II. Between the wars most young people in their early to mid-teens went from the local elementary school straight into the workforce. The children of wealthy parents might attend fee-paying independent secondary schools, while a small minority—like Ruth Apps—passed entrance exams into selective public high schools. A tiny minority (around 14,000 students in 1939, about 0.2 per cent of the population[1]) attended a university.

1 Alison McKinnon and Helen Proctor, 'Education', in Alison Bashford and Stuart Macintyre (eds), *The Cambridge History of Australia, Volume 2, The Commonwealth of Australia* (Port Melbourne, Cambridge University Press, 2013), p. 438.

After the war, as state and federal governments funded educational expansion, most young Australians attended the new comprehensive public high schools or Catholic secondaries, with a small but increasing minority at independent schools. Educational opportunities were still framed by social inequalities, expectations and prejudices. In the late 1950s Les Robinson struggled with homework in a chaotic Sydney working-class family that had little space or concern for learning, and his brothers were relegated to a non-academic stream because 'they weren't interested in school at all'. In the early '70s David Cooper, an undiagnosed dyslexic who struggled with reading and writing, was sent to the local technical school rather than the new high school in the hope that he might be 'good with his hands', and Rick Galea from a straight-laced Sydney Catholic college was astonished by his rough rugby league, public high school mates who sniffed school ties soaked in paint thinner. In the 1980s a year coordinator in Lisa Jackson's high school expected Aboriginal kids like her to muck up and fail. Young Lisa was determined to prove her wrong.

Whatever type of secondary school you attended, caning and other forms of corporal punishment were brutal and common, especially for boys, until outlawed in the last quarter of the twentieth century. Les Robinson explains that every week a line of students would be caned in the classroom for not doing homework; Rick Galea recalls the 'massive thunder sound' of the cane and was 'bloody terrified'. Former students remember the very bad *and* the very good teachers who transformed their lives for better or worse, such as the 'fantastic' mini-skirted feminist English and History teacher at Kim Bear's brand new high school on the Gold Coast in the early 1970s, a woman who taught her to question a woman's role. Students might be inspired or disaffected, like Les Robinson who left school as soon as possible, or Bronwyn Macdonald in 1980s Canberra who had been told that she was 'stupid' and acted up to be noticed and 'make my way through with kudos'.

Between the wars and into the immediate postwar decades, many young Australians stayed at home after finishing school and starting work, often contributing much of their income to the family budget. Ronnie Gauci recalls that 'it never occurred to me to leave home' when he started in the Sydney panel-beating trade in the early 1960s. Most young women, like Ruth Apps in the late 1940s, only moved out once they got married, though Trish Barrkman overcame limited opportunities for young women in rural Victoria in the early 1950s by moving to Melbourne for work and rented lodgings. By the late 1960s changing attitudes and opportunities were shifting the pattern, with some young unmarried workers earning enough to buy their own homes and rental and shared housing becoming more widely available.

Tensions between teens or young adults and their parents were not a new phenomenon in the 1960s and '70s, but by this time it was becoming easier to leave a turbulent family home. Kim Bear left school at fifteen in the mid-1970s, and then left home on the Gold Coast to escape her mother and live with a boyfriend in Sydney. Hanging out with his 'Goth' mates around Sydney's Campbelltown, having left school early in the mid-1990s to escape bullying, James Finnegan went to live with relatives when his father responded to a freshly-pierced lip by declaring 'you can't live here'. Parents were loved and hated, in different measures and with multiple causes, as we see in the section on 'Teen family life'. Rhonda King's father died when she was fifteen, and she wished she'd had a chance to say 'I love you, dad' and 'I'm sorry that I was such a horrible teenager'. Teenage Kirsty Wallett was 'very close' to her mother in the 1990s, and when her mum contracted multiple sclerosis she '*wanted* to be involved' in supporting both her parents and '*never* resented' what sometimes didn't seem like a 'normal' teenage life. In the Kimberley in the 2000s, Arthur Hunter experienced the violence that was endemic in some Aboriginal extended families, and left home to complete schooling and start work in Broome, but he could always tell his mum 'anything' and they sustained an intense bond. As Arthur concludes, 'Fuck, I love her so much.'

In 'Youth culture' our narrators recall the pleasures and risks of young adult life and the changing influences and attitudes that shaped behaviour. Trish Barrkman recalls that in Melbourne in the 1940s and '50s respectable young women still wore gloves and hats on social occasions. Trish cried at King George's death and waved flags for the new Queen Elizabeth's tour in 1954, but she also enjoyed the American music and movies that were '*very*, very big' in mid-twentieth century Australia: Bing Crosby and Frank Sinatra, Ava Gardner, Katharine Hepburn and 'the Clark Gables, the Gregory Pecks, the Gary Coopers'. Teenagers with disposable incomes began to enjoy new types of music, from Australia and abroad, that were not so popular with their parents. In Sydney in the early 1960s, fifteen-year-old Les Robinson spent his first pay cheque on a record player and an

LP (long playing) record special deal that started with Elvis Presley and included Australian rock and roll singer Johnny O'Keefe's *Greatest Hits.* On an isolated farm in central Victoria, Russell Elliott received a transistor radio for his twelfth birthday which offered a lifeline to the world of 1960s music. Indeed, most Australians recall the sound track of their youth as an audio signpost for their changing times, from rock and roll in the 1950s and '60s, through heavy metal, protest music and disco, and into Abba in the 1980s. As Canberran Rhonda King recalls, 'Abba *were* better than the Beatles as far as I was concerned'. She 'knew all the words, had all their albums, dressed like them' and identified with the dark-haired Frida.

Music and fashion were markers of distinctive, evolving and sometimes embattled youth sub-cultures, many of which worried older Australians. In the working-class La Trobe Valley of the mid-1960s, Polish migrant teen Donat Santowiak witnessed 'ugly scenes' between long-haired Mods, shaven-headed Sharpies and gangs of young Italians. Struggling to belong, Donat grew his hair long and then cut it short, until he morphed into the hippy fashion of bell-bottom trousers and waist-length hair. In Sydney, Rick Galea's older brother became 'an absolute disco freak' in the 1970s, with 'the Afro, tall shoes, the flares, the sports car'. In the early 2000s, after he had come out as gay, former Goth James Finnegan tattooed stars on his arms filled with the rainbow colours of gay pride.

The motor car enabled and signalled the free-wheeling independence of Australian youth, and by the later '60s and 1970s cars were a central feature of young adult life. Donat Santowiak nick-named his first, long-suffering Holden 'Torana la Bomba' and was torn between 'wanting to be a motor mechanic and driving fast cars and hanging out under trees smoking pot'. Drugs, alcohol and cars were a dangerous mix. Before the seatbelt legislation and drink-driving campaigns of the 1970s began to have an impact, road accidents cut a brutal swathe through Australian lives, with young adults worst affected.

Alcohol features in many stories of Australian youth across different generations, while the use of addictive drugs of different types and intensity has been more variable. Rick Galea recalls the 'massive parties' at their south Sydney home in the late 1970s when his parents went to the local Leagues Club, with the house full of smoke—'I'm talking not just cigarettes'—and 'alcohol just like nothing'. Rick and his mates felt 'totally impregnable'. While some young men and women managed occasional or even regular drug habits, others suffered serious damage. Donat Santowiak was an alcoholic by his late teens. Lynne Sanders-Braithwaite began drinking too much as a lonely country-town teacher in 1971, and after a failed affair she 'fell to pieces' and spiralled into heroin addiction. Jay Logan, who was working as a Canberra security guard in the early 2000s after a tour of duty in East Timor with the Australian army, was 'constantly fighting and drinking' and only narrowly avoided a gaol sentence. Jay 'got *very* lucky' and learnt lessons that turned his life around. Australians who are still suffering the worst of drug and alcohol abuse were less likely to share their stories with our oral history project, and their lives perhaps represent the sharpest edge and long-term consequences of risk-taking youth.

Contrary to popular mythology, sexual pleasure was not invented in the '60s, though the experience and consequences of love and sex have certainly changed across time. In the section on 'First loves', older Australians who recall dating in the mid-twentieth century decades explain that 'nice girls' were chaperoned and introduced to partners. After Ginette Matalon arrived in Sydney in the late 1950s, her aunt arranged a queue of suitors who 'came with chocolate, who came with records', 'who came in cars'. For Ginette 'this was the nicest part of Australia'.

Sectarian and other prejudices often governed relationships. In 1950s rural New South Wales, Protestant Trish Barrkman fell in love with a young Catholic man, but when the priest advised her to change her religion so they could marry she decided instead to 'put the ocean between us' by leaving for New Zealand. Up in the Kimberley in the same decade, Brian Carter had to go through 'a lot of rigmarole' with Native Welfare officials to be allowed to marry his Aboriginal love, and though Brian recalls that 'ordinary people' accepted the mixed-race relationship and that his mother approved because they were both Christians, the marriage was 'frowned upon' by the 'station people'. When Donald Grey-Smith told his parents about his teenage homosexual experiences in late 1940s Melbourne, they sent him to a psychiatrist who said he would 'grow out of it'. Geraldine Box had boyfriends while growing up in rural New South Wales in the late 1960s because 'that's what you *did*', but when she fell in love with another female nurse in Darwin in the 1970s they had no role models for a lesbian relationship, assumed they were 'the only people like them in the world' and kept it secret.

Older generations of Australians also recall that sex education was non-existent or inadequate and that there were powerful moral expectations against sex before marriage. Yet we know from stories and statistics about abortion, illegitimacy, adoption and shotgun weddings that sex before marriage was not uncommon in the mid-twentieth century decades and that pregnant single women suffered cruel stigma that might have tragic consequences. In 1951 Fred Henskens' pregnant Catholic girlfriend was told by her priest that Fred was a 'bad' man and she should put the child out for adoption; Fred never knew what happened to his child. Conversely, Suzie Quartermain, born to an unmarried teenager in 1975, never met her mother because her maternal grandparents enforced adoption despite the paternal grandparents' offer to raise Suzie. When fifteen-year-old Rhonda King became pregnant in Canberra in 1980 she took her mother's advice to terminate the pregnancy. Years later she has 'erased bits of it' so she doesn't have to remember a traumatic experience and a decision she regrets. By contrast Kim Bear, who hadn't been taking the contraceptive pill long enough when she got pregnant to her soldier boyfriend in Sydney in the mid-1970s, was terrified that her mother would find out that she was 'one of those girls'. Kim was determined not to have a baby at that stage in her life, and her aunt helped arrange a termination which Kim did not regret.

Women in particular recall contradictory expectations about sex and relationships. Veronica Schwarz describes women's magazines of the 1950s and '60s 'telling you how to behave and how you ought to make a man feel good' yet also condemning sex before marriage. When Veronica succumbed because boyfriends kept pressuring her to have sex and she couldn't 'keep saying no all my life', the sex wasn't very satisfactory. She also realised that Australian men didn't take responsibility for contraception.

By the 1970s, as the contraceptive pill (released in Australia in 1961) and feminism began to impact upon women's sexual decisions, Australian society became more open about sex, though the rate of change was uneven across different regions and social groups. At her Gold Coast high school in the early 1970s, Kim Bear's feminist teacher showed the class how to put a condom on a carrot. Kim was '*absolutely* blown away' by Germaine Greer's book *The Female Eunuch* (first published in 1970), and the frank writing and pictures about sex in *Cleo* magazine (launched in 1972) were '*absolutely* life changing' (though Queenslanders had to cross the New South Wales border to buy copies that were not censored by Queensland's conservative government). In Melbourne in the early 1980s the parents of David Cooper and his girlfriend allowed the young couple to go away together, unchaperoned, for the weekend, though other adults were 'absolutely disgusted'. By the mid-1990s Christian Bow and his girlfriend Ellen agreed to an 'open relationship' when she left Mackay to study in Brisbane. With long distance phone calls still prohibitively expensive, they sustained their bond through old-fashioned love letters, and when they finally got together and married it was '*so* worth it'.

Coming out may never be easy, though the stigma and discrimination around homosexuality has changed since the days of Donald Grey-Smith and Geraldine Box's youth. In Sydney in the late 1990s James Finnegan struggled with his sexuality and became depressed, suicidal and addicted to drugs. It was James' mother who helped him kick the drug habit so that James could take 'control of his life' and find a boyfriend while starting to 'become me'.

Our youngest narrators like James reveal both change and continuity in the Australian experience of love, sex and relationships. In 2008, twenty-three-year-old Rachel Brown had been with her Brisbane boyfriend for five years when she decided that what she really wanted at this stage of her life was travel, adventure and independence rather than the stable marriage and suburban life expected of earlier generations of Australian women. In 2006, when a young Broome woman asked Arthur Hunter to 'hook up'—through an intermediary, according to 'Kimberly style'—Arthur's shaking and speechlessness reminds us that while the patterns and expectations of intimate relationships change across time and culture, young love has always been anxious *and* thrilling.

Our oldest narrators, born in the 1920s, went 'From school to work' after the worst of interwar mass unemployment was over. Apart from occasional economic blips like the brief recession of 1961 (when Les Robinson left school in Sydney and joined long queues for work), most recall plentiful jobs in the immediate postwar decades. As Donat Santowiak explains, 'jobs in those days were on every corner'. When Donat left school in the La Trobe Valley in the mid-1960s he was offered three different jobs and chose the apprenticeship in mechanical drafting because that was closest to his love of cars.

Even in good times young workers faced ill-treatment. Starting work in Sydney as a secretary at the end of World War II, Ruth Apps suffered sexual harassment from her first employer and then, after returning to work following a short period of absence for marriage, she was forced to leave 'the instant' she was pregnant. As we will see in a later chapter, Ruth would resent and resist the lower wages offered to women. The young migrant workers who underpinned Australia's postwar industrial growth also experienced discrimination in employment, whether through stints of indentured government employment or the rejection of overseas qualifications. In 1954 Connie Shaw started her first job as a housekeeper in Perth soon after her Dutch family arrived in Western Australia, but walked out when she realised her employer didn't want Connie to improve her English for fear of having to pay a higher wage. Dutch East Indies migrant Fred Henskens worked hard to keep his first job on Canberra building sites in 1949, and was disconcerted by the foreman's request that he not work so 'hard and quick' because it upset fellow workers. In the mid-1970s Ouranita Karadimas was one of many second generation European and then Asian migrants whose parents encouraged study beyond school so they might enjoy better educational qualifications and employment opportunities.

These men and women who started work during Australia's long postwar economic boom often highlight their pride in their skills and achievements as workers. Ruth Apps recalls with tremendous satisfaction and vivid detail each of her secretarial jobs and her progression to senior roles in industry and government. Donat Santowiak 'loved' drawing and designing for the Victorian State Electricity Commission and Fred Henskens talked with an expert's satisfaction about the intricacies of his work as a drainage contractor. Geraldine Box recalls the bravery and skill of young nurses who staffed the operating theatres during the terrible aftermath of Darwin's Cyclone Tracy in 1974. Ouranita Karadimas 'loved it' when she became the 'Good little Greek girl' metallurgist in a Sydney foundry.

By the 1990s, with the shift towards a mass higher education system intended to skill new workers for the knowledge economy, an increasing proportion of school leavers attended college or university and higher education qualifications became a prerequisite for more and more jobs. When Christian Bow started as an apprentice electrician in 1996 he earnt more than his student mates, but as their job prospects and wages outpaced his, Christian returned to study so that he could work in construction management. In uncertain economic times, such as the recession of the early 1990s or the Global Financial Crisis (GFC) of 2008 to 2009, a degree did not guarantee employment, as Rachel Brown found when she was laid off from her first job with a mining company at the start of the GFC. In an increasingly globalised economy, young workers like Rachel have had to adjust to the insecurity of short-term and part-time employment and shed earlier generations' aspiration of a job for life. Gemma Nourse, born in Darwin in 1989 and university-educated in Canberra, had worked at seven different jobs in four cities when she was interviewed in 2013. She notes the variety of a contemporary career and argues that mobile young workers 'are more able to be agents in their lives' by comparison with workers of her father's generation who enjoyed a stable long-term career at the cost of personal fulfilment. But she also recognises that there is 'something to be said for having fewer choices' and a more certain future.

The military has always been a youth employment option, and in 'Military service' several narrators consider their experiences of military service in times of war and peace. Kathleen Golder, who soldered Spitfire aircraft radiators in an English factory in the early 1940s, reminds us that in the two world wars women often did paid and volunteer work for the war effort, and that in many migrants' countries of origin both men and women might be conscripted. In Australia young men (but not women) could be conscripted for home service during World War II, undertook national service during the 1950s and, most controversially, were subject to conscription by a birth-date lottery from 1964 to 1972 during the Vietnam War. Russell Elliott recalls the tension and trepidation at his Teachers College in Ballarat when the conscription lottery was televised in 1969 and the 'numbers fell out' for three of his fellow students.

Bert Castellari's first attempt to enlist in the forces at the start of World War II was thwarted by a recruiting officer who was suspicious of his Italian surname. Called up for service after Japan joined the war, Bert describes the danger and confusion of combat and the long-term effects of war service on an ageing body. Half a century later, in 2001, Cairns labourer Jason Johnson couldn't see his life '*going* anywhere' so he enlisted in the regular army. Jason's strongest impression of service in Afghanistan is the camaraderie amongst the soldiers, 'this awe' and the mutual support of a team which has been through danger together and depended on each other in hard times. While young returned men and women may suffer immediate and long-term physical and mental damage, they also often miss the wartime peak experience of belonging and achievement.

High School

***RUTH APPS** (1926) won a place at an academically-selective Sydney high school in the late 1930s.*

Well my secondary education were probably five of the happiest years of my life. To get a place at St George Girls High School I had to do a test at the end of sixth class and of a cohort of some hundred girls in Year Six, there were *five* of us got a place at St George Girls High School. I had to catch a bus to get there, from Hurstville to Kogarah. It was a school run on academic lines. We were told the day we arrived there, 'You are now St Georgians. You are expected to study and at the end I want you to graduate as a girl who knows her place in the world, who knows that she can succeed in anything but, above all, who is a lady.' Now it's obviously a bit of a contradiction in terms. It was an extremely strict school as far as discipline was concerned. We were expected to behave ourselves, wore a box-pleated tunic with a long-sleeved blouse, a red and white woollen tie, gloves, black stockings and a hat of course. But they instilled a sense of pride in their school.

THERE'S LOT OF TALK amongst my family about the way I speak. Where did I get it from? At the grammar school every morning we were lined up and we had to say, 'A, E, I, O, U' and heaven forbid if you didn't get it right. So that set an establishment. Went to St George where good language, well spoken, was emphasised. So it has stayed with me. Lady who used to live next door to me said one day, 'I used to think that when I talk to you, you were putting on [the] dog trying to be flash,' she said, 'until one day I heard you yelling at your kids in exactly the same voice.' So that's it.

***LES ROBINSON** (1947) recalls the difficulties faced by a working-class lad at the local high school in the south Sydney suburb of Jannali in the late 1950s.*

At school we used to get the cane, not doing the homework. Every week, line up, we didn't even bother going to the classroom in the end. We just stay outside and wait for the teacher to come along, cane you, then go inside and get on with your work. 'Cause I didn't do my homework. It's pretty difficult. I had seven brothers and sisters. You get home and where do you do your homework? Four of us sleep in the same bedroom. We had double bunks in one bedroom, four of us slept in there. And during the afternoon the other kids would be tearing around playing or whatever else and you're supposed to sit down. 'Cause I *was* the only studious one in the family, none of the others worried in the slightest. It got to the point that sometime there I used to get my homework and used to go to next door neighbours. They had a big mulberry tree and we had a bit of a cubby house built up in it and I used to sit up in the cubby house and do my homework up in the mulberry tree, just to get away from the bloody noise and that type of thing.

But even then, well, I wasn't *that* studious, like I wasn't in an A class. In those days you had A, taking two languages, B was taking one language, C and D was the rest of us chopped in half. Rs were at the beginning of the second class alphabetically, so I was in the D class. Then in those days you had GA classes, which was General Activities, which was where Neils and Brians, the brothers went. 'Cause they weren't interested in school at all. So I spent three years, three years, which wasn't particularly happy time once again. I had a couple of mates. But I didn't enjoy school. I was glad to get out of it in the end. I can't remember any fond memories of school, at all.

Hamish Sewell: And you left at fifteen?

Yes. Actually before I was fifteen. I turned fifteen in the February and I left school in the December, for Christmas holidays, and never went back.

***RICK GALEA** (1958) completed the Higher School Certificate in 1976 at Marist Brothers Pagewood in east-Sydney Maroubra, and remembers the violence of corporal punishment by the Brothers.*

I was pretty bloody terrified to be honest. You only had to look sideways to get called up the front and get two cuts. Every cut was like thunder, 'cause it come off the hand on to the cloak—that made that massive thunder sound. It seriously sounded like an explosion as it hit. And everybody, they'd all go out of there just in agony. It was really quite brutal.

We actually went through the last year of what they call corporal punishment. When we left Year 10, that was the very last year [in] New South Wales, of caning or hitting of any description and the change from that year to Year 12, when we left, between the children, the discipline in that school was, it was just infinite. Like, infinitely worse. The cheek, the talkback, the lack of manners was just *unbelievable*—how quickly it went downhill in that time. Kids just talked back to teachers knowing full well they couldn't do anything about it. Would verbally harass them at times. It was just mindboggling how quickly it changed. I really to this day think they ballsed up completely with going from one extreme to the other.

I LIVED A BIT OF A DOUBLE LIFE. I spent time—a lot of school holiday time—with boys that *did* go to the public system when I was in the thirteen, fourteens, because I actually played in a rugby league team involving all these guys. They were great mates, but living and seeing their lifestyle, it was just *so different* to the life I was living. They were smoking marijuana openly at age fourteen. They had pornographic magazines which I never ever, I couldn't even comprehend to be honest.

They used to actually—at one stage—they were soaking their ties, their school ties, in a paint thinner. They used to buy these cans of paint thinners. And it was called tollyrene [toluene]. Something like that. It smelt like just rip the nasal straight outta ya. They would actually dip their ties in it and go to school and suck on it during class. They were level-headed guys but they, this is the absolute nuttiness of it at the time, that was just almost standard practice for these guys. It was just so bizarre.

Elena Volkova: But they were also your friends?

Yes, oh yes, they were great friends. Yes, and we used to do a lot of things together during the holidays. Listen to music, go to movies and stuff like that. But then when the holidays were over I'd go back to the Catholic school and I'd be with my school mates, who I loved dearly. It was chalk and cheese, it was just so different.

In Melbourne's south-east in the early 1970s ***DAVID COOPER*** *(1959) attended a technical school that was aimed at teenagers who were heading for a trade rather than an academic education.*

I went to Aspendale Technical School. The reason I went there was basically, in Grade 6 my mum went to the Grade 6 teacher and said, 'Should David go to the Bonbeach High School or Aspendale Technical School?' And I still remember the teacher's answer, it was, 'Send him to the technical school 'cause if you're lucky he'll be good with his hands.' So I wasn't very good at school and the hope was that you'd become a motor mechanic or a carpenter. That was how people made their decisions back then.

KIM BEAR *(1959) recalls an exciting time at her new high school on the Gold Coast in the early 1970s.*

High school I hit when I was on the Gold Coast and it was also when I was thirteen, it was 1972. That was *such* a momentous time to turn into a teenager. Particularly on the Gold Coast, being in Queensland and happily quite close to the border. It was Gough Whitlam, it was feminism, it was *Cleo* magazine. They were *incredible* times. Moratoriums, people protesting and always the sense that the world just keeps expanding, and your exposure to it. How blinkered have you been till now? I guess too, moving out of primary school into high school—although we'd moved around a bit you've got your group and it's fairly small—and that moment when you go into a high school where suddenly its kids from lots of different schools, that funny kind of pecking order that becomes established.

What I loved about my high school was it was the very first year that the school had opened. We were the first students in Grade 8 which I *loved* because *nobody* had written on the desks and *nobody* made mess anywhere or carved their names on things. I loved that our school was all new and fresh.

We did have one teacher who was the absolute *radical* feminist, *incredible*. Was the first person I'd ever seen who didn't shave under their arms and wore very, very, very short skirts. She took us—we had one period of the week where she was English and History together, and we loved it because *all* she talked about was feminism. So it was kind of like this subversive undercurrent in our class and she was fantastic. It was the first time I'd really come up against somebody who really questioned the traditional authority over women.

BRONWYN MACDONALD *(1964) grew up in Canberra, the youngest of eight children of a German Jewish refugee who had come to Australia on the* Dunera *and been interned along with other German 'aliens'.*

I didn't like school. I always thought I was pretty stupid actually and in fact that was dad's word. Dad said, 'Are you stupid?' *Clearly* thought we'd have the guts to say no, but we didn't. And I did think I was very stupid. So I was very quiet in school and in primary school I just didn't do much of anything. Then by the time I got to high school I thought that probably being naughty was the only way to make my way through with any kudos, I guess. M'mm. So, didn't do well at school. Didn't fail anything because I am actually quite clever. But I never made an effort.

Getting kicked out of class was always fun. Took up smoking and, you know, slowly put it out while the teacher walked up. You know, just challenging, pretty challenging behaviour. I wanted to be noticed, I think. Which I was, for all the wrong reasons. Yes. Took German and failed and --- (laughs). I thought dad was German. I mean, he was German. I wasn't thinking. That's what I mean. We didn't really understand. And this is Year 7. Didn't really understand that that would be a horrible language for me to be speaking around the house. So --- (laughs). How mean. Had no idea. None. Proudly came home and said, 'Look, I can count to ten.' Must've horrified him. He never said a word. Neither did mum.

LISA JACKSON *(1972) started her secondary education in Sydney and completed Year 12 in Perth when the family moved to Western Australia.*

Aboriginal kids were always treated differently than non-Aboriginal kids. There were about forty to fifty Aboriginal kids in one of the high schools I went to. So we were in a majority but, academically, we weren't. We weren't smart. Well, there were some people that were but the rest of us were not really. We were just average run-of-the-mill kids I guess, but we were always subjected to, you know, differences in terms of comments made to us.

I remember one comment. I had a year coordinator tell me, by the time I was eighteen, she said, 'Oh, you'll be a drug addict, alcoholic, and you'll be a mother.' I think that pretty much set the tone for the rest of my life. I basically said 'No, no, I'm not'. I'd love to go back and just say to her, 'Well, look, I'm nearly forty now. I haven't got any kids, but I've still got influence and I have an education behind me and I'm not a drug addict or alcoholic.' I'd love to do that. That's the kind of the mentality that we all had to go through and that was the kind of stuff. Aboriginal kids are expected to get into trouble, they're expected to muck up in classes, and I never did.

JAMES FINNEGAN *(1981) recalls the challenges of being 'different' at a western suburbs Sydney high school in the 1990s.*

I got bullied at school. They would all call me gay before I even realised that that's what it was. Somehow *they* knew. I don't know why. It was probably because I was a quiet person and, you know, I liked hanging out with the girls and I wasn't into sports and all of that. So I guess they equated that to being gay. Even though they wouldn't have even really knew what gay was (laughs). That definitely affected my own perception of being gay. I always felt like it was wrong and it was a bad thing.

It happened all the time and, and I never actually spoke to my parents about it. It was something that I was embarrassed about. I didn't want my parents to know that I was being bullied because, I guess I felt like that made me less of a person. It was extreme. I still have a lot of fear of those people. I still do fear quite a lot and I think that led to a lot of struggles in my life.

I ended up leaving school at the beginning of Year 10, because I couldn't handle it anymore. I guess the pity about that is I was a very good student.

Further Listening on High School

Bert Castellari, 1923, http://www.nla.gov.au/amad/nla.oh-vn6252044/0-3019
Veronica Schwarz, 1939, http://www.nla.gov.au/amad/nla.oh-vn6290927/0-2736
John Murphy, 1940, http://www.nla.gov.au/amad/nla.oh-vn6504268/0-4958
Greer Bland, 1944, http://www.nla.gov.au/amad/nla.oh-vn5972533/1-585~1-677
Lynne Sanders-Braithwaite, 1949, http://www.nla.gov.au/amad/nla.oh-vn6290876/0-3398
Donat Santowiak, 1950, http://nla.gov.au/nla.obj-220175608/listen/0-4036
Peter Galvin, 1951, http://www.nla.gov.au/amad/nla.oh-vn6252046/0-365
Alison Fettell, 1952, http://nla.gov.au/nla.obj-220185705/listen/1-2
Gina Polito, 1954, http://www.nla.gov.au/amad/nla.oh-vn6421369/0-2405
Michelle Cripps, 1960, http://www.nla.gov.au/amad/nla.oh-vn6252075/0-4413
Rhonda King, 1965, http://www.nla.gov.au/amad/nla.oh-vn6390877/0-6124
Jodie Bell, 1970, http://www.nla.gov.au/amad/nla.oh-vn6290885/0-2474
Christian Bow, 1978, http://nla.gov.au/nla.obj-219896923/listen/0-3324
Jay Logan, 1981, http://www.nla.gov.au/amad/nla.oh-vn6569699/0-1742
Arthur Hunter, 1989, http://nla.gov.au/nla.obj-219957349/listen/0-4659

Teen Family Life

RONNIE GAUCI *(1947) was the second eldest of seven children in a Maltese migrant family. He recalls that his parents were 'battlers', with dad working in a Sydney glass foundry and mum doing sewing and cleaning work, and that there wasn't much money around.*

> Well, if there was, mum wouldn't have to work. Not to mention then she gotta cook for us, feed us, do our beds and what have you. But when my first sister started work she used to give mum the pay packet. Never opened it. The year after, I started work. I did the same. Now she did it for three years and I did it

for two years. She then got married and left home so the last year was just me. I never, ever expected anything from it. It was just part and parcel what me and my sister did to help out. But mum started—soon as we started giving her pay, like that—she started a bank account. She's give me five dollars a week in case I wanted to buy a bottle of coke or whatever I can do it. Whatever she wanted to put in my account, she can, the rest was for the family. And that's how me and my sister did it.

After that things got easier 'cause then me younger sister got married not long after leaving school. I stayed at home till I was twenty-one—that's when I got married—or twenty-two. Right up till then I was giving as much as I could. Help them out as best I can. That's just something we did. Never dawned on me to leave home or anything like that.

*At fifteen, **KIM BEAR** (1959) started a summer holiday job. When her widowed mother's sewing piece-work dried up in the mid-1970s because much of the textile industry moved offshore, Kim continued her job after the school holidays finished, to 'fund the family'. When her mum found new work Kim decided not to return to school. Within a year she had left home on the Gold Coast and moved to Sydney to live with a young man she'd met during the holidays.*

Once you know you can function in a work capacity, it's like, 'Oh well, okay I can obviously do what I want and I'll get a job' and, very optimistic about it all. It changed the dynamic again at home because suddenly I was less beholden to her, and I think there was that sense of some of the controls slipping away, which she didn't like. It just always seemed to take her a long time to adapt to a change and I think—you did ask me before and I don't know if I've answered—the kinds of things that would tip her over the edge or warrant a hiding would be weird things where she'd say, 'I'm going out. I've got washing out on the line. Bring it in, because I think it's going to rain later.'

Well that was actually the argument that forced me to leave home. I'd gone to my room. I'd read a book. I'd fallen asleep and of course it rained and she came home and the washing was still out on the line and I woke up to her hitting me. Frightened the life out of me. I was so scared I'd no idea what was going on. Then I think I just got the courage to just stand up to her and just say, 'If you ever hit me again, I'll hit you back. I will hit you back and you will regret it.' I've never done it before. I never stood up to her and by that stage the hitting implement was the fan belt of the car.

I JUST DECIDED, THAT'S IT, I'm going to Sydney. I remember being, you know, I really wanted to go because I knew I had to get away but I was a bit worried about leaving my sister and what would happen to her. I thought about it and thought about it, and I thought no, I will go. I was probably also a bit worried whether I'll get a job or whether I'd be able to cut it in the city, the Coast was so different. Anyway I booked my bus ticket and mum wouldn't even take me to the bus station. I packed up my few books, sorts of things, and my friend Leonie came around in her dad's Valiant Station Wagon to get all my stuff down to the bus. She said goodbye to me. When I left mum at home, she just said, 'Well if you go just know you can't come back.' So I kind of okay, so --- (laughs) getting on the bus and bawling my eyes out halfway to Sydney, at what I'd done.

Then when I got to the other end, he was there, and he had a flat that he shared with another guy, so I just moved in with him. I think a week later I had a job and that was like, okay, new life begins, just get started. So yes I was very young, really when you think about it, although at the time it just didn't seem to be that unusual. I guess one of the good things about the upbringing I'd had was that I was very self-sufficient. There wasn't anything I didn't know how to do in terms of looking after myself.

I had started taking the pill. I obviously hadn't been taking it long enough (laughs), and I got pregnant. *All* I could think of was, 'Oh my God! I'm going to be one of those girls.' I was also *absolutely* terrified that my mother would find out. That was the overriding thing that concerned me, that my mother would find out, that all the things that she told me about, you know, don't get pregnant, don't do this, and all other things she said, I'd done it. And I was like, 'Oh my God!' I didn't even realise at the beginning I was, because I was away from home and I was eating stuff—like we ate very healthily at home whereas, when I moved to Sydney I started on Tim Tams—so I thought I was just putting on weight (laughs).

RHONDA KING*'s (1965) father, who ran a mobile crane business in Canberra, died when she was fifteen.*

I remember we were out at the farm one day and I said something like, 'But what if you die dad?' And he goes, 'Oh I'm going to be round for years and years yet.' It was only a couple of weeks later he died. I was like, 'Oh that's a bit ironic', that he had said that. But we were always fighting—he and I. Always at loggerheads with one another, once I became a teenager. To the point that one day I said, 'Can I have a hug dad?' and he goes, 'What do you want?' And I said, 'I don't want anything. I just want a hug.' And he wouldn't believe me. He just insisted that I must want something. I'm like, 'No, I just want a hug.'

It had a really huge effect I think on my younger brother and sister. Well it had a huge effect on everybody obviously—losing someone like that in your life. I didn't have a reaction of crying till a few days later when my older brother—from my dad's first marriage—came to Canberra and we were going through the wardrobe in the office, because he used to have a sleeping area in the office from when he was in Canberra. So he'd stay there while we were at the farm. I was getting his clothes out and I was looking at his boots that were next to his bed where he'd obviously just left them. I looked at them and I just suddenly—he had this funny—because he had quite a round stomach—he had this white singlet that he would wear like a, you know, wife-beater style. It had this print on the front of it and it said, 'Jogger.' Had these people jogging. I always used to watch him wearing it with this big tummy and I was like, that's so the wrong singlet for you. But whatever. You can live in hope (laughs). I remember getting that out and looking at it and realising it was just this limp singlet hanging in, that he wasn't going to fill that up any more with his body. Then looking at his boots on the floor and seeing—you know when you buy a brand new pair of shoes or boots, they're all pristine, there's no creases in them—and seeing those creases from his feet walking in those shoes and that those creases were made by *his* walk, by *his* body, by *his* being on the planet and being here. Realising that neither of those things would have his being inside them anymore, and at that moment I just broke down and just burst into tears.

It was really hard in the year following that—because we had been at loggerheads with one another—to come to terms with the fact that I didn't get the chance to say, 'I love you dad' or 'I'm sorry that I was such a horrible teenager' or, you know. He just was gone just (clicks fingers) like that.

***SUZIE QUARTERMAIN** (1975), who had always known that she was adopted, received her first communication from her birth parent when she was sixteen.*

Mum and dad made me go into the lounge room to talk to me. It had to go via my parents because I was underage. So he sent it to the adoption agency. The adoption agency rang my parents. Said, 'Is it okay?' They were allowed to read it first—whether they did or not I don't know—and then they said, 'We've got a letter. Do you want it? We've got a letter from your father'. And for sixteen years I'd been waiting for my mother. I assumed my father wasn't in the picture. You just assume that she was left by herself with a baby. So I was like, 'Oh well what about my mum?' And they said, 'Oh your mum died'. I was crushed. Was, yeah. I didn't really react but I was crushed that I'd never get to meet her. But anyway I read this letter from my father and he explained everything.

After that came a letter from my grandparents who are just the be all and end all of everything to me. I just *adore* them. They're the ones that wanted to adopt me. 'Cause they're *everything* that you expect your grandparents to be. Every time I see my nan now she gives me this great big cuddle and --- (sniffs) 'My beautiful girl. I'm so glad to have you and precious little Ava', and, you know, everything that grandma should be. I've known them about twenty years now so there was no feeling of betrayal with them like there is when you get to know your dad and you've already got a dad. Both my [adoptive] nans died shortly after I met my grandparents so they were just able to be my grandparents (sniffs).

Katie Holmes: Do you want to pause it?

Oh it's okay. It's all right. I don't even know why I'm crying. I've never cried about my grandparents before. But they just love me unconditionally. There's no, you know, with my mother's side of the family there's all this *guilt* that hangs over their heads and it's stopped me from getting to know them.

Why? What sort of guilt?

Well 'cause my grandmother made Wendy give me up so --- (sniffs) any time I've met my grandmother she, she's never asked me about myself. She doesn't talk to me. She just treats me like someone she's having lunch with. Yeah. She just doesn't care about me at all. Which is okay. She doesn't have to. But it stops me from getting to know who my mum was.

So has your dad been able to tell you?

He doesn't really talk about it. That was just devastating for him. My nanna tells me most stuff. Because Wendy spent a lot of time at their house, and I'll do things and she'll go, 'Oh my goodness. You're so much like your mum when you', you know, 'use that expression' or --- (sniffs) So I only know little bits and pieces. But Chris has been very good to me.

So Chris is your biological father and Wendy's your biological mother?

Yes. And I look exactly like Chris so I finally found that person that I look like. I look like my nanna.

***JAMES FINNEGAN** (1981) recalls the consequences of bullying at his school in western Sydney.*

So in Campbelltown when I was at school and didn't want to go, I just wouldn't go. I'd stay at home. And there wasn't really much my parents could do because I just wasn't going (laughs).

Roslyn Burge: And your mother was there at home?

Yes, she just didn't know how to make me go to school. I would just refuse to go. Sometimes I'd be at school and I'd just walk out. I think she was at a bit of a loss. She didn't know how to make me go to school. So eventually I just left. And then when I hung around Campbelltown it was pretty much me and my cousin and Amy. We were Goths back then so we'd be all dressed in black, piercings everywhere and makeup, and I guess it was our whole, well if people are going to pick us, pick on us for being different, well let's be *really* different. We'd hang around Campbelltown Station. And a lot of the other kids in the area that identified in the same way started gravitating towards us. So we ended up having this big group of Goths that hung around Campbelltown Station. I'd say all up there was probably about ten to fifteen of us. And we'd just hang out there. People would try and make us move along.

I ended up getting an interest in piercing, and so I would give everyone in the group piercings. I had this little tin that I carried around with a whole bunch of safety pins in it (laughs). One of the chairs at Campbelltown Station—on the back of it—it says,

'Jimmy's Piercing Parlour' (laughs). So just grabbed whatever I was piercing. So whether it be an ear, an eyebrow or a lip or whatever. Just pulled it out, got the safety pin and whacked it through (laughs). You'd be surprised how easy you can get a safety pin through the skin (laughs).

What was your parents' reaction to that?

They didn't like it but at the same time there was nothing they could do. I pierced my lip and my dad said, 'If you don't take it out, you've got to leave. You can't live here if you've got that.' And I was like, 'Well fine. I'll leave.' And so I went and lived with my cousin and her parents (laughs). Yeah. So that lasted a little while until my mum made him let me come back.

When she was a teenager, ***KIRSTY WALLETT****'s (1982) mum was diagnosed with multiple sclerosis.*

We're very close. And we always have been. Do I think that I was leaned on? Not necessarily by her, but by everyone more than I should have been at that age? Absolutely, but I don't think there was any other alternative. I *never* resented what was going on. I *wanted* to be involved. I wanted to be supportive.

There were a lot of periods where I could tell my dad wasn't coping. I know I knew that at the time because to imagine the woman that he loves being that debilitated and not necessarily being able to process that emotionally, I can look back on that now and see that that's probably what it was. But he couldn't handle it all on his own. I know that he couldn't. I don't necessarily think that what I did—whether *he* even recognised that or whether it actually helped him—but I had a lot of responsibility at sixteen and seventeen. I would take my mum on school nights into the hospital at midnight. I think my seventeenth birthday I took her to—my eighteenth birthday maybe?—I remember having an argument with some doctor in the hospital who didn't want to give her pain medicine because of all the stigma around that. I don't regret any of that. Was it a normal experience for someone at that age? I don't know, but what is normal anyway? That was my experience and that's what it was.

ARTHUR HUNTER *(1989) was a teenager in the Kimberley in the 2000s.*

I'm single, yeah. Single for about two years. Two years man—that's pretty long (laughs). Some people have been single for ten years or something. I'm kind of happy that I'm single. When you got a woman or a man—I'm straight but, just to make it clear—but with me, with my past relationships which was three, four maybe, I just felt I was violated. Well not *that* stuff. Like it's bad. I've been abused a lot. I've been hit, physically hit, I'm abused and mentally and verbally you know.

They say that I'm doing it to them but for me it's like that's all been pushed onto me, and I had bruise marks, I had everything. When I was fourteen, thirteen, maybe fifteen, I seen that happen to my mum. She got hit by her brothers and all that stuff you know. I told my mum I'm *not* gonna do that *ever* in my life. I'm not gonna abuse my wife or woman or my kids. Till that day till now it's like I'm gonna keep the promise I made to my mum. And my uncles that did that to my mum, now they staying back because I confronted my uncle when I was fifteen. My mum was crying, really crying. I tell her, 'Mum, just leave it. Don't worry about it anymore.' That's my relationship with my mum. Me and her have, you know I can tell my mum *anything*. The most *embarrassing* thing you can say to anybody, I still tell my mum. I have more relationship with my—I feel, you know that girlfriends and anything you can have, you can get married—but the relationship and the bond with your mum, for me you know I care about that more than a girlfriend or a wife. That thing—the connection is always going to be there whether you're sick, old, ugly, fat, skinny, you know, anything.

My mum's a very special woman. I went off one part. I don't know why. I was sober and I hardly drink. So I can prove that. I went off, and my mum was going mad too for something else. What made *me* smile and made me feel happy that I went up to her, I was shouting at her to tell her to be quiet and I lost it. My aunty—my mum's younger sister—said, 'Get away brothers. Get away, he's going to hit you or anything.' And what made me smile—well not at the time—was she said, 'He's not going to hit me. He's my son.' And it's like that has a lot to say for --- Fuck, I love her, so much. And for her to say that, for me it's special.

Further Listening on Teen Family Life

Trish Barrkman, 1933, http://www.nla.gov.au/amad/nla.oh-vn5972545/0-4055
John Murphy, 1940, http://www.nla.gov.au/amad/nla.oh-vn6504268/0-6061
Michelle Cripps, 1960, http://www.nla.gov.au/amad/nla.oh-vn6252075/0-4577
Phil May, 1962, http://www.nla.gov.au/amad/nla.oh-vn6569680/0-316
Jason Johnson, 1981, http://nla.gov.au/nla.obj-220115636/listen/0-3582

Pleasure and Risk: Youth Culture

TRISH BARRKMAN *(1933) grew up in south Gippsland and moved to Melbourne as a young woman. She studied at a business college in Caulfield and then did office work and staff training at G.J. Coles in the first half of the 1950s.*

I remember King George VI dying. I know I was living at Kew and I know I cried and we all went into a state of great mourning because he was a very much loved king who had stood very hard and fast during the Second World War, and that was a very sad, sad time. Then of course the Queen came '54. That was *huge*, huge. We lined the streets. We sold the flags. We took every opportunity to see our Queen. She had beautiful skin. I encountered her on several occasions. Didn't matter where she went. If you were close by, whether you were working, we would all drop whatever we were doing and you'd grab a fruit case or *anything* you could to stand on to go and see the Queen passing by.

Hamish Sewell: So it was like a forerunner to a rock concert?

Well (laughs), we didn't break out into song. We were still quite reserved and I think we young ladies were still wearing hats and gloves.

Did you scream or did you wave flags?

Oh we waved. I don't think there was, well there was a certain amount of screaming. But it was the waving of the flag.

So it was quite restrained.

In a sense yes and we were still rather a restrained country. As I say, we still wore the hat and gloves and my social life in Melbourne in the years that I lived there and I was single, it was hat and gloves all the time. Daytime, and a little hat of an evening when you went out. We went to the movies a lot. The movies were *very*, very big at that time. Well, we saw the Clark Gables, the Gregory Pecks, the Gary Coopers, the wild west of America. They were all American movies. Ava Gardner, Katharine Hepburn, all those great, great—Bing Crosby, Frank Sinatra. I've been a fan of Frank Sinatra's for many, many years.

***LES ROBINSON** (1947) started work in Sydney in the early 1960s as an electrical engineering apprentice, and suddenly had money to spend.*

When I first started work, fifteen, at Trevan Products, I was getting [the equivalent to] nine dollars fifteen a week. I bought my first record player, which I had to pay off. I think it was thirty-five pounds for the record player. My first LP, first records actually, that I bought—I had an account, used to pay a pound a week or something and get a few records—it was *Blue Hawaii*, that was released first time at the time. I did want that LP and to get up to my limit for what I could buy for what I was paying off, I can get another LP so I bought *Johnny O'Keefe's Greatest Hits*. I've still got both records, and out of both records Johnny O'Keefe's one is my favourite now. *Blue Hawaii* is good but ---

Hamish Sewell: Who sings Blue Hawaii?

Oh, that's terrible. Elvis Presley. Whole movie, Elvis Presley.

Right, forgive me.

Yeah (laughs).

And Johnny O'Keefe, of course, was an Australian, wasn't he?

Oh yes, Johnny O'Keefe's Australian. You're New Zealander?

Yeah.

I thought I picked up ---

But still no excuse for not knowing who Elvis was, isn't it?

No, it's not really. Johnny O'Keefe was Australian. He never had a great voice but he had a good voice for what he used to sing. At the same time you could say he's a larrikin but then what you get later on, what he got up to, he was a bit of an idiot, you know, drugs and that type of stuff and he ended up getting killed very young in a car accident.[2]

---

2 Johnny O'Keefe was terribly injured in a car accident in 1960. He did recover to continue singing, but died young in 1978 from a heart attack induced by prescribed drugs.

Radio was a lifeline for ***RUSSELL ELLIOTT*** *(1950), growing up as a teenager on a farm in central Victoria in the 1960s.*

I have a thing over there on the mantelpiece, a little AWA radiola transistor radio that I was probably given as a birthday present when I was twelve. I'd hate to think how many miles it travelled around with me but it was a sort of window to the world. Because you could pull in the local radio station at Maryborough. That had all the songs. I'll ever maintain that '60s has the best music ever (laughs). Favourite bands, I suppose it started with Bill Haley and the Comets and *Rock Around the Clock*, and had Beach Boys and Buddy Holly. Things like that, but a fairly wide range of music. Elvis Presley, he was going then.

Nicole Curby: Much Australian music?

Johnny O'Keefe occasionally, but beyond that no, no. I guess it was just what came over the radio. But as I said it, every time from about twelve when I was out walking around the farm, carried it with me, *all* the time. And so I listened to music, listened to the radio and ninety per cent of it was music, there wasn't too many ads. And I suppose interestingly enough the news that appeared every hour—I was talking to the kids the other day about the --- I know it's a bit later, the Cuban Missile Crisis, that was unfolding then [in 1962]—I said to the kids and they seemed a bit astounded that we were out on the farm and as a family watched, and I suppose to some degree agonised with the rest of the world as that was unfolding. It would've been via the little radio.

DONAT SANTOWIAK *(1950) and his Polish parents arrived in Victoria's La Trobe Valley in 1964.*

Alistair Thomson: What was youth culture like in Morwell in the late '60s in your late teens?

Well you had the so-called 'goodies' and the 'baddies'. They came in all shapes and sizes. In the '60s we had the Mods. They were a peer group and they were the kind of aspiring hippies, came with the long hair and the flared pants and all that. Well in Poland there was none of that. There were young people that would dress up, whatever the fashion was at the time—which was ahead of here—but there wasn't kind of, you know, where you'd see a dozen of them standing on a street corner all wearing the same things and stuff like that.

When we came here, very quickly, we had the Mods. Then we had the Sharpies which were like a version of the Skinheads, and they had their own outfits. They had very baggy grey pants—pinstriped—and maroon was the predominant colour. And the two didn't mix. I was sort of struggling for an identity. I ended up growing my hair long and then getting it cut off. You know, this desperation to fit in somewhere (laughs).

But the Sharpies were the ones that were the ones to stay away from because they're the ones that came out of the pub at ten o'clock and came to the local dance and you didn't look at them in the eye because that was the beginning of the end of the night (laughs). There were also little subcultures. There were a lot of, particularly Italian migrants—see, because the Dutch and the Italians are the most prominent not just in the Valley but across Australia—so a lot of Italian guys—probably just a little bit older than I was—they had their own encounters with the broader Aussie community. There were some pretty ugly scenes here. I remember one night there were cars overturned on their rooves in the streets. One bloke was stabbed with a screwdriver, so some of it got a bit tacky.

I certainly identified with the Mods. That carried on then later into my life. Even in my mid-to-late twenties I had hair down to my waist.

YOU KNOW, WITH THE PLATFORM SHOES and the great big long bell-bottom pants. The horrible thing about platform shoes used to be that if you went somewhere where you had to take your shoes off, your pants were about six inches too long. So you had to roll them up at the bottom not to trip over your feet. When you got home and you unrolled your pants you usually found cigarette butts in them. It was like a collection, like a rubbish bin (laughs).

I HAD DESIRES IN MY LATE TEENS to go to Nimbin to join the hippy communes. Bit of a clash between wanting to be a motor mechanic and driving fast cars and hanging out under trees smoking pot (laughs).

I bought my car in my first year at work. I started dating my first I guess real girlfriend. So I spent a lot of time with her and her family. My first car was my mother's choice in the end, because, well it was a combined decision. I wanted a sports car—obviously a two-seater—but it had to be a family taxi. So it ended up being a Holden Torana, and I had that car for eight years, and after the first three years it was so unreliable I almost pitched a tent at the local wrecking yard. I affectionately called it in end, 'Torana la Bomba', because it was the most awful thing ever designed. I modified it. Interestingly I was a bit of a devil of a driver and—by the grace of God—I didn't wipe myself off or anybody else. But I did lose my licence about four weeks before I turned twenty-one for alleged speeding.

There was a few times where I might have turned up home drunk. One night I got the car bogged in the middle of the bush and I just came to—I was in a blackout—came to and I had the car sideways on this bush track not knowing even where I was and how I got there. I somehow managed to get home that night. I remember that I was read the riot act, 'You do this again and you're out of here.'

It's pretty extraordinary you survived really.

Oh gosh, yeah. I rolled the Torana when I was drunk. Yeah, oh God forbid. Then my second car, I crashed that into a road post and it could have been a tree. Went into a blackout and (sighs), oh gosh. It wasn't till the '80s that the .05 and all that came in. And, you know, for all the times that I drank and drove, never got pulled up.

After growing up in the south-west Sydney suburbs, **LYNNE SANDERS-BRAITHWAITE** *(1949) went to teachers' college in inner-city Balmain. Her first teaching posts were in the New South Wales country towns Tumbarumba and Queanbeyan.*

Ah, '68 and '69. They were really crucial years societally as well. I would have been eighteen, nineteen. So it was into the city and the fashions and got myself my first three-piece pinstriped suit pants. Hair cut really short. And the moon of course, we had the moon walk, a lot of things happened in those two years. Woodstock. Plus I've got access to the city and ferries. I *knew* that I wasn't going to be locked into what I thought I was going to be locked into, which was the suburban housewife life. *And* I was lucky because I didn't have parents saying I had to do that either, even though they enjoyed it themselves. I knew that.

Exciting times. It was daring, we were all crazy. Crazy. All of a sudden, you didn't have to have a particular type of hair style. You could have *whatever* you wanted. Just after is even better but that was the beginning of that for me. It was like, oh, I can just get my hair cropped really close. And I can wear, you know, John Lennon glasses, listen to music—I was never a big music person—but listen to music, walk around the city streets. When was the moratorium, '69?[3] We also encountered that at the same time, the Vietnam dispute. I had the old soldiers, *incredibly* anti-Vietnam, *really* anti-Vietnam. My father and his friends would just, 'This is *not* what we'—as they would have put

3 The first nationwide United States Vietnam Moratorium marches were in 1969. The Australian Vietnam Moratorium marches were in 1970 and 1971.

it—'This is *not* what we fought for, to send our boys over there again.' So I had that back-up.

I always had a camera so I was behind the lens all the time, photographing city streets. We'd go down to the pubs in Balmain and talk, so we'd be knocking theories around. Balmain then was still a poor working suburb but it was also a student suburb with all the excitement that that means. So there'd be everyone sitting around discussing the war and causes and feminism and, yeah, it was marvellous.

Jo Kijas: And who was we?

A very small group of us that nearly got expelled. There was this massive percentage that was still just being very nice little teachers and then there was this small group of us, or one did get, my boyfriend got expelled.

I WAS TRANSFERRED to Queanbeyan South Public School in 1971. It was like being back in the suburbs for me so I began to lose hope and I began to drink. Alcoholism and addiction weave a thread right through my adult life. I began to drink at home behind closed doors in a brick flat. All I had was work and come home and drink, really sad sort of drinking really. No one *knew* that I was drinking like that. Ended up in hospital one night and I still have no idea why or how, what happened. But I became, probably almost agoraphobic. I was capable of going to work and home and that was quite a sad year, well sad beginning to the year, but it's also when I fell madly in love ---

But he went to London and I fell to pieces. I went to visit [a friend] Leslie, and by then she was heroin-addicted and living in a commune in Drummoyne. I suppose it took about—from being a young school teacher—it took about a month before I was living with a drug dealer and heroin-addicted. That fast, you know, kaboomf. Hilary [Lynne's boyfriend] stayed in London. That was hard really. Life changed on a dime.

***RICK GALEA** (1958) grew up in south Sydney, where his Maltese parents had a house in Botany and the two teenage sons partied on Saturday night.*

My parents religiously went to Souths Juniors Rugby Leagues club every Saturday night, from when I was five years old till virtually two years ago. I'm talking solid fifty years. Our house was basically a party house. Every Saturday night, when they were away, mum would actually call me on the phone from the foyer of South Juniors and let me know—as dad would walk off to get the car and pick her up from the door—she would let me know, so I'd have about twenty minutes. She didn't mind, as long as I was safe at home. Dad didn't know about it—we kept it a secret.

Some of the parties were just massive. I mean we're talking about seventy people. House full of smoke—and I'm talking not just cigarettes. Everybody drinking. All they had to do was ask the neighbours. He somehow just turned a blind eye to it. We used to buy couple of flagons of wine. And every sixty seconds we'd have a two ounce glass, basically until the last person was ready to fall over. I was hungover like, Sundays were just usually a nightmare. We just thought we were just totally impregnable, just totally --- alcohol was just like nothing. It was just music. Just music and dancing. Oh, we danced our heads off! We used to love Jimi Hendrix. There was a lot of heavy metal—Creedence. My brother was a real music guru, and later become an absolute disco freak, in a nice sort of way. He was seriously used to disco. He had the Afro, tall shoes, the flares, the sports car. He really went disco.

We had the *best* stereogram—a big old Kriesler stereogram. Better than any of my mates. And had massive speakers, pumped out this huge sound. Six stack vinyl—vinyl records in those days were the only form. *God* it was loud. Just shake the place. It was brilliant.

As a young woman in Sydney in the mid-1970s ***KIM BEAR*** *(1959) recalls the culture of smoking.*

Well we all smoked at work. We smoked on public transport and for quite a long time we were still smoking in the movies. I guess because I had an aunt who smoked it didn't seem that unusual to me that women smoked. My mother hated it. I took it up probably about fifteen, sixteen, I took it up very young. It stopped you being hungry (laughs). That sounds ridiculous. And it wasn't, you know, there were ads everywhere for it. I can still remember ads for Virginia Slims, 'You've come a long way, baby', so very, very much targeted at women. Then we went through all the lovely cocktail cigarettes, all nice different colours and very much for women to buy. I certainly wasn't aware of, well I hadn't thought of long term health impact of it. I smoked quite a lot. I used to get up to about a packet a day and more if you went out in the evening.

It was almost like Pavlov's dog for me. If I heard the telephone ring or I had to make a phone call—and I guess because I smoked at my desk too and I was taking calls all day—if I had to make a call I had my own little ceremony about making sure my ashtray was ready, my cigarettes and my lighter, and I'd light the cigarette and dial the number and I could sit there smoking happily while I had my conversation. And I got to the point where if the phone rang, the first thing I do would be think about where are my cigarettes. It was *exactly* like Pavlov's dog.

I did try a few times to give up and finally managed to do it when I was about nineteen just because it was starting not to make me feel very well and I'd cough in the mornings, and it was getting expensive. It was really starting to get expensive and that's a *long* time ago.

MICHELLE CRIPPS *(1960) was a music-loving teenager in Burnie on the north-west coast of Tasmania in the 1970s.*

> I did most of my homework listening to music on the radio. I guess that filtered out every other sound, so I would often study with the radio on. Having my teenage years through the '70s and '80s was a time when lyrics were very strong, so the lyrics of Elton John, Billy Joel, in Australia Johnny Farnham, Russell Morris, people like that were really important to me and I grew up with their songs and their lyrics and so I've always loved the words to the songs as well as the music.

In Canberra in the late 1970s ***RHONDA KING*** *(1965) was an Abba fan.*

> I think Abba had a huge influence on me (laughs). Abba was enormous. Abba *were* better than the Beatles as far as I was concerned but now that I'm an adult, I can see that they both were as awesome but different. But at the time you couldn't beat Abba as far as I was concerned. I knew all the words, had all their albums, dressed like them, identified with—can't even remember her name now—Frida, the dark-haired girl, she was the one that I wanted to be like. I guess popular music, peers, that kind of thing, in my teenage years were more of an influence, yeah, than anything. Yes, that's right (laughs).

CHRISTIAN BOW *(1978) was a teenager in and around the north Queensland coastal town of Mackay in the 1990s.*

> We were certainly getting into The Doors when we were started experimentation with marijuana. In Mackay there was a lot of pot was getting grown at the time and it was just cheap and most of the time free. And so I first started smoking when I was fourteen and --- smoked for longer than I didn't in my lifetime.

At the time also in Mackay, acid was pretty available, pretty prevalent. So we put in a bit of acid. LSD. I loved it. I enjoyed it much better than things like speed or ecstasy or cocaine or anything like that. It appealed to my artistic side, into my open-mindedness and yeah, you just want to give the world a big fat hug, you know? (laughs) I really enjoyed it. It was good but it was pretty full on you know, lasts a long time. We would go away to Airlie Beach for the weekend or something like that and a group of us have a good time. I'm not quite sure but I think the bikies moving into town changed what was available and so it started becoming harder to come by and then speed was very available. The first time I ever had speed I injected it. I took it for years, I had it for years without having it any other way except through intravenous injections. It became very commonplace. You know, on the weekend, go uptown, shoot up. At the time for me it was just what we were doing, it was what was happening, it was okay. Looking back, it was pretty full on.

Upon completing his Year 10 Certificate ***JAY LOGAN*** *(1981) joined the Australian army. After a tour of duty in East Timor, Jay left the army and was working as a security guard in Canberra when he was arrested for providing back-up for an ex-army mate who was owed some money.*

Even though I may not have broken into the place, I still got charged with the same, as if I had. Because I was there. Not inside perhaps, but I was there as a part of it, so you get charged with the same charges. I got charged with possession of a firearm in a public place, possession of an illegal firearm, break and enter with intent to commit, intent to gain money by intimidation, possession of a knife, possession of a baton.

Matthew Higgins: Now the case eventually took three years to go through the system?

Oh it took a long time. It took a long time. Now Bernard [Jay's lawyer] thought that was fantastic because the longer you leave it, the more it shows you're capable of—while you're out on bail—the more you're capable of being a member of the community. You're not doing anything wrong, you're abiding by your bail conditions—which I did to a t.

You have to go and see the police every week is it or ---

Yes. It started off being every day. And then Bernard arranged for a hearing when it got dropped off to every week. And that's how it remained. Every week I'd go and sign in. It was a funny experience signing in to Civic Police Station on Anzac Day in a suit with gongs. And I'd go in there, and they said, 'What are you, what did you do?' I said, 'Oh I don't really want to talk about it' (laughs).

It was --- wearying beyond all belief. I was working three jobs, trying to keep up with the payments. Bernard did a discount for us. I think he knew we didn't have a huge amount of money but I sold everything I owned. I sold my car. I bought a cheap old bomb. Well, if I wanted Bernard, I had to pay for him. If you paid Legal Aid you get whatever lawyer Legal Aid gives you, you know, some of them don't have a lot of experience, they have maybe a lot of petty experience.

So I got a two-year non-custodial sentence. It was a suspended sentence. So if you screw up in your life and in any sense, like say I got, done DUI [Driving Under the Influence] or something like that, straight to prison. But during that two-year period, you're on a good behaviour bond, you're out. You're free to do what you want as long as you don't break any laws and you live the life of a exemplary citizen, which is what I did and I endeavoured to do.

So what's your overall impression of the legal system as a result of this experience?

For me it worked. I think I got *very* lucky. I think I could have been put in gaol—if I had a different lawyer. And I think I might be a *very* different person if I had. I'm hugely grateful. Grateful to them for giving me the chance to resurrect myself as the person I am now, rather than that person I was, who got out of the army, who was hot-headed, who was constantly drinking and fighting and doing all the things that, you know, who'd work at a nightclub and then detested people for coming in pissed and behaving like an idiot and then, when he had an off night would go out and behave like that person that he detested. Go out and cause trouble.

***JAMES FINNEGAN** (1981) explains how his tattoos illustrate significant people and issues in his life.*

I've always been a bit of an artist. I remember during school I used to draw tattoos on myself. Like big wizards or a kind of drawing like that. And I always knew I'd get tattoos. I actually waited until I was twenty-one just to be sure, and ended up getting a little tattoo on my shoulder. Since then I've gotten more and --- but they all mean something to me. So on my arm I've got a large number of stars—big ones and little ones—and a few of them are coloured in with the colours of the pride flag. But also the big stars represent my parents and my brothers and sisters and the little stars are all their kids. That's something that means a *lot* to me. But I also like the way it looks.

Roslyn Burge: Just for someone listening to this in a hundred years' time, James, what are the pride colours on your stars?

So the pride colours, I guess the gay community has a pride flag so they're the colours of the rainbow. I think it actually started out a protest and now it's just something that I think the whole gay community identifies with, to be proud, and to be proud of who we are.

Further Listening on Pleasure and Risk: Youth Culture

Leo Cripps, 1923, http://www.nla.gov.au/amad/nla.oh-vn6290880/1-144
John Murphy, 1940, http://www.nla.gov.au/amad/nla.oh-vn6504268/2-1441
Greer Bland, 1944, http://www.nla.gov.au/amad/nla.oh-vn5972533/1-3524~1-3598
Alison Fettell, 1952, http://nla.gov.au/nla.obj-220185705/listen/1-739
Ouranita Karadimas, 1958, http://www.nla.gov.au/amad/nla.oh-vn6252080/2-416
David Cooper, 1959, http://www.nla.gov.au/amad/nla.oh-vn6290926/0-4603
Phil May, 1962, http://www.nla.gov.au/amad/nla.oh-vn6569680/0-3413
Lisa Jackson, 1972, http://www.nla.gov.au/amad/nla.oh-vn6252067/0-811
Jason Johnson, 1981: http://nla.gov.au/nla.obj-220115636/listen/0-4122
Adam Farrow-Palmer, 1988, http://nla.gov.au/nla.obj-219982656/listen/1-801
Arthur Hunter, 1989, http://nla.gov.au/nla.obj-219957349/listen/0-5812

First Loves

*For **RUTH APPS** (1926), coming of age in Sydney in the early 1940s, boyfriends were supposed to be introduced and marriage was an expectation.*

We did a lot of sewing and that type of thing, what we called fancy work which was embroidery. Once I went to school—I was in an academic school—there was very little time for hobbies as such. There was a *lot* of study to do. We had an enormous number of assignments to do. After I left school I went back to this fancy work to get my glory box ready for the boy that I was ultimately going to marry.

You started off at a *very* early age and you started off with just a box—a wooden box—and into it you gathered tea-towels or cups and saucers, anything to do with your house. Later on then you got—generally for your twenty-first birthday—you were given a camphor wood box, which was your glory box, and into that went all the sheets and towels and dinner sets, that embroidery that we had slaved over. I've still got embroidered table cloths which my grandchildren think is *hilarious*. But all those things were saved up, waiting for that boy to come along. It's quite a different attitude now but then you had your eye pinned on that white knight in shining armour and you had to have all that household goods ready for his pleasure (laughs).

I WAS WORKING IN THE CITY in Clarence Street in an office. On this particular afternoon I had to stay back. The cables had come in from overseas and one of my jobs was to decode the cables. I had done that and it was about a quarter to six. I lived at Hurstville so I used to get the train from Wynyard to Central and change trains. So I got on at Wynyard, got off at Central and I knew there'd be a train to Hurstville waiting and I had to climb up the stairs, and I was *racing* up the stairs and the train was in. I jumped on the train and the guard pushed the bell. In those days the guard was accessible to the passengers. Oh, this handsome man of my dreams came in—he was the guard—and I said, 'Oh, thank you for holding the train, guard.' And he said, 'Oh, I couldn't have let those fairy footsteps miss the train.' He said, 'May I sit down?' I said, 'Yes by all means.' We chatted on and off all the way to Hurstville. I got home and said to my mother, 'Oh, I met this gorgeous guy.' She said, 'Were you introduced to him?' I said, 'Well, no, I don't even know his name.' So she thereupon delivered a lecture about nice girls don't go out with boys who are not introduced.

The next day I didn't have to work back but I waited so that I could catch that same train. I had to walk very slowly and I did that for the rest of the week. By the end of the week I knew his name and all about him. He said 'I'll give you a ring.' We exchanged phone numbers which was very naughty. He rang me and that was it. We went out together for two and a half years before we were married, but there was never another boy in my life after that.

In 1951, ***FRED HENSKENS*** *(1929) was a young man working on building sites in Canberra.*

I had a girlfriend named Joy, and I loved her very much and we went everywhere. Anyway, I got her pregnant. She was very religious Catholic. She went to confess and the priest told her that I was bad and then he told her to go to Melbourne. They adopted the child out to a Catholic family because they needed children for Catholic families and that's what happened.

I had no say in it at all, I had no say in at all, and them days you couldn't say anything. I didn't know what to do but anyway she left. She went there and I used to write letters to her and back. Then she never came back to Canberra. I don't know what happened to her. She came back, oh, three years after that, when I met Helen, the lady I got married to. That was the end of relationship and I don't know what happened to the child.

I often think about it but it's best to leave sleeping dogs sleep, you know what I mean.

After farming in the Victorian Mallee, ***BRIAN CARTER*** *(1931) got 'the flying bug' and worked as a commercial pilot around Australia before he settled at Derby in the Kimberley where he met and married Violet, a Bardi Aboriginal woman, in 1960.*

I fell in love with a Bardi girl who'd been born on Sunday Island. There were three of them, three young ladies were working for the mission. They'd take it in turns doing washing one week—for all the kids—and cooking, ironing. There was actually three, three flowers actually. There was a Daphne, there was a Rosemary and there was a Violet (laughs). Fell in love eventually with the Violet. Her parents were living still on Sunday Island. We knew each other for a fair while before we got together. Over a year.

It was pretty strange—I think—in those days. Not like today. It took a fair bit of arranging 'cause being Aboriginal she was under Native Welfare and I had to go through a lot of rigmarole to get permission to marry her. I just had to answer a lot of questions. They didn't have rights in those days. That came later. Quite a bit later, I think. It was frowned upon more by station people—I think—than ordinary people, than general people. We had no problem.

I remember buying a pram in Perth when Andrew was a baby, when we moved over there, and living in half a house. We wanted to buy a pram, no a cot, and I remember the lady in the shop complimenting me on something or other, 'Oh, you're a brave man. Oh, so brave', for marrying Violet (laughs). So, I don't know whether that was an attitude, different attitude anyway. I asked my mother before I was married—dad was dead—and I said, 'How would you see me if I married a Aboriginal girl?' Only thing she asked was, 'Is she a Christian?' And I was fortunate to be able to say yes. That's all she worried about.

After finishing school on the Mornington Peninsula in the late 1940s, ***DONALD GREY-SMITH*** *(1931) moved to Melbourne and got a clerical job with the Union Steamship Company. He lived in a YMCA hostel in Northcote and joined the Northcote Dramatic Society, where he met a 'whole new set of people' and had his first sexual experience with a man.*

When I first told my parents, they were very distressed and felt that in some way it was their fault, that they'd done something wrong. Perhaps their troubled relationship had been the cause of all this and that it was something which I would probably grow out of or be cured of. So they sent me to a psychiatrist.

Peter Donovan: So how old were you at this stage when you came out?

Oh, probably seventeen or eighteen. I was in Melbourne. It was only after I went to Melbourne that I had my first sexual experience and it was around about that time that I told them and they sent me to a psychiatrist. Which I regard as a waste of money because all he did really was tell me that I would grow out of it and he didn't believe that I was truly homosexual. So nothing much came of that. But that was the level of their concern.

In the early-1950s ***TRISH BARRKMAN*** *(1933) had a job which took her around Victoria and New South Wales to train staff for the retail business G.J. Coles.*

I went to work in Deniliquin and I met this young man, Des, who taught me to play golf. And that became a romance, a very serious romance. But he was Catholic and I was Protestant. But anyway, you're in love and, you know, there's nothing that can't be solved, is there? So we were planning on getting engaged (laughs). And I shouldn't laugh. His mother was a descendant of Ned Kelly, so they were very Irish. And everyone was keen for me to go and talk with the priest.

So we went to the priest in Deniliquin and had this very interesting conversation about me changing my religion and becoming a Catholic. I can't recall lots of the conversation but—and I don't know who said this, I think it might have been the priest or might have been a thought that popped into my own head—but somewhere along the line, there was something about, 'if you can't change your religion, put the ocean between you'. Now, I don't know where this came from. But it gave me food for thought and I finally decided that I was brought into this world a Protestant and I was going to go out of this world a Protestant. So there was nothing, you know, I made that decision, that I would not change my religion. I decided that I'd put the ocean between us and that's what I did. I got on a boat, on the *Wanganella*, and I went to New Zealand with my friend Lesley.

***GINETTE MATALON** (1936) and her mother fled from Cairo to Paris, and then to Sydney in 1958, escaping the persecution of Jews by Egyptian nationalists. In Sydney they moved into two rooms in a terrace house in Glebe shared with Ginette's uncle and his wife, Aunt Becky.*

Wednesday we arrived here. The next Monday I had a job. On Saturday firstly, the young men started coming. My aunty did such marketing work about me to the whole Jewish community with available young men. She said, 'My niece is coming from Paris, she's the most beautiful girl in the world. She can dance, she can sing, she can do this, she can do that.' And on Saturday afternoon they all came. Who came with chocolate, who came with records, who came --- they all came. I thought this was the nicest part of Australia was all these. One came with a motorbike, one had a car and they all started inviting me out. So that was a good start socially—I had my fellows lined up.

MY HUSBAND HAPPENED TO BE BECKY'S COUSIN—first cousin—as well, and he came and I said he bought chocolates, words of songs—in French the song at the time was called *Bambino*—he bought me the words to *Bambino* and took me out on his Vespa. One night we went to Chequers to dance on the Vespa—I had this beautiful night, evening dress—and we went on the Vespa.

So, twenty-six days after I arrived, we went on a ferry cruise for Australia Day with the All Nations Club. The boats stopped a little distance from Parsley Beach and the people started swimming from the boat to a rock. When we reached the rock, Ralph said to me, 'I have to apologise to you. I'm really, really sorry, I can't marry you straight away, I have a few commitments.' To which I replied—I was really surprised—I said, 'But I have no intention of getting married now.' I mean, I had just come here. And this was the twenty-sixth of January 1958.

He proposed to me on a rock at Parsley Beach. That was his first proposal.

His second proposal was the next year. The year was early 1959 and my mother had been diagnosed with breast cancer. Obviously she wanted me to get married—very badly. *Very*, very badly, and very quickly and this fellow was not proposing officially as yet. So one afternoon, I went to visit my mother in hospital, with Ralph, and she said, 'You know, my friend, Florette McDowall just came to visit me in hospital and she has two brothers coming from overseas'—that's my mother saying in front of Ralph, you know—'and they're very, very keen—the whole family's very keen—that you should meet them.' And Ralph said, 'But Ginette and I, we came here today to tell you that we are getting married.' So that was proposal number two. It was a bit forcing his hand. We got engaged and that September we got married.

***VERONICA SCHWARZ** (1939) recalls her mother's unusually frank sex talk, and then her early sexual experiences when she was a primary school teacher in Brisbane in the early 1960s.*

My mother sat me down at the age of twelve or something, or younger—eleven—told me all about menstruation and sexual intercourse and having babies. And I thought, 'All right, well we've done that now.' I had no further interest. Well, I didn't. I didn't *need* to go off and explore it. But I have not come across anyone else in my age bracket whose mother told them anything.

I MET THIS GUY ONE WEEKEND at the Gold Coast. He wanted to see me again and we spent time together. Then I told him I was going to go overseas and he—as I found out later—he was quite a ladies' man and --- womaniser is probably more the term. I think it offended his sense of his attractiveness for me to say I was going to leave him and go overseas. He asked me to marry him and I said yes --- Stupid (sighs). I didn't expect it at all—no. Took me totally by surprise. Anyway, I said yes and I cancelled my trip—so I was twenty-three at the time.

Once I'd said yes and cancelled my trip, he just cooled down pretty much immediately. I felt that was strange and odd, and I just felt that he was withdrawing from me. So in the end I just separated from him. It was only *after* that that I found he had actually *three* of us on the go at the same time! (laughs) One of whom ended up in an asylum with a nervous breakdown and the other one got pregnant so I think I got out of it quite lightly.

Katie Holmes: So did you have a sense of being in love with him?

Yes, I was very, very attracted to him, and he was gentle, and he could say all the right things and put on such a good front. It was really weird. The first time we had sex he was so drunk he didn't know what he was doing. He didn't realise I was a virgin --- and I wasn't too sure what he'd done, 'cause when he stopped I said, 'Am I still a virgin?' (laughs) God help us! Anyway, no, it wasn't very satisfactory!

Did it get better?

No! (laughs) No. He did drink a lot which is not all that good for a man's potency.

I'd had several boyfriends before this and some of them had *wanted* to have sex. I suppose I thought it was what you did when you got married. Although my mother had never said that, but by God, there was a lot of stuff in the women's magazines telling you how you ought to behave and how you ought to make a man feel good, and how you were to downplay your intelligence, and blah, blah, blah. It was all around you that you were expected to get married, and probably not work.

So I fell into this relationship with this guy pretty much because I'd said no to a couple of other guys and I thought, 'Well God, I can't keep saying no all my life, can I?' I think there was a large element of that in it—more than love, as you asked me before, did I love him? You might notice I answered, 'I was *attracted* to him', and that certainly isn't love. I've experienced love since then and that certainly wasn't it. M'mm.

That was another thing that used to surprise me, the way boys and men would want to leap on me—they'd never say, 'Is this a good time of month?' or anything. Just want to leap on me, and in those days *Australian* men did not take responsibility for *condoms* or contraception. It wasn't until I got to Europe that I found that men actually used condoms. It wasn't something Australian men thought about.

***GREER BLAND** (1944) left school at sixteen to work first as a bank clerk in Melbourne and then, from 1963 to 1969, as an accounts auditor with the Royal Australian Air Force. In 1970 she returned to Gippsland in Victoria to work on the family dairy farm.*

I remember about the age of twenty-four, twenty-five I've been nearly driven out of my mind with relatives and friends saying, 'Well aren't you married yet?' They'd want to know the ins and outs of everything and I had nothing to say. I didn't find it unusual. I never thought about it, to be quite honest but of course it was *amazing* how the attitudes of people would get to you at times.

Till the point where you sometimes when you're down in the ebb, at your lowest, sometimes you think, oh, is there something wrong with you, you know, and you'd start to doubt yourself even. But I'd soon get out of that. I'd come out of that and think, well I wouldn't be any good at it anyway. So you just reply to yourself like that. But I do remember the pressure didn't let off until I was perhaps in my mid-thirties and it was, I'm nearly over the hill and it was too late, and they give up. But I do remember a great deal of pressure.

During my air force days, I think I was in the eligible period. I was that keen to get on and strive for a career, and you weren't allowed to be married. If you got married in the air force you got out. So in those days you weren't allowed to be married. You are now.

***GERALDINE BOX** (1949) left the family farm on the New South Wales Riverina to train as a nurse because it offered travel and excitement. After completing her training she spent a year working as nanny in England and travelled overland back to Australia through Iran and Afghanistan. In 1974 she was working as a nurse in Darwin and, at the age of twenty-five, realised that she was a lesbian.*

I didn't want to have boyfriends and thing, and yet I did it because that's what you *did*. But it was never right, they were always just good mates, they were always chaps that you just wanted to go out and have fun with. If they went climbing or something I'd be there because I thought that was great fun, but I didn't really want to be there as their girlfriend.

I didn't really have a concept, and in that era—the '60s growing up—even though I had all literature at home, there was nothing *really* out, there was nothing *overt* written, or even television didn't arrive until much later anyway in the late '60s, or for us the late '60s, early '70s, at home. There *weren't* programs about being *gay*, or 'gay' wasn't even a word very much here in Australia. I didn't think I knew anybody. I had no concept for it. I had no role models or concept of what was going on, until I *met* somebody and that was, ah, right. So the light went on but, you know, we thought we're the only people in the world anyway. We absolutely had to be the only people like this in the world and so it had to be a secret. So it was a secret for some time, especially living in nurses' quarters you've to be really quite careful.

However subsequently learnt from people who lived around us, they all knew, it was all fine but nobody said anything. We thought they didn't know and they knew, so there's a strangeness about that.

***ALISON FETTELL** (1952) married in September 1970 and had her first child the following April.*

Roslyn Burge: Your husband—did he propose?

He proposed that maybe we should get married seeing as I was pregnant (laughs).

So I was about seventeen when I fell pregnant. Marriage did *not* figure in the picture at all. I suppose at the time I felt that I loved Brian. We were going out for two years. We didn't have sex the whole time. We'd only *really* probably just started having a sexual relationship when I was around seventeen. I obviously thought that probably was fair enough. I had a lot of pressure, there was a lot of pressure from him to actually have a sexual relationship. Because he was a good deal older. He was five years older than I was. When we got married I was seventeen, he was twenty-three. So although that's young for a man, it's still a lot older than seventeen.

So, the relationship was, you know, the normal sexual relationship without full-blown sexual intercourse for quite some time. But then, I don't think we had been actually having sex for very long when I fell pregnant. Because I didn't know what the heck was going on. I trusted him to know.

*As a teenager on the Gold Coast in the early 1970s, **KIM BEAR** (1959) recalls a changing yet contested openness about sex and sex education.*

I remember reading *Female Eunuch* and being *absolutely* blown away by that, and *Cleo* was life changing, *absolutely* life changing. The hilarious thing was the Queensland editions had lots of things blacked out or had little black boxes printed over them and sealed sections taken away and there's all this weird censorship that went on for the Queensland *Cleo*. I'm still thinking back to 1972, I don't know how long it actually continued there because all the smart people just knew you went to Tweed Heads and got a New South Wales copy (laughs).

Nicole Curby:* DID THEY TEACH YOU *about contraception and all?

I think there was some discussion about condoms in the film [shown at school] and that would kind of make it boys' responsibility, which I remember thinking was a bit dodgy (laughs) since there was no penalty for them if it didn't work. I think probably just about everything else I learned to do with sex or contraception or *anything* came out of *Cleo*. That was kind of the Bible really, because not only would they talk about it but there'd be pictures, and discussions, and it wasn't always about, you know, the *wrongness* of it. It was that it's just natural and, I've always felt much more comfortable about my own body after reading *Cleo*. And, you know, that these things were normal and not everybody did everything in the same way and it didn't matter. I thought *Cleo* was just absolutely fantastic from that point of view.

Although I do remember my radical feminist [teacher] showing us how to put a condom on a carrot. I had no clue when that was going to be helpful for me, but (laughs) it was a very interesting conversation. Yes, I remember everyone was terribly embarrassed, but she just ploughed on regardless and by the end of it everyone was laughing and then it seemed to be okay.

Mind you, some girls didn't pay attention and did get pregnant, so --- (laughs)

***RHONDA KING** (1965) recalls an unplanned pregnancy in about 1980 when she was fifteen, not long after her father died.*

This guy that I'd asked to come and hop in with me, nothing happened. Later on—on another occasion—things did happen. So then when I was pregnant I wasn't sure if it was him was the father or my ex-boyfriend because I didn't take any notice of when I had my period or what dates it happened. It was just like, 'Oh, here we go again.' I never was a hundred per cent sure which was the father. I told my mum and her advice was to have an abortion. I didn't know what to do because I was fifteen and I was like, ah, what do you do with this? I don't know what to do. At that point in time I hadn't come to the, 'I want to be a mum' (laughs). I was just like, 'Oh my gosh, I'm going to be a mother.'

So yeah, fifteen. Pregnant. Not sure who the father is. Dad's not around anymore. Mum's freaking out. And we'd come not long out of—I've just been reading a lot of information about the forced adoptions thing that went on up until the late '70s, early '80s even I think—so I think we were coming out of that period and my mum was from that generation and she's seen me unmarried, fifteen years old, pregnant, thinking, 'This is what you need to do.' Not a forced adoption in this case, an abortion. So I had an abortion and it was really horrible. It was, I never --- sorry. I never don't regret doing it. I always think --- excuse me.

Mary Hutchison: We'll have a pause. Just wait for a second. Or do you want me to turn it off?

No it's fine. I just, whenever I reflect on that, I think that was probably the only choice I've ever made in my life that I regret. That if I could go back and turn it around, I would. But especially because you see so many young girls having children at that age these days and they're fine. They cope. There's no big deal. They come to terms with it. But I guess in the environment and the situation I was in at the time, we didn't, *I* didn't know what to do. I had *no* idea. What, what do I do? And so you turn to your mum to ask for the advice and it was her advice that I took and she came with me to Sydney to have it done.

I think my mum did most of the enquiries about it. I think. I feel like I kind of erased bits of it so I didn't have to remember, but I remember it was in Challis Avenue in Potts Point. That's near Darlinghurst and Surry Hills. We stayed in this tiny little—went up on the train—stayed in this horrible little smelly hostel, because mum was on a single parent pension because my father had died and we'd just kind of lost everything so we had no financial anything. I walked to the clinic and I went in and I sat there with this group of people. I was by myself. There was a woman there who was there for her fifth or sixth abortion and was raving on about it, like, and I was just like, 'Okay'. And then there was another young couple there. She didn't look like she was much older than me or maybe the same age.

Then they took me to a room where they asked, you know, explained to me what I was about to do and did I know what I was going to do, and they were showing me diagrams and pictures. I think if they had've showed me something more graphic I might've changed my mind but it was just, it was like being at school and them saying, 'And your ovaries are here and your cervix is there', and I'm sort of like, 'Okay.' Didn't really get a concept or idea of, you know, I guess it was meant to be pre-counselling but it didn't seem to really help very much (sniff).

Then the next thing I was getting changed and I was on a hospital bed and they just said, 'Lie down' and I was out. Then I woke up and they sent me home. I walked back to the hotel on my own. Just feeling crap (laughs). 'Cause I just came out of an anaesthetic. It was really traumatic and really horrible, but I just kept going with life. I mean I didn't sit there thinking, 'Oh my gosh. What have I done?' The 'what had I done' didn't really hit me until I had my own children. That's when I was like, 'Oh. This is what I did, and that's really bad.'

DAVID COOPER *(1959) was engaged to be married in the early 1980s.*

I remember thinking that I was lucky, like her parents let us go away to Perth for a weekend. My wife's *girlfriends'* parents were absolutely disgusted. So there was still that bit of, you know, let's just pretend this doesn't happen. But I was lucky with her parents. And my parents, it was never discussed with my parents, but her parents were happy. They weren't worried about that. They were a bit more open thinking, but at that time there were still parents who would have not liked that, wouldn't let you go away for a weekend somewhere and stay in a hotel with your girlfriend or something like that. My wife and I's attitude towards that was, how stupid's that because people are doing it in a car park down the beach. It's more unsafe if you know what I mean. So it's all a bit silly really.

Then I look back when I trace my family tree and you find out that your own mother was pregnant when she got married, and that my grandmother and her and her sisters left Tasmania to come to Melbourne so that you wouldn't disgrace the family's name because you were pregnant. I even found out that my grandmother's sister got pregnant to her sister's fiancée. So all this stuff, it's always gone on. You're never going to stop it. It's just all a bit silly really.

CHRISTIAN BOW *(1978) recalls a long distance relationship in Queensland in the mid-1990s.*

We each have a ring-binder that's quite full of the letters. We haven't really gone back through it because there's a lot of dark teenage stuff there. A lot of the time it's just ramblings of what was in our heads at the time. But they were really important to us, to getting through that long distance relationship. We kind of just did the old suck it and see approach with it because you know, we got together just after school finished and then that—the Seventeenth Summer we refer to it—was pretty special for us. It was movie-like. Summer nights in Mackay can be pretty magical. You get on the beach and you get away from this, the lights, and the stars really come out and the sound of the ocean and nice breezes. You really do get carried away to another place. We knew that Ellen was going off to uni and we just put it in the back of our minds.

Then she went away in late January and we said, 'Oh look, let's just see how it goes.' It was a little bit of an open relationship. We knew that we were young and restless and there was a lot happening. It made it a bit easier. We weren't having to lie to each other or we weren't having to be celibate eighteen-year-olds for long periods of time. But at the same time we weren't going out there and chasing other people and that. Well, a couple of things happened but nothing serious.

At the time long distance telephone calls between Mackay and Brisbane were quite expensive—this is '96, start of '96 she moved away—and a long distance phone call for the period of time that we wanted to talk to each other each night was literally prohibitive. So letters was our main communication. We would have averaged two to three letters a week. Sometimes more than that. And it wasn't just letters. It was drawings and poetry and scribbles and tea stains and it was, it was just ---

Hamish Sewell: Testaments to the time.

Yes. I certainly got the feeling that whatever I could put down on the paper, or whatever ended up on the paper, was reflective of what was happening to me at the time. It was something that Ellen could read into and take something from. A letter on a typewriter is pretty sterile whereas your own handwriting—with scribbles in the margins and changing sentences and a picture here and there and going away and coming back to it—it gives a lot of context around where you are and what you're doing. Even just what's on the back of the page. It was just bit of paper that was not used anymore, so on the back of it you write your letter but on the other side it was, you know, a phone bill or something.

We do cherish those two folders. They're symbols. They're symbols of our commitment to each other over a difficult period. And then we finally get together to live together and make a go of it, it was so worth it, so worth it.

***JAMES FINNEGAN** (1981) describes how he began to get involved with the Sydney gay community in the late 1990s.*

I guess at the time I was *very* confused. So I was with my girlfriend [Amy]. I loved her. I was seeing a guy—his name was Christian—and I felt like I was falling in love with him too. So I was very, very confused. My relationship with my girlfriend, she really, very much loved me as well and she wanted to kind of, I guess, make it okay. In the end there ended up being three of us in the relationship. I guess it all came to a head and it became too much. I was jealous of them and I wanted both of them. I didn't want one or the other. And I guess, yeah, that's where it all happened and I tried to kill myself and just after that I ended up turning to drugs. Because after I tried to kill myself Christian kind of disappeared. I haven't seen him since.

From that point when I *identified* as gay with myself, and me and my girlfriend were kind of getting together but not together, and we started going to a youth centre in Campbelltown—which I'm not sure is there anymore but it was called Trackside—they had a gay men's support group. So I started going to that and meeting other gay guys, and that's really when I started going out clubbing in the gay community. But I guess the danger of the gay community is there is a lot of drugs and I found a liking for them. So I actually spent nearly a year taking a lot of drugs. I very much became addicted to speed. Even to the point where I started injecting it.

There was so much *turmoil* at that time. Eventually, my mum helped me get off it. I spent the next couple of years really in deep depression. I cut off all my ties so I actually didn't speak to Amy again for a number of years. I couldn't be around any of those people anymore. In that time of depression I definitely thought about killing myself a lot. I felt like I'd thrown my life away, and then I would have blame, so I'd blame society or blame the people that bullied me. Eventually I took control of my life and made myself a stronger person and went out and got a job and found a boyfriend and we lived together for a long time. I guess I started becoming me (laughs). All that time I wasn't me.

***Rachel Brown** (1985) recalls the challenge of combining her aspirations as a young woman in Brisbane in the 2000s with the expectations of a relationship.*

We grew up together. We knew of each other but we didn't hang out just because he was a few years older than me. And when I was eighteen—just before I got into university—we started having a relationship together. It was at the start of the summer holidays. He was living in Rockhampton at the time, going to university up there, studying engineering. Then by the end of the summer holidays I found out I got into university down in Brisbane and so around the end of February I moved down here. I remember he drove down with me when I was moving my stuff, to help.

I was eighteen and I think he was twenty-one and he said in the car on the way down, 'I think I'll move in with you.' And I said, 'Oh --- okay.' And I was—just because I always thought, like I really liked him and sort of my first relationship—but I just wasn't sure and I guess always had in my mind like, 'Okay, well, we can live together but, you know, something is going to happen in the future I know and we'll break up.'

So we moved into this one bedroom studio apartment in Newmarket and he left uni in Rockhampton and ended up getting a job down here. And we just stayed together for five years. Nothing ever happened, it turned out. We got along really well. I mean he was just, he was great and I just think the problem was that we wanted different things in the end. I guess I felt like I had compromised a lot of myself and I lost myself in that relationship.

When I finished university that was really the time for me to take stock and, 'What do I want to do next?' So I decided that I just couldn't be in this relationship because I couldn't see myself being happy and living the life that I wanted to, so I had to leave. That was really difficult actually 'cause I was twenty-three and he never did anything wrong. Like, there was no reason on the outside and my family really liked him, my mum really liked him. She really liked me being with him. He was this great influence because he was an engineer and he was hard-working and he was always so caring towards me. But I just knew that this isn't what I want and I wanted to *travel* and I wanted to have *adventures* and I wanted to live like I was twenty-three not like I was thirty.

I remember, I received a text message from him one night and it happened to be our five-year anniversary. This is going to sound horrible but I remember he said, 'I just wanted to say, it's our five-year anniversary and the last five years have been the best and I hope the next five years are going to be even better.' I just thought, 'If the next five years are anything like the past five years I will regret it.' I knew that I had to get out of the relationship because he was already talking about buying a house and living in the suburbs and that *wasn't* what I wanted at all. So I made up my mind that day.

After the relationship I just became much more confident in myself, much more confident in my ability to make decisions for myself. I really began the process of like asking the question: 'What do I really want to do with my life?' And yeah, so that's when I went to Korea actually.

***ARTHUR HUNTER** (1989) describes dating culture amongst young Aboriginal men and women in the Kimberley in the 2000s.*

Broome had this this competition called Kimberley Girl in 2006. Oh, me and my mate and my teacher, we built this black border for the staging, to help the Goolarri mob set up. And there was one girl that was in the competition. Her name was Anjay Phillips. She was checking me out, from what she telling me. Then on the finals night she got someone to come up and ask me, you know, if you want to go out or hook up or something. I was a good boy. The girl came up to me and said like, 'Oh

> this girl want to know.' I'm thinking, 'Fuck.' I was thinking, 'Gee.' Then I asked this other dude here—my cousin—but I was shocked that the girl wanted to go out with me or something, like go out with me. I was speechless. I was shaking ---

Elaine Rabbitt: Can you explain that that's a bit of Broome style or Kimberley style—about how Anjay didn't come up to you direct.

> Up here in the Kimberleys we don't—well some people do but most people don't—they get someone to, they get a friend or a cousin to ask a girl or a guy out. So they don't go directly to that person and ask them because they're scared to get shut down or get rejected and people don't like that—getting rejected. So she did that to me and she got someone else to do it for her. And I said, 'Yeah okay, might as well.' I was really shy, and a little good boy.

Further Listening on First Loves

Ronnie Gauci, 1947, http://www.nla.gov.au/amad/nla.oh-vn6290910/1-769
Les Robinson, 1947, http://www.nla.gov.au/amad/nla.oh-vn6504265/1-1799
Lynne Sanders-Braithwaite, 1949, http://www.nla.gov.au/amad/nla.oh-vn6290876/1-715~1-765
Donat Santowiak, 1950, http://nla.gov.au/nla.obj-220175608/listen/1-2998
Ouranita Karadimas, 1958, http://www.nla.gov.au/amad/nla.oh-vn6252080/1-3714~1-3783
Rick Galea, 1958, http://www.nla.gov.au/amad/nla.oh-vn6535733/2-3299
Michelle Cripps, 1960, http://www.nla.gov.au/amad/nla.oh-vn6252075/0-5398
Phil May, 1962, http://www.nla.gov.au/amad/nla.oh-vn6569680/2-56
Barbara Krickl, 1962, http://www.nla.gov.au/amad/nla.oh-vn6252047/3-2762
Lisa Jackson, 1972, http://www.nla.gov.au/amad/nla.oh-vn6252067/2-4687
Suzie Quartermain, 1975, http://nla.gov.au/nla.obj-220022403/listen/0-4629
Gemma Nourse, 1989, http://nla.gov.au/nla.obj-220049717/listen/2-1709

From School to Work

***RUTH APPS** (1926) wanted to join the army during World War II but was just too young. She studied to work as a secretary and then discovered some of the challenges faced by women in the workforce in the 1940s.*

Once I left the Secretarial College—I'd come out with eight As in my diploma and a very bright little budding secretary—and my first job was at a very small office called Ealing Studios—they were film studios—and I went there straight from college. That was an unfortunate place. There was only one other girl there. I could do the work, that was no problem at all, but the manager, who was the New South Wales manager for the Ealing Studios—which was a British studio—turned out to be far from nice. Look I'm nineteen, not very worldly wise, stayed back one night and we were doing some shorthand and he started manhandling me. I knew enough to get up and walk out. I went back because I thought, 'Oh it's only one off', but the incidents became more and more sexually oriented and I knew it wasn't for me.

I went back to the headmistress of the college in tears and she said, 'You must never go there again. Here you are, here's another company.' I never went back. I didn't resign I just left. I went to an import export company called Swift & Company. I went there as a stenographer and was very lucky because the lady who was the private secretary to the governing director decided to resign and leave. She was an older woman and I heard later that the governing director, Mr Treloar, had said, 'Who's that cute little blonde down in the stenographers' pool?' And they said, 'Oh that's Miss Fleming'. He said, 'Right, well she can come here'. And I got that job as a private secretary. I suppose I've been there about six, nine months. So the cute little blonde got that job and it was a great job. He then went overseas—this is just after the war when they were trying to establish contacts overseas—he went overseas. While he was away the managing director poached me and moved me to be his private secretary. I stayed there until I was married. I went back for a short time after I was married but of course the instant I was pregnant you had to leave. That was the thing.

After coming from the Dutch East Indies to Australia following the Japanese surrender, sixteen-year-old **FRED HENSKENS** *(1929) and his older sister stayed on in Australia when the rest of the family went to live in the Netherlands. Fred worked as a share farmer in market gardening on the outskirts of Sydney until in 1949 he moved to Canberra where his sister was working.*

I used to come to Canberra to look Rita my sister up. I had a friend, actually he was her boyfriend once. He told me, 'Canberra's a good place,' he said, 'the money's good, it's alright.' So I come to visit my sister and then I decided that I'll come to Canberra and live. So I got a job at Havelock House where Jack McCarthy was the foreman and he give me a job there.

First I was helping digging some of the foundations with a pick and shovel and then I was a brickies' labourer. At first I used to have to stack timber and then the bloke said I was working too hard. The foreman—Jack McCarthy—the foreman used to give me a job and he said, 'You *can't* of finished that already?' I said, 'Yeah', because I was used to working hard and quick. He said, 'You don't work that hard here.' The men were a bit upset with me because they said, 'You don't have to work like an idiot, just take it easy.' Even the union boss used to say, 'Well you have to cut down because you don't work like that here, you'll kill yourself.' I said, 'Oh well, I thought I have to work hard, you know, like I might lose my job.' Because that was the first [paid] job I ever had.

***CONNIE SHAW** (1937) arrived in Western Australia in 1954 with her Dutch family. On the second day at their migrant hostel near Northam, about 100 kilometres north-east of Perth, Connie went to a welcome talk by migration officials.*

They talked about different things. Everybody should join the hospital benefit. If girls needed something, you know, what to buy and things like that. Then there was a list of jobs. One of the jobs was housekeeping in Perth here and the wages was three pound a week, plus keep. And English wasn't necessary. So off I went the next day. I got the train to Perth and I was met in Perth by this lady. My first job in Perth, on the esplanade. But she said she was only going to give me two pound ten because my English wasn't very good, which was a bit of a disappointment because on the boat out I'd grown out of everything I owned.

I was there for quite a few months and --- I was talking to the lady because she told me off for getting a book. They had quite a large shelf of books which belonged to her husband. I'd asked him, I said, 'Oh can I borrow some of the books?' And he said, 'Oh yes.' She wasn't very happy about it, when I said, well I'd asked could I read the books. It turned out that she didn't want me to learn English because, she said, 'Your English is not very good and you can't get yourself another job.' It was like a red rag to a bull to me. Next time I had this half day off, I walked from Subiaco to East Perth, along Hay Street, asked everywhere for a job and I got a job in the printers in East Perth in Hay Street. By that time mum and dad were living in West Perth so I went and lived with mum and dad in West Perth and worked at the printers until the Christmas.

They knocked off before Christmas and I got a job starting at Royal Perth [Hospital, as a nurse], which was living in, all trainees had to live in. Then I saw a bit more from Perth and I had a little bit more to do with the people in general and I quite enjoyed it. I got in some ridiculous problems at times with the language, but apart from that. My basic English reading wasn't bad, you know, for basic things. But what we had learnt was Oxford English and it sounded different. So it was hard sometimes to pick up the words in the sentence.

After leaving high school in southern Sydney at the age of fourteen, ***LES ROBINSON*** *(1947) found his first job in a nearby suburb.*

I was getting four pound sixteen a week. That was my starting wage when I was a kid, which is about nine dollars. That was my week's wage. I started at Trevan Products in Sydney, at Taren Point. They were electrical engineers. When I was first going for work, there was only the trades. That's all you thought about. There was electrical, plumbing, carpentry, you know, we were very naïve in another way that we didn't know of all these other little bits that might be around, which there weren't that many little bits around. So I thought, I might be an electrician, so I'd be getting electrical. I got this job actually after searching numerous places which, like I said, very silly at times. Applying for jobs in Sydney, they say they've got to wait for jobs these days when they apply, and send emails away or whatever else. Well, we had to stand at the door. And we'd be standing outside, you know. I remember standing outside Avery Scales once applying for a job and the queue would have been a hundred metres of people down the street, lined up, waiting to go into an interview for a job.

So I ended getting this job with Trevan's to go in as electrical apprentice. When you first get into a place you're shoved anywhere, you're given anything. You swept the floor, you carried this, you did that, and they'll find out if you're going to work, and if you're not going to work, well, goodbye. I was put out in the paint section to give a hand out there and I liked it and I stayed there. And I was there in the end for six years. I was foreman in the end when I left. And in that six years I paid my way through coach and motor painting at Ultimo Tech. Used to go of a night time three nights a week.

Young Polish migrant **DONAT SANTOWIAK** *(1950) started an apprenticeship in the La Trobe Valley in the late-1960s when the Victorian State Electricity Commission was at its peak with upwards of 11,000 workers.*

I got to Form 5 and jobs in those days were on every corner. I applied for three, as a—of all things—as a male nurse, with the old Yallourn Hospital, as a fitter and turner with the Australian Paper Mill, and as a draftsman with the State Electricity Commission. And I got all three. So chose drafting 'cause for me there was mechanical drafting and the closest [to] motor mechanicking, where my heart was.

I ACTUALLY LOVED THE ACT OF DRAWING at tech school. So for me it was a great, it was excitement. We worked at an office in the old no-longer-existent township of Yallourn. There were five trainees and I was one of the five. There were three streams of drafting. There was the mechanical, electrical or civil. And so we—the five of us—had different directions.

We spent the first year just learning how to basically draw properly. You know, coming home with cramps in my fingers, and being able to letter neatly, and join up lines so you couldn't see the join, all that basic stuff that after a while became so automatic. That's *before* we designed, because our qualification in the SEC was what they called a 'design draftsman'. So we were not just drawing. We were actually doing the computations—like engineering computations—so designing for strength, for durability, and all those sort of things, as well as concept design. Often with other engineers, but we didn't just draw. That came later.

But I loved it. I loved drawing and as the years rolled on, the SEC being such a large enterprise, the variety of work it offered was just most incredible. One minute I could be doing a job in the Yallourn open-cut mine—on a dredger—and then the next week I could be at the Hazelwood Power Station doing some pressure piping on a boiler. Or then the week after in the central workshops in Yallourn redesigning a lathe or something. *It was just great.* It was great.

After finishing teachers' college in Sydney, ***LYNNE SANDERS-BRAITHWAITE*** *(1949) began her teaching career in the early 1970s at a bush school near Tumbarumba in the foothills of the Snowy Mountains.*

I had the Mini, Mini Cooper S, British racing car green. But I'd never driven so far by myself and my little brother came with me and we started driving and the car blew up. You could drive at any speed limit too, which I think is something that's forgotten. 'Cause I was hitting a hundred miles per hour in this Mini, feeling quite joyful about life and it blew up.

Got there, got to Tumbarumba, and my dad had said, 'Get a room at the hotel, don't go and board with anybody.' Which I think was pretty good advice 'cause, he said, 'You board with people and you become part of the family whether you want to or not.' So I went and got a room at Tumbarumba Hotel.

Went and saw this two-teacher school in the bush. Like I've got the suede boots up above my knees and miniskirts made out of half a metre of material. I was trendy by then. And I arrive in this town that has three prison farms feeding into it, really, really in the sticks. Pretty funny. Pretty scary. Book into the hotel. Ladies didn't drink in the main bar. My father once again, my mentor. 'They don't let you drink in the front bar. Don't you take that. You go straight up to the bar and you order your drink.' Which in a way did pay off in the end but it was pretty scary, 'cause I'm five foot tall.

So I end up a teacher in this two-teacher school with a really difficult man. Really difficult. And I don't know what happened to me that year. It was pretty scary. They did things. I don't think they wanted me there. They did things like put a kangaroo head out of the front of a letterbox and a tail out of the back. Snakes in the drawer. It was pretty violent. For once in my life I was really glad that an old soldier brought me up 'cause I knew how to shoot really well, knew how to knife fight and other assets that I had not expected to use as a young school teacher. Very isolated.

GERALDINE BOX *(1949) was working as a nurse in Darwin when Cyclone Tracy devastated the town on Christmas Eve and morning 1974.*

'74 was a great year. '74 was the year that I met my first same-sex partner and we were together for twenty-three years after that. I think Cyclone Tracy cemented the relationship for a time. Tracy, I think, it's one of those moments—and I'm sure people had them when they've had an event, if they've gone through the floods in Queensland or fires in Victoria or wherever—and for me Tracy was one of those moments. Fortunately as a twenty-five-year-old I don't think I've been emotionally scarred by it although I still don't like to be anywhere near cyclones. I don't like high wind very much or the screeching sound of corrugated iron, that really sets me off. But it threw one into having to work with the basics basically.

We stayed up all night in the third floor of the nurses' home trying to work out what was going on with this noise and the wind and the windows blowing in and the screeching, only to have a *phone* call—an internal phone call—no power, I don't know how the phones worked but no power—the internal phone went about five o'clock and it was my colleague—junior colleague, same, I was a junior theatre nurse—calling saying, 'Gerry, you've gotta come over to theatre.' I said 'Jenny'—Jenny Beat is for me the hero of what happened in the operating room in Darwin Cyclone Tracy—I said, 'But who could come into hospital in this?' I was thinking somebody's come in with an appendix or something. I thought, 'What's going on?'

Opened the door to casualty and went, 'Oh --- my --- goodness!' and there were just people everywhere and there were bodies, there were people with their internal organs out. There're people with limbs hanging off, it was just *horrendous*. There were few staff there. A couple of the resident doctors were, must've been there on duty for the evening. There were some nurses there and I just went straight through to theatre. So Jenny was there and she said, 'We've got to set up for theatre, we've got to.'

Mr Bromwich was our senior surgeon. He was an ex-British army officer—medical officer—fantastic surgeon, in and out sort of surgeon. Bromwich came in and said, 'You'll have to get the theatres ready, we'll run the theatres and we'll start.' But he said, 'I can't be here,' and I said 'What do you mean you can't?' He said the person who was the head of the triage was our senior anaesthetist and he'd been killed in the cyclone, which Bromwich had found out somehow, and he said, 'He's dead. I'll go down to casualty, I'll take over triage', which is basically deciding who's going to go to theatre and who's safe to leave and who's not going to be resussed [resuscitated]. 'You two get the theatre set up'. As other staff managed to drift in we set it.

Some of the doctors had managed to get in and I was working in one theatre as the nurse, the running nurse if you like, not the scrub nurse. I can remember our first case, it was a young woman who had her whole belly basically out. She had a cut that had obviously, probably corrugated iron had ripped her open from fore to aft, everything was on view. So she was seriously ill.

I can remember we just worked straight through. We did all the lifting and laying and running around. I think we worked like that for forty-eight hours until a team from Woden Valley Hospital flew in. I can remember them walking in and saying, 'Right just go'. Go? You know, go where? (laughs)

During the mid-1970s, daughter of Greek migrants, ***OURANITA KARADIMAS*** *(1958) studied part-time for a degree in metallurgy while undertaking a traineeship in a Sydney foundry.*

They did not have any specific educational aspirations for me. I will quote my mother here, 'na parete ena kalo harti', which means to get a good certificate or diploma of some sort in your hands, that was what was important. 'Yana mini sustame sustomagazi', so you don't have to go back to being the fish and chips shop proprietors that myself and your father were, yeah. What they wanted was for their children to be qualified in some way with a legitimate qualification that did not involve them having to do manual labour of the sort that they had to do. Yeah, it was that sort of thing. Beyond that, I don't think they thought very much about it.

AS THE ONLY FEMALE on the foundry floor at Austral Bronze Crane Copper, I was working with some of the roughest of the roughest men you could ever get. So I was exposed really early on to some very rough ways of talking and language and all that sort of thing, and I *loved* it. It was the good little Greek girl in amongst all these, you know, factory-hardened types, and I absolutely loved it.

We had a lunchroom, an office, where the metallurgists and the technicians used to sit for morning tea. And there was a large pornographic calendar up above the door, that was just like a standard thing there. And one day, I don't know, some time during my first year, one of the bosses came in and turned around and said to that, 'Look *that's* inappropriate, you can't have that up there anymore if you're going to have a young woman in here.' And all of the guys just said, '*What*? We're not going to change because of that, leave it up there. She's going to get used to it.' And it stayed up there. It wasn't an issue. I never thought of it as an issue, but can you just imagine, today, walking into an industrial workplace and having *Playboy*—wall-to-wall *Playboy*—everywhere, with women in the workplace, how unbelievably offended and offensive that would be considered.

Seriously, I was not insensitive, I was not stupid. I knew what it was. It was just not an issue.

DAVID COOPER *(1959) hated school on the Mornington Peninsula and left as soon as he could, in 1976.*

I just wanted to get out of there. I was lucky really that I wasn't born today because, you know, I'd be bloody pushing a broom around or something. I remember reading the careers book, and all I was looking, the job criteria was you had to be sixteen and you didn't need Leaving English and Maths. That was what I was looking for.

I think it's a funny story, but I went through this career book every lunchtime for a week or a fortnight, couldn't find anything. And I was walking home from the railway station at Seaford—'cause we lived in Seaford by then—and just near the milk bar, there's this really attractive blonde walking towards me hanging off the arm of this guy, and the guy was in a uniform, and that's the only reason I looked because I was perving on the girl unfortunately. As he walked past, I saw he was in uniform and I read what was on his shoulder and it had that he was a paramedic. I thought, 'Gee, he doesn't look very old.' *That's* what made me go to school the next day. I looked up the careers booklet and it had Cadet Ambulance Officer. You had to turn sixteen on the thirty-first of March of the first year when you joined or you were too young. Well my birthday was the thirtieth of March. So I got in on the last day and I thought that's the job for me. 'Cause I'd been in the lifesaving club. I'd been doing CPR [cardiopulmonary resuscitation] and mouth-to-mouth resuscitation and learning a little bit of first aid.

By mistake really, I ended up in a career that actually really suited me, 'cause in those days it was a practical job. Everyone was either an ex-motor mechanic or a tow truck driver or a factory worker. People went to university wouldn't become a paramedic because the wages were so lousy back then.

***IAN REID** (1961) recalls applying for his first job whilst completing a degree in maths at Adelaide University in the early 1980s.*

In my third year of my degree I started to do the careers program things. I'd settled on this actuarial field, like, 'Oh that's something I could do'. So I wrote lots of letters off. Had them all typed up professionally as you had to do in those days. No word processors. A professional typist did it for me. I took it to a printer and had them offset print properly. Not just this cheap photocopying business. And sent them off to various insurance companies. I remember I had a reply from MLC [the National Australia Bank's wealth management division] who said, 'We're interested'.

So I went off to the interview with nice tie and a nice chocolate brown polyester jacket (laughs). Thinking that was pretty, you know, formal. Off to this interview, really I think just, was I sensible and well enough presented to get a job. And they offered me a position, at North Sydney in the head office. So that was pretty good. I remember the starting salary was 12,000 dollars a year and I thought I was an absolute millionaire. In fact that was in the early eighties in the time of the boom in salaries. There was a bit of hyperinflation happening in the early eighties. I think I was offered a salary of 12,000 something and by the time I started the job—that was about October or something like that—by the time I started the job in January it'd gone up to 14,000.

***CHRISTIAN BOW** (1978) recalls the difference that a university degree made to work opportunities and salaries in the mid-1990s.*

I did an apprenticeship as an electrician and I started off on—that was 1996—I was on five dollars and fifty-five an hour and that was pretty tough to live on. My girlfriend who's now my wife, she moved to Brisbane for university and so we had a long distance relationship. I'd spend all my money coming down to Brisbane on holidays. But then I went to university as a mature-aged student at twenty-seven and got a construction management degree. Now I'm a project manager and I'm earning a good salary. When I was an apprentice, all my friends who were students were getting paid nothing and I was rich compared to them, you know. But then they started getting into their jobs properly and became professionals and started earning big dollars, or better dollars, and so all of a sudden they outraced me. Then I went back and studied and caught up.

A double degree did not guarantee employment for Philippines-born ***Rachel Brown*** *(1985) when she left university in Brisbane during the Global Financial Crisis.*

I graduated back in 2008 and I had done a double degree in International Business and Asian Studies. So was really interested in business in Asia in particular and I wanted to live in Asia and do something business-related.

I graduated in mid-2008. I had a job with a mining company and they were even going to send me to their subsidiary in China and it was all going well and then the financial crisis came to Australia. The company lost funding for the project and so everyone was just let go after that. That was my first job really out of university and I remember at the time I thought, 'I will keep trying to get another job here in Brisbane.' And it was just really, really difficult having no experience, just out of university—I was twenty-three I think at the time.

So my options were really limited and I decided to answer one of those job ads to teach English in South Korea. And that's how it happened. I thought, 'Well, it's not the *field* I wanted to be but it's *where* I wanted to be anyway.' 'Cause I have studied these places for so long and I wanted to live there and travel there and understand the area. And this was the best way I could do it.

Up in the Kimberley, ***ARTHUR HUNTER*** *(1989) was among the first in his family to complete Year 12 schooling.*

I was the second child in the whole family, and the first in my dad's kids' family, so I was the first to complete my Year 12 studies. It was a pain in the bum but I did it. And I was happy and I was glad.

2005 I wanted to quit school and go work in the station with my family or, you know, do something, because I thought I was dumb and I couldn't learn much. My teacher telling me, 'Arthur stick into it. Next year will be a good year for you.' You know, 'You'll really love it.'

But for me I was really shy. I couldn't really talk and when he telling me about this place called Goolarri that we are in now—Goolarri Media in Broome, Goolarri Media Enterprises—back in 2006, he said, 'We gonna go to Broome, do school-based training. We gonna go into radio.' I was like, 'What? Radio? That's gonna be shame.'

School-based training it's kids going to school, they also get paid for it. You come to school and you go away. I was seventeen at that time. I was really shy too, so I was getting there. And then I went onto the Mary G Show—radio show—in 2006. I was talking and my family, they was blown away because on the radio they heard me talking. And my dad was like, 'Is that my son? Is that my son talking?' You know, because I don't really talk much. My family was like, 'Is that my nephew?' You know, 'Was that my grandson?' I went back home, that's what they were like, were saying to me. 'Was that you on radio?' I'm like, 'Yeah it was me.' And I started talking a bit more. Went on radio and that's when I started coming out of my shell. School-based training was the end of it.

At the end of it Goolarri Media said there's two vacant positions. They say, 'If you want you can sign up for it and see if you can get it. And we do an interview and see if you want it and everything.' They gave me I think three or four months to think about it—maybe five months—to think about it. But what I did, I did up my resumé and I wrote up a document saying why I would like to do it. I sent it off. Prior to that I was thinking, 'Broome?' Well, this is what I was thinking at the time, I was thinking about Broome with girls and you know—me being young—and yeah. I was thinking about that, Broome and girls and different scenery. Or the other option was this mine, this diamond mine up in the Kimberley. It's called Argyle Diamonds. It has the rare pink diamonds. I was thinking about working there. But I was like, 'Nah, I'll go to Broome just for the girls.'

When she was interviewed in Sydney in 2013 at the age of twenty-three, ***GEMMA NOURSE*** *(1989) had already completed an Arts degree and worked in seven different jobs in Darwin (where she was born), Canberra, Adelaide and Sydney, where she was now working in a café, studying film-making and hoping to pursue opportunities in music.*

People my age are more able to maybe be agents in their own lives. To know that they can make decisions about what they do, their lives and how they unfold. I think that's really valuable for people. But I don't think it necessarily makes people happier, necessarily. I guess it's a balance. Because I was talking about my dad earlier and saying that maybe he's forgone a lot of personal fulfilment or personal growth by being in this field of work for so long.

I think that those opportunities are more available to people my age. But I think there's also something to be said for having fewer choices so that you know your days or years of your life aren't taken up wondering what else you could be doing or whether it's better or whether you'd be happier. Which is something that I've been grappling with (laughs) in the last couple of years.

What is it that you want? Would you prefer to stay in one job for your whole life? I know a lot of people who would. Just trying to sort out what your own expectations of yourself are, and trying to figure out enough about yourself to—and your own values—to work out what kind of career life would suit you.

I don't think those are questions that a lot of people in my parents' generation had to think about at twenty-one or twenty-three years old.

Further Listening on From School to Work

Kathleen Golder, 1920, http://nla.gov.au/nla.obj-219908851/listen/1-963
Leo Cripps, 1923, http://www.nla.gov.au/amad/nla.oh-vn6290880/2-15
Bert Castellari, 1923, http://www.nla.gov.au/amad/nla.oh-vn6252044/0-3293
Trish Barrkman, 1933, http://www.nla.gov.au/amad/nla.oh-vn5972545/0-2155
Veronica Schwarz, 1939, http://nla.gov.au/nla.obj-220011117/listen/1-174
Greer Bland, 1944, http://www.nla.gov.au/amad/nla.oh-vn5972533/1-988
Geraldine Box, 1949, http://www.nla.gov.au/amad/nla.oh-vn6190857/0-2737
Russell Elliott, 1950, http://nla.gov.au/nla.obj-219850973/listen/4-340
Peter Galvin, 1951, http://www.nla.gov.au/amad/nla.oh-vn6252046/0-626
Alison Fettell, 1952, http://nla.gov.au/nla.obj-220185705/listen/1-2
Gina Polito, 1954, http://www.nla.gov.au/amad/nla.oh-vn6421369/0-2405
Rick Galea, 1958, http://www.nla.gov.au/amad/nla.oh-vn6535733/2-2948
Kim Bear, 1959, http://www.nla.gov.au/amad/nla.oh-vn6190847/0-6226
Phil May, 1962, http://www.nla.gov.au/amad/nla.oh-vn6569680/1-658
Jodie Bell, 1970, http://www.nla.gov.au/amad/nla.oh-vn6290885/0-3810
Benjamin Peek, 1976, http://nla.gov.au/nla.obj-219981628/listen/1-306
Adam Farrow-Palmer, 1988, http://nla.gov.au/nla.obj-219982656/listen/1-2898

Military Service

*At the start of World War II, **KATHLEEN GOLDER** (1920) was working as a hairdresser in the north of England and though she was about to become a single mother she ended up working in an aircraft factory.*

The day war broke out I was one week overdue giving birth. That day I remember very well --- I used to hear what my father had to say about the First World War. I think he impressed me quite a bit. I didn't like to think at that young age that there was to be another war. It made me realise, I think, that I wasn't a young girl any more, that I had to grow up. It wasn't long after that my brothers left, one for the air force, one for the Grenadier Guards, actually.

I did odd jobs actually to begin with. There was no hairdressing done. One of the jobs I went to do, I was asked if I would do something because they said, 'You've got in this house your mother, one baby, your father and your grandfather. They can look after all that. We'll give you a job.' They had a factory—I got quite good at it—where I was taught to solder casings on Spitfire radiators. So I did that one after the other (laughs). On a line. I'd be paid, but it was never very much. Women didn't get paid much in those days really and it was work for the army, for the good of the war. We were awful bad state then, you know, with rationing and --- crikey. How we came through it all, I've no idea.

This little girl that I had a week after war broke out, she actually remembers the bombing, as a little girl of perhaps three. We'd go to bed—she and I in bed—and we'd hear the, oh dear me, I can hear it in my mind right now. These Germans coming either to bomb Liverpool to hell, those docks burned for two solid weeks, and Manchester was bombed and all different other places. But we'd hear this drone coming in, 'Mmmmm,

mmmmm, mmmmm, mmmmm.' And it would get louder and oh --- (thumping noise).

Get out of bed and she would get out of bed and I more or less threw her onto my grandfather who was under the stairs there for him to look after, while we went out because they often dropped—many times did—the incendiary bombs. We had a thatched roof and we would *pray* that they never dropped on the roof. And do you know, they never did. Not one. We were very lucky because if it had dropped on our roof it would've gone straight through because it was only straw (laughs).

***BERT CASTELLARI** (1923) was working as a newspaper copy boy when he was called up after Japan joined the war. From 1943 he served in a tank crew in New Guinea and Borneo.*

Mostly you didn't really know what was going on around you at any time. I've found that reaction in people in other units. You're in something. You don't know what you're doing. In fact, I think it probably applies—from the extensive reading I have done for years—that's how a lot of war is run. Nobody really knows what's going on.

The Matilda—although it was obsolete by then—had been a very good tank in the beginnings of the Desert War because it had extremely thick armour around the turret and filler hole, and was shaped so that rounds would bounce off instead of penetrating. Certainly the Japanese had nothing which penetrated. Quite frankly—I've not said this to anybody else except my dear late wife—I never felt afraid because I knew the people that really were copping it were the infantry. Although we were at risk—we had trouble with mines and stuff and we did have people wounded—but they were outside the tank. I never felt it was --- I knew there was danger but it's something, something happens to some people. In great danger you don't feel the danger. But I never said that to anybody. You know, they may think, maybe you'd say, 'It just happens'. It was the same in Borneo.

There was a very high noise level from the engines. Put a non-tank crewman in one day with me. He couldn't cope with the noise of the engine, it was just so enormous. It's worse than any rock band because it's beating. Then if you're firing the guns you got a gun that's going off there and a machine gun noise is a very loud noise. Even just the noise of a rifle. The Veterans' Affairs Department belatedly accept the fact that if you'd been a rifle man, you could claim a deafness disability pension from the effect of the rifle going off. And I think that was fair enough.

Well the Vet Affairs can be difficult people. I applied for a disability pension—I have it because of my deafness—but it took three years because at first they refused. I've built it up to about seventy per cent because my hearing, you know, is bloody lousy. And it has affected, denied me many things I'd like to have had. Mainly where good hearing is required. I don't want to labour that, but it destroyed my—ultimately—my appreciation of music. I listened to some LPs we had there one day, Bach, Beethoven. I thought, 'I'm not hearing this right'. I've never heard music properly for a long time.

***RUSSELL ELLIOTT** (1950) was at teachers' college in Ballarat when his name and birth date were in the mix for the conscription draft during the Vietnam War.*

I can vividly remember I was involved with the conscription sign-up. The year or the intake that would've affected me, they had—I don't know what you would say—the temerity, for want of a better word, to televise it as the marbles dropped within each month. I can vividly remember that day, because I was at teachers' college, and I can remember when they did it because they did it live—it was like a TattsLotto thing, we're playing with people's lives—and the numbers dropped out.

Nicole Curby: How did that feel as you were watching it?

Yeah, pretty intense to be honest, pretty intense because I'd signed up for, you know, had to fill in the conscription thing and I suppose there was enough information coming through to show it was a fairly horrendous conflict with perhaps no great resolution but a fairly horrid theatre of war to be involved in, and now it was within the range of everyone.

It must've been '69, '69 yes. A couple of momentous things we watched at Teachers College. That was one, balanced by Armstrong landing on the moon, which was quite the opposite. That would be forever etched there too I think. But the Vietnam one was only I suppose a fleeting moment but I guess it brought for that fleeting moment to being that close to being part of something that would not have been good, not been good. Yes, I can certainly remember that with great relief in hindsight but fair bit of tension at the time. Out of the group of us that were watching it, I think three, their numbers fell out.

JASON JOHNSON *(1981) was working as a labourer on construction sites in Cairns when he joined the Australian army in 2001.*

I was watching television and the army ad came on and it sparked my interest. I'd tried to enlist about twelve months earlier. I thought, 'You know what? I can't really see myself *going* anywhere. I can see myself just sitting around Cairns and not doing anything interesting with my life.' So I picked the phone up and made a phone call and dropped into the reserve unit in Cairns, 51st, and explained the whole situation to them. They were pretty quick to chuck me on a bus and send me to Townsville. Sat the testing again. Sat through all the interviews. It was interesting. I know looking back on hindsight now the guy that I spoke to in there was an infantry senior NCO [non-commissioned officer], 'cause he wore the red sash.

He pretty much told me right from the start, 'You're joining infantry son. Sign here. Get on the bus and away you go.' So that was me.

I SUPPOSE THE BIGGEST THING coming out of Afghanistan, and I know it's the guys, they talk about it a lot, you come back to Australia, it's the camaraderie, it's the mateship. Probably the easiest way I suppose for people to understand it is, you watch some show like *Lord of the Rings*, for example, the guys will go out and do what they got to do and when they come back it's a big—everyone's back and everyone's met and there's going to be a feed prepared for you and you'll sit down and you'll have a meal and you'll sit down and you'll talk about the day's events that transpired. It's that, it's that *mateship* and that sense of belonging, not only amongst ourselves as the Australians, but we would involve the Afghanis in that as well. You create this awe, this atmosphere of that's your team, that's, you know, we're going out to go and do this.

Examples of where we were in fights and we'd call for reinforcements and the guys, the Afghanis that were back in the camp, would load up in the vehicles and come screaming down the roads and pull up. We'd look behind us and they'd be sitting up on the hills and we knew that was our chance to break. We'd be running back to the hill and they'd be standing on the hill firing RPGs [rocket-propelled grenades] and weapons over our heads while we were running back to the hill that we were at. We'd all get up there and high five each other and a couple of the guys would shoot back at the village and we'd go, 'Rightio, that's it. It's done and dusted. It's time to go home.'

I used to eat all the time with the Afghanis. The food that the Afghanis prepared, I loved it. A couple of us guys who they got to know quite well, we'd go and sit and eat with them all the time. Lamb, chicken, rice, primarily for every meal. The vegetables that used to get grown that they'd prepared. Cucumber and tomatoes and carrots and shallots and different things like that. Unbelievable. Pomegranates. I think I ate more pomegranate in Afghanistan than I care to ever remember. But it was a great custom to sit down and eat pomegranates with them. But the meals that they cooked, I can't believe it. The T-bones, the Australian cooks when they'd cook, they'd cook a T-bone. My test now in Australia is if I sit down near the T-bone steak, if I couldn't eat that T-bone with a plastic knife and fork, it's not good. And I'll be sitting in a restaurant where I'm paying 200 dollars for a meal and these blokes are preparing better meals on very rudimentary stoves and cook tops and stuff.

It's amazing. It's that mateship, I suppose, that sense—I get a feeling that the guys coming back from Afghanistan and they miss that camaraderie, that sense of belonging, and achievement, I suppose, of every single day, knowing you go out the front gate, there's a chance, there's a very high chance, that you won't be coming back. So you work very hard to support yourself and the guys around you. You work *harder* to support the guy to your left and right than yourself, knowing that if you're in a team of ten, for example, there's now nine other people working just as hard for you. That's what it all comes down to.

Further Listening on Military Service

Leo Cripps, 1923, http://www.nla.gov.au/amad/nla.oh-vn6290880/0-6106
Greer Bland, 1944, http://www.nla.gov.au/amad/nla.oh-vn5972533/1-2113
Jay Logan, 1981, http://www.nla.gov.au/amad/nla.oh-vn6569699/0-3396

Further Reading on Youth

Arrow, Michelle, *Friday on Our Minds: Popular Culture in Australia Since 1945* (Sydney: University of New South Wales Press, 2009).

Bongiorno, Frank, *The Sex Lives of Australians: A History* (Collingwood: Black Ink, 2012).

Campbell, Craig and Proctor, Helen (eds), *A History of Australian Schooling* (Sydney: Allen & Unwin, 2014).

Crotty, Martin and Larsson, Marina (eds), *Anzac Legacies: Australians and the Aftermath of War* (North Melbourne: Australian Scholarly Publishing, 2010).

Cuthbert, Denise, Swain, Shurlee and Quartly, Marian, *The Market in Babies: Stories of Australian Adoption* (Clayton: Monash University Publishing, 2013).

Davison, Graeme, *Car Wars: How the Car Won Our Hearts and Conquered Our Cities* (Crows Nest: Allen & Unwin, 2004).

Douglas, Louise, 'Becoming an Adult', in Bill Gammage and Peter Spearritt (eds), *Australians 1938* (Sydney: Fairfax, Syme & Weldon Associates, 1987), pp.187–96.

Driscoll, Catherine, *The Australian Country Girl: History, Image, Experience* (Farnham: Ashgate, 2014).

Garton, Stephen, *The Cost of War: Australians Return* (Melbourne: Oxford University Press, 1996).

Gerster, Robin and Bassett, Jan, *Seizures of Youth: The Sixties and Australia* (Melbourne: Hyland House, 1991).

Hetherington, Penelope, 'Childhood and Youth in Australia', *Journal of Australian Studies* 10, no. 18 (May 1986), pp. 3–18.

Holmes, Katie and Pinto, Sarah, 'Gender and sexuality', in Alison Bashford and Stuart Macintyre (eds), *The Cambridge History of Australia, Volume 2, The Commonwealth of Australia* (Port Melbourne: Cambridge University Press, 2013), pp. 308–31.

McCalman, Janet, *Journeyings: The Biography of a Middle-Class Generation 1920–1990* (Carlton: Melbourne University Press, 1993).

McCalman, Janet, *Struggletown: Public and Private Life in Richmond, 1900–1965* (Carlton: Melbourne University Press, 1984).

McKinnon, Alison and Proctor, Helen, 'Education', in Alison Bashford and Stuart Macintyre (eds), *The Cambridge History of Australia, Volume 2, The Commonwealth of Australia* (Port Melbourne: Cambridge University Press, 2013), pp. 429–51.

Murray, Suellen, *After the Orphanage: Life beyond the Children's Home* (Sydney: University of New South Wales Press, 2009).

Savage, Jon, *Teenage: The Creation of Youth Culture* (London: Chatto & Windus, 2007).

Twomey, Christina, and Boyd, Jodie, 'Class, Social Equity and Higher Education in Postwar Australia', *Australian Historical Studies* 47, no. 1 (2016), pp. 8–24.

Lawrence Zion, 'The Sound of "Australia"', in Verity Burgmann and Jenny Lee (eds), *Constructing a Culture: A People's History of Australia since 1788* (Melbourne: McPhee Gribble/Penguin, 1988), pp. 209–22.

CHAPTER 5

MIGRANTS

Immigration has reshaped modern Australia, and migration experiences have shaped the lives of many Australians. While Australia has a long immigrant history stemming from European occupation of Aboriginal land, this chapter focuses on first or second generation migrants and refugees in the second half of the twentieth century. Some migrated to Australia themselves, while others had parents or grandparents who chose to journey to this country. We learn about the trials and tribulations of building new lives and homes in an unfamiliar land, from managing family life to working through changing identities. We also hear from Australians who witnessed the country diversify with each wave of immigrants.

Kathleen Golder, Fred Henskens and Connie Shaw started new lives in Australia after World War II. During this period, the Commonwealth government wanted to grow Australia's population, and encouraged British migrants through an Assisted Passage Migration Scheme which offered a subsidised fare to eligible citizens. The cost of the journey was just ten pounds and those who signed up became known as Ten Pound Poms. Kathleen Golder and her husband took up the ten pound passage because they were scared of the European Cold War and had 'only just got over the last one'.

The government also offered a home to Europeans affected or displaced by the war. There were never enough of the British migrants preferred by both Labor and conservative governments, so the migration net widened to include non-English-speaking Europeans. At sixteen, Fred Henskens decided to stay in Sydney when his parents returned to Holland from the Dutch East Indies, via Australia, after the war. 'I thought I'd be more a *burden* to them if I go back to Holland'. After spending a night in Sydney's Central railway station, Fred quickly found a job in a market garden and eventually settled in Canberra. In 1954, teenager Connie Shaw and her family, travelling from Holland, spontaneously abandoned their plans to settle in Melbourne and disembarked from their ship in Fremantle when Connie's mother learnt 'that the sun always shines in Western Australia'. Connie recalls arriving at a migrant camp: 'the first thing they said to us: "The football match between the Dutch and the Italians on this afternoon at the Italian camp. You've got to be there!" And we thought they were crazy (laughs).'

Some migration journeys involved risk and danger. In 1956, Michael Bicanic left his family and village in Bosnia—'after war, everything was destroyed'—in search of a better life. Late one night, Michael and his army-trained friends crossed the border into Austria on foot. They arrived unscathed. After gaining political asylum, Michael migrated to Australia where he worked on the Snowy Mountains Scheme, among other jobs, before settling in Tasmania.

Many migrants recall discrimination and the difficulties of fitting into the 'Australian way of life' as expected by the government assimilation policy of the 1950s and '60s. Rick Galea, born in Sydney in 1958 to Maltese migrant parents, recalls his distress when he was called a 'wog' at school, and how he 'just always wanted to be Australian.' In 1964, Polish teenager Donat Santowiak and his parents arrived in country Victoria to join his mother's family who had come under the Displaced Persons Resettlement Scheme in 1950.[1] After a few months with his mother's family in Maffra, Donat and his parents moved to Morwell. 'It was a very lonely time' for Donat. His parents were experiencing relationship issues and his father was humiliated when his overseas qualifications were not recognised in Australia. Donat recalls that 'the price of admission was a denouncement of my heritage'. He 'used to take the Polish-English dictionary to bed with me every night and just hammer away, memorise words', and he attempted to shed his accent. In later life, Donat, who worked in Gippsland community development, instigated a project that led to the establishment of a migrant memorial at the site of the former West Sale Migrant Holding Centre. This memorial activity impacted on Donat's *own* migrant identity: 'It was like coming out and saying, "Well, this is who I am and I'm now *okay* with it."'

1 The Displaced Persons Resettlement Scheme enabled over 170,000 people to migrate to Australia between 1947 and 1953. Many came from Eastern Europe and had been affected by the war and its aftermath.

By the time of the interview in 2014, he had decided 'to revert back to my full Christian name of Donat rather than being called Don'.

Ruth Apps and Alison Fettell witnessed European migrants move into western Sydney in the 1950s and '60s. Alison's father's migrant workmates introduced her to 'the most amazing different foods on Sundays', and Ruth's children started to meet migrant kids at the local primary school. Ruth's explanation for widespread ignorance about these new members of Australian society hints at the insularity and racism of the old Anglo-Australia: 'we were not given enough information to say that these people were normal people who were coming here for help'.

In the 1960s and '70s the Commonwealth government's immigration policies slowly shifted away from the White Australia that had been institutionalised by the Immigration Restriction Act of 1901. The Whitlam Labor government passed legislation in 1973 that ensured race was no longer a criterion for migration, and in 1975 the government enacted a Racial Discrimination Act. As immigrants from the Middle East and refugees from south-east Asia reached Australia in the early and mid-1970s, Russell Elliott was beginning his teaching career in the northern Melbourne working-class suburb of Broadmeadows. Russell faced an ethnically-diverse classroom of mostly non-English-speaking migrant children who had arrived in recent weeks. He recalls the barrier of language and inadequate support from school management. 1959-born David Cooper, whose mother was English, recalls a less diverse school environment on Melbourne's Mornington Peninsula: 'There weren't any little Chinese boys when I went to school if you know what I mean. I had one girl in the grade that was Greek.' By the 1980s, one of David's son's best friends at school, in the same area, was Chinese.

Not all Australians—migrant or native-born—have perceived the 'multicultural' policies prevalent from the mid-1970s in entirely positive terms. In 2013, ten years after his arrival as a refugee from South Sudan, James Mayol has made the most of his Australian opportunities yet recognises the limits of a multiculturalism in which other languages and cultures are acceptable as long as they don't 'have anything that will affect Australian lives'.

In this chapter our narrators discuss complex migrant identities. Barbara Krickl, who left Germany for Australia in the early 1980s, and married an Australian, concludes: 'as far as identity goes, it's sort of really *schizophrenic* in a way. Because almost as if I have two different people that I have to adjust to different situations.' Fred Henskens, who came to Australia in his teens after barely surviving the Japanese occupation of the Dutch East Indies, reflects: 'I class myself a fair dinkum Aussie (laughs) since 1949 after I met all the people at work and everybody treats me like, just, you know, *Australian*.'

Ouranita Karadimas, Milijana Stojadinovic and James Finnegan ponder their second generation migrant identities. Ouranita describes her 'really problematic relationship with Greece and with being Greek', while Milijana, who was raised with a strong Yugoslav identity, recalls how the break-up of Yugoslavia, thousands of miles away, reverberated in her school classroom in the 1990s. Her Yugoslav identity was challenged and fractured as 'the climate that was in this country made people like my family choose to either be Serbian or Croatian'. By contrast, James Finnegan—born in Sydney, raised by Irish parents—explains how he's 'always probably identified with Irish more than Australian.' 'I feel like my parents actually just brought Ireland to Australia. So I've always been Irish (laughs).'

Departures and arrivals generate potent memories. They are remembered in vivid, sensory detail. While Donat Santowiak was impressed by the Melbourne cityscape as he sailed into Port Phillip Bay in 1964, his first impressions of 'little old Maffra' in rural Victoria were less positive: 'it was like life stopped. The silence was deafening. I'd never heard crickets in my life. The smell of freshly mowed grass, never smelt that.' We can hear the emotion in Kathleen Golder's voice as she describes the difficult task of leaving her home and family when setting off on an old troop ship on a dark, wet, London night. She recalls the uncertainty of what was to come: 'We had no idea really, what it was like.' Although, in that moment, she didn't want to leave, she explains 'it was the best thing I ever did.'

If you listen to the extracts in this chapter you will hear other layers of migration experience. You'll catch the north of England in Kathleen Golder's voice, or perhaps even the difference between Fred Henskens' East Indies Dutch accent and Connie Shaw's Netherlands Dutch. You can hear how Donat Santowiak's self-taught English lessons paid off, for better or worse, and how more recent arrival James Mayol is still developing his English proficiency and occasionally reverts to the Dinka words that best express his meaning. In all of these voices you will hear the emotion of migration: the pain or excitement of leaving and the surprise or shock of the new world; the hurt of racism or the relief of acceptance; the complex pride of fusing old and new cultures and the poignant memories of places lost and found. The sounds of migrant stories perform the tangled diversity of contemporary Australia.

In 1946, ***FRED HENSKENS'*** *(1929) father came to Sydney for a leg amputation following a motor accident. Fred and the rest of his family travelled from the Dutch East Indies, where Fred was born and raised, to join his father. When his parents returned to Holland, sixteen-year-old Fred and his older sister Rita decided to stay in Australia. Fred found work in a market garden in western Sydney, then settled in Canberra in 1949.*

> I was very homesick at first but I couldn't leave. Working for this Mr Goldis on the farm, I was very lonely and, you know, it was a shock because you're out here all by yourself and trying to—I couldn't speak English very well. I could a bit. Having to learn working in the market garden. I was used to having a good life because my father had a good job and the mother, after the war we still had everything good, but after he lost his legs he was pensioned off. So I thought I'd be more a *burden* to them if I go back to Holland because I had a brother and one sister they had to look after and Holland in that time was very bad to live in, in the '40s after the war. They had trouble getting place to stay and all that.

Matthew Higgins: So you have no regrets about having become an Australian?

> Never, never, never any regrets. No. I class myself a fair dinkum Aussie (laughs) since 1949 after I met all the people at work and everybody treats me like, just, you know, *Australian.* Because when I first come to Canberra there were no foreigners here. I was one of the first foreign people here in the working gang because there were no immigrants coming. The first immigrants [who] came to Canberra were the Poles—they

call 'em the Balts because they're from the Baltic countries, Balts. I worked with some of them, nice people, but they had contracts with the government. They had to work for two years to pay their fare with the government and they used to go on to pick and shovel, and digging trenches, and that sort of thing. But before that I come to Canberra. But coming to Canberra first, oh I go in a pub and everybody wants to pick a fight with you, I don't know what it was. Everybody wanted—the local people here—they always wanted to have a fight. I don't know why (laughs).

I used to go to the Causeway Hall to the dance on the Saturday night and you can bet your life there've been at least two fights every time at the old Albert Hall sometimes (laughs).

I LIVED IN A HOSTEL, at Riverside Hostel, for a while first. I lived at Eastlake when I came here—Eastlake Hostel.

So these were government run hostels for the workers?

Yeah, government.[2] That was thirty shillings a week board. And then I went to Riverside but at Riverside, you only get one meal, you couldn't back up. Yeah, I lived at Riverside. At Riverside, a lot of Dutch people come. Young Dutch people came in. So I met them, I mixed with them but I couldn't get mixed with them because I didn't really like real Dutch people. Because when you live in Indonesia, the Dutch were like snobs to me. They're different. I speak a different sort of Dutch. I'm like a colonial Dutch, I sound different than them, because speaking a lot of Indonesian—the words are different. You'll use different words like an Australian and an Englishman or a Scotsman—the same difference. And I never really got on with some of these Dutch blokes.

---

2 Riverside and Eastlake were two of several government hostels which provided accommodation for those new to Canberra at a time when the city faced a critical lack of housing.

KATHLEEN GOLDER *(1920) reflects on why she and her husband Peter—who was a prisoner of war in Poland during World War II—decided to leave England in 1953.*

The atomic bomb had already been dropped in Japan. We *knew* what could happen and we were in the middle of this. Oh, *no*. I was and many others were. And we left. A few of my friends left to go to—one went to America, another one went to New Zealand and such like, another one went to France actually. So, oh yes, the Cold War was *very* prominent. It was very—made its presence felt. We were scared. It wasn't going, and I could understand he didn't want to go through another war, he's only just getting over the last one. So, no.

We were always poking around to see what we could do, when we could do it and come to Australia. Well, we couldn't come unless we were married. So we were married by then, and oh he pushed it. But they were very *choosy* in coming, in letting us come. You had to be healthy, well, and all the rest of it. They didn't allow us any delinquents or disabled people come. You had to be fit and healthy before they'd accept us into this country. Then we became the Ten Pound Poms. Oh well, that's how we come out, how we were able to come out.

After deciding on Australia, which 'seemed to be a warm place of new beginnings', they set off on their journey from London to Queensland.

IT WAS ON THE *MALOJA*. It was an old troop ship. It was a merchant ship coming out from Tilbury docks. It was on November 5th. There again, I was on the ship. It was dark. It was evening. I'd said goodbye to my mother and Maureen—my first daughter—because she stayed with my mother because of schooling and one thing and another, to come out later. But I was on the *Maloja* and it was slowly going down the estuary from Tilbury docks and I had this new baby in my arms. It was two weeks old. He was born on 22nd October and this was 5th November. I just bundled him up and he wasn't, he wasn't *registered* to come. So I had a bag. I popped him in a bag and hid him and got on the boat. And said nothing to anybody because they did not like you to travel with new babies or if you were past six months pregnant. The date for our departure did not come as early as it could have done and I was getting onto six months pregnant and I said, 'I'll get on that boat if it's the last damn thing I'll do. I'll get on. I don't care if I'm in labour, I'll get on that boat.' But I happened to have had the baby two weeks before we got on the boat. So I got on the boat with this new baby. And I was, stood—it was raining, as it would be in London in November—with this baby and I was crying, crying, 'Oh dear me'.

I *didn't* want to leave really. You know, it was my home. It was my family. My brothers and every—all my family were there. I didn't want to leave but it was the best thing I ever did. But I didn't know it then. One of the emigrants said to me later on that journey, 'Were *you* that person crying on the boat at the back of that vessel?' I said 'It was, yes.' He said, 'I often, I did see you crying and I knew you had a new baby, it was you.' I said, 'Yes.' So there was one witness to that very moment of my leaving.

With Peter, we did not know what we were coming to. We had no idea really, what it was like. It was just an *escapism* for Peter. It was *leaving* the country and he was *scared* of another war so I had to come. And that's when we left, in 1953 and it was the time when, on that same ship came some of the Queen's equipment including her car. Because she followed in 1954—early—and that was her first visit.

In the mid-to-late 1950s in inner-city Melbourne, Kathleen found a place where she felt at home.

I FELT QUITE AT HOME in Carlton. But I was just about the only English-speaking person in that whole block because all the others were Italian. *They* had started to come out by the boatload and they were a *great* lot of people and that used to excite us all. Their children and my kids, they used to play up the back alleyway and we used to go in the wide nature strip in the middle of the road—the Italians and myself—in a hot evening. They were always coming out with food and wine.

They were a wonderful bunch of people, very homely, very entertaining and very helpful. Especially when I had my last one there, my last baby there. Was a little girl after all those boys. Along came this little girl. I had about forty or fifty little dresses. They *all* came with dresses. They were wonderful times there.

And the children, they had become Aussies. They didn't know *anything* about England as they were growing up, the older ones. So it was home to them. And it became home to me, in a way.

When **CONNIE SHAW** *(1937) was sixteen-years-old, her family left Holland on a ship called the* Sibajak. *After a sudden change of plans, they disembarked in Fremantle, Western Australia in March 1954, then travelled to an immigration holding centre in the wheatbelt town of Northam, 100 kilometres north-east from Perth.*

Well, we were supposed to go to Melbourne. Somebody told mum about three days out that the sun always shines in Western Australia (laughs). Mum pricked up her ears and we got off at Fremantle (laughs). And we stood there (laughs) on the wharf with about four suitcases (laughs). Nothing else. We were offered a lift to the camp in Northam. So we got to Northam, I think it was 108 degrees or something. It was *dusty* and it was *hot*. Near the camp we could see this guy who seemed to be a road worker or something—he had a shovel and he was standing along the road there. We looked at him and I thought 'Well it's very hot. He's not actually doing anything' (laughs). Then we got to the camp and the first thing they said to us: 'The football match between the Dutch and the Italians on this afternoon at the Italian camp. You've got to be there!' And we thought they were crazy (laughs).

Having married an Australian, had three children and settled in Perth, Connie considers whether she missed Holland.

I MISSED THE FAMILY. We had quite a lot of uncles and aunties and cousins and that sort of thing. The fact that there was nobody that could relate to anything from your growing up—that was a bit lonely, I suppose, in some ways. When I got married, my husband didn't like anything to do with or want to know anything that happened in Holland or anything to do with that. He didn't like the fact that when the kids learned a few Dutch words from my father. He was totally against another language being spoken. Not that my parents and I used to speak Dutch among ourselves—we all spoke English if there was somebody else around. But yes, the children said later on, they said, 'Well why didn't you teach us any Dutch?' But it was --- that was uncomfortable (laughs). Yes. Yes, that was the part we missed, having a lot of family of my own. But he had enough to make up for it (laughs).

MICHAEL BICANIC *(1937) was born in a small village in Bosnia. His father fought in World War II and did not return after the war ended. Michael's family never learnt what had happened to him. In 1956, when Michael was a teenager, he left his mother and older brother in Bosnia to cross into Austria. He arrived in Australia in 1959 and eventually settled in Scottsdale, Tasmania.*

So I went to Austria with another five fellows. All the others they was in army, finished army. They knew the borders. We had to go night time across the borders. Take a risk. You get caught—three year gaol. That's *automatically* three year gaol. Or you get killed on the border.

Ben Ross: Why was it so important that you left Bosnia to get to Austria? If you were to risk your, you know, to go to gaol?

Yes. But better life. We were told, 'That's a much better life'. And it is. That's why we're here.

After war, everything was destroyed—buildings all burned, all flattened out. There was hardly anything left. All the men, nobody come home, more or less. Kids and women, you know, children, young ones—I saw them running down the roads and things. Yes. No clothes. Nothing.

Do you remember the night when you crossed the border into Austria?

Oh, yes. We organised all that. We had a leader and everybody had to pay the leader so much money. So I sold a little bull to get the money. We went to a place in Yugoslavia—Maribor—that's in Slovenia close to Austria border. I had a rellie there and we was hiding there. And I was one—I can, go on the streets, if police would stop me—'I'm visiting a rellie'. He was a Bicanic—Bicanic like me. I was actually known as 'Bichanich' but we changed it slightly in English country. And then we stayed a couple of days there till when we learn about border.

One night—after midnight—get up. Cross the border. We saw border patrol pass with their big German Shepherd dog. One lot went one way, one lot of two men went the other way. So we gave it fifteen, twenty minutes on foot. Went across in Austria. We were told, 'Just keep walking. There's a little place there. You will find a police station'. In Austria, was Sankt Maria. Anyway we found the place. We reported. Doors open. Nobody in police station. Bell on the table—we ring the bell. One man comes. He get on telephone. Another four, five of them come with the cars that picked us up—checked us all for weapons, things, first—picked us up and took us in a camp. Well, I had a cousin there and a priest who christened me when I was a kid, he was there. They knew I was coming. They come on the camp and took me out. That's how I, straight away—after about two weeks—went to do my job. Finish the trade as a joiner. Then I applied for United States where my uncle was—well, my uncle's older son. Visa was so slow for United States and my rellies was in Australia so that's it, I come to Australia.

At the end of the interview, Michael addresses an omission from his earlier telling of this story.

I MISSED A PART THERE because --- maybe would mix other part in politic. In case somebody like other side listening they say, 'Oh he was that and wasn't that'—'cause we was armed, you know, a lot of us.

When you were going to Austria?

Yeah.

You had guns.

We had automatic ones. We had everything. Yes. Hand grenades. If you run into it—let's handle it.

Were you expecting to have to fight?

We didn't expect anything, you know. When you're there, five of us, four of them been in the army and I'd been trained as a kid. In the country where I come from, soon as you are eleven, twelve—after ten—you go out on training camps camping week, every month. Use the weapons, everything.

Who did you expect that you might have to fight when you were leaving?

Well that's the part (laughs) I missed out. Because can drag like politic. If somebody else is listening maybe say, 'Well, he's anti-communist'. Well, really I was anti-communist. That's the reason I left the country. I didn't like the system. Because we couldn't survive under a communist regime and that's why we went for a better life.

***RUTH APPS** (1926) remembers the arrival of post-war migrants in the western Sydney suburb of Westmead, where she still lived at the time of the interview in 2012.*

My children went to Westmead Public School—Primary School. When they went to school—starting in 1955, the first one—the children of these migrants started coming. So they started coming to birthday parties and you've got to mix with the parents who would come to pick them up. And *we*—I say we, my generation—suddenly discovered that these people were pleasant, they had two legs and two arms, and it was quite a strange getting-to-know-you thing.

In the early days they had it hard and well I'm going to say, we had it hard. We were not given enough information to say that these people were normal people who were coming here for help. There, there was a lot—I didn't do it—I claim I didn't do it but they could be in shops and be trying to buy food and you'd have some stupid shop assistant *laughing* at them—not *fair.* I don't think that happens much now as it did then.

Let's face it, apart from—when I was a child living in Wagga—there was a Greek café and an Italian café and their children went to school with me, but that was about the extent of—as an Australian—of knowledge. We did very little travelling in those days. You had to be pretty wealthy to take a ship to go to Europe. We as Australians in those days were pretty insular. We lived here. We didn't know anything beyond our own little world. It has changed but that's how it was then.

THIS HOUSE WHERE WE'RE SITTING IN TODAY and across the road, we are the only two white Anglo-Saxons in this block of some twenty houses. On one side of me I have an Indian family, the other side a Filipino family, then there is Indians and Cambodians and I've got some Indian-South Africans and another Asian family. Across the road is much the same mix—there's people from Mauritius, from India and Sri Lanka. Now we all get on well. I'm the oldest person living here and they will *all* if they see me, ask 'Are you alright? Can we help you? Do you need anything?' From time to time they will drop in with a plate of whatever food they have. I am accepted and I accept them.

My youngest daughter as I told you married a Polish boy. They were not keen. Bronwyn is an Anglican—from my family type. John—the boy she married—was a Catholic. Now his parents wanted John to marry a nice Catholic, Polish girl and instead he married a nice Anglican, Australian girl. But having done that that Polish family has enfolded Bronwyn and me and my husband with all the love in the world. They said after the wedding they didn't know that Australian Anglicans could be so nice. So that was a good mix. Now my granddaughter—the daughter of the Polish-Australian family—she has married a Lebanese Christian boy. So their children are very involved—they are Polish or Lebanese or Australian or Irish or something.

At my church we have a Persian service that is conducted in Farsi, we have an Asian service which is conducted in Mandarin and Cantonese, and we all mix together very happily so multi-culturally. And I worked for years for a Maltese. So I have *no* problems or any difficulties with other religions or anything like that. Very fortunate.

In the spring of 1964, thirteen-year-old **DONAT SANTOWIAK** *(1950) and his Polish parents left the city of Katowice in southern Poland for country Victoria. They came under the family reunion scheme to join Donat's mother's immediate family who migrated to Australia as Displaced Persons in 1950.*

Oh, I was excited. I really didn't think about leaving behind stuff at the time. It was exciting. I remember we used to get lots of Christmas packages from Australia with food and stuff from grandma. They always had like an interesting smell and I don't know what that was about, whether they used to put some kind of a perfume or something in there.

So I had this vision as a kid thinking Australia smells like that when you get here. So I had these naïve kind of, I don't know, just looked forward to the whole idea. But I had no, obviously no consultation in terms of, 'Well do you want to? What do you think?' No. Just came.

Alistair Thomson: And presumably what you were told was, 'We're going to join your mother's family?'

Exactly. Yeah, yeah, yeah. We vaguely heard about kangaroos and crocodiles like a lot of people do.

From then on—as soon as we landed here particularly—it was like a disenchantment. It was like being slapped across the head with a shovel. It was like, you know, not really having a firm idea what to expect apart from just thinking, 'Well maybe it's like Poland except that the climate's different and that there's maybe people dress a bit differently or whatever.' But the whole, how we felt we were accepted into the community and all that—that was a real shock. Because in Poland foreigners as such, were—at least the area that we came from—were actually highly regarded. So if there were tourist-like people the hospitality would be extended to them beyond reasonable, almost.

When we came here we felt the completely reverse. I know today that a lot of that was real discrimination at its --- I mean, I remember getting belted up at school. Gosh I got so beaten up once I ended up nearly losing all my teeth. And being physically thrown out of shops because I couldn't pronounce the name of a particular product the way the man expected me to say it. Yeah, bloody awful. Yeah, it was awful.

Donat recalls his first impressions of Australia and the challenges of adapting to a new culture.

COMING INTO PORT PHILLIP BAY, I remember the pilot's boat pulling up. Also the banks' agents were actually getting on board when the boat was about to go through the heads. They were doing currency exchanges on board before we actually pulled up at Princes Pier. The sight of Melbourne and the cityscape—with the high buildings and all that—I thought, 'Oh wow, this is more like where we came from'. Not knowing that we were going to live like about five hours by car in those days, from Port Melbourne to little old Maffra.

And it was like—when we got there—it was like life stopped. The silence was deafening. I'd never heard crickets in my life. The smell of freshly mowed grass, never smelt that. Yeah. In those days—'cause I was placed with my aunty, and my sister and my mum and my dad lived with my grandmother, so there were two separate houses. And where my aunty lived—it was a modern new home but there were still no articulated sewage lines or anything. So there was the midnight can arrangement. And wow, was that primitive.

Then of course, I had to go to school. So I ended up going to Maffra Catholic school with my sister who was eight years younger. She was in Grade 1 and so was I. Physically I couldn't even fit into the little desks. The nuns put a chair beside the desk so I could sit in the chair beside my sister.

Why do you think that was? Why did they put you in Grade 1?

'Cause I couldn't speak English. I'm assuming, never asked the question. But my academic level could have *easily* fitted into Form 4 which is Year 10 then. Easily. So over, I think, a period of about seven weeks I kind of jumped a grade every week. And I can't remember exactly but we probably lived in Maffra about three months—with our mum's family—before dad was offered a job with the State Electricity Commission here in the La Trobe Valley. And hence we came to Morwell.

SO I WAS IMMEDIATELY PLACED into secondary school at Morwell Tech School. I remember the first day vividly because again, you know, my English was very limited and they actually ended up putting an announcement through the PA for any kids at school that may have spoken Polish or German. I was really fortunate that I'd cottoned on to a couple of—one of them turned out to be the only really friend that I had. They kind of acted as interpreters—if you like—for me.

But that was the beginning of a huge disenchantment of not really being welcomed. Really being *stunned* by the fact that there were people that not only didn't want to associate with me at school—like students—but at the other extreme actually being verbally or physically violent towards me. There were a lot of children from an immigrant background at school—particularly Italians and Greeks—but they hung together in groups. Whilst I was, in many ways, the odd one out. I didn't have a --- and I see that today maybe as really, probably—in the long run—as a healthier thing. Because I made an unconscious decision there to assimilate to the most convincing way that I could in terms of becoming invisible, undetectable, verbally, physically. I just wanted to be part of the mainstream.

So really the price of admission was a denouncement of my heritage and who I was, you know. I didn't see it like that but that's what it was. So it was a very lonely time. Mum and dad were going through—not just some of the relationship issues that they brought with them from Poland—but now there was the added pressure of my dad's qualifications not being recognised, being offered work which was really demeaning for him. And they just did not cope well.

But in the beginning --- for me, there was nowhere to run. I wasn't welcome outside and it was a bugger of a place to be in the house. So it was a really difficult time for me. I guess from there, it was just basically head down bum up. Used to take the Polish-English dictionary to bed with me every night and just hammer away, memorise words, try and put sentences together. I had a part-time job in a milk bar. Worked for a Polish Jew—of all things, around the corner—whose wife owned a milk bar. Got some pocket money. First thing I bought was a reel-to-reel tape recorder, which I've still got, and started recording my own voice to try and, you know, minimise the accent and stuff like that. In some ways I'm sorry that I've done that now. I wish I really had a stronger accent than I do have. But, yeah, it was all full steam ahead, academic kind of achieve --- wanted to be a motor mechanic, mum wouldn't let me.

SO IN MORWELL TECH ***there weren't enough other Polish kids for you to have a group?***

No. No. Probably, there *were* but I didn't connect. I had this Polish/German friend to start off with—Alfie—and we spent time together outside of school as well. Oh and just another thing that I've just remembered that I'm really, really fond of—I spent some time with the Koori kids. I used to visit a particular household in Morwell. Just sit on the lounge room floor watching TV and there was no conversation 'cause I could hardly speak English and yet I really felt safe and I felt like I belonged. We used to go swimming down to what was known as the Eel Hole Creek together. So I don't know whether that was a natural fit because obviously the Koori community was on the fringe. And so they're very fond memories. In fact as my career path evolved, I've worked with some of the relations of the people that I spent time with.

At the time you knew they were Koori kids?

Oh yeah. Of course, of course, yeah, yeah. Sadly, they were my age but none of them are alive, they all sadly died pretty early. But yeah, I did. It all just seemed so normal. You know, there was no racist or separatist thoughts about them or them about me. It was wonderful.

Any friends with Anglo-Australians?

No. No. Not at all.

ALISON FETTELL*'s (1952) father worked in an aluminium-casting foundry when she was growing up in western Sydney in the 1950s and 1960s.*

What I loved about my father—and that I take with me—is his relationship with his work colleagues who were multicultural. We were introduced as children to the most amazing different foods on Sundays. We'd walk 'cause we didn't have a vehicle and we'd go to, you know, Billy's place, but he was Italian and so we'd have this feast. Then it was another weekend, we'd go to somebody who had a Greek background and then it would be Yugoslav background and my father admired these men because of their work ethic. Yes.

Both mum and dad, *I* think, were very welcoming in a sense and quite non-discriminatory. I think—I like to think—that that's opened my mind for completely accepting people as human beings rather than where they come from and what they choose to believe. I think that wasn't even in the mix with my father—it was how you treated another human being, how hard you worked. That seemed to be very important to my dad. And I think he's left that with me.

RICK GALEA*'s (1958) parents and his elder brother left the Mediterranean islands of Malta in 1955. They settled in Sydney, where Rick was born. He recalls his childhood meals and Catholic school days.*

We would have meat probably every second day—steaks or lamb or pork. Baked dinners were very, very frequent—as in baked meat dishes. A lot of pasta dishes. A lot of stuff was done in the oven. Baked rices which I still do today, a lot of them based on the corn beef that I mentioned early—the bully beef was a main part of the ingredient, not so much because it was cheap or anything, it was just traditional flavour.

WHEN IT COMES TO BAKED DINNERS and stuff I've tried to instil in my children how simple it is. They do it now and they're celebrities with their friends when they come up with a big baked dinner.

GENERALLY WHEN THINGS GOT A BIT ROUGH that's when the terminology would come out. There was one guy in particular that I remember and he was such a --- he was so much bigger than me that it was ridiculous that I could actually, that I actually stood up to him.

Elena Volkova: Was it at school?

Yeah, during school hours. He, he was seriously twice my size and we had some huge fights together in the school grounds.

But nearly always it was because of the wog word or as I say the competition to be, you know, in a group.

How did you feel when you heard this word?

Oh, used to be just very, very painful—*very*, very hurtful. It was probably the worst word in the vocabulary actually, for me. I just always wanted to be Australian. All my friends—my best friends—were second, third generation Australian, the ones that I mainly hanged with. Very well-spoken, very educated families, lovely people—give you anything. I just wanted to, basically wanted to be an Australian, to be honest.

Did your parents encourage it?

I virtually asked that English was spoken at home. Mum found it quite difficult—she would basically think in Maltese, first, and then have to decipher it herself to speak it in English. So it was always quite hard for her and she'd intermittently be speaking Maltese and English at the same time and wouldn't even know it. My father—because he was in the workforce, working with a lot of Australians—his grasp of the English language was a lot better. He would definitely speak to me only in English. And made a point of it.

RUSSELL ELLIOTT *(1950) recalls the challenges that came with his first permanent teaching job in the northern Melbourne suburb of Broadmeadows in the early 1970s.*

A lot of housing commission areas, working class people—no aspersions on any of those—but it was *noted* as a very tough area. It even came to the fore in news as an area of *gangs* and problems and I thought, 'Oh, my goodness, what have I let myself in for here, what's happened here.'

I went down to the school, it was quite a small school. I had a look at it. I was given the privilege of a Grade 6, which obviously *no one else* wanted—thirty-four kids. I thought this is going to be sink or swim material. But the whole thing was made worse the first day because in marched the thirty-four Grade 6 students and a very quick sort of glance around I could realise I literally had the United Nations in front of me. Considering these were Grade 6 children, there were probably *eight* ethnic backgrounds in that classroom. That in itself would probably be a good thing but the problem was that all of them had landed in Australia within the last fortnight. They were living in the army barracks beside the school which was the first marshalling point for them, and East Meadows was the school that they were sent to. So, thirty-four children, eight ethnic backgrounds or probably two Australian kids in it that spoke English, the rest spoke anything from Turkish to Greek, you name it. And they had no understanding of English and here they were sitting in a classroom.

It was just impossible to say the least. Exacerbated by the fact there was no support either from the principal who was a guy just about to retire and who lived by the motto, 'Children should be seen and not heard.' No language support teachers at all. It was just beyond belief. It just staggered me how I was going to impart *anything* to them because a) ninety-nine per cent of them couldn't even understand anything I was saying, let alone try and teach them. It was obvious from the day one that there were frictions between the groups because they'd just arrived here. They were in a totally new environment with cultural backgrounds that were as diverse as, as they're spread.

So most of the time was spent keeping them away from one another in the classroom because they would speak in their language. Few of the other ones that could speak English would turn around and tell them to shut up, they didn't want to listen to their stuff. They didn't understand and started to remonstrate and then you'd literally had a brawl almost constantly in the classroom—to which I did try and extricate them away from one another. In the midst of all this again, *still* no support from principal or anyone who just used to bellow down the PA system that you could hear *noise* coming out of our room. It was a nightmare to say the least.

It just went on almost in another world where even in that ridiculous state of play within about three months, there was the first parent teacher interview after school. And notes or something was sent home to the parents and I remember saying to the principal, 'If the parents come along to this, you realise that all are going to be of migrant background. We're not going to be able to talk about anything. What are we going to do?' He basically said, 'Well, that's for you to work out.' I came to that interview—and to their credit most of the parents came, of all of these kids. But it was just an absolute farce because they came, they shook my hand fifty thousand times, we smiled and looked at one another and that was it. We could not communicate beyond that point. That is just plain macabre almost, let alone sad. But they all *did*, walked away and I thought, 'What on earth is going on here? This is just beyond, beyond belief.'

***BARBARA KRICKL** (1962) first came to Australia to participate in a year-long cultural youth exchange programme in 1982. She met her future husband during this trip. After returning to Germany in 1983, she decided to migrate to Sydney the following year. In 1992, Barbara's parents joined her and husband Stephen in the south Sydney suburb of Blakehurst. Here, Barbara considers her cultural identity.*

I find myself saying things a certain way because it's *simpler* to say them a certain way, and I will explain this in a minute. Also, because English isn't my native language and I haven't been in the workforce for quite some time now—I stopped when my younger son was two—so I worked for about twelve years or so and went to university before that. So I had a reasonably long time of exposure of talking to people and talking bilingually. *Now* I'm basically not talking to anyone. My father has gone to a nursing home so I don't speak German much anymore either. So it's getting quite difficult to say things in English.

And I cannot argue or speak sometimes—I can speak to my children but I find arguments or emotional things quite difficult to express in English because I didn't learn that language as a young person. I came to English as a fifteen-year-old, fourteen-year-old. Then came here, then did academic English, always talked to adults, talked about issues but that's sort of *other* language that you have to have to get things across. I don't think in German but occasionally now I suddenly know, 'Oh this is exactly how I would say it in my dialect', not even in High German. *In my dialect*. Similarly when the Germans were here last week I suddenly thought, 'Oh I can't say that in German but there's a *perfect* English expression for it.' Now that's a bit of how I really feel, as well.

I say certain things without meaning to put Australia versus Germany or Germany versus Australia but that's how it comes across, at times. It's *dismaying* to me because I don't intend to do that. But I will say things like, 'Oh, they can't even make decent windows or blinds here.' It's easier to say that because it's not 'us' and 'them' but it's the language we've developed in the house for example, because I'm a German—I migrated—my husband's Australian. Sometimes it gets a bit confusing when we say 'we' and 'you' and 'them' and 'us'. But always to say 'Australians', 'Germans' or 'the companies who make blinds here'—so it's much easier to say 'they.'

Now interestingly, when my children were little—and really the blinds did come off and that was really simplistic stuff and thirty years later, there are still no decent insulated windows and you still have to pay a fortune if you want anything else that works better. And I was up there and a thing fell off and I was really frustrated and my son said, 'You know we do make good stuff in Australia' and I said, 'Oh, my goodness!' (laughs) Like, I didn't want it to come across like that. And ever since then it's been—now that they are older they understand—but I thought, 'Oh yeah I have to be', you know. They're just little things but as far as identity goes, it's sort of really *schizophrenic* in a way. Because almost as if I have two different people that I have to adjust to different situations.

***OURANITA KARADIMAS** (1958) was born in New South Wales to parents who had migrated from the Greek island of Ithaka. Her father came to Australia as a child, and her mother arrived intending to marry Ouranita's father. Ouranita's husband John also migrated from Greece to Australia as a youngster. Ouranita considers the family's connection to Greece and the Greek language.*

Frank Heimans: Do the children speak Greek to each other?

They don't speak Greek to each other, no. In fact, all of us—our common language is English. John and I spoke English to each other right from the beginning. When the children were young—before they went to school—we used to speak to them in Greek as did all the other members of the family. Once they started school a lot of the language interaction changed and it was very clearly observed that we spoke more and more English to them as they grew older. So our common language now is English. So there is a generational language shift between the second generation and the third generation. So the family language now is predominantly English with a little bit of Greek every now and again.

I HAVE A REALLY PROBLEMATIC RELATIONSHIP with Greece and with being Greek. I feel very strange going to Greece. I feel even stranger going back to the island that my parents came from, and I've been back there many times. While I want to feel like I belong there, I don't. Nobody sees me as belonging there, nobody *treats* me as though I belong there and that's very obvious. Why? Because I'm from Australia (laughs). Especially when we first started going to Greece—the first few times—I thought, 'Gosh, why, why don't people think I'm one of them?' You know, clearly I was a tourist (laughs). So I don't feel a connection to Greece at all. There is very little about Greece and Greek life that I actually identify with, or like, in many ways. I love the passion and the earnestness and the honesty of

Greek people—those who I have met—but I'm not one of them. For so many years of my life I lived as a person here in Australia always separating myself from other Australians by having that Greek identity tag on me.

Milijana Stojadinovic*'s (1985) parents were born in Yugoslavia. Her maternal grandparents came to Australia at the end of the 1960s, with Milijana's mother in tow as an infant. Milijana's mother met her future husband while holidaying in Serbia and they both moved to Perth, where Milijana was born. Milijana's paternal grandparents also relocated to Australia to be close to the family. She considers how the political conflicts in Yugoslavia, and its later breakup, affected her when she was growing up in Perth, Winton (in Queensland) and Adelaide in the 1990s.*

When I was little I was Yugoslav. And I was never taught any other way. The things that I did and the way that I was—it was just Yugoslav. Then '91, the war broke out in Croatia—the conflict—and then the civil war broke out in Bosnia. When that war broke out, that was when there started being quite severe consequences for me and my family.

Susan Marsden: And what were they?

I remember being made to tell someone, you know, they asked me—it was an adult and I think it was at school—and they said, 'So what are you?' And I said, 'Well I'm Yugoslav. What do you mean?' I didn't know that Croatia and Serbia even existed. They said, 'Well what are you? Are you Serbian or are you Croatian?' And I said, 'Well (sighs), you know, I'm Yugoslav, that's it'. Then I remember going home and saying to my mum, 'What does this mean?' She explained it to me and she said, 'But you're Yugoslav and you just tell people that you're Yugoslav, you don't have to tell them anything else.' *That* was really the point where my family had to choose what they were. I'm not just saying my immediate family—not just my parents and my grandparents but also my aunty and my uncle and that side. That war here and the climate that was in this country at that time made people like my family have to choose to either be Serbian or Croatian—so either to be a bad guy or a good guy—and that was really hard.

Especially when you're both (laughs).

Yeah, exactly. Especially when Yugoslav meant something a lot more than that. As a kid I never knew about that stuff. I didn't understand that that's what existed there.

All of that, I think, ended towards the end of '96 and I was in Year 6 at that stage. I had had a few things said but I was just like, 'Yeah, I'm Yugoslav' and whatever and that was my protection. It wasn't until the bombing of Serbia—the NATO bombing of Serbia in 1999—when I really felt the effects of the *racism*. Not only *me* but my sister and my mum and my dad, and even my grandparents to an extent. I just think that that decade of that ongoing conflict really was a very tense time for all former Yugoslav people in the country. I remember in 1998 when all of that stuff started happening in Serbia in Kosovo, I remember one of my friends saying to me, 'Oh those effin Serbs. They're effin killing everyone over there.' You know, 'They're barbarians and they should all be locked up and put away'. And I was like, 'Well'—I had no idea as a twelve-year-old kid—I was like, 'What the heck is this person talking about?' I just left it at that and then I went home and I told my mum and my mum said, 'Well this is what's happening. There is this conflict. There is this issue and someone's always gonna choose one side of the story to go by.'

Then in 1999 when the bombing happened and when—you probably would have heard about Arkan and how he was arrested and killed.[3] I have one really vivid memory—and I'll never forget this. So this was Year 9 for me. I was walking down

3 Known as Arkan, Željko Ražnatović led a unit known as the Serbian Volunteer Guard (or Arkan's Tigers) who fought during the Yugoslav Wars. His men were accused of ethnic cleansing and he was indicted for war crimes conducted in former Yogoslavia by the UN. He was shot dead in Belgrade in January 2000.

the corridor out of drama class and a boy started running down the corridor and he was saying, 'Arkan is dead! Arkan is dead! Thank God, I hate all Serbians. I hate all Serbian people, Thank God he's dead.' Then he turned around to me and one of my friends was like, 'You know, she's Serbian. Shut up.' And then he's like, 'Oh are you Serbian?' And I said, 'Well yeah, sort of.' And then he's like, 'Well I don't wish you were dead but I wish everyone else was.' And I was just like, 'Oh. Okay. What the hell do I say to that?' I didn't know what to say so I just left it at that. Then I guess I had other experiences just with teachers making comments and just always being made accountable for what had happened over there. I never understood that.

I always felt very guilty. I felt very ashamed of being Serbian because of everything that was said *to* me about those people and about that time. But I shouldn't have been made to feel that way. But as a kid you don't know that, you think that what other people are telling you is the truth. So I just accepted that that was the view of people and I really tried to hide that part of myself. I really *tried* my best to assimilate in the culture, to the point where I didn't even want to speak the language anymore. I really distanced myself from everything that was Serbian. The racism and the discrimination, those experiences have continued on. To this day it still happens. But for me and my family, the first war—that civil war and everything—it was a very terrible time and it was a time where we were *forced* to choose.

***DAVID COOPER** (1959) considers the changing experiences of multiculturalism in Australia.*

My son's best mate at school was a little Asian boy—Chinese he was. Comes to school, can't speak any English and my son took him under his wing and they're best of mates. You've got a little Chinese boy—well Chinese boy with an Aussie accent back then—he's not a boy anymore. And that's normal. They don't see any different to that. He's a person and he's who he is.

There weren't any little Chinese boys when I went to school if you know what I mean. I had one girl in the grade that was Greek. *I* grew up thinking that all Greek people owned fish and chip shops and all Italian people owned fruit shops. That's the world I knew because the kids in my grade—I had one Italian kid and one Greek kid and that's what their parents did. I thought that was their purpose in life, if you know what I mean. It's a bit more complicated than that (laughs).

JAMES FINNEGAN *(1981) was born in Sydney. His parents migrated from Dublin separately around 1969–1970 and met in Australia.*

Roslyn Burge: What does Irishness mean for you?

Family, I think. Yeah. I've always probably identified with Irish more than Australian. I think that's just the way I've been raised. I feel like my parents actually just brought Ireland to Australia. So I've always been Irish (laughs). It's like our house was a little piece of Dublin (laughs).

How did they bring Ireland to Australia?

I think it's because they only left *physically*. So the same way they lived in Ireland, the same culture came with them to Australia and I guess that means the music, and the family togetherness, and the drinking (laughs). It was all still there. Nothing really changed in that respect. They were just in a different place (laughs).

I guess they never really assimilated with Australian culture. My dad probably did more than anyone. He feels very proud to be an Australian. He got his citizenship and he identifies very much with the Australian bush and he's even—much to my dismay—a Liberal (laughs). I remember when growing up, I was sure he was always a Labor supporter, now he swears he wasn't (laughs). But yeah, I don't know. We were just always very Irish. Friends would come over—when I went to school—and they wouldn't be able to understand my parents. They're like, 'What did your mum say?' And it was like, 'What do you *mean,* what did she say? It was very clear!' I never realised how strong their accents were.

Was there any cultural opposition to things Australian?

I guess my mum never really liked Australia Day. She liked to call it Invasion Day. She didn't think it was something to be celebrated. There was a bit of an opposition to, I guess—for lack of a better word—bogan culture. My mum always wanted me to be with someone who was Irish (laughs).

JAMES MAYOL *(1974) was born in Aweil in north-west South Sudan. In 1983, the Second Sudanese Civil War between the Sudanese government and the Sudan People's Liberation Movement/Army (SPLM/SPLA) began. In 1986, militias kidnapped James and sold him as a slave. He escaped around 1988 but couldn't return to South Sudan because of the ongoing war so he joined the military garrison. After completing his training, he escaped from the army and became involved in political movements that were connected to the SPLA. In early 2000, James was in Eritrea. He was about to represent the country as a sprinter in the Olympic Games, which would have given him access to Eritrean travel documents, but these plans fell through.*

We moved—I and John Garang[4]—we come to Egypt together. We come to Egypt on day 12 of May 2000. Then from there he started telling me, 'You are a very brilliant boy. You need to have education. So people like you, in future you will be something.' But I didn't want to become educated. I just find myself—I'm okay. Changing the government, maybe everything will be good. That's what my limit. But he wanted me to go to

4 John Garang was a Sudanese leader and politician who led the SPLA during the Second Sudanese Civil War. Garang briefly served as the new South Sudanese government's First Vice President in 2005, but died shortly after his appointment.

school. And I felt like this guy maybe doesn't want me but in contrary he wanted me to be educated. So when I come to Egypt, he told me to go and stay with the SPLM chapter and then 'I will come back to you soon'. Then he never come back to me. I was in Egypt for almost a year. I was able to contact him. He sent me a letter and he said, 'Take this letter to any human rights office.' I took the letter to human right office and they gave a reference to UN. They said, 'Take this reference to UN Office or Australian Embassy. Whatever you will choose.' I took the letter to Australian Embassy. Then they accepted me to come to Australia.

Atem Atem: So what was in the letter?

The letter actually just stated that I was a victim in the old Sudan government. And if I returned I would be killed. So it just—combination of words like that. And then 'I would like to see a solution for this young man to go and study.' So that's how I got accepted to come here.

So what year did you come to Australia?

I come in 2003.

SO REALLY YOUR COMING TO AUSTRALIA WAS, from the word go, about education?

Yes. It was just because I have good reputation that they, first, are very good people. Secondly, they have a good system of education. That reputation drove me to come to Australia. While America in that time, they have a bad reputation that there's too much crime in America and too much headaches. That has impact on where to choose and where not to choose. So some people they just choosing to go to America just because they know that America is a strong country. But finally, they go to opposite side. They went there, they struggle in life. They have to pay for their education. They have to struggle to be there in America, otherwise you will be homeless. Later on when I met them ten years later—they can see a difference in me. You see? Now I can write, I can read, I can talk. Some of my friends who left to America and they just went to job because it's on the way. American system, you need to become independent and work.

And if you want to get education you have to pay for it.

You have to pay for it. You want to go to medical, you have to pay for it. When I met them there, they still very horrible. They still can't speak well. They still have trouble with writing. Maybe speaking is okay, but sometimes have trouble with writing and reading.

Now, if I see my government in South Sudan, the majority of people working in government, they're all coming from Australia. Because they come with qualifications and they come with a system of working in a government to provide support and a positive approach.

MULTICULTURAL IS A WORD that we are promoting in Australian society for everybody to see that we are a multi-culture. If you come and you speak whatever you language, we treat you as it is. We provide you with a translator. If you come with your language and cultural background, we accept it. We don't say, 'Don't follow on your culture'. We can say, 'Yes, your culture is acceptable.' As soon [long] as your culture doesn't have anything that will affect Australian lives, okay.

But if I tell them now, 'Can you open a school in a Dinka language? Open a centre for me so that I can practise my cultural issues?' Then you're going to get now some obstacles on how you're going to say what are Australia's rules for education. 'We have English as a language. And now you want to impose that language to become second? *No.*' So we have to go back and study about what you say. If you want to open any organisation or any association you need to have Australian models of constitutions. So all these things now you're going to come to deal with, and find out what Australia is (laughs).

But this you need to find it maybe in your first few years—Australia's a multi-culture. But go to street and say, 'Chi Bak' [spoken in Dinka, translates to 'good morning' or 'how is your morning'] in your language—nobody will answer that. Even some people when you go and say, 'How are you?' they don't know English and they live in Australia. Probably, that's what they mean. And that meaning: yes, we can accept Australia is a multi-culture society because we accepted different cultures to come in. Different people from Chinese, from everywhere, to come in and become part of Australia. But in Australia we have a system. We have a system that we have to follow. You see? English is number *one* if you want to work in an Australia institution. It's number one.

Further Listening on Migrants

Bert Castellari, 1923, http://www.nla.gov.au/amad/nla.oh-vn6252044/0-1517
Doug Fong, 1938, http://nla.gov.au/nla.obj-219960559/listen/0-1376
Greer Bland, 1944, http://www.nla.gov.au/amad/nla.oh-vn5972533/1-30
Gina Polito, 1954, http://www.nla.gov.au/amad/nla.oh-vn6421369/2-1870
Michelle Cripps, 1960, http://nla.gov.au/nla.obj-219910905/listen/0-854
Phil May, 1962, http://www.nla.gov.au/amad/nla.oh-vn6569680/2-6063
Adam Farrow-Palmer, 1988, http://nla.gov.au/nla.obj-219982656/listen/0-2146
Gemma Nourse, 1989, http://nla.gov.au/nla.obj-220049717/listen/2-1069

Further Reading on Migrants

Andreoni, Helen, 'Olive or White? The Colour of Italians in Australia', *Journal of Australian Studies* 27, no. 77 (2003), pp. 81–92.

Damousi, Joy, *Memory and Migration in the Shadow of War: Australia's Greek Immigrants after World War II and the Greek Civil War* (Cambridge: Cambridge University Press, 2015).

Haebich, Anna, *Spinning the Dream: Assimilation in Australia, 1950–1970* (North Fremantle: Fremantle Press, 2008).

Hammerton, A. James and Thomson, Alistair, *Ten Pound Poms: Australia's Invisible Migrants* (Manchester: Manchester University Press, 2005).

Jupp, James, *The English in Australia* (Melbourne: Cambridge University Press, 2004).

Jupp, James, *From White Australia to Woomera: The Story of Australian Immigration* (Melbourne: Cambridge University Press, 2002).
Lack, John and Templeton, Jacqueline (eds), *Bold Experiment: A Documentary History of Australian Immigration Since 1945* (Melbourne: Oxford University Press, 1995).
Markus, Andrew, Jupp, James and McDonald, Peter, *Australia's Immigration Revolution* (Crows Nest: Allen & Unwin, 2009).
Markus, Andrew, 'Everybody Become a Job: Twentieth Century Immigrants', in Verity Burgmann and Jenny Lee (eds), *A Most Valuable Acquisition: A People's History of Australia since 1788* (Melbourne: McPhee Gribble/Penguin, 1988), pp. 87–105.
McMaster, Don, *Asylum Seekers: Australia's Response to Refugees* (Melbourne: Melbourne University Press, 2001).
Neumann, Klaus, *Across the Seas: Australia's Response to Refugees: A History* (Melbourne: Black Inc., 2015).
O'Hanlon, Seamus and Stevens, Rachel, 'A Nation of Immigrants or a Nation of Immigrant Cities?: The Urban Context of Australian Multiculturalism, 1947–2011, *Australian Journal of Politics and History*, forthcoming 2017.
Ricatti, Francesco, 'Elodia and Franca: Oral Histories of Migration and Hope', *History Australia* 7, no. 2 (August 2010), pp. 33.1–33.23.
Richards, Eric, *Destination Australia: Migration to Australia Since 1901* (Sydney: University of New South Wales Press, 2008).
Tan, Carole 'Living with 'Difference': Growing Up Chinese in White Australia', *Journal of Australian Studies* 27, no. 77 (2003), pp. 101–108.
Tavan, Gwenda, *The Long, Slow Death of White Australia* (Melbourne: Scribe, 2005).
Thomson, Alistair, *Moving Stories: An Intimate History of Four Women Across Two Countries* (Sydney: University of New South Wales Press, 2011).

CHAPTER 6

MIDLIFE

In midlife, adults create homes and families, whilst also breaking up, moving on and starting new relationships. Many become parents and raise children (who transform into teenagers), then reconsider life after the nest empties, while often still caring for ageing parents and dealing with the ill-health or death of loved ones. Careers are established, progressed or lost as the world of work changes around us, and new learning by mature students sometimes leads in unexpected directions. The circumstances and expectations of midlife also change across time. Our oldest narrators entered midlife in the 1940s and '50s, and their experience of this life phase is markedly different to that of younger Australians who are starting families and developing working lives in the 2000s.

The dream of owning one's own home has animated Australian men and women across all the postwar generations, though the opportunities for home ownership have varied across time and social class, as we see in the first section about 'Making homes'. The immediate postwar home buyers and builders were driven by memories of shabby, insecure rental housing during the battling 1930s, and then frustrated by the acute shortage of building material and available homes in the decade after the war. Ginette Matalon recalls that home ownership was 'the dream of all Australians in those days'. For refugees and migrants escaping European conflict and austerity that dream was especially potent. Ginette and her husband secured a block of Crown-release land on Sydney's north shore in the early 1960s, wanting to avoid the more crowded older housing of the eastern suburbs. 'Buying part of Australia' was 'our dream'.

For most Australians, buying a house has never been easy, but across the postwar decades the shifting ratio of average wages, house prices and interest rates has changed the equation of home ownership. In the early 1980s David Cooper could afford an outer-suburban Melbourne house on a single man's paramedic wage and savings. As interest rates shot up in the 1980s, Rhonda King and her panel-beater husband bought a house in the northern outer-suburbs of Brisbane, but on a single wage, with Rhonda at home with two small children, 'it was just survival'. By the 2000s, young Australians were struggling to join the housing market. Milijana Stojadinovic and her partner lived with Milijana's parents for two years while working and 'saving like maniacs' to buy their Adelaide home. The prospect of home ownership, or even secure, good quality rental accommodation, is increasingly remote for many young Australian families.

Negotiating married life across decades of changing personal circumstances and social expectations is sometimes a joy and always a challenge. Our narrators managed this negotiation more or less successfully, as we discover in 'Intimate relations'. Married in 1947 and now a widower, Bert Castellari explains that a long, happy marriage is based on an 'equal and complementary' relationship; indeed, in 1969 Bert moved from Melbourne so that his wife could study in Canberra and develop her own public service career. When Ouranita Karadimas and her future husband met as adolescents in the mid-1970s they were 'as experienced and clueless as each other', yet despite their different interests and characters 'somehow we managed to work together' and balance each other's needs. When Ginette Matalon's husband Ralph died after twenty-five years of marriage she 'missed him as a companion in life, very, very badly'. Other long term relationships survive serious challenges. In the mid-2000s Jay Logan was 'an absolute pig' to his partner when he was 'on the turps'. He realised he was close to repeating the abusive behaviour of his father, and was scaring the person who loved him 'most in the world'. Jay determined to change his behaviour as a starting point for marriage in 2009 and then raising his own family in a better way.

Married life does not always work out, and women in particular recall its tensions and failures. Veronica Schwarz met her German husband while travelling in Europe in the mid-1960s. They started married life in Canada, and though they enjoyed the adventure of travel the marriage was 'a disaster'. Veronica's husband suffered from mental illness, he tried to isolate her from friends and then became violently abusive. They moved to Australia in 1970 and Veronica ended the marriage. After two decades of marriage, in which she followed her husband's retail career around Australia and raised their three children, Trish Barrkman discovered he was having an affair. Trish got out of the marriage with the house and car but had little money and no obvious work prospects after years out of the workforce. In mid-1970s Brisbane, as she soon discovered, society still frowned on divorced women and was not supportive of single mothers and their 'latchkey' children.

As social attitudes about marriage and sexuality shifted in the latter decades of the twentieth century, some men and women embarked on new types of relationships. As a young man in the 1950s, Donald Grey-Smith had repressed his homosexuality, and in the 1960s he established a successful family life and career as an Anglican clergyman in South Australia. In the late 1970s, as the gay community became more outspoken and his church began to consider 'the matter of homosexuality', Donald made the difficult personal and theological decision to accept his sexuality and acknowledge the value of intimate relations with men, while still maintaining his married life. After Alison Fettell separated from her husband in the early 1980s, and while she was still raising their three children in Sydney's west, she discovered to her surprise that she preferred sexual intimacy with women and decided to 'jump the fence'.

For gay *and* straight men and women who are single in midlife and searching for intimacy, there are new ways of creating relationships and ongoing issues about commitment. Now in his thirties, James Finnegan describes online dating in the 2000s and the impact on gay men of the smartphone app Grindr. At the same age, Kirsty Wallett has been 'anti-marriage' for most of her young life because of the 'ridiculous expectations' about love and romance in popular culture. Australian marriage rates have declined since the 1950s, though the rate of decline has slowed in recent years. Despite their reservations, Kirsty and her partner do plan to marry because they see value in a formal commitment. 'We're not doing it in a traditional way but there is a tiny part of both of us that is traditional in the sense of family.'

In 'Maternity and childbirth' our narrators explain how having babies has changed over the past seventy years. When Ruth Apps' first child was born with 'multiple malformations' in 1949 there had been no ultrasound to pick up defects in utero, and there was little that medical science could do to help. When baby Elizabeth died after twenty-two days she was buried in a hospital cemetery to which the parents had no access, and instead of support for the grieving young couple there was family recrimination about fault. Just over a decade later, Trish Barrkman recalls a medical catastrophe and how she narrowly avoided the drug for morning sickness that caused deformed 'thalidomide' babies. In 1989, Bronwyn Macdonald was appalled that medical practitioners took five months to diagnose the intellectual and physical disabilities that she had noticed in her baby almost from birth. By contrast, in the late 1990s in vitro fertilisation (IVF) enabled Phil May and his partner to have children, and then two months of intensive hospital care ensured the survival and well-being of their triplets. In the early 2000s recently-retired Sydney teacher James Box donated sperm to both members of a lesbian couple so they could start a family in which each would be a mother and James an occasional father. Their modern type of family showcases dramatic social changes in parenting and current ethical debates posed by emerging scientific ways of creating babies.

Parents' experience of childbirth has also changed, perhaps most obviously for fathers, who were not often present at childbirth until the 1980s. Most importantly, under pressure from community organisations and childbirth educators, health practitioners have increasingly focused not just on the health of the baby but also on the positive experience of the mother and the bond between parent and child. After the humiliating and 'horrendous' birth of her first child in the early 1970s, Alison Fettell finally enjoyed 'the perfect birthing moment' when her third child was born a decade later. After the arrival of that third child Alison suffered debilitating postnatal depression, but unlike an earlier generation of women that suffered in silence she was directed to support that 'saved my life'.

In 'Family life' our narrators recall continuity and change in parenting. Throughout the twentieth century Australian women took primary responsibility for raising children, and despite moves towards wage equality, improved childcare options and both maternity and (more limited) paternity leave, in most twenty-first century families that is still the case. Ruth Apps was unusual in the 1950s when she returned to full-time work as soon as her children were at school, though her experience as a working mother became more common later in the century. Like Ruth, Ginette Matalon recalls the domestic and workplace challenges faced by mothers who opted to work outside the home. By choice or necessity, many migrant women like Ginette wanted to work so they could contribute to buying a home as soon as possible. Ginette expected her mother to care for the new baby in 1961, but when her mother died just after the birth, and limited childcare options proved inadequate, she stayed at home. Following the introduction of childcare subsidies by the Federal Labor government in 1972, Ginette recalled her earlier difficulties and broke with family tradition to become a Labor supporter.

Not all women have wanted to be a mother, and some have had no choice because of infertility or circumstance. In the 1990s Kim Bear was worried that she would turn out like her own mother and not be a good parent, and despite a period in her mid-thirties when she 'bawled her eyes out' at the sight of a pram, she decided that motherhood was not for her. In the latter decades of the twentieth century, as women's educational and career opportunities improved, an increasing number of women did not bear children. Where two parents were present in a family, they were more likely to both be working. Working women especially struggled to balance career and family. When she was interviewed in 2013, thirty-five-year-old Kirsty Wallett had a successful career in social media and was soon to marry. Though she would be 'devastated' if she could not have children she agonised about the impact of childcare on her career. 'I want to have a family but I don't want to give up my freedom.'

For much of the twentieth century most married mothers assumed that their husbands would work full time as primary breadwinners, and that fathers would only have a limited role in childcare and other domestic work. Given the difficult economic conditions of the first half of the century, and the disparity between men's and women's wages, a dependable male breadwinner was essential for family well-being. Leo Cripps learnt that lesson in Hobart in the early 1950s when his wife threatened to walk out with their child because of his regular drinking after work. Leo realised that he 'had a job to do to look after the family' and decided to stop boozing with his workmates. Fred Henskens' wife had separated from her drunkard, gambling first husband. By contrast, hard-working Fred proved to be a reliable and much-loved step-father to Helen's three children. In the mid-1970s Donat Santowiak was 'elated' when his first daughter was born, but Donat's dysfunctional upbringing had not prepared him for fatherhood and his drinking impacted on family life. After five years Donat's wife left with their child and found another partner and parent. An addictive mother might also destroy family life. After two decades of drug and alcohol abuse, Lynne Sanders-Braithwaite realised that she needed to leave her two small children with relatives so she could go away and sober up.

In the latter decades of the twentieth century some fathers sought a greater role in child care. In the mid-1980s Melbourne paramedic David Cooper wanted to be more hands-on with his children than his own father had been. Shift work helped, and David was able to take the children to and from school. But though the contact with his children was 'ten times more' than that of men from his father's generation, David also realised that in other domestic work 'we might not have moved as much as what the average woman would like'. Twenty-first century surveys confirm that women still do most of the work in the family home, despite the fact that in recent decades a small minority of men have been primary carers for their children. Russell Elliott was one such pioneer house-husband after he suffered ill-health and was superannuated out of teaching. In 1992 Russell agreed that his wife Mary, who had been raising their young children, would return to her work as a teacher while he stayed home with the kids. Russell found the kindergarten run 'interesting', and his relationship with his children deepened. A few years later Russell was a sole parent after Mary died from cancer.

Though children are less likely to lose a parent and parents are much less likely to lose a child than they were at the start of the twentieth century, illness, disability and death can still rock family foundations. In Michelle Cripps' own battle with cancer in the mid-2000s, her immediate and extended family, as well as workmates and friends, were 'really, really critical' to recovery. A few years earlier, Peter Galvin, not long turned fifty, the father of two teenagers and at the peak of a trade union and public service career, suffered a stroke and was forced to stop work and slowly rebuild his body and his life. Bronwyn Macdonald describes the tremendous effort of caring for a severely disabled son and battling for improved government support, and Phil May explains some of the challenges of living with an autistic teenager—as well as the modern parent's anxiety about managing their children's internet access. Ian Reid ponders the profound impact of the death of his elderly mother and concludes that he 'didn't expect it to feel quite so lonely'. Rhonda King recalls a different kind of family loss when the eldest of her four children left home in the 1990s. Though thrilled with her daughter's adventurous new life, Rhonda's feelings of loss were 'all there, knotting around inside your heart'.

'Working lives and transformations' focuses on changes in the experience of work across the past century. Ruth Apps identifies perhaps the most dramatic transformation, the increased rates of married women's participation in the workforce. In the 1950s Ruth was something of a pioneer as she battled discrimination and argued for equal pay, and though she felt guilty about leaving her children to fend for themselves after school while she was at work, she 'didn't feel guilty enough to give it up'. In 1973 Veronica Schwarz left school-teaching for new opportunities and enrolled as a mature student at the University of Melbourne. Before fees were abolished in 1974 she funded her study as a part-time taxi driver, despite the prejudice of male drivers who did not believe a woman could put petrol in a car. Amongst her fellow students were scores of older women who had left high school early, 'got married, had children, looked after their families' but 'had not looked after their *own* education' until now.

Sometimes re-education was forced upon older workers. Just as her children were leaving home in the early 1980s, Connie Shaw was in a car accident that ended her career as a nurse. Connie's husband left because 'he couldn't cope with the fact I couldn't do everything'. Connie was broke and miserable, until she enrolled in a degree in community studies that led to a passion for computers and a new paid and volunteer career using computers for social care and community development. When computer-aided drawing was introduced at the State Electricity Commission in the mid-1980s, Donat Santowiak hated the move from hand design to mouse, keyboard and screen, and shifted sideways into training and human resources. Here he witnessed what he called 'the holocaust' of privatisation and redundancy from the late 1980s, with grown men in tears or suicidal as they contemplated life without secure employment.

The experience of Connie Shaw and Donat Santowiak testifies to the impact of computerisation and other new technologies in the Australian workforce. Greer Bland was working with the air force in Gippsland in the mid-1960s when she encountered a giant teleprinter that was linked to a bank of computers in Melbourne. It took up a wall forty foot long and eight foot high and 'you'd swear blind' that the machine was 'jumping up and down and smoking'. One person's excitement was another person's deskilling. Kim Bear loved her work with an evolving range of computing technologies, but she also witnessed their impact on 'terrified' hot metal master typesetters in the printing industry who were expected to adapt overnight to new computers. Kim recalls that from the late 1970s and through the 1980s an older generation of workers, with all their experience, 'vanished' from the workforce and was replaced by youngsters who could 'get stuff out of the computer'.

Other workers describe how digital and online technologies have transformed the pace and expectations of work. Construction manager Christian Bow explains how 'the old guy with the pencil' is long gone. Modern businesses expect rapid turnarounds by 24/7 workers now that information is 'all on our phone, it's all on our watch, it's all inserted in our brain'. Like many contemporary workers (and not unlike interwar employees who worked long weekdays plus Saturdays), Christian wants to 'slow down a bit' and spend more time on the beach and mucking around with the kids. At the other extreme, more and more work is casual and part-time, often to the disadvantage of workers and their rights. The ideal of a job for life is now rarely an option. For some, like young Sydney television producer Adam Farrow-Palmer, it's 'pretty fun' to move around 'whole new worlds' of work. Others born in the 1980s, like social media professional Kirsty Wallett in Brisbane, highlight the insecurity that comes with this freedom, and how economic changes boost some industries while upending others. The flexible career can be a risky proposal, perhaps especially for young women hoping to start a family.

The final section of this chapter shows how midlife Australians still manage to have 'Fun!' in myriad ways, whether through fishing trips or bike-riding, playing in a band or amateur drama, as football fans or online gamers. Such pastimes might offer blissful solitude or a precious connection with friends, family or even household pets; they might focus on personal development and pleasure or involve volunteering at junior sports clubs and community associations. Sometimes these pleasures are transformative, for the fisherman or woman who reconnects to nature, the performer who rediscovers their voice, or the parent stuck at home who makes connections through new communication technologies.

Making Homes

***TRISH BARRKMAN** (1933) recalls the postwar housing shortage when she moved from Gippsland to work for Coles in Melbourne during the early 1950s.*

After the war, housing was a *huge*, huge problem. When I first went to live in Melbourne, accommodation for *everybody*, for young married people, for men coming back from the war, it was just so difficult. I was fortunate enough that I had people that I boarded with. Freedom still wasn't a big thing 'cause you were living with other people and, virtually in many cases, you felt I guess the need to be home reasonably early, to conform to the way of life of the people you are living with. But for many people in that time they would have just, they'd live in one room in a home. Even married couples often rented just one room.

I lived in Melbourne for approximately eight years. There was a lot of sub-letting going on in flats and houses and highly illegal as far as the landlord was concerned, and I remember one time we shared a flat with a lady. She had a bed-sitter. We had a bedroom and a lounge room and both parties shared the kitchen and Dorothy, the lady that rented the flat, she would have her dinner at a certain time so we could use the --- That sort of thing was all over Australia. It was going on all over Australia. It was so difficult. People used to pay key money to rent houses. I remember this because this house that my father had bought, straight after the war, he would advertise that for rent and there'd be *queues* of people lining up. And it was often the person that had the most money that got the house.

After arriving in Sydney via Paris from Egypt in 1958, ***GINETTE MATALON*** *(1936) married another Egyptian Jewish refugee and lived in rented accommodation until they could afford to buy their own home.*

My second son Steve was born in October '62. At that time we had already purchased—it was our dream, my husband and I—of buying a part of Australia. Which was the dream of all Australians in those days. So we started looking, and my husband didn't like the old homes of the eastern suburbs. He really had an aversion for the eastern suburbs and all this living almost next door to you. He loved the North Shore.

There was at the time a lot of Crown release land. So when we started looking at land to build our dream house, we went to a neighbourhood called Beacon Hill—not Jewish at all—and they were releasing blocks. We bought a block of land. My first outing after my second son was born, my first outing out of the hospital to go home, was to have a look at the pegs which had been put in on the block where the foundations of our home would be. And this was at Beacon Hill. The whole neighbourhood had three houses. That was it—at the time. Then it filled up. And people had bought like us blocks of land and when they could get a loan to build then they would start building. And we stayed in this area for seventeen years.

OURANITA KARADIMAS *(1958), daughter of Greek migrants living in Sydney, married when she was twenty in the late 1970s. For the young married couple, buying a house was a top priority.*

My siblings and I were so determined that what happened to my parents would *never ever* happen to us. It goes back to the blithe statement that my father used to make when my mother used to say to him, 'Peter, it's really time we bought a little house as well.' And my father would go, 'Well, why do you want one of those for? We can get one of those anytime.' My mother regrets that just so much because in retrospect if they had have had their own little roof over their head, they would not have spent forty years with the domineering aunt. My mother still doesn't own a house. She lives with us now. So my parents did not ever own a home and my father never really considered that a big issue because he eschewed those who aspired to property.

So from very young, we children were not going to be like that (laughs). And my husband, coming from a peasant agrarian family who were subsistence farmers who owned *nothing*, that was even more urgent because he had actually lived in poverty, where they used to receive Red Cross packages in the late '50s and early '60s in the part of Greece where he lived.

WE COULD GET BY with just my husband working, but it was *just* get by. It made life much easier for us when both of us worked because then we were able to save up enough to pay off—that's what's extraordinary now—in Sydney, to pay off our house. Our house cost $42,000 in (laughs) 1981 and now it's valued at, let's say, $550,000 or $600,000. And that's a very average price for a house in our area now. So my son now has to pay half a million dollars for a cute little house in the western suburbs of Sydney near where we live.

Frank Heimans: Do you see him being able to do that?

Yep, because banks are likely to *lend* a lot more than they were. We could no way borrow the sort of amount that you can borrow today from banks. We had to have a thirty per cent deposit and that took a whole lot of doing to get that thirty per cent deposit and then we could borrow the rest. So we got this *massive*, for us, $25,000 loan (laughs) and we had *no* idea how we were going to pay that off. But it got paid off. I tell you what's astonishing, it got paid off in one year. In 1982 I made a decision to go back to work full time, because we worked out that if I went back to work full time we could *wipe out* our mortgage in one year, and you could. We owed $17,000 at the time and that's what my earnings were going to be. And in one year we could wipe out our mortgage.

Nobody that I know of my son's generation is going to be able to earn four hundred odd thousand dollars in a year—or his wife, his partner—yep, four hundred thousand odd dollars a year to wipe out their mortgage in one year, no.

DAVID COOPER *(1959) recalls beginning to save for a house as a young teenager with earnings from part-time jobs in shops, factories and pubs, and then raising sufficient funds within a few years of beginning an ambulance cadetship aged sixteen.*

I started with the ambulance service and living at home. So I was saving with a plan to buy a house. I wanted to make sure I got my house.

Alistair Thomson: Where did that plan come from, from such an early age?

I think that came from my dad, and my mum. My dad's whole ambition—he grew up in rental accommodation and having to shift all the time—from a young age the two things I was taught was join superannuation the day you start work because you're going to need it, and make sure you own your home by the time you retire because once you own a home, it doesn't matter what happens, no one can take it off you. That was it really I think. That just made sense.

I had $10,000, which was from working. Bought a house for $43,000, so I borrowed the thirty and been poor ever since. I just bought this brick veneer house and re-tiled it and fixed it up a bit, and I would have only lived there for six months probably, or a year maybe at the most, before I got married and then my wife came into the home with me.

Her parents wouldn't have minded if we'd lived together but it wasn't something that either of us wanted to do. And I thought, oh, that was my big adventure, like cooking for myself and all that sort of stuff. I didn't want to go straight from home, with mum doing all my meals, straight to a wife. Token gesture really, because that's what happened. My wife ends up doing all the cooking but it was just something that I wanted to do. In fact I remember buying TattsLotto tickets and thinking, 'Gee I hope I don't win this year because I want to get my house before I win.' I didn't realise that you didn't have to wish that you didn't win TattsLotto because it doesn't happen anyway, but (laughs).

Twenty-one-year-old ***RHONDA KING*** *(1965) had a toddler and was pregnant with her second child in the mid-1980s when she and her panel-beater husband moved from Canberra and bought a house in Deception Bay on the northern outskirts of Brisbane.*

Mary Hutchison: Just tell me about being a mother. You talked about being the earth mother and so on. Did that stay as your ideal for being a mother?

Well it did stay as my ideal, whether or not it got put into practice is another thing (laughs). I mean it still is my ideal of a way to live but, I don't know, life gets in the way of all those things. I tried to, you know, *be* that kind of a person but living on a single income, with a mortgage, in a time when the interest rates on housing loans was like seventeen per cent or something, it was really, really hard to be earth anything (laughs). It was just survival. Just trying to make sure there was food on the table each night and that the mortgage payments were paid and that the bills were paid and that the phone wouldn't be cut off. We didn't have the phone for a very long time because we just couldn't afford it. No phone. Can you imagine that? Wow (laughs). No phone, no internet back in those days. No entertainment whatsoever. So it was just me and the girls entertaining ourselves. It was really, really tough. Financially it was really hard.

Milijana Stojadinovic *(1985) and her partner bought their first house in Adelaide.*

I think there have only been three owners in this house and we're the third ones. Now our neighbours across the road have lived there for, well *her* whole life anyway. She remembers the first owners who was, she says, 'A beautiful Polish man'. And he made this house. It's made out of bricks.

Then after that there was a young couple, and they had kids. And then after that was me and Danijel. I think, you know, I really believe—like just going back to spirituality and stuff—like I really believe in energy and I believe in spirits, and I believe that spirit energy is sort of the same thing and I think the man that built this house had a really beautiful energy about him, because this house has such a lovely energy as well. I mean the house is a lovely house in itself, but I think that that's what makes it even nicer, is that it was built with love and kindness and that's what filters through, in the house.

So we bought the house in 2009. We lived with my parents for two years—saving up like maniacs for a deposit. I was working and studying and Danijel was working fulltime.

Having lived in rented accommodation in four different cities in the previous five years, ***GEMMA NOURSE*** *(1989) would like to stay put and have a place of her own.*

I kind of feel a bit homeless at the moment.

Frank Heimans: Are you interested in ever owning your own home or having a mortgage and so on?

I've always said that I don't understand that, until the last year, where I think I've moved house on average once every six months for the last probably five years, just due to circumstance and share house issues and moving cities and all kinds of circumstantial things. Not by choice necessarily, like all the time. But at the moment—having just moved to Sydney and having been in this house for four months now in Newtown, or thereabouts, and moving to Adelaide and all of that—I just feel like it'd be really good to stay put. The concept of having a place of your own that you can set up your life in and not have to move that around all the time has become really appealing. Having had so many experiences with landlords and real estate agents and all of that through renting I think has made me appreciate that a bit more.

Further Listening on Making Homes

Kathleen Golder, 1920, http://nla.gov.au/nla.obj-219908851/listen/4-10
Ruth Apps, 1926, http://www.nla.gov.au/amad/nla.oh-vn6252043/2-5665
Brian Carter, 1931, http://www.nla.gov.au/amad/nla.oh-vn6290887/3-683~3-837
Connie Shaw, 1937, http://nla.gov.au/nla.obj-219992795/listen/2-3381
Lynne Sanders-Braithwaite, 1949, http://www.nla.gov.au/amad/nla.oh-vn6290876/2-2440
Alison Fettell, 1952, http://nla.gov.au/nla.obj-220185705/listen/1-1977
Bronwyn Macdonald, 1964, http://www.nla.gov.au/amad/nla.oh-vn6390885/0-3695
Lisa Jackson, 1972, http://www.nla.gov.au/amad/nla.oh-vn6252067/0-4353

Intimate Relations

***BERT CASTELLARI** (1923) married in Sydney in 1947.*

We were seriously interested in each other. We had a party at my parents' place. They were still living in Randwick then and they'd gone off on a tour and to meet my uncle and his family in Geelong. Gloria came out to that party and I was gonna ask her to marry me. I took her to the laundry so it'd be private (laughs). I told her I was a member of the Communist Party because she should know that. I asked her to marry me. And she said, 'Yes!' Well Gloria was only nineteen when I met her but she wasn't your average nineteen-year-old. For a start she had intellect. And the thing was she grew up in a family of musicians.

IT WAS A HAPPY MARRIAGE. It couldn't have been happier. We rarely in our marriage had a row. We were so well matched. The only two or three times we had a row we couldn't make up quicker. She was a woman of considerable intellect. They recognised that at Angus and Robertson where she worked before she was in the photo studio. She became a copyholder with them at their Halstead Press. She was a reader. She read a lot of books. Copyholder used to check the punctuation and capitals with the proof-reader.

I said to her in the beginning, 'We're equal and complementary'. I was always, had the outlook of equality and I never felt men were superior or having any special qualities. The very fact that men had this great special belief about themselves—it had really contained a great number of men—it stereotyped them and a huge number of men were that stereotype. Hiding an inferiority complex it used to be, what it was. And that was the way a great number of men were in Australia then.

I think we developed each other. She's been used to go into gatherings of musos, and musos generally had a different intellect and mostly they were interested outside their craft. So right from the beginning we had an understanding. We never had any problems. We told each other everything.

We were like a lot of young couples then. The family began without planning despite what we thought was reliable contraception. But I thought later, we raised our kids while we were young and still developing.

Matthew Higgins: What sort of contraception did you use?

I've forgot what they're called. It involved a tablet. We never used a rubber.

But obviously the tablet didn't work.

Not until we had three kids and looked like being in danger of more. She went to Doctor Weintraub, who's a doctor in Dulwich Hill. He fitted a diaphragm and we never had any trouble after that (laughs). We were quite happy to have the kids. We didn't want to abort them. So the first was born twelve months after the marriage, then three years and then two years. So we were pretty young people with not much experience of the world with three very young children.

After working with Qantas in New Guinea in the mid-1950s, ***DONALD GREY-SMITH*** *(1931) studied theology with the Anglican Society of the Sacred Mission in South Australia and was ordained in 1965 (he did not take a vow of celibacy like 'professed' members of the Society who continued to live in a religious community). In 1964 Donald married Else, a German national he had met in New Guinea where she had been working with a Lutheran mission.*

Eventually, when it was quite clear that I was not going to be joining the Society, I got permission to renew the correspondence with Else. We started to talk about the possibility of marriage. So when I graduated from St Michael's I went up to New Guinea. Actually it's just fifty—Else reminded me—it's just fifty years ago. I arrived in Lae on Advent Sunday and I was met by the son of one of the New Guinean pastors who was at school in Brisbane but who was home for the holidays. Actually Else *met* me at the airport, but because the custom was that women sat on one side of the church and men sat on the other side, Bartholomi sat beside me and translated the service for me.

So I spent that summer holiday as a guest of the Lutheran mission. Else was still working during December, so I acted as her chauffeur and drove her around to the various meetings and things that she was involved in. It was while we were there that I told Else about my sexuality. At that stage I really genuinely believed that that was probably all behind me. My experience as a theological student had convinced me that my sexuality was unacceptable, to God, and so I set about repressing it, and I was very successful at repressing it. I confidently believed that that was all in the past and that Else and I would have a fulfilling life together. Else was disappointed to hear such news. She'd had no experience—even though she's one of eleven children—she'd never had any close contact with such a phenomenon. She didn't understand. She was hurt in some ways by it but --- being the person she is, she accepted the reality. I suppose I can't speak for her, but set that into a much wider context of shared values and shared vision, I suppose.

While travelling in Europe in the mid-1960s, **VERONICA SCHWARZ** *(1939) met a young German man and rather reluctantly agreed to migrate with him to Canada, where they married in Toronto.*

Oh, the marriage was a disaster. I'm not good at it, am I (laughs)? He turned out to have some sort of personality disorder which in those days was called neurosis. We'd have a great time. We both loved travel and all the other things I've told you. And when it was good it was very, very good. Then he would get these depressions. This is when I became *very* interested in psychology, because I started reading books trying to understand what was going on.

Katie Holmes: What started to happen for you? You're twenty-five, six, when you marry?

Twenty-five. Yes. Well, sex was a surprise, it wasn't all that much fun. Just seemed to be mainly about the man and what he did and when he was finished. So I thought there was something wrong with me—that was one aspect of it.

Had you thought that would be different?

M'mm. Well the people I'd had sex with before it was much the same as well so it's hard to know at what point I thought it should be different. I just began to think there was something wrong with me—there isn't—I didn't have orgasms. And I now know that many women don't. Particularly just through penis-in-vagina sex—doesn't always do it. Anyway, nothing changed about that so ---

Could you talk about that with him?

No. Again, because I thought it was my fault and he was very experienced at sex. He'd told me he had lots of sex with lots of women but obviously hadn't noticed that maybe he wasn't doing enough (laughs). Also, I think most of us know that a man's ego's very fragile and we try not to go there. Yep.

He would have these moods where he would start becoming depressed. He would start becoming paranoid. I did notice that he didn't have any friends and he didn't like me to have any. He did like to keep us isolated, which a lot of reading I've done now shows up in abusive relationships as the way the abuser first *isolates* the other.

Then there were times when he was violent. End up with a black eye. One time he strangled me and I couldn't speak for days and another time he pushed me down the stairs and I sprained the ankle. I left him a couple of times. Again it was difficult in a strange country where I had no friends and no relatives. As I said, he managed to keep it that way. He would persuade me that he would change and I would go back.

But when it was good—as I said—it was very, very good and we travelled a lot and we travelled all over most of Canada and the United States. We had a great time when it was good.

So what was the balance between good and bad? How often was it good?

Three times good to one time bad.

***TRISH BARRKMAN** (1933) married in 1958 and lived in several different states with her husband and three children.*

In 1972 we moved to Queensland. My husband had left Woolworths and he had been offered a position up here and was very keen to come. I did not want to come to Queensland. I'd been here once on a holiday and I didn't like it and I didn't want to come. There was nothing about Queensland that I liked.

But suddenly I found myself in Queensland. We came in January and we moved into this present house that I'm in today and I honestly felt that I'd gone backwards in my life. I hadn't gone forward. I'd gone backwards thirty-odd years. From Sydney to Brisbane in early '70s was a huge shock to my system. I *never ever* really settled in and two years later I was separated and looking at divorce. Divorce in this country at that time was either two-year separation—desertion I think it was called, it had to be two years—or it could be done through adultery. Adultery meant that you had to raid the purse and get a photograph of them sleeping together and you could then get a divorce.

There was a lot of discussion going on in society. By this time the Labor Party had come into power and there was a lot of discussion going on about changing the law. I had instigated the separation. I couldn't handle what was happening in my marriage any more. I saw a solicitor who said, 'Right, we'll get this divorce on adultery.' I refused. I was not going to get a divorce with private detectives and all that. It was *horrible*. It was absolutely *horrible* what they expected people to do. So I opted for the two-year separation and then suddenly somebody came up with 'confessed adultery'. Oh right. Anyway, I got divorced on confessed adultery.

Hamish Sewell: Who confessed?

My husband (laughs). I wasn't one to confessing to adultery.

And he willingly confessed?

Well, as it turned out, he had to get his new mistress/lover/partner/whatever to sign a form to say that she'd committed adultery. I thought all this had been done until just three or four weeks before the court case was due in court. And no, nobody had signed anything and here I was confronted with going into court with no confessed adultery. So we had to find someone. It was horrible, absolutely *horrible*.

Was he a willing partner in this divorce?

He always said he didn't want it to come to that. But he was living with this other woman. So --- He could have got it all sorted very quickly. But anyway, I had to find someone that knew and could stand up in a courtroom and state the facts. I did, and they stated the facts. So I got divorced, I think it was the fifteenth of May or somewhere about that, '74, and here I was with three children. The house was in both our names at the time but a big mortgage was on it. The house was transferred into my name. I'd never owned a motorcar. We had an old motorcar and that was transferred into my name. I think it cost about five dollars. I had no prospect of a job. I had very little money but I had three children and a lovely old house and no family. Wasn't easy. But somehow or other, I ended up, I went out, I found work. But being a divorced woman in Brisbane, in Clayfield, at that time, *well* (sighs), oh dear. Society really frowned on divorce.

South Australian Anglican clergyman **DONALD GREY-SMITH** *(1931) recalls how he reconnected to his homosexuality in the late 1970s.*

1978 was a very important year. It was the year when I discovered the gay press, the newspaper campaign which was being published in Adelaide, and that put me in touch with things that were happening in the gay community. It was also the year when the Lambeth Conference met in England. The Lambeth Conference being bishops of the Anglican Communion coming together as they do every ten years to discuss various issues. And the matter of homosexuality had come up. They had suggested that the time had come for the church to discuss this issue from a theological perspective. I heard Archbishop Keith Rayner who had come back from Lambeth talking about the Lambeth Conference in general and mentioned this issue. At the time I was on the Social Questions Committee and it was decided that we should have a taskforce to look into issues of homosexuality.

Then I started reading the latest writing in that area and was influenced by several people in my thinking. I began to change my view. I began to *believe* that the church had been wrong in much of its teaching about sexuality and particularly about homosexuality. I began to see that a lot of the church's teaching about sexuality comes from pagan sources in which the dualism, and the body, anything to do with the body, is inferior to things to do with the spirit, and sexuality is so much part of the body that it's something that drags our humanity down instead of building it up. I began to see that that dualism is still part of the church's official teaching. So I began to move away from thinking that way. In all that literature that I was reading, people were looking at the Biblical passages which have been traditionally used to *condemn* homosexuality. I saw a different way of interpreting them.

The archbishop knew that I was reading all this material. So he invited me to present a paper at a clergy conference in 1981, which I did, under the heading of Making Sense of Sex. People listened in embarrassed silence. I had a phone call from the archbishop a few days later to say, 'Donald, I've had some people get in touch with me and they're concerned because they think that your paper is actually a statement of the church's new teaching about sexuality. And I feel that I need to speak to the clergy and let them know that that is not the case, that we have not changed our official teaching.' I went back to the clergy conference and I was sitting near the front when the archbishop spoke about my paper and went through point by point, demolishing every argument that I had put forward and reinstating the church's official position.

But of course that didn't mean that I accepted in my own mind his disagreement with what I had presented. Of course, having come to this new theological insight meant that that had effects on my own personal life. It had a liberating effect. I no longer felt bound to repress my sexuality, and began a search I suppose you'd say to find a responsible, moral way of expressing that. I'm still working on that, I suppose.

The main issue is --- how does all this fit in with my marriage? That's the main thing. That's the area where I've had to work through and I think I have worked through it. I'll never be completely at peace because I know I'm swimming against the tide and many people just see me as a self-deluded sinner. But I believe that marriage is such a rich and multi-faceted relationship that I'm still happily and, yes, happily married. For me, fidelity means much more than sexual exclusiveness. There's much more to it than that. When I look around I sometimes see marriages where there might be sexual exclusiveness but not much fidelity in that other sense of the word. I'm aware that it's been difficult for Else at times, but again, because of our mutual love and respect, we've been able to work through that together.

I believe that my sexuality is a gift from God, and it has more than one facet. I rejoice in its reproductive nature. I have two wonderful children with spouses that I love and grandchildren that I love and that's been a wonderful aspect of this gift. The other gift is that I'm able to relate in a very deep way with other men and that's quite different and it's not productive, but there's something about—not just men as sexual objects—but there's something about the male personality as well as the male body which I'm attracted to. I see that—as a positive thing in my life. I no longer feel sinful about this part of my life. I feel that it's given by God and has brought enrichment in those relationships that I've experienced with other men. And so, in many ways, I'm at peace.

In the early 1980s, ***ALISON FETTELL*** *(1952) had three children and was separated from her husband when she had her first sexual relationships with a woman.*

Some of this memory is murky. It really is murky. But it was around that time, that the option of another lifestyle was in my face. So I wasn't divorced, when I decided I would possibly try what it was like to be with a woman. Right, so I was still in a family home. Left him, but there was this possibility.

It was around that time that I did the deathbed scene. There was a woman that was attracted to me and she was in the soccer team. She verbalised that attraction and I was somewhat shocked but, I quite liked her, and I thought, 'Oh, I don't know what it would be like and do I want this, am I interested in this, like, you know, am I interested?' I thought, 'Well, I'm more interested than any *man* around.' I wasn't interested in looking for another relationship particularly. I thought, 'Oh, what if I liked that lifestyle? What if that was my comfort?' I thought this could be a huge thing. I in my mind saw myself laying virtually next to a coffin. I had to be really clear in my mind—I was old, like I was in my eighties, nineties, I was wrinkled up and I was old—and I was laying there and somebody asked me, 'Do you have any regrets? Is there something you regret?' I wanted to verbalise, so I was that person and I was saying --- 'I don't have any regrets. I tried something that turned out to be right but if I *hadn't* have done that I would now have regrets.' I wanted to see myself there at that age having chosen not to try this possibility of a change of lifestyle.

I kind of did the two and I was far more comfortable with the, 'I have tried this.' Even if it turned out that it wasn't the lifestyle I wanted. But I wanted, I guess, jump the fence, I guess, the expression. Jump the, or bat on a different team or whatever people call it.

I've spoken to a lot of my friends since and some of them have admitted having attractions to women, to their other friends. But they'd never ever, ever, *ever* go over that line. So cross a line, jump a fence, whatever. Heterosexual women. Their line was very clear. I knew there was a line too but I was prepared to see what was on the other side of that line or over the other side of the fence. Knowing full-well that if I wasn't comfortable, I would come back. And I will have just said, 'I've tried.' But I didn't want to not try to see if I was comfortable with a woman.

I think what had happened was that I had read a book. It was a book that had a scene in it, a love scene between two women. This is being incredibly honest, because I had never come across that option of two women having a sexual relationship ever, before I read this book. I think it was a Harold Robbins book, was it *79 Park Avenue* or something? But I remember—it's disgusting!—but I remember reading it and I remember how I felt when I read this scene. And it affected me very differently than a heterosexual love scene had affected me. I mean it was exciting. Incredibly exciting. It was like, '*Wow*, I didn't know you could do that!' Well, that's how naïve and in a sense dumb I was in relation to what options there were. But it did, it was like, 'Oh my God, I didn't know that was an option.' It's almost like when a word doesn't exist the thing doesn't exist.

Roslyn Burge: So did you have a relationship?

Let me just say I tested the water, to some degree. I suppose it was a friendship that had a sexual connotation, yes. But it wasn't a relationship, that I'd call a relationship in a sense. But my first experience making love with another woman was that other defining moment where I decided that I'd be staying on that side of the fence. It was a no-brainer, for me. Once I had experienced that I realised that although my sexual relationship with my husband—in the early days especially—was fine. We had no problems. I didn't have a sexual hang-up, I enjoyed it, I enjoyed sex. It wasn't an issue. So it wasn't like it was like, 'Oh God, I haven't enjoyed that therefore, I'm enjoying this so this has to be.' It was just the feeling that I had through the sexual relationship. It was so much more for me. It seemed righter. It seemed, I fitted better there.

What made it righter?

(Sigh) The softness. I have a very strong sense of smell—of olfactory. There's something about the female smell that for me was more comforting than the male. So there were physical reactions that I had, and something that was really important for me, obviously. But I also love women, and always have. I relate really well with women even though I adored my father. School teachers, people I got on with, were women, and I admired them. Discussions, friendships, women, yes. Even though I can get along really well with fellas. A contradiction somewhat. But yep, I don't know how else to explain it. The whole package was, 'Oh my God, I'm home.' So when you're home you don't want to go somewhere else.

GINETTE MATALON *(1936) recalls the impact of the death of her husband in 1984 after twenty-five years of marriage.*

Ralph's death was bad but I grieved with a whole family. I really missed him as a companion in life very, very badly. But I had the opportunity to grieve with the children. To tell them I miss that and this and to tell his sisters. Which I didn't have with my second husband—I'll come to it. But I grieve for three and half years and then it became all of a sudden—because I was thinking how long did it take me—I became whole again after three and a half years. It was as if something had broken and there was a part missing in me. Because when he went, all the things that I used to be to him and to myself went as well. And then after these three and a half years I became whole again.

So that was that and I was sure I was never going to remarry or love another person again. But another year and a half after that, after I've been whole—and I was working, and also his death was instrumental to full-time employment, that I can come into the field of my big involvement with work—and a year and a half later I met up with Victor and I fell madly in love—madly in love—with Victor and we started a relationship.

OURANITA KARADIMAS *(1958) looks back over several decades of a relationship that began in the late 1970s.*

John and I have in a way grown up together because we met when we were basically adolescents, really, both of us were about as experienced and as clueless as each other. So we have grown up together in many ways. My parents met when they were already formed adults—my mother was twenty-eight, my father was forty, forty-one—so they had a very different relationship. My relationship with John, first of all we met, we were both working and studying at the same time so we had all of those formative growing up in Australia experiences together. We also had the Greek family experiences together and then we made our way through our twenties and our thirties and our forties and into our fifties very much complementing each other. We have diametrically opposed interests—his interests are in technical, in engineering, mine are in literature and language and the creative and the humanities—but somehow or other we managed to work together. I think my relationship with John is a lot more sharing life experiences together rather than my parents who were working partners and bringing up children partners and that was their focus.

Frank Heimans:* SO HOW WOULD YOU CATEGORISE THE RELATIONSHIP *you [have] had with your husband during your marriage?

Oh absolutely brilliant, absolutely brilliant. How can I, where do I start? M'mm (crying), I don't know where to start. I think, 'How do I love thee? Let me count the ways.' I think this is how you describe that relationship. It's really ironic because my husband is not at all literary and I'm thinking of Elizabeth

Barrett Browning now. John is an amazing, *really* amazing human being and I didn't think I'd cry when I talked about him of all things, yeah.

He is an incredibly empathetic human being. Unbelievably patient and unbelievably *balanced* in his approach to almost anything. He is able to put the brakes on me when I'm off on some tangent or other. He always is able to bring me back to the middle ground and get me to look in a very balanced way at any situation. He is so rock solid dependable that it's not funny. He's so understanding and so wonderful in all ways with his in-laws, with my side of the family, with our children. He is incredibly courageous. He has taken some business and work decisions that would make your hair curl and he's been in such difficult situations—particularly in the work and the business environment—that it would make I think pretty much anybody else just give up and walk away but not John. John, I think to his detriment, fights those battles to the bitter end not out of stubbornness but out of a feeling of doing something properly to the very last minute. When you start something you do it properly and that's him.

JAMES FINNEGAN *(1981) discusses a relationship that started in his thirties and reflects on dating in the 2010s.*

So we've been together over two years. I guess not long in the scheme of things but we kind of hit it off straight away and lived with each other for the majority of that time.

Roslyn Burge: How did you meet?

We actually met using an app on the phone. It's an app where you can talk to I guess like-minded people and meet up if you want to. We met each other on that. Started talking and decided to go on a date and hit it off from there.

Had you used that app before to meet people?

I had. So we'd been using it for a while and we both saw each other on there but never actually said anything to each other for a while and just randomly one day we started talking to each other.

DOES ANYBODY MEET ANYBODY STONE COLD, ***face to face anymore?***

No, I don't think so (laughs). I know a *lot* of people who have either met that way [using the Grindr app], and even just for recreation (laughs). A lot of the periods while I was single, it was easy. I think particularly in the gay community, it can be hard to find people without really putting yourself out there at the risk of danger unless you restrict yourself to gay bars and areas. So it was interesting. You're able to meet a lot of people around your area that you wouldn't have even known were either there or gay.

So where would you meet?

It depends. I must admit sometimes I have taken that risk and let them just come over. Other times you would meet out and maybe go to the movies. It's definitely made things easier for a lot of gay guys in particular.

But it's even more and more so in the straight community now, but those kind of apps originated with the gay community as a way of identifying each other. Although it does have its downsides where people don't really go up to each other and talk any more. It's like you see someone, even *in* a gay bar, and a lot of people, rather than going and say hello, they'll open their phone and see if they're on Grindr (laughs).

Former soldier and barman **JAY LOGAN** *(1981) met his future wife six months before he spent time in remand and received a suspended sentence. Jay describes how he needed to become a different man before they married in 2009.*

She just had no idea that I had this anger in me. She'd see it sometimes. Like we had some *big* arguments. For some stupid reason she used to think I was shagging everybody. Like I was some sort of a Casanova or something. The truth is, I was an absolute pig, when I was on the turps. Even when I was working at the pub, I wasn't engaging in conversations with other women or anything but I worked with a lot of good-looking women and it worried her. I think she was a little bit self-conscious about that. She had nothing to worry about. But it would cause huge arguments there. I was the type of person who had a snap temper so I'd try and get away. I'd try and go out to the car, go for a drive, cool down, you know. Fleur was the type of person who would follow and want to resolve the argument. But I wasn't like that. So, I punched holes in things. Punched holes in doors. Basically I nearly strangled my cat once. It was wailing at the wrong time, and I felt so bad after that. I thought, 'Jeez, you're just like your father.' I thought, 'No more.' I said, 'That's it.' So you get that glimpse of yourself in the mirror looking like a complete animal, behaving like an animal. You're scaring the person who loves you the most in the world. No. So yeah, you've got to change.

At the time of her interview in 2013 ***KIRSTY WALLETT*** *(1982) was newly engaged to be married.*

Hamish Sewell: So Dean didn't just pop the question and give you a ring?

No, we went shopping, yep. And that's fine with me. I didn't need there to be any grand gestures like in a Hollywood movie because I think a lot of the time (sighs), like a lot of my friends—not everybody, I don't want to generalise—but a lot of women can be really unhappy in their relationships because of the ridiculous expectations they place on it because of Hollywood movies. It's not to say I'm not a romantic but I'm very realistic

I think about our long-term relationship and that we're going to have our ups and downs.

And Dean's a very shy person in personality and I think he wanted to get married but he was quite afraid to go ring shopping on his own and do the big gesture but felt the pressure to. Certainly not any pressure from me because it wasn't something we talked about all the time. So we just decided to do it the low-key way—the same way we're gonna get married. I mean we are travelling to an overseas location and making it special. It's not—the wedding isn't important to us, I mean we want it to be nice and fun and all of that sort of thing, we want to include the people we love—but we were also quite open to not actually getting married. If I had been pregnant before we were married, we wouldn't have had a shotgun wedding. We don't feel that pressure to. We're choosing to get married I guess because we do see some value in the commitment.

But you know, since we're engaged, it's definitely made both of us feel more secure. Which is interesting and I hate that because I was very anti-marriage for most of my young life, but it is nice. It's nice. I guess we're creating a family and we're not doing it the traditional way but there is a tiny part of both of us that is traditional in the sense of family. That's why we're doing it I guess.

Further Listening on Intimate Relations

Ruth Apps, 1926, http://www.nla.gov.au/amad/nla.oh-vn6252043/3-1352~3-1429
John Murphy, 1940, http://www.nla.gov.au/amad/nla.oh-vn6504268/2-5680
James Box, 1946, http://www.nla.gov.au/amad/nla.oh-vn6252081/2-881
Ronnie Gauci, 1947, http://www.nla.gov.au/amad/nla.oh-vn6290910/1-2025
Geraldine Box, 1949, http://www.nla.gov.au/amad/nla.oh-vn6190857/3-3604
Lynne Sanders-Braithwaite, 1949, http://www.nla.gov.au/amad/nla.oh-vn6290876/1-4304
Donat Santowiak, 1950, http://nla.gov.au/nla.obj-220175608/listen/1-2673
Kim Bear, 1959, http://www.nla.gov.au/amad/nla.oh-vn6190847/5-3363
Michelle Cripps, 1960, http://www.nla.gov.au/amad/nla.oh-vn6252075/0-5651
Rhonda King, 1965, http://www.nla.gov.au/amad/nla.oh-vn6390877/1-4619
Suzie Quartermain, 1975, http://nla.gov.au/nla.obj-220022403/listen/0-5525

Maternity and Childbirth

Sydney mother ***RUTH APPS*** *(1926) recalls her birth of a severely disabled baby in the late 1940s.*

My first child was born in 1949 and she had multiple malformations. She had spina bifida, a cleft palate, and a clubbed foot and she couldn't digest food. She lived for twenty-two days. I was in this small private hospital. My prenatal care had been with a GP, which is what most people did then, and in hindsight he did not pick up on the fact that the developing baby was extremely small and it wasn't until she was born that the defects were noticed. In his defence there were no ultrasounds, X-rays were few and far between and it may've been hard to pick out. We never took her home. She stayed in the hospital and died there basically because she had no food. They were tube-feeding her but it wasn't being digested.

It was our first baby. We found it very hard to take. What happened were recriminations. Bill's family decided that it was all the fault of *my* family. My family decided it was all *his* family's fault, when in actual fact it was just a defective birth. As doctors have told me since, there's a percentage of children that are born that way.

I probably managed it better than anybody. My view was, 'Well, let's see what we can do about it and then have another baby.' But it was hard to take because all my friends were having babies and their babies were alright. There was no post-mortem, nobody tried to work out *why* it had happened to her. She was basically buried and, not exactly forgotten, but she was buried in a section of the cemetery for what they call newborn babies which has no access. So we don't have any access to her grave.

It was hard to take, but we went then to a specialist who took some tests and everything and said, 'I think it's just one of those things. Have another baby', which we did, which was Julie. And from Elizabeth—the first baby who was never going to walk or talk—we had Julie who turned out to be a brilliant academic. So there you have it, and the other two subsequent children were much the same.

Ruth remembers the impact of the introduction of the contraceptive pill to Australia in 1961.

I HAD THREE CHILDREN but that wasn't my original intention. When my first child was—we didn't undertake any family planning before she was born. She was born two years after we were married, just arrived, and then of course we had our second child immediately afterwards. That was on medical advice, 'Just have another baby.' Then after that you could go to the chemist and get various tablets and different contraptions and that kind of thing. So I had my second and third children with that *basic* family planning. Then after the third one was born, I said, 'I didn't want any more' and that happily coincided with the introduction of the pill. I think I rejoiced. I was the first one on it because I didn't want any more children. When I heard about it I hightailed it to the doctor and very quickly got on that and stayed on it until I no longer needed it. I think it was a brilliant invention. It gave women the *choice* that they were looking for.

As a young woman ***TRISH BARRKMAN*** *(1933) was told she had spots on her kidneys and should not have children. She ignored the advice, but concern about her kidneys stopped her using a 'magic pill' for morning sickness that was later linked to the thalidomide birth defect tragedy.*

The morning sickness was a very big thing and I was very, very fortunate. There's always been somebody looking after me.

My second daughter was born in 1961 and that was the year that they had this magic pill to help you overcome morning sickness. I'd suffered morning sickness with Jenny and I had it with Joanna and there was all this talk about this wonderful pill to stop morning sickness. I can't remember what the name of it was but for some reason or other, I decided I wasn't going to take it. It was the pill that caused the thalidomide that deformed children. So, you know, pigheadedness, I don't know why. I knew that kidneys were organs that all these pills and things, they all had to go through your kidneys. Whether that was in my subconscious that this doctor had told me I had something wrong with my kidneys, but I didn't take it. I took very little medication and so she was born happy and she was very healthy, my Joanna.

ALISON FETTELL *(1952) contrasts her experience of bearing three children between the early 1970s and the early 1980s.*

The birth in and of itself was horrendous—my first child. That was like a labour of twenty-four hours and I was eighteen and that was tough. That's another defining moment. When you've got a male nurse—and there weren't many around—giving you an enema. This wasn't pretty at eighteen. It was horrible. It was really embarrassing and I felt --- I was incredibly shy and it was awful. I suffered a lot through the labour. It was a difficult, difficult birth. Now I think it would have been a caesar [caesarian], because I was exhausted and they had to use forceps. Yeah, so it was a difficult birth.

Roslyn Burge: Was your husband there for that?

No, no, they weren't allowed in in those days. This was forty-odd years ago. Nup, no support. Nobody. Not even, you couldn't have a support person so everybody that was around you were strangers. I was physically sick through the labour. I wanted to vomit. And they kept saying, 'Look, get up, walk around.' 'Oh,

I feel so sick.' There was one nurse who was really horrid and she said, 'Look, just get out of bed and stop complaining. Get out there and sit with the other women that are going through it, right.' Next so I vomited all over her uniform and on her shoes. I didn't do it on purpose but she insisted I stood up. I must say that I didn't really want to continue that. I would have been quite happy to not be pregnant right at that point in time. Didn't really want to go through that and I thought, 'What is this about? The pain is horrendous.' Anyway, I eventually gave birth and I was fine after that. But I had split. So I had some sort of episiotomy. It was *horrendous*.

And then, in those days, they used to put you on the bed and, and have ray lamps. Everything's showing and you'd have a ray lamp aimed at you, behind your legs, and then people'd walk in and like, 'Hello, I'm shy!' Dreadful (laughs). This was Bankstown Hospital. So dreadful, dreadful, dreadful.

Did you anticipate that for your second child?

I did. I thought it was very brave for me to go back but that birth wasn't quite as difficult. It was probably about ten or twelve hours. Still hard but not quite as hard. There's moments, if you've ever given birth, you'll always remember parts of it.

Then Casey's birth was probably—if you could have the perfect birthing moment then Casey's was—that's my youngest. I can't explain it except that when I actually gave birth it was like the most amazing orgasm. It was incredible. I've never known anything like it, and yet some people have explained that to me. Because the other two were so difficult this was just amazing. Easy. But I was very fit then.

I SUFFERED SOMEWHAT FROM POSTNATAL DEPRESSION with her, but I *didn't* with my first two. So after Casey, my youngest, who is now thirty-two, I suffered. I knew I needed help because I knew that both her and I were at risk. There was no question. I was suicidal I think and I was worried about the little one. So for me it was like, 'This is dangerous, I've got to do something.' I was still with my husband of course at the time. That was my first sojourn into therapy. But what came out of that was lots of things. One of these therapists—I think I went to a couple—but one of the therapists taught me self-hypnosis, and like a meditation. That has played a huge part in my life from that point. I still meditate now. If I can I meditate every day but when you work you can't so it was always weekends. So over thirty years, thirty-four years I've either meditated or done a relaxation therapy or self-hypnosis of some sort. I think it saved my life.

PHIL MAY *(1962) recalls the arrival of triplets in 1999 after successful in vitro fertilisation (IVF) treatment.*

Matthew Higgins: Now it was twelve years before you had children. Did you have plans for having children from day one?

No. (a) I wasn't getting married and (b) I was *definitely* never having children. That was something that was not on the cards and I made sure Fiona knew that well before we got married. She was comfortable with that at the time. She said, 'Oh maybe down the track I might be able to talk you into one.' So we got married actually stating zero / one *children*. That was our agreement. I maintain to this day that that was a loophole that was interpreted as zero / one *pregnancies* because—as I have told you earlier—we were blessed with triplets when we decided to go for children because we actually had some scientific assistance.

We were on the IVF program after a few years of being unsuccessful. Eventually we I suppose hit the jackpot. We ended up with three children which neatly side-stepped a major concern of Fiona's. She was a middle child and *never* wanted any of her children to be middle child and that was a way around it I guess.

FIONA MOVED OUT OF THE WORKFORCE. That was a very conscious decision. She wanted to devote her energies and time to the children and raising them. Again, another statistic for you—there are 168 hours in a week and 193 hours a week required to look after triplets. They were born premature. They were two months and one week premmie. My smallest daughter fit in my hand when she was born. I could literally hold her in one hand and she was safely snuggled inside. They required a *lot* of energy. We didn't get them out of the hospital till they were two months old. They spent the first eleven days in the intensive care unit and all of them did well. We have unfortunately been to a large number of funerals where the coffins are far too small.

The middle of ***BRONWYN MACDONALD****'s (1964) three children, born in south-coast New South Wales in 1989, was diagnosed with Cerebral Palsy and a profound intellectual disability.*

Elena Volkova: When did you first notice that something was wrong with your child?

Straight away. Straight away in the hospital. He wouldn't open his eyes. Didn't open his eyes more than like this little crack for the whole time we were in there. And he wouldn't feed and his urine was just like one little dark brown spot and they sent us home like that. They said that, 'Don't worry, your milk will come in.' As if that was the only—but I knew I had plenty of milk. Then there was just a struggle for five months. Luckily we had a very good nurse. Can't think what they're called now. Like a community nurse that looks after new babies in the area. She knew that there was something wrong too so she was really a bit of a lifesaver because the doctor just kept saying, 'He's fine.' She's the only one who understood that he wasn't. And kept pushing with us, well you know, 'We better go and try another doctor' and 'Let's go and try a paediatrician'. It was only when we went back to—because where we lived was between Narooma and Bega, and we'd been using the Bega facilities, the Bega doctors, the Bega Hospital and our pregnancy was diagnosed in Narooma—so we finally went *back* to Narooma and we went back there because Jethro had diarrhoea and he was *clearly* not coping and the doctors in Bega had just gone, 'Well you know, he's okay. Just make him have water.' Well he would *never* have water. The doctor in Narooma didn't have hospital privileges but she sent us up to the hospital in the town north of that—at Moruya. And from there he was sent to Canberra and that's where he was diagnosed.

So yeah, we knew straight away. Knew straight away. But coming to that firm understanding that, you know, someone's got to tell us something, took a long time. Yeah, yeah.

How did you feel when he was diagnosed?

Oh, over the moon. I laughed. I thought it was the *best* thing because we'd gone these five months where everyone's going, 'Well, don't know what's wrong with you but there's nothing wrong with your child.' And suddenly we had a name. We had a name. It was *magical*. It couldn't have gone better. Yep. Yep. The doctors were horrified because I actually did laugh. Because I thought they were going to tell me he was dying.

Further Listening on Maternity and Childbirth

Kathleen Golder, 1920, http://nla.gov.au/nla.obj-219908851/listen/4-3793
Russell Elliott, 1950, http://www.nla.gov.au/amad/nla.oh-vn6223258/4-5926
Gina Polito, 1954, http://www.nla.gov.au/amad/nla.oh-vn6421369/0-2958
Kim Bear, 1959, http://www.nla.gov.au/amad/nla.oh-vn6190847/1-945
David Cooper, 1959, http://www.nla.gov.au/amad/nla.oh-vn6290926/1-2802
Michelle Cripps, 1960, http://www.nla.gov.au/amad/nla.oh-vn6252075/1-1222
Suzie Quartermain, 1975, http://nla.gov.au/nla.obj-220022403/listen/1-50
Jason Johnson, 1981, http://nla.gov.au/nla.obj-220115636/listen/3-3075

Family Life

***LEO CRIPPS** (1923) married Pat in 1952 and lived in Hobart where they raised four children and Leo learned about fatherhood.*

Ben Ross: How did you take on the role or the job, if you like, if you thought of that in that way, as a father to your children?

> Ah, I don't know if I can explain. The only thing I can explain is one Christmas when I was still plastering then, one Christmas—and we only had the one daughter then, the older daughter—we were working down at the government printing office which was down towards the wharf area, you see, and couple of blokes I was working with they'd said, 'Oh, we'll go over to the pub and have a couple of beers before you go home', you see. I used to catch the ferry home. We'd be going on, and they always worked it so that when the ferry was coming in it was my shout. They didn't realise what a *favour* they'd done me in the finish because I went home and here's me wife just off out the door with the daughter. Of course I said, 'No, you can go but I'm keeping her.' That was the only real blue we ever had but that taught me a big lesson. Wake up to yourself, mate. You've got a job to do to look after the family and not get out boozing with these other blokes, yeah. And from then on, I was always very restrictive in me drinking, not only for driving but for other things. I was very restrictive from there on.

*In Canberra in the 1950s, **FRED HENSKENS** (1929) became a stepfather to three young children whose mother had left their drunkard, gambling father.*

Matthew Higgins: So you lived together for three years before you got married. Now in the 1950s that was pretty unusual, wasn't it?

It was, yeah. It was. I wanted to get married but we went to—wanted to do it in church—and I used to take the kids to Sunday school at St Paul's at Manuka, right. But the priest there, the reverend there, wouldn't marry us because she was a divorcee and he didn't like marrying me there. So we just waited for a while and then I went to St John's Church one day and I saw someone named Archdeacon Arthur. He was a very nice bloke. He had a good talk to me and I told him I couldn't get married in the other church (laughs). He told me to come back with Helen and he talked to us, and then he called me back again and he said, 'You know what?' he said, 'I'm going to marry you myself, because you deserve to be married more than any of these, some of these people are marrying.' He said, 'Because you've been looking after this woman and these kids love you, and you're doing the right thing,' he said, 'I'm going to marry you.' So I got married in St John's Church.

Anyway, they were very fond of me the kids. Even now if you say I'm their stepfather, they go off their head, they say, 'He's not my stepfather, he's my *real* father (laughs).'

Jewish Egyptian migrant ***GINETTE MATALON*** *(1936), recalls the importance of extended family and then its loss around the time she and Ralph had their first child in 1961.*

When we got married, we moved out of the terrace where we were—my mother and I—and we rented a small, two-bedroom apartment at Glebe Point Road. This was considered a *big* improvement on the terrace. It was our apartment but my mother—it wasn't a question of she not living with me. So there was, the second room would have been my mother's room and the baby's, and the first, the largest room, would be mine. Their room would have been a sort of sunroom full of lovely windows and we painted and we decorated with bright curtains and everything. My mother was looking forward to staying home—she was only fifty-two—and minding the baby while I was going back to my job three months after birth.

Unfortunately she died one month after I had the baby. On 4 February 1961 she passed away. So she died. It was a big loss for me—the loss of my mother. Then I had to stop working also—I had to stay home with the baby—and there was no childcare. I remember I had read a little ad of a lady—she turned out to be a lady, a Greek lady all dressed in black—minding babies. I went to have a look at the premises and really it wasn't a place where I would have wanted to leave my baby so I stayed home and minded Richard—my first child—at home.

So, one of my theories in life is that there is nothing that stands on its own. After I had desperately tried to find childcare for my son, came in a Labor Government and [in 1972] they introduced childcare. Free childcare, or at an affordable rate. And all of a sudden I turned from my entire family's—most of the people who came from Egypt were voting Liberal—and I was no longer a Liberal person. I became a Labor supporter.

By 1974, ***TRISH BARRKMAN*** *(1933) in Brisbane was a divorcee with three children. She recalls local attitudes to single working mothers and the increased prevalence of divorce after the Family Law Act of 1975.*

The Family Law Act came into being and that was a whole new ballgame. So, suddenly *everybody* was separating. They were going mad (laughs). It's interesting because I can look at my children. Jenny the eldest, her class in school, Jenny was probably one of the few, of the very few children that came from a divorced family. My other daughter, who was two and a half years younger, suddenly (laughs) they were getting divorced and separating. It was incredible. And Joanna ended up with four close friends and they were all from broken marriages. And yet *most* of Jenny's friends still were intact as far as their marriages were concerned. It was just *unbelievable*.

I can remember my youngest daughter was a very good swimmer, and I had to work on a Saturday morning. They had a rule at the school that parents had to attend Saturday morning. You had to attend so many Saturday mornings, otherwise your child was punished, was not allowed to swim in the final races, in the championships. I took them to task (laughs). I really did battle on that one. I thought it was so unfair. Children were called 'latchkey children'. I used to go to school meetings and these people would get up and talk about latchkey children.

Hamish Sewell: What's a latchkey child?

A latchkey child was someone that came home to an empty house, from school. There was that *stigma*. There was that moral undertone that you were leaving your children. What else were we supposed to do? How else were we supposed? I had people say 'Get your mother-in-law, get your grandmother to come and help.' I didn't have a grandmother, I didn't have a mother, I didn't have anybody. I had no relations here whatsoever. And these people were standing there telling me. I even had a woman come around from this swimming club telling me what I should do, in my own home. I couldn't believe it.

I fought, I battled and I said 'The only person you're punishing is my daughter.' And she went on to win every championship of her age group (laughs). They eventually changed the law. Their argument was that if they didn't have this strict law—rule—that no parents would turn up. So they altered it and if you had a good reason, you could put an application in and state your reason. And do you know what? There were two parents, the next year, that couldn't attend and I was one of them.

In Victoria's La Trobe Valley, teenage Polish migrant **DONAT SANTOWIAK** *(1950) was an only child in a dysfunctional family. By the time he married and had a young daughter in the mid-1970s he was already an alcoholic.*

Being a father, well that's again a very deep and interesting question. Because I was elated. I remember when my daughter was born, it was at the old Traralgon hospital. I remember skipping stairs—like four at a time—with the joy of it all happening.

But as time rolled on I realised that my upbringing started really affecting on how I was going to be as a father. So, a lot of those issues that I had with my wife were about, you know, tidiness in the house and my daughter leaving toys behind. All that real crappy kind of really insignificant stuff, as I know it today. But at the time it was a significant thing for everyone.

My daughter was five years of age when that marriage ended. So I really only had zero to five with her. Now that I've got grandchildren—and one's twelve and the other one's ten—when I spend time with them they're kind of—in a way—they're teaching me on how to be a dad. This is a profound statement in a way. But I'm kind of like, now I think I could be a quite a different father. I think a much better father. I'm sure I could be. But at the time, it was all that really not knowing much about anything. I really had no modelling in my own childhood on what it means to bond and all that stuff.

So I jumped off the cliff and realised I didn't really have a bloody parachute. Being a father in the fatherly sense I really didn't have much clue.

Alistair Thomson: Do you think your drinking affected your fathering at all?

Oh yes. Yes. But if anything I would say that it probably helped because it would have taken some of the tenseness out of me. Because I was a lot more passive and accommodating when I drank. So it would have taken maybe—you know, if there was something that bothered me—it probably would have done the antidote to that. Would have relaxed me. I mean, there were obviously—for the marriage to have failed in the end—there were some disagreements and disharmony.

Donat gave up drinking in the late 1980s.

IN THE END—before I actually stopped drinking—it wasn't uncommon for me to sneak out to the shed out the back and drink sweet sherry out of a jam jar that was disguised as some form of solvent or something. Just to even start the day. Yeah. Then I had extremely bad blackouts that would last sometimes a whole weekend. The fear of what may happen drove me to Alcoholics Anonymous. I despised the power it had over me. Deep down I knew that life had more to offer and I had more to offer life if I didn't drink.

For me to ring AA, God it was like the end of the world. It was death or AA. That first phone call, a lady answered the phone and she had this really kind of a worn voice. And she said, 'I'm so and so and I'm an alcoholic.' I thought—not knowing anything about AA—I thought, 'Oh my God. That's the last thing I need. An alcoholic (laughs). I wanna get together with sober people.' But thank God for that.

*Former school-teacher **LYNNE SANDERS-BRAITHWAITE** (1949) was a drug user and heavy drinker for most of the 1970s and up until 1987, when she left her husband and, for a time, her children on the north coast of New South Wales, to get clean in Sydney.*

I had these two beautiful children that I adored but it was caravan parks and farm houses and evictions, lots of violence within the home, lots of fear. A constant feeling of failing at everything that I'd ever believed in or wanted.

I think for the earlier years --- that the community was able to absorb them as long as I stayed down here where we were known in Bellingen and Urunga. Going into Coffs, we were fairly conspicuously a combination of feral and—I was always drunk as well as drug addicted. The children were --- they had a place here and they had mum and dad and they had their other grandparents and my sister.

But in the last two years, when they were about seven and nine, things started to change. They weren't being asked to parties. The very last, 1987—just before I left my marriage and took off to Sydney to get clean and sober—we had to go to Coffs Hospital. They had ear surgery coming up and something went wrong with the equipment. One of the doctors said, 'Even children of women like this deserve better treatment.' I realised then that it was beginning to impact on them. I knew if they were to stay in the world that I was offering them, they would become children of the local drunk or the local junkie. I hated that. I knew I'd be showing them the world of hotels and not a world I wanted to show them.

I've never forgotten that day, that burnt into my memory. Going 'Oh no, it's come to this', you know. I think that's the day that was—I'd been married nine years, that was 1978—and I think the process that led me to deciding to do something. To me there were a whole lot of stepping stones towards it and that was one of the ones that went, 'I have to stop this lifestyle for them somehow', whether it meant suicide, whether it meant, I didn't know what else it could mean. But that was one of the days I can—I was gone within two days of that.

I knew nothing about life without drugs by then. Certainly knew nothing about life without alcohol because all the family had drunk. Well not mum, everyone except mum. But that was the beginning of life turning a corner completely. I still think—in later years I was still ashamed of leaving the children and an old lady in Maroubra said to me that she'd left her son and it was the single most honourable thing she'd ever done. That was a real gift. 'Cause I knew they—where I'd left them—they were going to be safe and they were going to be loved. There wouldn't be danger any more, you know, and they'd be fed and clothed and all those sort of things, which they were of course.

That was the end of the marriage. We tried hard. I look back sometimes, I feel, it wasn't that, we tried, you know, we fought and struggled trying to beat it and you can't beat it, not that way. You just, yeah, put up a good fight and it won. And I left, on the train.

I was in the halfway house and I got a job down at the beach, which was just—coming from the back of the hills up here to selling clothes and souvenirs at Bondi Beach—was just so much fun. It was a halfway house. There were twenty people, usually about seventeen of those were male. 'Oh, this is pretty good' (laughs). I just ate my way along Bondi Beach and swam and just *healed*, healed from the hard years. Just travelled around Sydney and reclaimed my own city, the city I'd been born in.

Then I got a letter one day saying that my in-laws didn't want to care for the children any more. It was time that I took them back. But I was still in the halfway house. So I had to get my act together fast. They came back to me, I think it was about a year and a half, the children were sent to me from the country. They came down to live in—first in Bondi in a little flat thing that we had. Life became very hard but I think it was the making of me as well.

I know the first place we had, my income was 145 a week and the rent was 135 a week (laughs). So I learnt a fair bit about humility and op shops and charity vouchers and things that I really didn't want for my world. They'd come from, you know, being the mayor's grandchildren here and living in a really nice house, with my family down here, to living with mum in a one-room dive really in Bondi. But, you know, they came down and they walked into this place they'd never been before, they'd never been in a city before, and I was so worried and they threw the bags on the floor and went, 'Oh thank God we're home.' But it was hard, you know, it was pretty hard.

In rural Victoria in the early 1990s, ***RUSSELL ELLIOTT*** *(1950) left school-teaching aged forty-one and agreed with his wife Mary that Russell would become a house-husband.*

We'll continue on from probably 1992, obviously the three children had been born at that stage. I was no longer teaching, had been superannuated. We made a decision—Mary and I—that we would have a role reversal. Because she had been a primary teacher, an art-trained teacher, she was keen to return back to the workforce. She was a brilliant teacher—I was envious of her capacity to work with children, community and parents—and she said, 'I'd like to go back teaching. That would mean that you would have to look after the three children, be responsible for their kinder runs and all of that sort of stuff. Are you in agreement to that?' And I said, 'Yeah, I would be happy to take on that mantle if *you* would be happy to go back full time teaching.' She applied for a position that was advertised as a Shared Specialist Art and Science. She got the position and it meant she travelled around to eight or nine little rural schools in this area delivering an art science program to the children.

I assumed the mantle of looking after the three kids, doing the kinder run which was yeah, interesting, interesting. Going to the kinder functions, I probably was the only guy there at that stage and used to have to try and sit down on the floor and worm my way through a tunnel that they'd built, but yeah, it was a great experience and on reflection I guess a great time to connect with children on a very personal level at a very interesting time in their life. Prior to that when I'd been teaching and Mary had been home with them, I'd see them early in the morning, leave to go to work, come home at five o'clock, see them, they'd be fed, bathed, put to bed. So there wasn't a lot of interaction going on other than at weekends. So this was a chance to really connect with the three of them as part of the activities of school and kinder that they were involved in and also when they were home with me during the day.

In 1994, Mary was diagnosed with a brain tumour and died while the children were still young.

MY UNCLE, MOSS STREETER, who has been a mentor all through my life, was staying with me at the last time. He had spent Christmas with us in the last few weeks when Mary was going through the final stages of her life. After the funeral, everyone else had gone, he was still here and he got up the next morning after it and he said, 'I'm leaving Russell, I'm going home.' I looked at him and I didn't say but I thought, 'No you can't go home. This is the time I *want* some sort of support from someone like you.' He said, 'No, I'm going home'. He said, 'You've got three kids there who need you and', he said, 'you have to start to work with them. They're your future. I'm going home, you take it on.' And I—because I know him so well—I just thought, 'Oh, that's a bit harsh, he's a bit harsh.' But it was only after spending the first few weeks that I realised how prophetic his words were. I *had* to make a start and if he'd stayed there as a support—and he would've been a support—it would've been an artificial crutch that wouldn't have helped me make those first initial steps, that yes, it's now in your court, you're going to have to do this.

And the first steps are simply the routine, wash for them, cook for them, take them to the functions, support them as best you can, go out to their sport, continue the things that they were doing. They were interrupted enough, don't interrupt them anymore. Look that's simply the way, and over time, that you work through it.

I have absolutely indelible memories of her but your life has to move on. You can't live in the past, you can't. I have seen people who've lost loved ones young and early who can't get beyond visiting the cemetery. I don't often go there. People say, 'Oh that's not all that respectful, perhaps is it?' But Mary is not in the cemetery. She is in a sense of her remains are in the cemetery, but that's not where I see her. I look at three kids, and I look at a store of memories and things, and that is her and for me that is what I focus on and use going forward.

About ten years before his interview in 2012, former trade union organiser and government advisor **PETER GALVIN** *(1951) was working in Canberra with the Industry Training Advisory Board when he suffered a stroke. At the time, he and his wife had two teenage children and Peter had an adult child from an earlier relationship.*

After I had a stroke one of the things I couldn't do was use a computer. I could have the computer in front of me and in my head I knew what to do, but I couldn't make my body do it. So part of the rehab, they'd have this computer thing at the hospital for people to learn the computer after their rehab. I used to go and do that every day, and then suddenly *it all came back*. It was like, you know, like a waterfall. I could do everything and all the stuff in my brain I could actually do physically. And it became—I wasn't a great one for the email before the stroke, because it wasn't all that common a way of communication before I'd had the stroke—I found I could communicate with all these people that I knew or that I didn't know, but wanted to know or wanted to talk to. It was amazing. I felt like I was back in life again 'cause I could contact all these people. I contacted lots of people, people that I hadn't seen for twenty, thirty years. For me it was just unbelievable. And I could organise things, I could organise travel to go to Adelaide or wherever my wife wanted to go.

And I think the mobile phone has been, for me it's been a real asset. I'm not a great telephone talker, but with a mobile phone, I ring my daughter up in Sydney for example a lot more. Now my children have left home, I talk to them more than I used to when they were at home. Or it seems to me that I do. For a long time after the stroke, I had a fear of going anywhere by myself in case I—once you've had a stroke your fear is always that you're going to have another one. So, my wife got me a phone so that I could go out by myself so if I had felt a stroke coming on, I could ring her or ring someone to come and get help. It's been like a—what do you call those blankets that you carry around?

Matthew Higgins: Comfort blankets?

Yes. It's like, I feel like if I've got it with me, I'm safe.

***ALISON FETTELL** (1951) recalls a conversation with her elderly mother when Alison was in her late thirties that cast a different light on their relationship.*

We were driving home from my grandmother's funeral—the grandmother I adored. I don't know how the conversation got to it but she said, 'Well Al, you know you were my favourite.' My partner was sitting beside me, and I was driving, and she ribbed me and said, 'Ask her why.' I went, 'I don't want to know, I don't want to know.' Because I never wanted to be the favourite. I thought it was unfair for the rest of the family that there was a favourite because, you know, I just think it was, I thought it was fairly awful to be honest. But then I said, 'Mum, okay, why was I the favourite?', thinking, you know, I don't know. Anyway she said, 'Well, when you were conceived it was the only orgasm I ever had.' Course I'm driving along and trying to think this through. I'm going, 'Okay, so it was *nothing whatsoever* to do with me! It was (laughs) something to do with mum's only orgasm.' And I'm thinking, 'One, you poor bugger and, two, yeah, okay, nothing to do with who I am.' So it was very eye-opening. I've gotta tell, I didn't pick it. I didn't pick it.

***OURANITA KARADIMAS** (1958) contrasts the parenting she received in the 1960s and 1970s with her own parenting from the 1980s onwards.*

The relationships that I have—or that my husband and I and that we individually have with our children—are very, very different from the way that our parents related to us. We could never talk to our parents about anything to do with boys or girls or relationships. I tried once, no, I'll never do it again (laughs). I wasn't young. I was in my first year out from high school and I tried to tell my father that this boy was coming to pick me up that afternoon and all hell broke loose. I thought, 'Ah, it's too hard, I'm not doing this again.' So I found talking about relationships, talking about anything to do with sexuality, almost anything to do with those kinds of relationships with people, that that was just a no-go area with my parents. You did not talk about it.

I encouraged—my husband and I—encouraged my children—our children—to speak to us about those sorts of matters much more openly. Whereas I had a very mum-dad-us relationship with my parents, I feel that with my children I have much more of a team effort kind of relationship. Our family, our nuclear family—my husband, myself and my two children—we call ourselves the awesome foursome because we see ourselves as a cooperating team and that is how we brought our children up, and that's entirely different from anything that my parents did with us.

***KIM BEAR**'s (1959) mother was widowed when Kim was a toddler and then struggled to support two children as a single parent. Kim explains that her own difficult upbringing influenced the decision not to become a mother herself.*

I think she really felt the burden of parenthood—single parenthood—and because she wouldn't ask for help. She had to *do* everything herself. I can't imagine what that's like, to be the breadwinner and make sure everything is hunky dory in clothes and food and entertainment, and the twenty-four-hourness of it is quite astonishing to me. I think parents deserve a medal and I don't know how they do it, I really don't.

I think probably aspects like that of my childhood were more than likely the reason that I didn't become a parent myself. I was always convinced—despite whatever partner it may be who would be the other parent—I was always terrified that I would be her, that I wouldn't be able to put enough time between being the child under that influence and becoming a parent and not repeating it. I just wasn't convinced that I could do it and it never seemed to be any point to experimenting in it (laughs). If I couldn't be sure that I'd do it properly, I just decided it's probably not for me. I think kids are great, love other people's kids, but it just wasn't a persona I could see for myself, being a parent. I probably have fairly strict ideas about it which was probably another good reason why I didn't do it (laughs).

But I had a long period in mid-thirties—I used to think that the biological clock was a lot of rubbish—then (laughs) I had this weird few months where I found myself bawling my eyes out at the sight of a pram and I'd think, 'My God what's happening to me?' But I worked through that and didn't end up being a parent and luckily also had a partner who for him having kids was never a priority. So I didn't have to *battle* anyone else close to me and just thought I could probably be a lot more useful as a, just me myself, and not becoming a mum.

Melbourne paramedic ***DAVID COOPER*** *(1959) married June in 1982 and they had two children. He contrasts his own experience of fatherhood with that of his father in the 1960s.*

I was a very hands-on father and the shift work helped with that. When my daughter, our first baby, was born, the nurses at the hospital laughed at me because I was in there rolling my sleeves up. I was wanting to bath the baby before my wife did and change the nappies and all that sort of stuff. Working shift work really helped with that because I could take the kids to school, I could pick them up, I would be a reading dad and do the things that a lot of mothers would only normally get to do.

So I was very much hands-on doing all that sort of stuff. I was *very* determined to make sure my children loved books, and all that, and that's where you decide what went wrong in your life and you want to make sure it doesn't happen to your kids.

I DEFINITELY PARTICIPATED MORE with children, and part of that is 'cause of shift work, 'cause you can. I would probably do a tiny bit more housework than my father would, but he never would have been home to do it even if he'd wanted to. So mum definitely was, she did the budget, she did all the cooking, all that sort of stuff. She ran the house. Our mother raised us really. The father earnt the money and the mother raised you. We have moved since then. In my particular house, we might not have moved as much as what the average woman would like us to, but we both work, and she works part-time rather than full-time. I used to do all the bills, but over the years I've let her do that.

I don't think the shift is enormous, if you know what I mean. The contact with the children is definitely enormous, and driving the kids, so yeah, that's the biggest difference I reckon is my contact with my children is ten times more than my father's was, mine's much more hands-on and conversations with the kids. *That* would be the biggest difference. Between the tasks that my wife and I do and what my mum and dad did, I don't reckon there's a big difference.

***RHONDA KING** (1965), who'd left home in Canberra when she was fifteen and became a teenage mum, recalls what it felt like when the oldest of* her *four children decided to leave home.*

As soon as they said they wanted to leave home, my heart kind of got in a knot because they were my babies. You know, I don't want them to leave. I was like, '*No.* Why do you want to leave me?' But when Shelley said she wanted to go, she was being the rebellious teenager where it was like my mum with me.

'Just go,' I was like, 'Fine. Just go.' I can remember it clearly. She was ironing her shirt in the laundry and she's going, 'Mum, I want to move in with Amber. I want to move into the city.' I'm sitting there thinking, 'She's seventeen years old. I was fifteen when I left home. I'm sick of this argument. I'm sick of *talking* about this.' And I was like, 'You know what Shelley? I think you should.' She stopped ironing and she was like, '*What?*' I was like, 'I think you should go. I think you should move out. If you can manage finishing off Year 12, that's all I ask, finish Year 12 then go ahead.' I think she was in a state of shock.

She ended up moving out and it was really hard but fun too. I could sense her sense of adventure of the new part of her life starting. So in one way it was a relief because she was being really rebellious and hard to manage and it was taking its toll on me because I've got these three other kids to look after. Then there was also that sense of adventure that she's starting the new part of her life and then there's that sense of loss that she doesn't love me anymore. She's *leaving* me. So yeah, there's a lot of mixed emotions that come up when they go. But they're all together, all at once, none stronger than another. They're just all there, knotting around inside your heart (laughs).

A few years before her interview in 2013, ***BRONWYN MACDONALD*** *(1964) moved from south-coast New South Wales to Toowoomba, where she describes life with a son in his twenties with severe disabilities.*

Jethro is completely dependent. So he needs help. He needs to be showered, dressed, fed, changed, moved for comfort, like seating adjusted all the time. Need to make sure he's not too hot, not too cold, he doesn't need a drink, yeah, so that's pretty constant. You have to do everything. His combination of disabilities can make that difficult at times. He suffers some *pain* which would be muscular but we can't really pinpoint it and we don't know exactly which muscle is sore, so you can't really do a lot for him. That can be very long, difficult days. He may be screaming all day or he may be rocking, trying to get wind up. He may need you to tap his tummy all day. It can be really demanding, m'mm, very stressful.

Elena Volkova: And he's a grown-up adult.

That's right. Yes, a lot harder to manipulate his body now. It was quite easy at one point. If you thought he had muscle ache, you could just pick him up, put him on his bed or even on the floor and stretch his muscles and rub him. That's not anyway near so easy anymore. Like if his muscles are contracting, you're not going to just simply smooth it because those muscles are big now.

Do you have any support from the disability office?

Jethro's been assessed as having high level needs and he was given three hours a week of care. That's like a day service that he could go to. We objected very, very strongly to that, to the level of taking it to the Minister. At that point they doubled it. So he's got six hours a week that the government pay for, and the day service that we send him to gets some block funding and they use part of that to fund another day for Jethro. So he gets sixteen hours a week.

What exactly does it consist of, the day care?

There's not a lot they can do with him really. They mostly take him for a walk through town or a walk through the parks, which he enjoys. They have a choir once a week, which he goes to. Not that he sings, but music's one of his things that he really loves. So that's enjoyable for him. And they have groups. Not that Jethro can participate in, but he can be a part of a group, you know, they might play board games or that type of thing, so there's lots of fun and laughter and jostling. That's pretty well what they do with him. They give him lunch and they bring him home again.

Did you notice any change in personality since he started the group?

We did actually and he went from full-time school, where we used to live, to this group up here and he became much more social when we came here. The first two houses we lived in, although they weren't fantastic *houses*, they were fantastic locations and it was right in the centre of town. Everything was flat, so we could just push him all around whenever we wanted and we'd go out every single day. There was a *lot* of input all of a sudden that really made him very aware of everything. I think he was fairly complacent and nothing was ever changing in his life before. But now things are often different. Yes, different people around, different carers, different people in the groups. They go to big shopping centres to visit and yeah, it's pretty full-on. He just seems to be more aware of what's happening around him. Sometimes he hates what's happening but that's okay, you've got to hate something to know what you love.

Eight years before his interview in 2012, and around the time he retired from teaching, gay Sydney man ***JAMES BOX*** *(1946) was asked by a lesbian couple to help them have children.*

I was asked by a lesbian couple who were in their late thirties so the clock was ticking. They'd been looking around for quite a long while, in terms of having children, both of them. For various reasons the people that they decided would've been okay weren't interested or the ones who were interested weren't okay for them (laughs). So they ended up asking me and I had no philosophical objections to it and it was very open in terms of my involvement. They were quite happy for me to have *no* involvement after that or at whatever level suited me. I was a little bit chuffed at being asked, because they were quite particular about who they picked in terms of, I don't know, being the father anyway. For some unknown reason they both wanted to have babies at the same time. Fortunately for them it didn't quite work out that way, there was eight weeks between them.

Frank Heimans: How's the process of being a father, what has it meant for you? How has it been for you?

It hasn't been much at all (laughs) other than the fact that they call me dad, because I'm not living with them and seeing them day to day. Occasionally we might have a weekend or a few days away in a holiday house somewhere. They see far more of their one set of grandparents because they live close by. So, yeah, I don't have a particularly strong paternal instinct, I don't think. I've decided that, it's not like I feel I've got to go and become part of their lives. I think I'll enjoy getting to know them when they're a bit older, maybe in their teens. Relating to children who are really young is a bit more difficult unless you're living with them.

In 2006 ***MICHELLE CRIPPS*** *(1960) had been working in state government as an electoral officer, and had narrowly missed election to the Tasmanian Parliament, when she was diagnosed with breast cancer.*

From the minute you're told, your automatic pilot kicks in and you're fighting. So it was, right, how do we get through this? What do we do? So the operation, I was fine with that side of it. I had to have chemo afterwards and I found the chemo very hard. Watching them put bright red toxic stuff into your arm that you know doesn't belong in your body and you know is going to have a *massive* effect on what happens to you over the course of the next four weeks, got harder and harder with each session and, mentally, I found it really, really tough going.

After the first chemo, I sat around waiting for what would happen and that was the worst thing I could possible do. I was physically ill. I decided, I can't live like this and so I organised, for me, the right thing was to go back to work and to be as normal as I could. So, I'd get up and go in the morning. Often I'd be home by two o'clock absolutely exhausted. But I *had* to get back to daily routine. For me, that was the most important thing and up of a morning, saying goodbye to the kids, sending them off.

What was really good is they knew that when I came home, I couldn't physically do anything. I couldn't do the washing. I couldn't cook a meal. I physically couldn't do anything. They just picked that up without a blink. One of my older son's mates even shaved his head in friendship and I thought that was so sweet of a nineteen-year-old boy to do that because, occasionally at home I'd have the scarf off when they'd drop in. Most of the time I kept it on 'cause sometimes they'd come home with people we didn't know really well and I was conscious of it being an awful shock for other people. But for me, that was important.

One thing I learnt is *everybody* experiences it differently and you have to do what's right for you and that would be my big message. So for me going back to work which meant I felt I was still contributing and 'cause we used up very quickly all my—luckily I had holidays coming—so we used up all my holidays and holiday pay, all my sick leave and then some. At least being able to go back and work part of the day, I was able to contribute financially, 'cause it's not only the cancer that knocks you, it's the worry of the finances and the not helping around the home and it's all those other things as well.

Karen George: What do you think got you through?

Definitely family. I would not have been able to do it without their support. From mum cooking meals to offset the strain on Eric working and cooking and all the rest of it, and the kids sharing in all of those tasks. That definitely helped. And friends. I had the teachers from the school that—at that stage I'd left but they were still friendly—put a basket together for me of things to pamper myself with. A couple of them had been through and knew that the chemo was pretty rough and so, nice bath salts and things like that, couple of good books to read. So the support of family and friends was really, really critical. And the *amazing* support from the breast care nurse who came to visit at home and would talk anything, you know, was on call when you needed her. I found that that was really good.

Adelaide educationalist **IAN REID** *(1961) describes the impact of the death of his elderly mother, who had raised three children as a widowed single parent.*

My older sister is now the oldest member of our family, and the relationship between us as children has changed a lot, because everything we did together—as siblings—was around mum's welfare. We'd ring up and, 'Oh what's she like today?' And, 'How's she going? Has the doctor said anything about this or that?' All that sort of stuff. 'Cause she was in Perth as well, so we had lots of phone calls and lots of strategising around that. Now that she's gone and we are three little islands much more now, we don't talk to each other as much. We're not on the phone to each other as much. We're still very close but there's no need to do that as much.

It's quite an amazing feeling actually. I didn't expect it to feel quite so lonely, in a way. Which sounds like a strange thing to say but I did feel that as well. It was quite a profound thing, when you lose your parent and you become an orphan.

In Canberra, one of **PHIL MAY**'s *(1962) teenage triplets (born in 1999) was diagnosed with high-functioning autism. In his interview in 2014, Phil describes some of the challenges of parenting teenagers with or without special needs.*

He's actually, IQ is above average—quite well above average actually—but his social skills and development and emotional maturity are way behind what you'd expect for somebody his age. He's probably four or five years behind in emotional development compared to his sisters. Which, when you package him with a somewhat large young man he's growing into, can be difficult when he's emotionally distressed. He's now physically larger than Fiona and we have to manage him differently now.

One of our ways of managing some of that stress is we've actually—at the moment—taken him out of the education system because it was causing too much stress. We're no longer fighting the Department, we're no longer fighting the school and we're no longer fighting Simon. It was wearing us out. A statistic—because I work for the Bureau of Statistics I'm actually kind of statistic mad—the statistic that was scaring me a lot is more than ninety per cent of couples with an autistic child don't stay together. And having had the stress of trying to keep Simon in school, it's a stress our relationship can do without. It's just hard work.

Now, because we're not forcing him to do something he doesn't want to do, he's *more* like a normal teenage child. He's not stressed therefore he's not as reactionary. And we're coping a lot better.

Matthew Higgins:* YOU'VE WORKED IN AN IT CAREER FOR YEARS. *You can certainly see the benefits of technology and the internet. So what are your concerns as a parent?

The amount of material that's available to them that we don't approve of—that would obviously be porn sites, but also hatred sites. But our children, well Simon has had a young man's interest in what a woman's body might look like and we've had to have a chat and say well, 'Some of these sites are not so good to go to. We'd rather you didn't.' 'But how did you know I go to them?' 'Well I'm your father and I'm in IT and I have a log of every keystroke you've ever made on your computer—would you like to see?' 'Yes I would because you don't do that.' 'Okay well you went to this website and then you clicked on this button and that took you and showed you this picture and you spent this many seconds looking at that picture.' 'Okay dad that's enough. Thank you.' And I said, 'Well you don't want me to go any further because some of these pictures are pretty --- and I'd like to talk to you about it.' 'No I don't want to talk about any of those pictures.' 'Right we wouldn't have to talk about that again, would we?' 'No dad.' And we haven't.

So yes, down to the button click for access. I know that's hard for a lot of parents to do because they lack the expertise to do that and there aren't the products available to them, and it does require a certain bent I guess. But the purpose of the exercise was actually to scare him into realising that the internet wasn't free access for him while he was living here. The other thing we do is that the internet—when Fiona and I go to bed—the internet is turned off.

As a mother of four and an Aboriginal media manager living in Broome, ***JODIE BELL*** *(1970) reflects on family life in the 2000s compared with family life in the 1970s and 1980s.*

Maybe this is a generation thing, but I find the way Vincent and I manage our family unit is probably a lot more flexible than what we were managed as kids. So very much with mum and dad, we were—it was a nuclear family with mum and dad, myself, and Jeremy my brother—every dinner we sat down at the dinner table, had to discuss the day, did our homework, watched TV, went to bed. That was the routine. Whereas with our—I think life just gets a lot more busier—so quite often it could be that I'm not getting home until six because I've had a late day at work, and it's takeaway in front of the TV, or my kids are texting me from lunch time saying this is what we are doing at school. So you don't tend to have that whole concentrated effort of sitting down and communicating with each other because you're doing it more often. My kids start talking to me the moment they get home, you know, 'Mum, I want to do this' or 'This is what's happened.'

Sydney man ***JAMES MAYOL*** *(1974) reflects on roles within the family in the South Sudanese community.*

Well, the concept of fatherhood as well, in South Sudanese, is still exist that the father still is a father and he's a number one in the family. Even the families, the children now are getting up with that knowledge, that they know father is still number one in the family. Women also, even though they try to control everything they still know that the role of the father is number one. Even when you bring the conflict into that issue, you see, they didn't want to accept the responsibility saying that I'm number one. They do problems, to become number one in the family, but the reality, they don't accept it and say, 'Yes, I did this because I want to become number one.' You see? Many still have that mentality of responsibility. To become number one in the family as a father would.

JASON JOHNSON *(1981) from north Queensland has Irish and Indigenous ancestry, and his wife is of Melanesian and German descent. He reflects on raising their three children in multicultural Australia.*

My children are growing up and it's been a difficult thing for my eldest son, and Calef is going through it a little now, in understanding the (sighs)—I suppose the easiest way to summarise it is—the multicultural aspects of Australia, and I say that noting they know that I have white skin and my wife has dark skin and their grandmother who they refer to as 'nene' has quite dark skin. She grew up in Rabaul. They don't see people any different to anybody, they just understand there's a different colour, in skin colour, and they don't quite understand that difference in skin colour sometimes. I've taken the time to explain to them, it just depends on the part of the world that you grew up in.

At the time of her interview in 2013, ***KIRSTY WALLETT*** *(1982) was about to get married. Here she reflects on the prospect of conceiving a child as a woman in her thirties, and on the challenges for women combining parenthood and other aspirations.*

I definitely have worried about whether that will be possible. I am assuming that—because I haven't had any other issues—that I'll be okay. I'm not going to worry about it before it happens but I know women a lot younger than me in their late twenties who have had problems. I have lots of friends who have had fertility problems. If I couldn't have children it would be devastating for me. I'm sure that there are other options and that myself and my partner would look into that. But it's never been a big enough fear for me to make me have children earlier.

We're a good match in the sense that we're both happy to do the family thing later in life, and committing to each other. But I have absolutely had that conversation with him, talking about, 'Well how long are we willing to wait?' In case I'm thirty-five and we can't have a family because that would be a big loss. So it's hard to balance it. There's a lot of external pressure. I do worry for my career at that point. I've seen lots of people struggle with that. And then we've got pressure from my mother-in-law who just wants grandchildren.

I tend to feel very torn about it. I want to make a commitment to my partner but I don't necessarily want to give up my name. I want to have a family but I don't want to give up my freedom. So yeah it's definitely a challenge.

I DEFINITELY THINK THAT WE'VE GOT a lot more time to explore what we want in life, which is a great freedom. We've had a lot of freedoms—and especially as a woman—that previous generations haven't had, but a lot of pressure comes with that as well.

Further Listening on Family Life

Kathleen Golder, 1920, http://nla.gov.au/nla.obj-219908851/listen/4-2004
Bert Castellari, 1923, http://www.nla.gov.au/amad/nla.oh-vn6252044/3-31
Ruth Apps, 1926, http://www.nla.gov.au/amad/nla.oh-vn6252043/2-4783
Connie Shaw, 1937, http://nla.gov.au/nla.obj-219992795/listen/2-3060
Veronica Schwarz, 1939, http://nla.gov.au/nla.obj-220011117/listen/3-1037.
Gina Polito, 1954, http://www.nla.gov.au/amad/nla.oh-vn6421369/2-2165
Barbara Krickl, 1962, http://www.nla.gov.au/amad/nla.oh-vn6252047/4-2702
Suzie Quartermain, 1975, http://nla.gov.au/nla.obj-220022403/listen/1-4272
Christian Bow, 1978, http://nla.gov.au/nla.obj-219896923/listen/1-5407
Jay Logan, 1981, http://www.nla.gov.au/amad/nla.oh-vn6569699/2-1211

Working Lives and Transformations

Mother of three ***RUTH APPS*** *(1926) rejoined the paid workforce in the 1950s.*

I don't know that I was a terribly good mother. I often say my children were dragged up but they weren't, they were cared for. As for saying my children are my whole life, that's not true for me. I've looked after them. I've had them educated. I've taught them to be strong and I've loved them. I still love them even though they're now in their fifties and sixties. I love them very much.

But I stayed home with them until the youngest one went to school. When she was five she went to school and I then thought, 'I've got more to do with my life than this', and Blacktown Council, which is just a little way up the road there, desperately needed a stenographer and it was to be for three weeks. A friend of mine told me about it and I went for an interview and they said, 'Oh you'll do very nicely.' So I started working there and it was three weeks and then Christmas time came and I left, and they rang me after Christmas and said, 'That position that you were doing casually is available, would you like it?' I said, 'Yes please' and I went back to work.

I'm now glad I did. I *thoroughly* enjoyed it. It made a lot of financial difference to the house. I started in a stenographers' pool and then I became the secretary to the engineer and then I worked for the Mayor. I stayed there for about eight years and then was offered a job with the firm of surveyors in Parramatta which I took. By that time I was in charge of what they called the development section and I was climbing up and earning more money.

As a parent, I could not have done it without my mother who came once a week and cleaned the house and did the ironing, and Bill did *all* the shopping. He was on shift work obviously so he did *all* the shopping and so I had that assistance.

So what does that mean for me as a mother? In those days a lot of my neighbours thought I was a fallen woman, you know, I had left my children. But they were *always* cared for. On the afternoons that Bill was not here there was a strict rule. You come home from school, you buy an ice block at the corner shop and you come in. You can play on the backyard but you must never be seen out the front. In all those years, people used to say 'We never see them'. They'd play in the backyard but not out the front. So the rules were there, and I would come home and cook them a meal. As a parent I did my job. In hindsight maybe I should never have been a parent because I was so happy being a worker.

I did at that time feel dreadful. I felt I was letting them down. I probably overcompensated in many respects, like they never had to wash or iron their own clothes. I did that, whereas my daughters now—their children once they get to about fifteen, sixteen they do their own ironing. So yes, I felt guilty but I didn't feel guilty enough to give it up.

IN THE EARLY DAYS when I first went to work at Blacktown Council being a woman was a problem. In fact, I went for one promotion and didn't get it and I had a letter from the chief clerk. I said I wanted to be paid the same amount as the other clerical men who were there because I was doing the same job as them. In fact I was teaching them some of the job but I was being paid less and I said I wanted to be paid the same. The letter came back from the chief clerk, 'Unfortunately you cannot be paid at the same grade because you are a woman.' That was put down on paper. So I promptly put my resignation in, which was declined and I got the money. I got the same money. Equal pay had to be fought for then. I didn't want equal pay with somebody who was doing better than me but I feel doing the same job I wanted the same money.

As an accounts auditor at a Royal Australian Air Force base in Gippsland in the mid-1960s, ***GREER BLAND*** *(1944) witnessed the beginning of a technological revolution in the workplace.*

At this time the Vietnam War had started. All accounting and all ledgers and records were done by hand up to this point. I was about twelve months, eighteen months in my course when they started to build a room out the back, and we all wondered what it was going to be, and why it was detached from the rest of the building. Anyway, we later found out it was to house a teleprinter—what they called a teleprinter—which was just like a gigantic typewriter, except it made four times the noise, the sheets of paper that went in the roller. It was electronically run, you know, technology was starting to come in. This teleprinter—as it turned out—was to be linked to a bank of computers in Melbourne. Computers that you can fit in your pocket today took up a wall forty foot long, eight foot high and each machine—well you'd swear blind—they were jumping up and down and smoking.

These teleprinters would send the messages through from the different bases and they'd come out on a ticker tape machine on wheels and pulleys and God knows what. We know now why the little hut round the back was built so far away. There was no such thing as ear muffs and I'm sure the operator—I never volunteered—but the operator that went down there, he would've been deaf in no time. It was very hard to stay in the room with those machines. Then at Point Cook, Point Cook couldn't have been linked up because after I went to Point Cook it was back to hand auditing. I never saw a computer at Point Cook.

After working as a primary school teacher, ***VERONICA SCHWARZ*** *(1939) went to university in Melbourne in 1973. At first she had to combine study and part-time work.*

I did resign from the Education ministry and decided to go to university full-time. I'd never been to university—I'd only been to teachers' college. The first year I enrolled at university it was 1973 and I needed to work. So I got a job as a taxi driver. I started work at four-thirty in the morning and ended at midday and went to lectures in the afternoon and then took in typing to make money in the evening. So that was a pretty hefty schedule.

But I remember when I went to get the job, previously women hadn't been able to be taxi drivers. The Premier, Henry Bolte, had said it wasn't a job for a woman, but they were desperate for taxi drivers. So Rupert Hamer—the next Premier—made it legal for women to be taxi drivers. I think when I went and applied there were five, six of us in the whole of Victoria—female taxi drivers. I went into this room to apply for the job and there are about fifteen to twenty other people—all men—mostly non-English speaking. They put us through our paces. We had to find how to get to a place on a map and we had to do some simple arithmetic and we had to explain where certain places were. I was the only one who passed (laughs)!

So I got my job and off I went. The first time I went into the depot to put petrol in the car—you may find it hard to believe but at that time women didn't put petrol in cars—you believe it, you might even remember it then.

Katie Holmes: I do.

Oh! It was not what women did. I drove in and all these guys, other taxi drivers, all lined up to watch me. To see if I could do it. It's rather reminiscent of what happens to me now when I back that caravan into a caravan site. They all line up to watch to see if I can do it. Anyway, I managed to do it. I'd never done it before. But I just kept on at it till I got it right without too much fuss.

Then the great Whitlam made university free. And I didn't have to work at taxis anymore. I went to university and took four subjects instead of two. The people who came to university as a result of it now being free—in my observation—many of them were mature women who had maybe quit high school at Year 11 or something, got married, had children, looked after their families but had not looked after their *own* education. Now with the families either in tertiary education themselves or at work, these women realised they wanted to do something more with their brains.

So a lot of them had to do the HSC exam—Year 12 exam—before they could then get into university. The year I met all these wonderful women, they were forty and fifty and sixty. I was in my thirties and they were all *nervous* that they would not be able to study, they hadn't studied for so long. They wouldn't be able to write an essay, they wouldn't be able to do this or that or the other. They were all scared. Every one of them got honours. They were just amazing. And we ran rings around the eighteen-year-olds—we really did. And I think it's not because we were cleverer than they, it was because we already had more experience.

An accident in Perth in 1983 kick-started a transformation in nurse ***CONNIE SHAW****'s (1937) life.*

In 1983, I had a car accident. A truck went in the back of us. My daughter and I were going down to get a permit or a book or something for her driver's licence, and I was waiting to turn at Russell Street and this building truck went in the back of me. It was about one o'clock on a Friday. I'm pretty sure he came from the pub.

I ended up with actually multiple fractures on my back, although at the time they didn't realise 'cause they thought it was all torn tendons and damaged nerves and everything else. But I went through rehabilitation for quite a few years. Went to court and the judge thought that all nurses have bad backs so I was compensated for whiplash which didn't really cover the bills. My husband couldn't cope with the fact I couldn't do everything and we parted company. Whereas before we were actually looking at a reasonably comfortable retirement, all of a sudden, I was broke. No income, nothing (laughs).

It was about the time that the kids were leaving home. My eldest daughter was already married at that stage. My youngest one was just turning eighteen. The other one was at university at the time. But she was in the car with me and she had some spinal injuries and she left university because sitting in classrooms and that, she just couldn't cope with it at that time.

I spent quite a time learning to cope with everything. I thought I'll have to do something with myself when the rehab finished. I sat here in the corner for about three days and I thought 'This is it. I can't sit here for the rest of my life.' I was looking in the paper and I saw an ad about an open day for a degree in community studies at Edith Cowan. I thought, 'Oh. That looks interesting.'

IT OPENED A WHOLE WORLD up really.

*In the 1980s **DONAT SANTOWIAK** (1950) moved into a new role in training when his work as a draftsman with the Victorian State*

Electricity Commission (SEC) was challenged by both computer-aided drafting (CAD) and privatisation.

For me drafting was about the act of drawing. To me, it was the drawing. And when computers came along it, drawing on a monitor with a keyboard just lost completely its meaning. That was one of the driving points of wanting to move in a different direction, as it turned out to be, adult education. Yep.

So about '85, '86 we were seriously starting to transition from drawing boards to the 'CAD' systems as they were known in those days. Hated it right from the word go. In those days of course the technology wasn't anything like what we have today. So it was terribly laborious and unfriendly, and I could see other people really taking it on like with gusto. I, perhaps I just felt that, 'Well, gee, I mean this is a race. I'm gonna be last.' It was bloody awful. You know, pressing things and things just not doing it and this highly specific stuff. Working in layers, and all this. I thought, 'Oh no. No, this is not me,' So that training centre secondment I think came along in time (laughs).

It was about that time—'89—we also had the first offerings of voluntary departures. The so-called dark cloud of privatisation was starting to pop over the horizon. A lot of people starting leaving. The entire SEC area was—I often referred to it as the holocaust—it was just awful because my role in HR [Human Resources]—a big part of it—was to work around that support for people who all of a sudden found themselves without a job but not being told to go.

I was coordinating what was known as the Help-a-Mate program. So I was in the epicentre of, you know, walking into the toilet and hearing a grown man cry. Walking through the carpark in the morning and seeing someone slumped over the steering wheel 'cause they've just attempted suicide. I was daily hearing people's stories about their wives threatening to leave them because they were about to get a windfall because of the voluntary departure package and, you know, they're gonna leave them and grab their money. Then others who dreamt about leaving and starting a lawn-mowing business or whatever, and then that not working out for them.

KIM BEAR *(1959) had left school and home on the Gold Coast in the mid-1970s and trained for clerical and commercial work. Her career in several cities ranged across office work, typesetting, advertising and editing, and she too recalls the impact of computerisation.*

Sometimes I'd be training *master* typesetters who were hot metal typesetters. These guys did it the old way, they're still working for newspapers of the day, creating in hot metal. They knew more about typesetting than I will ever know in my lifetime. But, the company was going to decide to come in to the computer age and these poor guys were going to go away from their desk on a Friday and come back the next week and this box was going to be sitting on their desk. The expectation was, they do what they'd been doing but now the skill of it was gone, it was down to a keyboard.

They were terrified. I saw—there was an amazing decimation of a workforce, in terms of, suddenly being old was a crime because you were not going to *get* the new technology, you were not going to be *able* to get it out of the computer. There was this amazing—I guess late '70s into the mid-'80s—where it's like anybody over thirty-five, forty disappeared out of offices. It was like suddenly old people vanished from the workplace. Wherever I went it was suddenly all these people barely shaving but they knew how to get it out of the computer. They didn't know the history of the company, they mightn't necessarily understand the history of the job they did, but they knew how to get that stuff out of the computer. I just remember this weird almost brain-drain where the people with the knowledge just vanished.

*After settling in Sydney's western suburbs in 2003, South Sudanese refugee **JAMES MAYOL** (1974) received government funding for training.*

When I come here the first thing they gave me 600 dollars for free to go to learn English, and because my English was very good they send me to computer school so that I can learn the basic in computers. As we know, generally when you come from Africa you don't have skills in computer. So I use my 500 dollars in computer. That was my first time to get into the Facebook, Googling and all of that, creating website, able to write—

Atem Atem: And your wife did the same?

Yes, did the same, and we went to improve of our skills in computer. After that I went to TAFE (Tertiary and Further Education), and then after the TAFE I went to uni. I did Social Welfare in TAFE.

How was the TAFE experience for you and doing the English classes?

Well for me it was very different than others because I was having a little bit of a skill prior to that. Because I did a lot of education through, sometimes I go to school. Then sometimes I have to stop. Sometimes I did a course, like that, you know, before I come to Australia. That helped me a lot when I come to Australia. I didn't require to any interpreters. I was just, go to office and do my own interview, read my own letters, carry on with my own educations. So it was very good.

My first job I work as a teacher aide at intensive English centre at Lewisham. So that also gave me a lot of opportunity to, educated myself on the field. The only difficult part was just an accent which is very different than our accent. But it become okay because I found other people in Australia been here for thirty years, they don't even speak English!

In 2014, towards the end of his career as a tiler in Sydney and north Queensland, **RICK GALEA** *(1958) reflects on his working life.*

Elena Volkova: What do you like about tiling?

Probably the money, actually. I do love the satisfaction of, as I said earlier, seeing a transformation of whatever we're working on. I've probably gotten to like it more as I've gotten older. I'm just getting wiser and doing things easier and, having more specialised tools, it has gotten a *lot* easier. The tiling today—as I said earlier, it used to be all sand and cement when I first started. That's almost past. It's very hard to find tilers now that are comfortable doing anything with sand and cement. So it has gotten easier in many regards with all the new adhesives and that.

But the money is—and the freedom of your own hours generally—has been a huge thing. I can seriously earn in one day what some people earn in a week when I'm organised and everything goes perfectly. So the money has been a big, big side of it. But saying that, you can earn a lot of money doing other occupations, but I haven't been able to find one (laughs) that's ready to throw money at me like that.

Not long before her interview in Toowoomba in 2013, **BRONWYN MACDONALD** *(1964), a qualified chef who had significant care responsibilities for her disabled son, started work in a government call centre.*

I'm in a call centre for Centrelink. It's not always terribly pleasant, but I quite like it actually. Customers who were like surly teenagers don't bother me. Actually, teenagers are my favourite age group. I really like them a lot. So generally have a good rapport with them by the end of each call, because someone's actually treating them like a person. So I do quite well at it I think. Lots to learn. It's a very complex system so, lots of mistakes to make yet. But I wouldn't mind that being ongoing for a little while. That would be good, because it's safe and secure (laughs). I get a pay cheque every week.

Elena Volkova: Is that the only reason?

It's a good reason (laughs), but no, it's not the only reason. It's always busy. There's always another call waiting for you. So you don't get a chance to feel useless. And you're definitely doing something for somebody. I like customer service. It's what I've always got the most satisfaction doing. And it's customer service with a good wage. So yeah, suits me really. And there's heating in winter and don't have to walk into walk-in freezers or horrible stuff like that. It's easy, easy work.

There's so much happening in the rest of my life, I don't really want a job that's going to take all my energy. It does take a fair bit of energy but it leaves you enough and you can go home at the end of the day and it's done. You don't have to think about it anymore till you go back. So yeah, it suits me on a lot of levels.

After starting his working life as an electrician, ***CHRISTIAN BOW*** *(1978) went to university as a mature student and now works as a construction project manager in Brisbane, where he reflects on changes and pressures in the modern workforce.*

I'm concerned that there's—because of the speed of internet and because of the amount of information available and because of the vast number of tools and applications and the like (sighs)—that there's a greater expectation on people and businesses and institutions to do what they've been doing forever in a faster way, in a more summarised format, dumbed down. The comparison between what I'm doing now at work and the old guy with the pencil, it's not just him getting used to the tools, it's him getting used to the speed of what we're doing.

So if I'm writing a program for a project and I say, 'Well okay. I can type this email and send it to him and he'll send it back to me within five minutes literally', whereas old mate would have written a letter, goes off in the post, takes two days to get there, they write the letter, it comes back and a week later he's got his response. The speed with which we *can* achieve things is just adding continuously to the expectations on what we should be able to do in a certain period of time. 'Why haven't you done that yet? It's just an email. It's just a spreadsheet. It's just, just do it. Get onto it. What are you doing?' You know, 'Stop fucking around.'

There's a potential exponential factor that can add onto that, and where do we stop? Do we keep designing devices that we don't need a computer anymore. It's all in our phone, it's all in our watch, it's all inserted in our brain. I'm not technology paranoid, but talking about my concerns about it and I'm concerned that it's just going to put more pace into society and more pressure (sighs).

Personally I'd like us to slow down a bit. I'd like us to knock off earlier and be able to go and have a game of golf and play in a park or go to the beach or do other jobs or chores or just things that we enjoy doing without having to get up in the dark, go to work all day, come home in the dark. You know, muck around with the kids. People expect you to work at night now. You've got a nine to five job but they go, 'Oh well you got a smart phone, you got a computer. Why can't you be doing that stuff at night?' You go, 'Well do you want me to book you for those hours as well?' Like there's just, 'Oh you're on a salary. You have these tools and you're on a salary so we expect you on call 24/7.' That's not said but there's a growing expectation that we're wired into this global connection.

At the time of his interview in 2013, ***ADAM FARROW-PALMER*** *(1988) worked as a producer with Sky News in Sydney. Here he reflects on the trend towards mobility in the workforce.*

My grandfather had a job for life. He stayed in his one job, one industry, and was there for the whole time and he always regretted it. My dad swapped a little bit from being an English teacher and being a writer but really, that was it.

I think with my generation, people are much more impatient. People want to try lots of things, and sample it, and it's much more common that people would stay in a job for maybe one year, maybe five max, and then jump out somewhere else, including swapping industries completely, and just try and find a place where their skills might be helpful there, or maybe just go for broke and change completely. I think that's pretty fun. I like that because you enter a new job, you'll learn all these new skills, get experience in a whole new world really. Then you can jump out and go and so you get another world later on.

I do intend to do that and move around, because we've got radio, TV—which is still fairly similar—but I think there are a lot of things out there that I would love to try and I feel that I really can.

By contrast, as manager of social media strategy for an online company, in 2013 ***KIRSTY WALLETT*** *(1982) in Brisbane was noticing inequalities and insecurity in her workforce and the risks of job mobility.*

Hamish Sewell: Do you think it's a level playing field out there?

In the workforce? That's a loaded question. No. Between males and females it's not, between women with children and women without children it's not, between corporate companies with big budgets and smaller companies that might be a little bit rewarding to work at, no it's tough. And it's tough at the moment. The job market's not fabulous for my industry at the moment and that's the first time in my lifetime it's ever been like that. I'm lucky because I have a job and I'm not unemployed but in the last few years I've known quite a few people and friends of mine that are very capable at their jobs—university graduates, professionals—who have been made redundant because of the economy.

I still realise that over the last hundred years we're very lucky to still be in the economic position we're in. But definitely, it's the first time in my working career—which I guess has almost been ten years now—that it's not easy to just go out and get something else. You don't have the flexibility that you used to. You can't throw caution to the wind. Perhaps that's about where I've worked myself up to in terms of the money that I'm earning and the freedom that I like to have in management roles. I've definitely noticed a change in the last couple of years.

Further Listening on Working Lives and Transformations

Bert Castellari, 1923, http://nla.gov.au/nla.obj-219871557/listen/3-3598
Fred Henskens, 1929, http://nla.gov.au/nla.obj-219905240/listen/1-1456
Ginette Matalon, 1936, http://nla.gov.au/nla.obj-219968733/listen/2-1603
Les Robinson, 1947, http://www.nla.gov.au/amad/nla.oh-vn6504265/2-3337
Russell Elliott, 1950, http://www.nla.gov.au/amad/nla.oh-vn6223258/4-3306
Peter Galvin, 1951, http://www.nla.gov.au/amad/nla.oh-vn6252046/1-2200
Alison Fettell, 1952, http://nla.gov.au/nla.obj-220185705/listen/2-165
Gina Polito, 1954, http://www.nla.gov.au/amad/nla.oh-vn6421369/2-28
David Cooper, 1959, http://nla.gov.au/nla.obj-220009702/listen/2-4486
Phil May, 1962, http://www.nla.gov.au/amad/nla.oh-vn6569680/1-2132
Rhonda King, 1965, http://nla.gov.au/nla.obj-220035263/listen/1-4719
Jodie Bell, 1970, http://www.nla.gov.au/amad/nla.oh-vn6290885/1-34
Lisa Jackson, 1972, http://nla.gov.au/nla.obj-219901040/listen/2-1338
Suzie Quartermain, 1975, http://nla.gov.au/nla.obj-220022403/listen/1-990
Jay Logan, 1981, http://nla.gov.au/nla.obj-220182115/listen/1-1006
Arthur Hunter, 1989, http://nla.gov.au/nla.obj-219957349/listen/1-2355

Fun!

Fishing became a passion and a life-saver for ***DONAT SANTOWIAK*** *(1950) in the 1970s.*

About the end of my first marriage I met up with a friend who—if I had a brother I would suggest that he would be, he was the sort of brother that I'd like—and I know on reflection today, he really fed the fishing fire in me and that really kept me alive in some ways.

He had a boat. So I ended up being the number one deckhand for him. Oh, I have some invaluable great memories. Sometimes we'd go as far as Narooma and Bermagui in southern New South Wales and do some *really* serious fishing, but more often than not, south coast of Gippsland here offshore. Did a lot of beach fishing off the surf.

Alistair Thomson: So what for you was the attraction of fishing?

I'm not really sure. There'd be some common elements with all the other fishos. The mystery and the excitement of catching something, not knowing what it is till it's on the surface. A day out—great day out—for the first time I think I was really starting to tune in to nature. I remember some of my language changing, so calling like 'a majestic scene'. Those more noble descriptions to the environment started popping up. And then stories, and the social connection that came with that. The drinking was obviously a part of it. We called ourselves the 'Happy Hookers'. It grew from probably half a dozen blokes that went fishing together to a point where we had our annual go-aways—a place called Cape Conran in East Gippsland—we'd have a swag of blokes, swag of boats, and in the end we had our own logos. That was a marvellous, marvellous thing.

The dilemma came when I stopped drinking. Those early trips became impossible for me. We say in AA that, 'If the Christians managed to get out of the lion pits they didn't go back to pick up their hats.' Or 'If you sit in a barber's chair for long enough you'll end up getting a haircut.' What I'm saying is I couldn't survive that without drinking again. So that was a really horrible kind of disconnection. A lot of people didn't understand that, some of them to this day. So when I stopped drinking that came to an abrupt end, for me.

By the late 1970s **VERONICA SCHWARZ** *(1939) had a young child with her partner Ian, was working in the Victorian Education Department and was active in the women's movement and party politics. She found a 'different dimension' through music.*

I joined a band that played at a women's pub in Richmond. Half of them were lesbians and only two of us were not—the other four were. We formed this band called Synergy and we used to play in the pub. It was mainly in the back of the pub that women gathered. It was an ordinary Richmond pub with men in the bar in the front. That was the beginning of my playing in the band, I suppose.

I played guitar. Later on after that, that band split up—a lot to do with the lesbian-heterosexual tensions actually—that band split up and then Ian and I and a couple of other friends formed another band which we called the Stump Jumpers. A bush band. We played for bush dances and I used to call the dances and act as the MC and Ian played the drums, and another couple who were our friends, Tony was the lead singer and his wife Deborah played rhythm guitar as did I. We also got a fiddler and a tin whistle player.

Well, we didn't need two rhythm guitars, but we didn't have a bass player. So I bought an electric bass and taught myself to play that. And that was wonderful. Bass plays a whole different texture to *anything* else. Absolutely amazing. It opened my eyes to a whole different dimension in the musical spectrum. I loved it.

After a divorce in the early 2000s, mother of four ***RHONDA KING*** *(1965) returned to learning in western Sydney, taking and then teaching fitness classes and eventually completing a degree and working in the arts. She recalls how she overcame her fear of standing out in front of other people.*

The thing that I did that really helped me break away this horrible barrier that I had was to join a theatre group—which was something I'd always wanted to do but again too petrified of getting on the stage and people looking at me—I joined this place in Richmond up near Sydney. Richmond Players it was called—or still is, still exists. It's one of the oldest constantly running theatre companies in Australia actually.

So I went and auditioned and I thought, 'Oh I'm not going to get the part'. They were casting, it was *Aladdin.* It was a pantomime though. So they cast this pretty young girl as the princess and this other pretty young girl as something else. I'm like, 'Yeah, I'm not a pretty young girl. They're not going to cast me as any of those things.' Then they're going through and then they're running out of girl parts. I'm like, 'Oh my gosh, there's no more girl parts. What am I going to do?' Then they said, 'We'd like to offer you the part of Ali Way.' I was like, 'What's that?' They said, 'That's a pirate.' And I'm like, 'A *pirate*?' They're like, 'Yeah, it's a *man*.' I'm like, '*What*? (laughs) Have to be a *man*? Really?'

Because I didn't know much about theatre, I suppose, I didn't know a pantomime, the whole idea is that people act in opposite roles, you know, boys are girls, girls are boys, and there was a lot of that in the play. But the character was an absolute ham and it was so funny. We had to sing songs and we had to dance and we had to act like idiots.

So I remembered the script and I'd practised and practised and practised so I wouldn't forget all these words I had to *say* on cue. The very first performance we did, and the very first thing I had to do in this play was—backstage there's a bit of a rise I think at the back, and I'm wearing these really huge pantaloons and I've got a scabbard and I've got a scarf thing around my head and I've got a drawn-on moustache (laughs)—and the first thing I had to do was run in and jump over this riser thing and then land in the middle of the stage and go, *'Aha'* (laughs).

I'm out the back going (puffing loudly), 'I'm going to die. I'm going to die. Why did I say I would do this? *Why? Why? Why?'* Anyway then I'm waiting for my cue, all the time going (puffing loudly), and I hear the cue and then I just take the big breath and I go, 'You can do it. You can do it.' I'm like, 'Big breath' and I jump in, I'm like, '*Ya ha.*'

Then I was off. It was almost like this big loud yell was the opening segment of this new part of my life. It was really, really funny. Then I couldn't get enough of theatre. I did as many plays as I could. I directed plays, I did backstage, I did front of house. I did everything and I just loved it. It was so much fun and to hear audience reacting to you when you do something, and I really love the comedy part. I thought that was so much fun and it really suited who I was as well. I just discovered this whole other person that I didn't know existed. I'm like, '*Wow.* There's this whole other person inside.'

PETER GALVIN*'s (1951) beloved Jack Russell Terrier, Chico, can be heard in parts of his interview recording in 2012, and prompted a discussion about the role of pets in Peter's life.*

I've had a dog from my earliest memory, from before I went to school when I was still living in Bankstown, we had a dog there. All the time until I left school and left home, my mother always had dogs. She had a dog all the time up until she moved, till her and dad moved into their own little flat in Sydney. They couldn't take the dog with them, so I took the dog off them. So I've always had one. The last dog before Chico, we had for seventeen years. Had him from the day he was born until the day he died.

Matthew Higgins: And how long have you had Chico?

Since, well Fella died in 2007, so about three years, just over three years now, nearly four years.

How close are you to Chico? I think yesterday when we were talking off the microphone about your recovery from the stroke, has Chico been very important to you during that period?

He has. Unlike any other dog I've had, I've spent a lot of time with that particular dog. Like when I had Fella—this was before I had the stroke, so he'd grown up used to me not being here when I was at work or away on business or whatever—so he thought of himself as a member of the family. He used to think—dogs have a pecking order—so at the top of the tree was mum, then me and then my daughter and then him and then Patrick [Peter's son] was at the bottom. He used to pick on Paddy all the time, something terrible. Whereas Chico's come into the family where he knows his place at the bottom of the pecking order. He knows that. And because I'm here all the time, he knows I'm at the top, I think, so he's my best mate. He's become my best buddy. He loves me unconditionally.

At the time of her interview in Perth in 2012, **GERALDINE BOX** *(1949) had recently retired. Bike-riding is one of her continuing pleasures.*

I've commuted for thirteen years actually, forty k's a day and I don't want to give up—that's I think helped contribute to maintaining a fitness and it certainly maintains my mental sensibility and just staying on track. Because I built into the day I didn't have to come home and go to the gym or do anything like that, and it was beautiful because I had a beautiful environment to ride in along the river, the Swan and then the Canning Rivers and I looked at all the changes, the bird life, the migratory birds, the whole thing, dolphins in the river. It's fantastic, it's a beautiful ride. I think it's probably—as I wrote in a recent bike blog—I think it's probably one of the best commutes in Australia. I plan to do some more touring. I've planned to do a ride along the Murray, the *other* Murray, the one I grew up on.[1]

As a working mother in Broome, ***JODIE BELL*** *(1970) takes an active role in sport and other community activities.*

I love the beach. I do a lot of stuff with my kids. I'm very involved in our football club that my son has played for before they went to boarding school, which is the Broome Saints (laughs). I'm currently—what am I? Fundraising coordinator, sponsorship coordinator, something like that at Saints Football Club and manage their canteen on the weekends at junior footie. My daughter now plays for Saints Juniors and Jeremiah plays for Saints Seniors. So, I do that. Also I try and do a bit of sport when I can though I'm not the best but I did play, when I got back here, I started playing netball again for a couple of years, didn't play this year because my knees were telling me that maybe it wasn't a good idea anymore (laughs).

I love the beach. I'm also member of the Broome Surf Life Saving Club now, I'm an age group manager for the Nippers. I've been doing that two years now which I really like that, and this summer I'm supposed to be doing my bronze medallion and stuff so I'm awarded safety supervisor for the Nippers, so, yeah, I enjoy that.

I've always loved the water. I want to try and get my boat license so I can buy a little boat. I don't mind fishing, and never catch much, but I like the peace of being sitting by the beach. Vincent [her partner] doesn't like the sea because he is—being a desert person (laughs). But I can get him out fishing now and then. We go fishing under the pretence of fishing and he fishes

1 Geraldine is here referring to the 'other' Murray River in south-east Australia where she grew up, rather than the Murray River near Perth in south-west Australia.

and I pretend I'm fishing. I just like sitting by the beach but I also just go myself with the kids (laughs).

Previously from Perth but now living in Sydney, ***LISA JACKSON*** *(1972) reflects on the importance of AFL (Australian Football League) footy in her life.*

Frank Heimans: I notice you're wearing an Essendon jersey there.

Yes, because it's one of the warmest jumpers I have. I do like Aussie Rules. AFL is my passion. I love AFL. I must admit I'm a bit of a geek and I do have a website that's got a blog. When I was a bit more functional than I am now I used to maintain a --- a record of all the Aboriginal players within the AFL and also the historical players. So players that made an impact like Polly Farmer, Barry Cable, all those other Aboriginal players that really impacted on the sport. I've got a page dedicated to them.

The reason why I got the Essendon jersey on is because—stupid little story—but Essendon and Sydney Swans play a game every year called The Marn Grook Cup which is the Aboriginal cup. They are the reason why I like AFL. It's a good story. AFL has its roots in Victoria and AFL came out of the traditional Aboriginal game where they would actually kick a possum skin to each other. Down in Victoria, they used to have this festival where all the tribes would get together and they'd play this possum-skin game kicking it to and from each other. During that time they would get together and they traded beads and animals, yeah women, but that was on the side. After they'd play the game they then break into this song and dance and they'd have corroborees and tell their stories and that. That's how they transferred stories and languages and stuff like that.

So for me, AFL has got a traditional side—an Aboriginal side—but also a modern side. So Essendon and Sydney Swans they have—in recognition of that—they have a game called The Marn Grook Cup and every year they'd play for this Marn Grook Cup. Since moving to Sydney a few of my friends are diehard

Sydney Swan supporters and my brother is a Sydney Swan supporter. And me, who I am, has decided that I'm going for Essendon. Every time they play I don't go for the Sydney Swans, I go for Essendon. But my home team is West Coast, so I've also got a West Coast jumper at home too.

In regional Victoria, single mum ***SUZIE QUARTERMAIN*** *(1975) extols the virtues of her smartphone.*

Well, when it comes to technology the iPhone is the best thing that's happened since I was born. I just think it's just the *best* invention. I saw something on Facebook the other day of all the devices from the '90s and then below, just the iPhone. It was all of those devices in one.

Katie Holmes: So what makes it so good?

Just because it's everything. It's a phone, it's internet, it's Facebook, it's games, camera. Like I don't know how I ever lived without a phone. I really *do* not know. My early adulthood there was no such thing. Well not in normal-day lives. So I have lived without and I've lived with it and everyone that I talk to that's my age agrees. They just don't know how they—you know, it's not just the young ones. They take it for granted I suppose. So I reckon that's the biggest thing. Because when I was a kid—like I said—we never had a video player. We never had a microwave. Colour telly, those things passed me by. By the time I got my own ones, they weren't new anymore so there was no novelty to it.

As a single parent—being on my own—it's like my link to the outside world. Most definitely. And because I haven't wanted to be physically social I can be from where I feel safe at home. I can still have contact with people without having to talk on the phone. Yeah. It's awesome.

In Sydney, writer ***BEN PEEK*** *(1976) plays online games with people around the country and across the world.*

I play this game called *World of Warcraft*, and it's basically a big online multiplayer game that you play with friends and stuff like that. I originally got into it with my childhood friends. One of them got addicted to crystal meth and we needed to do something that would basically while away the hours for him. So we all ended up (laughs) playing this game where you basically run around with swords and beat people up and it's online and we'd sit there with headphones and things like that and just basically kill time.

Most of my friends that I played it with at the time have actually stopped playing it. But I still play it. My girlfriend and I play it. We have like a little raid group that you go two nights a week for, it's a bunch of people we know from around the country. They live up in Queensland, down in Melbourne, out in Perth. There's a couple of people from Singapore and from the States and stuff like that in the little group that we have. And we kill bosses (laughs)—ten of us. It's pretty much like a—if you had to compare it to something—it's like a cards night. Where a bunch of your friends come over and you play poker and stuff like that and we just do that.

It's the most amazingly geeky pastime whatsoever but it's pretty cost effective, and fun.

Further Listening on Fun!

Alison Fettell, 1952, http://nla.gov.au/nla.obj-220185705/listen/1-2480
Gina Polito, 1954, http://nla.gov.au/nla.obj-220096095/listen/1-1510
David Cooper, 1959, http://nla.gov.au/nla.obj-220009702/listen/3-2194
Michelle Cripps, 1960, http://www.nla.gov.au/amad/nla.oh-vn6252075/2-730~2-847
Phil May, 1962, http://www.nla.gov.au/amad/nla.oh-vn6569680/2-2486
Christian Bow, 1978, http://nla.gov.au/nla.obj-219896923/listen/0-2562
James Finnegan, 1981, http://nla.gov.au/nla.obj-220176798/listen/2-3524

Further Reading on Midlife

Bongiorno, Frank, *The Sex Lives of Australians: A History* (Collingwood: Black Inc., 2013).

Verity Burgmann and Jenny Lee (eds), *Making a Life: A People's History of Australia since 1788* (Melbourne: McPhee Gribble/Penguin, 1988).

Davison, Graeme, Dingle, Tony and O'Hanlon, Seamus (eds), *The Cream Brick Frontier: Histories of Australian Suburbia* (Melbourne: Monash Publications in History, 1995).

Game, Anne and Pringle, Rosemary, 'Sexuality and the Suburban Dream', in Richard White and Penny Russell (eds), *Memories and Dreams: Reflections on 20th Century Australia* (St Leonards: Allen & Unwin, 1997), pp. 189–211.

Holmes, Katie, *Between the Leaves: Stories of Australian Women, Writing and Gardens* (Perth: University of Western Australia, 2011).

Murphy, John, 'Breadwinning: Accounts of Work and Family Life in the 1950s', *Labour & Industry* 12, no. 4 (2002), pp. 59–75.

Murphy, John, *Imagining the Fifties: Private Sentiment and Political Culture in Menzies' Australia* (Sydney: University of New South Wales Press, 2000).

Murphy, John and Probert, Belinda, '"Anything for the house": Recollections of Post-war Suburban Dreaming', *Australian Historical Studies* 36, no. 124 (2004), pp. 275–93.

Peel, Mark, 'A New Kind of Manhood: Remembering the 1950s', *Australian Historical Studies* 28, no. 109 (1997), pp. 147–57.

Reiger, Kerreen, *Our Bodies, Our Babies: the Forgotten Women's Movement* (Carlton: Melbourne University Press, 2001).

Reiger, Kerreen and James, Margaret, 'Hatches, Matches and Despatches', in Verity Burgmann and Jenny Lee (eds), *Constructing a Culture: A People's History of Australia since 1788* (Melbourne: McPhee Gribble /Penguin, 1988), pp. 1–17.

Reynolds, Robert and Robinson, Shirleene, *Gay and Lesbian, Then and Now: Australian Voices from a Social Revolution* (Melbourne: Black Inc., 2016).

Swain, Shurlee and Howe, Renate, *Single Mothers and their Children: Disposal, Punishment and Survival in Australia* (Melbourne: Cambridge University Press, 1995).

CHAPTER 7

ACTIVISM

Many of the Australian Generations interviewees have been activists of one sort or another. Some have had a formal role in parliamentary processes and party politics. Michelle Cripps, for example, recalls her time working in the Labor Party Senate Whip's office and witnessing what was for her a 'defining moment' of democratic politics—the federal debate over Work Choices and Fair Work legislation in 2008. 'I wish I could have bottled that moment because I think that really showed the democracy of Australia at work.' Though few Australians have such close, first-hand experience of the governmental process, many participate in different types of activism, ranging across party membership and politicking, single issue campaigning on local, regional or national issues, and community action close to home. This chapter spotlights examples of activism since the 1930s and the small and large ways in which Australians seek to make a difference beyond their personal or family life.

Examples from the mid-twentieth century showcase three different corners of party politics. In the 1930s Ruth Apps' parents were solid supporters of the conservative United Australia Party (precursor to the Liberal Party). As land developers their fortunes were dashed by the Depression of the 1930s and the populist New South Wales Premier Jack Lang, who backed laws restricting the rights of landlords to evict defaulting tenants. Ruth recalls that as a young girl she was so angry with Lang that she wanted to go to his house and 'really tick him off thoroughly'. At the other end of politics, Bert Castellari joined the Communist Party of Australia in the mid-1940s. The Soviet Union was still a wartime ally, many Australians were working for a postwar world that might transcend the economic and social disaster of the interwar years, and the Communist Party, with a significant base in Australian unions, supported radical change. But Bert was put off by the stale debate of Party meetings and soon 'drifted out'. In the

1950s and '60s John Murphy's Melbourne Catholic family were staunch supporters of the Democratic Labor Party, the socially-conservative anti-communist party that was formed after the Labor Party split of 1955. As a priest in the Philippines, John found his own political direction in the late '60s when he learnt about ownership, power and justice. 'That was a *real* eye-opener for me.'

The 1960s and '70s were decades of political ferment in Australia and around the world. New or reinvigorated social movements protested about war, environmental issues, and women's and Aboriginal rights, and young people in particular challenged authority and tradition and took to the streets. Australia's participation in the Vietnam War and the conscription of twenty-year-olds by a birthdate lottery were among the most contentious causes. Following reports of the United States bombing of Cambodia that commenced in 1969, and after her cousin was conscripted into the army, young Melbourne nurse Geraldine Box plastered anti-war graffiti over a local war memorial. In Sydney, Peter Galvin's involvement in a Catholic youth group forged his moral opposition to conscription. He refused to register for the conscription draft and spent several months in the early 1970s on the run from police until he decided to give himself up at a symbolic protest event outside Sydney Town Hall. Peter later campaigned against United States military bases in northern Australia and became a trade union organiser with the Builders Labourers Federation. Tensions within Geraldine and Peter's families highlight the generational divisions in Australian politics at this time. Geraldine's parents were 'aghast' when they heard about her protest. Peter's father, a 'believer in law and order and all that crap', was 'very hostile', though his mother's views changed after Peter and his brother were harassed by police.

Second-wave feminism exploded into life in early 1970s Australia. Brisbane divorcee Trish Barrkman 'became a bit of a women's libber' when her own experience in 1974 of divorce and single parenthood meshed with the ideas of Germaine Greer and other feminists who were '*talking about* the rights of women'. Greer's book *The Female Eunuch* (first published in 1970) was also 'startling and eye-opening' for primary school teacher turned university student Veronica Schwarz. In Melbourne Veronica was on the committee of the Women's Electoral Lobby, founded in 1972, and joined a consciousness-raising group with other Women's Liberation movement supporters. Through feminist politics she learnt that discrimination against individual women was part of a 'social pattern' that could be resisted and changed. Veronica's progressive politics also extended to party politics as a member and election candidate for both the Australia Party (established in 1966 by Liberals and independents opposed to conscription and Australian involvement in the Vietnam War) and the Australian Democrats (formed from the Australia Party and disaffected Liberals in 1977 to offer a centrist alternative to Labor and the Liberal-National coalition).

For Australians who lived through the 1970s, the election of the Whitlam Labor government in 1972 and its dismissal by the Governor-General in 1975, are potent memories that signify the promise (or danger) of a period of significant social reform. Ian Reid's South Australian family had 'strong Labor leanings', and he recalls riding his bike around a polling booth in 1972 with primary school mates yelling 'We Want Gough! We Want Gough!' Veronica Schwarz still reveres 'the great Whitlam' whose government abolished university fees and thus enabled her to study without having to work as a taxi driver. Trish Barrkman recalls the impact of no fault divorce introduced by the Family Law Act of 1975. Other Australians remember the chaos of the Whitlam government's final year and lament the negative impact of its reforms on 'family values'.

Social movements like environmentalism took root in the 1980s. Barbara Krickl, a young Christian exchange student from Germany in 1982 and 1983, joined Sydney's Palm Sunday peace and anti-nuclear march, and supported the campaign against the proposed hydro-electricity dam on the Gordon River that would have impacted upon the environmentally sensitive Franklin River and its World Heritage hinterland. Barbara recalls the interconnections and overlaps between the different social movements of the time, and her experience as a volunteer at a youth refuge in western Sydney introduced her to deprivation and inequality that was much worse than what she'd been used to growing up in a working-class family in Germany.

Barbara Krickl's voluntary work reminds us that volunteering in local organisations and campaigns is, for many Australians, their most important activism. For example, when a terrible accident in her forties forced Connie Shaw to stop nursing in the 1980s, a passion for computing that was ignited on a community studies degree in Perth underpinned a series of activist enterprises: creating flyers and databases for a local exchange service; providing computer-based assistance for people in chronic pain;

and introducing computers to remote communities. Connie's work changed people's lives but it also transformed her own life and identity. Alison Fettell and Jodie Bell describe their participation in community campaigns that have made a difference in the past decade, on both sides of the continent. On south-coast New South Wales sixty-year-old Alison describes a campaign against centralisation of health treatment and closure of local facilities. Jodie, who worked as a community trainer at Fitzroy Crossing in the Kimberley, recalls how Aboriginal women fought for restrictions on takeaway alcohol to reduce alcohol-fuelled violence.

All of our Aboriginal narrators recount episodes in Indigenous activism that have been important for their families and communities. Lisa Jackson, for instance, had tears in her eyes as she remembered two moments in 2000 that signified the pride of Aboriginal Australia and the hope of recognition and reconciliation. As a volunteer at the Sydney Olympics Lisa witnessed Aboriginal runner Cathy Freeman's historic victory in the 400 metre race, with her victory lap holding the Australian and the Aboriginal flags, and then a closing ceremony that showcased Aboriginal history. For Lisa, the Olympics was 'the *only* time Australia was *absolutely* proud to have an Aboriginal history'. Earlier that year, Lisa had joined hundreds of thousands of people walking across the Sydney Harbour Bridge on a Reconciliation Walk. It was freezing but there were '*all* these people walking for *my people*'. 'It couldn't get any better than that.'

The Al-Qaeda attack on the New York Twin Towers on '9/11' 2001 signalled a transformation of politics in Australia and around the world. The optimism that followed the fall of the Berlin Wall in 1989 and the end of the Cold War faded with the start of a 'war on terror', the fragmentation of states that had been held together by authoritarian regimes, and a series of refugee crises that tested border politics, ignited racism and spurred activism for and against asylum seekers. Michelle Cripps recalls thinking in the late 1980s that 'finally the world's coming together', but concludes that 'we definitely lost our innocence and realised how much part of the world we were with the September 11'. James Finnegan, born in 1981, describes 9/11 as 'one of the biggest defining moments in my generation'. At the time he was transfixed by the television footage of the Twin Towers, and on reflection he believes the attack 'triggered a very dangerous shift towards the right in politics'.

Young Australians in particular have been both politicised and disillusioned by recent developments in domestic and international politics. The 2000s have seen a decline of membership and electoral support for the major political parties and disaffection with conventional party politics. Interviewed in 2011 when she was in her mid-twenties, Milijana Stojadinovic was delighted by the come-uppance of the 'boys club' of Australian politics when Julia Gillard became Prime Minister in 2010, but she still thinks 'that at the end of the day, it's all the same crap'. On the other hand, non-party political, multi-issue campaigning organisations such as GetUp! have galvanised activism on a range of contemporary issues, and pioneered new forms of online and social media politics. In her late fifties, Kim Bear's membership of GetUp! has, for example, informed and connected her to campaigning on issues ranging from Aboriginal rights to same-sex marriage and Australian responses to asylum seekers. Activism may be happening in new ways, but activist Australians continue to influence social and political change.

***RUTH APPS** (1926) recalls her parents' and her own conservative politics in the early 1930s.*

> My parents as I mentioned before had been land developers. They were very solidly what you'd call Liberal today. In those days it was the UAP [United Australia Party], it was called, and they voted very solidly that way. When the Depression came and Jack Lang who was the Labor Premier at that time, he put a moratorium on rents and things which was my parents' downfall in the sense that they couldn't force their tenants to pay their rents and that was the result of Jack Lang. Well, they were *very* much anti-Labor in those days and very solidly Liberal.
>
> As a child I can remember on our trip to Sydney at Christmas time, I, as a eight-year-old the story goes, was so angry with that Jack Lang—I didn't know him but I was being told about him—that I said I was going to go to his house and 'really tick him off thoroughly'. So the story goes we drove through

a residential street in Sydney and my mother pointed out a house where there were people sitting on the veranda and she said, 'That's Jack Lang's house but oh look there are people there, you can't go in.' Now I believed that for years. She had confessed to me later that she didn't know who lived there. It was just a way to keep me quiet.

***BERT CASTELLARI** (1923) was conscripted to the army in early 1942. He fought overseas in Papua New Guinea and Borneo during World War II, and after the war served in the British Commonwealth Occupation Force in Japan. He joined the Communist Party of Australia [CPA] at the end of the war.*

Matthew Higgins: Why did you join the CPA? What was your motivation?

We'd been through a world war where we were learning more about what happened right across Europe. Very conscious of the war. We were going back to Australia which had come out of a Depression into a war. We didn't know what it was going to be like. The unions were very active, now that the communists were running several of the unions in Sydney. The coal miners, the iron workers, the transport workers, I've forgotten who they were, some of the unions that don't exist anymore. Fred [a friend] and I talked over these things and about Europe and about communism and he put it on me one day. He said, 'You want to join the Party?' I said, 'Alright, I'll join.'

***THIS IS A TUMULTUOUS PERIOD** for the Communist Party of Australia with the Menzies government trying to eradicate it through legislation. What do you remember of that particular issue and did you play any senior role in the party?*

Not much at all. I was a member of—I didn't find out till they pulled out my ASIO [Australian Security Intelligence

Organisation] file that I was regarded as a member of the journalist section. I didn't even know the Communist Party had a journalist section. I knew those on *The Telegraph* staff who were also members, and all of them like me drifted out. I didn't play any particular part. In fact I took myself up to a meeting of the Randwick branch. I lived in Randwick at this time and introduced myself. This was at the time when the coal strike was pending. That was a pretty tremendous era. I think I was still a member of the party in 1951, '50. I think it was probably 1949. I went to a meeting of the Randwick branch. I got there late and they were having a long, earnest discussion. When they finally dealt with—'cause you got to get used to the way communists discuss things—they were talking about a motion in support of something that was happening in Bulgaria which of course was a communist country. This went on for quite a while and we didn't seem to have other business and I finally left. I never went to that meeting again. It was 1949, the eve of the coal strike in 1949. They weren't talking about anything to do ---

So it wasn't relevant—they weren't relevant to Australia's issues?

No. Not a thing! But I might be unfair to the people who were there in that branch. They were locals and they might have talked about a lot of other things. But so *irrelevant*, I just left it.

Growing up, ***JOHN MURPHY*** *(1940) was 'culturally, Catholic DLP' (Democratic Labor Party). In the late 1960s, when John served as a priest in the Philippines, his politics became more radical.*

When I was in the seminary I would have been—my brother was involved with the DLP—and I'd be home --- I know there was a '61 election and Menzies *just* defeated Calwell. Morrie and his friends were counting, well working out, how-to-vote cards and all this kind of thing to take them to the different polling stations and all that. So he was full-on in the DLP. And

I was like osmosis, I was like a DLP fellow traveller, supporter if anyone had asked me. But the big turning point for me was going to the Philippines. Then a lot of things became clearer about justice and belonging and communities and differences and ownership and power and tenant farmers and slave labour. That was a *real* eye-opener for me but that was later on.

GERALDINE BOX *(1949) remembers her involvement in the anti-Vietnam War movement.*

I think I was swept up into the anti-Vietnam War sensitivities and feelings of the time. Certainly I felt that and acted on that end. I didn't attend any of the moratorium marches in Melbourne but I was certainly active and spoke out about what was happening in Vietnam and took a great interest in that. Also seeing—I think having a brother who was at the age when he *could've* been called up and fortunately he wasn't, his birth date didn't come forward but my cousin's birth date came forward and he was conscripted into the army. So I felt it wasn't --- a right thing for Australia to be doing. I came home from the nursing job that I was in and decided to do a late-night midnight run to the local war memorial and plaster it with anti-Vietnam War—I think it was actually just after the bombing of Cambodia and that really --- I thought that was it. I went up and wrote things on newspaper and spread it all, pasted it all over the war memorial. My parents who by that stage had moved into town and lived just up the road from the war memorial were absolutely *aghast* when I told them what I had done. But I felt very strongly about it.

PETER GALVIN *(1951) recalls draft dodging when conscription was legislated from November 1964 to December 1972. This was the beginning of his extensive involvement in political activism. The*

National Service Scheme required twenty-year-old men to register for the military and a ballot then determined which of these men would be called up. Peter's family lived near the University of Sydney, and he had become involved in student politics despite not being a student. His girlfriend, who he met through a Christian anti-conscription group, gave birth to their daughter just after Peter had failed to appear in court and a warrant for his arrest had been issued.

As I was growing up—from between the age of about sixteen and twenty—as the age for being called up/conscripted into the army grew nearer, I had to think more and more about it. I was always against the concept of --- conscription of human life. I thought it was akin to slavery. I was against it. I just was morally against it. No political reason particularly, I just thought it was conceptually wrong. Irrespective of what the war was about or anything else, I just thought that the idea of being able to conscript a person against their will to do something was wrong. And I still do.

Once they issued a warrant for your arrest—for, say, for example, stage one failing to register—they would come and arrest you. I didn't go to court so then they issued the arrest warrant. The *purpose* of it was to make a public stance, you know, 'come and get me' sort of thing. You've got to remember, most of us were twenty-year-old yahoos at the time and 'come and get me', so it was a bit of fun.

Matthew Higgins: So where did you move around? Where were you living?

By this time you see I had developed friends in this thing called the Draft Resistance Union, which was like a collective of people who had similar ideas about conscription. So through that, there was a whole network—through the Quakers and through the Save Our Sons movement—of people who would give you safe accommodation. Mainly I lived around the inner city of Sydney. I went to Melbourne. I went up to the country for a while and worked at --- was it a cattle station, I think? Bogan Gate, yeah.

Sheep station at Bogan Gate.

So I did a few different things until I finally gave myself up. After a while, you're sick of running around—in my case, I got sick of it. So we organised an event where I could publicly surrender. The police went berserk—I don't know, I mean I was giving myself up. It was the Commonwealth police. The New South Wales police, they wouldn't have arrested, they didn't want to know anything about it. They didn't care less. It wasn't a state crime, so ---

So where did you give yourself up to the Commonwealth police?

The idea was to do it in front of the Sydney Town Hall. But on the way there they saw us coming and they tried to grab me in front of the old Regent Theatre. It's not there anymore—it's now McDonald's—so that's a much-photographed event when they actually grabbed me.

So were you arrested outside the Regent or at the Town Hall?

No, I didn't make it to the Town Hall. So they arrested me, I was chained up to all these other people. Like *half* the people that were against conscription were against it for religious reasons, Christian reasons. So there were quite a lot of Catholics and Christians, of whom I was one. So we developed this thing with the chains—chains were common with the draft resistors—so following the example of St Paul who when he was in gaol in Rome said, 'When I am in my chains, I am most free', and follows the example of Dietrich Bonhoeffer in Germany and things like that. A lot of it was symbolic street theatre type activity.

Then you went into gaol for a period?

So then they locked me up, yep, they took me away. They arrested about a dozen other people at this time when they were trying to get to me. Then they eventually let them all go.

I was there, sitting alone in this police station in Phillip Street and I was wondering what was going to happen next. All my friends had been released. It was the first time I'd been alone in a police station—and it's now been turned into a police museum and I went there one day to look at it and show my kids the cell that I was in. But I got a bit lonely after a while and I didn't know what was going on, the police wouldn't talk to me. Then after I don't know how many hours this lawyer turns up at the gate. I can hear him arguing with the police out the front and they had some route to get me out of gaol. And they let me out.

So how long would you have been, if you like, on the run or on the move?

About three months, I think it was altogether.

So it's 1972 or '71?

'72.

What was your parents' attitude towards you evading the draft and how were they feeling while you were on the run?

My father was hostile because he was --- a believer in law and order and all that sort of crap. Whereas my mother was a bit on the side of mothers who don't want their sons to be killed in the Vietnam War and stuff, but she wasn't --- she was fifty fifty about it all. The police harassment of her house is what turned her against them, they turned her in my favour. They harassed her and did things to my—I've got a brother who was a year younger than me and they often mistook him for me, even though he had short hair and I had long hair. They used to give him a hard time. So that turned her against them, I think.

*Recently divorced and living in the inner-north Brisbane suburb of Clayfield with her three children, **TRISH BARRKMAN** (1933) recalls the impact of Germaine Greer in the 1970s.*

I did everything that I possibly could and life was great. But I must admit Germaine Greer (laughs), Germaine Greer had come into my life, hadn't she? We suddenly had in this country a female *talking about* the rights of women. Well, I really sat up and took notice. I think a part of me became --- oh I guess I became a bit of a women's libber (laughs). I wasn't outrageously so but I recognised the fact that there wasn't much out there for women. When I divorced, there was a widow's pension but I don't think in this country they had any *type* of support for women that were left in these circumstances with children. I still think today that women that are deserted with children are still very low on the economic arena in Australia. But we survived it all and I grew as a person.

Further south, Germaine Greer also influenced ***VERONICA SCHWARZ*** *(1939), who relocated to Melbourne from Brisbane in 1971. Veronica read Greer's seminal text,* The Female Eunuch, *in the same year that she joined the Women's Electoral Lobby (WEL).*

The Female Eunuch was probably the most startling and eye-opening. I went around calling her Saint Germaine for years. She seems to have changed strangely but (laughs). Don't know what's going on there but she certainly helped a lot of us at the time. And I joined WEL.

I WAS ON THE COMMITTEE OF WEL and I was the editor of their newsletter for several years. At one stage, I chaired a meeting in the Masonic Hall we were talking about last week. I had the five federal female Members of Parliament. We brought them down and they sat on a panel which I chaired. So that was a big event—Joan Child was among them. Couple of radio and television appearances speaking on behalf of WEL and putting across the feminist perspective. I'd travelled around a bit as a public speaker—Rotary, Lions Club, lots of clubs like that that were interested in knowing what this was all about. I remember once I was speaking at a Rotary club and about the discrimination that women had suffered and were still suffering. They received it all very well. I think that I speak in a fairly reasonable and logical manner and present facts. At the end of it they applaud and are very, very *impressed* I think. Then one man stood up and said, 'That was absolutely wonderful but you know you should smile more often.' I thought, 'Would you say that to a black man talking about black rights? I suspect not.' It was about we must smile and smile and always be sweet. I didn't feel any animosity towards him, he's just a product of the time.

Katie Holmes: There were different groups within the feminist movement at that time. There was Women's Liberation for example which was seen as being a bit more radical. Were you aware of the political differences within the women's movement?

Yes, I was also a member of Women's Liberation (laughs). I felt they were getting more at the root of the problem—hence the word radical I guess. I was part of a consciousness-raising group and that was great too. We mainly shared the experiences we'd had and found that they were all so similar. Again, it was this thing that you --- we think what's happening to you is just your problem and then when you start in a group like that to discuss your experiences as a woman you begin to realise it's not you at all, it's a social pattern. That suddenly lifts a sense of *blame* from *yourself* when you see that. Also probably gives a sense of, 'This can be changed.'

Veronica spent seven years travelling and living abroad before returning to Brisbane in 1970, politically awakened.

I BECAME VERY ACTIVE in the Australia Party—almost forgot that. I got into politics then. Having just not long come back from Canada, I first became interested in politics in Quebec with the Separatists, there. When I came back to Australia, I had eyes open to politics which I hadn't had before I left

Australia—well, I was only twenty-four at the time. I know some young people are very politically aware at twenty-four but I wasn't. So I went around, collected the policies of all the political parties for the 1972 election. I read them all and the only ones that I agreed with were the Australia Party, which was founded by a guy called [Gordon] Barton. I don't know if you even remember the Australia Party, but it was founded as a protest against the Vietnam War—was Barton's basic premise—but it also had a lot of environmental and socially-interesting progressive policies that *I* agreed with. So I went along, contacted them and said I was interested in the party. I joined the party and I ended up standing as a candidate. I stood as a candidate one year in Gellibrand which I think was the fifth safest Labor seat in Australia. Then the next election—it was '74/'75 election—I stood in the seat of Melbourne, which is also a very safe Labor seat.

It was very interesting, the people I met. The people I *most* liked in other political parties were the communists. They were the old-style idealistic communists who really wanted a society where everybody had a share and everything was fair—as the original communists probably believed but of course put into practice we know it hasn't worked. In fact you'd have to be an angel to have such a society, humans being what they are. But these were really lovely people. You also met some people in other political parties, particularly aggressive and horrible.

THE AUSTRALIA PARTY that I joined was the one that went on later to join with Don Chipp and form the Democrats.

After I came out of hospital with Crystal [1977] I stood as a candidate for the Democrats (laughs). I was breastfeeding Crystal at the time and I'd be up on the stage making a speech (laughs) and I'd suddenly start to leak (laughs). Somebody in the wings'd be holding Crystal (laughs) till I got off the stage. I thought to myself, 'These men don't know they're alive!' I've got a photo of me sitting with the telephone in one hand and the kid on the breast in the other hand (laughs) and the cat sitting on my knee as well, during the election campaign. So I stood for the House of Representatives, that was a way to help the Senate candidate who had more hope of getting in. Had a snowflake's chance in Hades of getting into the House of Reps but it was what you had to do to get the votes for the Senate candidate as well.

So what were the policies of the Australia Party that really appealed to you?

It was the way they looked at society as a different, *fairer* society. It wasn't a *socialist* view but it was a fairer, non-discriminatory view of society. When other people and parties were just talking a little about discrimination, the Australia Party was trying—and appeared to, in my observation—treat men and women equally. In fact we had as many candidates as --- of either sex. Also they were an anti-uranium party, an anti-war party. They were very much along the lines of a rationalist group. Perhaps the closest thing in more traditional politics I can think of is Fabian—the Fabian group of the left-wing Labor Party.

KIM BEAR *(1959) recounts her mother's political advice from 1972.*

I can remember when the 1972 election was going to happen. I remember they went out to interview people to ask them who they were going to vote for because this was a big election, and 'It's Time' and everything. The three of us, my sister, mother and I were watching on the couch one night. They went out and they were still interviewing people in the streets wearing *hats* which, long gone now—probably people in Sydney and Melbourne. I can remember they always seemed to ask *men* what they thought. I'm sure my mother made a comment at one point, 'Why don't they ask a woman what she thinks?' And then sure enough they asked this lady (laughs). They said, 'Hello madam and who you're going to vote for in the election?' I think she was probably quite startled and a bit nervous and she just said to the interviewer, 'Oh, I'll have to ask my husband.' My mother hit the roof! She said 'I don't know what happens to women when they get married, they just lose their brains, and they can't think for themselves.' She said, 'Now I want you two to pay particular attention to this and when you get married under *no* circumstances should you hand over your cheque book or your wages!' Off she went on this *huge* rant! It was absolutely hilarious and we were quite shocked. Then I'm thinking, no actually it's interesting to *know* that she felt that way. These things were obviously quite—had been bottled up for quite some time. It coincided with --- mum was out back in the workforce working—doing piece work, in sewing—and was working for somebody who didn't really have great conditions for his workers.

Growing up in inner-city Adelaide and from a small fruit-farm family background, ***IAN REID*** *(1962) became politically aware at a young age.*

Politics was very much a topic of conversation. We always had very strong Labor leanings. Mum grew up in a very Labor environment—like I said with the fruit properties and so on. She was very *against* people like Menzies and so on. Were public enemy number one for her really. Not in a vindictive or nasty way but she always felt strongly about Labor values.

I became more aware in the Whitlam era. '72 I was in primary school and I remember riding round on my pushbike on a Saturday morning. I think we were going to cricket on Saturday morning, had our whites on and we were going to cricket, me and a couple of mates. There was a polling booth in the school where we were waiting to go round. We were riding around on our pushbikes saying, 'We want Gough! We want Gough!' I think we got some stares from the election commission people—shouldn't be saying that sort of thing at the time. I remember watching the election coverage that night at my uncle's and aunty's place. They were equally strong Labor people. I don't know of any of my relatives who we used to visit who would not have been Labor voters. My aunty who was always saying *disparaging* things about Billy McMahon and so on. So I would have been about ten or eleven I suppose then. That was probably the win that really crystallised. Then of course with the Dismissal [of the Whitlam government, in 1975], again that had a very strong impact on me as well.

BARBARA KRICKL *(1962) came to Australia from Germany as part of a year-long International Christian Youth Exchange in the early 1980s. Having been involved in anti-nuclear activism in Germany, she became socially and politically involved in Sydney: volunteering at a youth refuge in south-west Sydney, participating in the Palm Sunday anti-nuclear peace march with her Australian boyfriend Steven, and demonstrating against the building of the proposed Gordon-below-Franklin dam in Tasmania.*

I got offered the position at the Stepping Stone Youth Refuge in Ruse which is just outside Campbelltown. That at the time was *literally* outside Campbelltown. There was no connection yet, there was no houses much, it was out in the bush and it was at the end of this *massive* drought in '82—well it's '83 by now. This happened in about March. I had to go. Now, I met my (laughs), I met Steven in March so we started going out at the peace march. The Palm Sunday peace march.

Also the *Franklin River* thing was on at the time. So we all had t-shirts and, you know, 'Save the Franklin'. Some people got quite annoyed because we were tourists and how could we --- But that's my first memory I have of Bob Brown because of course he was a very young man being *arrested*—well, not very young, but he was young—being *arrested* in Tasmania. I mean that was right up our alley having been on demonstrations in Germany. So we all went on those demonstrations.

There was this *stall* at the Easter Show that sold all these Franklin—there was all these Franklin stuff, *that's* right, that's what it was. I don't think I have it here, I used to have it here and it was this little pin. Steven got me a *pin*. Can't even quite remember what it was but it was a pink pin and then there was the female gender sign on it. I think people just wore it—at the time it was a feminist thing. And a badge, no it was a *sticker*. It said something like—a friend of mine always said this, she'd also been to Germany on the exchange and said she was politically awakened by having been on this exchange—it said something like 'A woman needs a man like a fish needs a bicycle.' That apparently was the saying at the time and they sold this sticker which we thought was very funny. Because I mean I don't necessarily agree with that but it was—there seemed to be all this feminist stuff happening. I don't even want to call it feminist, there was just a bit of a reaction I suppose to all this sexism that had been happening. So he got me these things and I mean of course I still have them now. It was funny because we hadn't --- I'm glad in a way we didn't meet earlier because I suppose it would have ruined my year 'cause I would've probably pined for him rather than *done* all those things, all those travels and that.

Then I had to go back to the Youth Refuge which I found very difficult—having met Steven, and we went on the peace march. I commuted from Ruse to Hurstville on the weekends. But Ruse again, the Youth Refuge was an amazing experience 'cause there were boys between sixteen and eighteen and I think they resented at times a little bit that someone like I who was only like twenty and came from overseas, basically *privileged*, could be a volunteer there. It was only a short-term refuge so they had to go after six months and where would they—they had nowhere to go.

That was the side of Australia when I realised that Australia has places --- at the time Campbelltown was totally different to what it is now. It was really stuck out there, no one --- huge expansion, *nothing* for anyone, for children to do or young people to do. The difference between richer and poorer and no social system like we were used to in Germany where everyone's pretty much taken care of. We pay high taxes but we're prepared to have a good system in comparison. Then I *realised* how inadequate the system was here. We've always told Australia is so easy-going, there is no class system and I found it was actually probably *worse* than what *I* was used to. Because I came from a poor family and I mean I never had to worry about my education. There was *no* question that I can have *exactly* the same education as everyone else because universities didn't cost anything, school doesn't cost anything.

CONNIE SHAW*'s (1937) back injury in the 1980s was a catalyst for change. She returned to university, immersed herself in computing technology and has been involved in voluntary work ever since.*

If you have to learn something yourself, you make every mistake possible. To work through that mistake, you learn an awful lot (laughs) I found out. So I started learning a bit of word processing. From there on I got interested in the LETS system [Local Exchange Trading Systems], which is the local energy exchange, people exchanging services on the basis like a babysitting club type of thing. I used to keep the records for that so I got into database and various other things. I did a bit of everything. I made flyers because I decided to run an introduction to volunteering as one of my projects. Of course I had to organise all that and I had to make flyers and distribute the flyers and all that sort of thing.

Also because I suffered with chronic pain, I was involved with a group with chronic pain. I found a young man with young children and he couldn't get out of a wheelchair. He was sitting there and he was talking to me and he said 'Well, the kids don't want to know me because I can't do anything with them'. I *thought* about that and I thought 'Well, the amount of use I got out of the computer.' So when I got thinking about that and somebody had an old computer so I got that one and

I went and I learnt a bit of programming and I programmed a computer and put some games and stuff in it and I taught him how to use it. They were just basic, very basic things. The next thing I saw, he was as happy as Larry because the kids were hanging around him all day (laughs). It just completely changed his life around.

Because I know it had for me because from sitting here I could—well by 1986 was the first time I had an email address. I didn't have many people to email because there wasn't too many around. But I could access what they called the bulletin boards. You'd ring up a local number and you put messages on there and they just during the night—it was in twenty-four hours, they went all around the world. People would interact that way. The next day or it might be a few days later, there might be a message back. Sometimes I was in bed flat on my back for weeks but I could still access this. It was almost like --- like people look at the Internet now, at that time you were looking at a black screen with some writing on it but the idea was the same. You could access programs and you could access all sorts of information from various universities. It opened a whole world up really.

***MICHELLE CRIPPS** (1960) remembers witnessing a special political moment in Canberra in 2008.*

I got to work in the Senate Whip's office with Senator Kerry O'Brien. My role was to make sure I had the speakers in order that were going to speak for the Labor Party on an issue, and coordinate with the Greens and the Liberals with their equivalent to me so that we all knew who was speaking when. I put the list together and would give it back to them so they knew when their people—they'd tell me who their speakers were and we'd order them and put them together. That was a real shifting feast and would change all the time. I also had to make sure that as soon as there was a vote that we had a system of—button to hit—to make sure everybody got back into the chamber in order to vote.

Because there were other people in the office working on strategy and planning, I *really* got to see the *thinking* behind putting legislation through and I guess how the game was played. I also got to witness what I think for me was a really defining moment that I wish I could *bottle* and take around and share with others. And that was the night that the Work Choices legislation and Fair Work was being changed over. At eleven o'clock, twelve o'clock at night, there was Joe Ludwig for Labor, Rachel Siewert for the Greens and Eric Abetz for the Liberal *debating* each point as they went through—people had obviously spent hours working through the entire legislation in each of those parties and them putting on record *their* beliefs. For me it was no guns, no fighting, no marching in the streets, just three intelligent articulate people who'd been given the mandate from their party to say their piece. That's when I thought, 'We're the lucky country.' Here we are, this massive legislation change. Some people didn't realise how big it was, but it was being done through debate, through discussion, agreeing to disagree, abiding by the rules that were set up for the country and to *me* that was a --- as I say, I wish I could have bottled that moment because I think that really showed the democracy of Australia at work.

KIM BEAR *(1959) was politicised in the early 1990s.*

I've thought a lot about what gets people to politics and even though I didn't go to university or have any political study of any kind, strangely enough it always felt that I was really dragged kicking and screaming to politics the minute I got a mortgage. I say that because *suddenly* when it is your back pocket, you become very interested in decisions that are made—fiscal decisions and anything that's going to affect you from a work point of view. Again, I guess noticing all those years earlier the effect that the unions had in improving my mother's work life, I always for quite a long time was satisfied that the Labor Party in particular was more for social justice and the worker and that made me happy (laughs) because I always really felt for the underdog. Once I got a mortgage of my own, it was about the time of the recession we had to have. Very scary leap in interest rates, and after a while it just --- you suddenly realise that, actually that is almost outside of politics to a certain extent. Particularly how affected we are globally by money.

I watched with horror in the Howard years of how mean-spirited we'd seemed to become as a nation, particularly to do with people seeking refuge here and Work Choices, all kinds of --- It was just a nastiness that I really didn't think we were. It wasn't who I thought we were. I almost lost faith in what it felt to be an Australian. We didn't treat, we don't treat people like this.

I also am a member of GetUp! and I like that because they bring things to my attention that I probably wouldn't know anything about. Through them I've got to know when significant Aboriginal sites are threatened by mining in Pickering WA. Lots of different decisions come up. Under GetUp! you'll have information about same-sex marriages. You have just a huge range of topics and I am very happy to support them.

***LISA JACKSON** (1972) reflects on two major events in Sydney in 2000.*

I was a volunteer at the Sydney Olympics and I—while I was not in the stadium for that particular thing—every time she [Cathy Freeman] had her race I'd be stationed on, so I'd watch the race on TV at the dinner times during the Olympics. But when her race was on I said to the supervisor I said, 'Look mate, I'm not going to be --- I'm going to be sitting down there with everyone else in the Exhibition Park' and he said, 'Yeah, I think everyone else is going to do that too.' I said, 'But I don't think you get the cultural significance of it.' He goes, '*I do*'. I went, 'Okay.' So I basically then took my hat off and sat there with everyone else. I watched that—her race—while listening to the sounds of people at the Stadium Australia, which you could never get another experience like that again. So I watched her win her race and I think I was more prouder as an Aboriginal person listening to that. And being, it's a historic occasion. Yeah, that had an impact.

I think the closing ceremony was a bit more impacting as well. You got Midnight Oil --- I'm sorry, I shouldn't be crying like this is not really good, makeup will run. You have Midnight Oil standing there making a political statement and all these people coming out with these Aboriginal flags and saying sorry on a world stage. You've got a Prime Minister sitting there going, 'They shouldn't have done that'. I think that was more of the way, Yothu Yindi coming out --- I think the Olympics was the only time that Australia was actually ever really proud of having an Aboriginal history. I think the way all that happened and I think the showcasing of Aboriginal culture, I think the Sydney Olympics was the *only* time Australia was *absolutely* proud to have an Aboriginal history.

Frank Heimans: What about the bridge walks? There was one in 2000 [the Reconciliation Walk] when 200,000 people or so walked the bridge for Aboriginal ---

I walked the bridge. On that freezing cold morning. I walked the bridge. I walked the bridge. I saw Geoff Clark who then was at the head of ATSIC [Aboriginal and Torres Strait Islander Commission]. We both bought coffee together and the grin on his face I think was even bigger than mine. The cultural significance of --- I walked with my two good friends, across that bridge, and I walked with the school that I was working in. I was just going, '*All* these people walking for *my people*'. It couldn't get any better than that. It was *freezing* and I remember ringing my brother up going, 'Walking across the bridge now.' Perth is two hours behind and I think it was the only time I've heard him say, 'I wish I was there with you.' 'Cause I was telling him, I remember saying to him, 'I saw a family of three, mum, dad and a baby and they're walking with their little 'sorry' written on the back of their jumpers. I saw Annita Keating [Prime Minister Paul Keating's former wife] walk past me and she was just strolling along the bridge. Like, this bridge has *stopped* for my people. *How* much better can it be?'

MICHELLE CRIPPS *(1960) considers the impact of the attack on New York's Twin Towers on September 11 2001.*

I think we definitely lost our innocence and realised how much part of the world we were with the September 11. Waking up that morning and seeing that on the television, knowing it was fairly well *live*. So being able to participate in a way in events that happened live now is something that I think is quite different. That one probably more than any brought it home. But at the same time, it also brought home that we still --- after growing up knowing that—fearing a nuclear bomb— and knowing there was a clock that they had that marked where they thought it was and the real worry of Russia. Then watching all that dismantling and thinking finally the world's coming together and then having that happen and knowing that no, there's another force at work. That I think was a defining moment. Just knowing you're really not safe. That probably was a *major* global event for me.

JAMES FINNEGAN *(1981) recalls learning about the attack, and considers its consequences.*

One of the biggest events that has impacted on what I can see in the world around me is probably the September 11th terrorist attacks. I think that they actually triggered a very dangerous shift towards the right in politics. They triggered a lot of inherent racism with a lot of people. I think a lot of our current troubles—as far as the political situation that we have in this country and which the flow-on effects are to all of our lives—are because of that and because of the outrage of what happened then and then allowing governments to do whatever they like to 'protect us'—air quotes—from that. I think it's set a dangerous precedent for governments to be able to do whatever they like and for media to allow them, if not help them. But I think that's probably been one of the biggest defining moments in my generation.

Roslyn Burge: Do you remember that event?

I do. I was in bed when it happened. I got woken up by my partner at the time. I remember because I wasn't in a fantastic place in my head at that time so I was a bit, I was a bit depressed and a little bit, didn't really quite know where I was. Then I remembered, I went downstairs and I saw it and I was *obsessed* about it. I watched it constantly and watched it from all different angles on the TV and I couldn't get enough of it. But at that time, it was one of those times in my life where I wouldn't go out. So I was living in this *bubble* where this all happened on TV, not in real life.

***JODIE BELL** (1970) explains how local women, with the support of the town's elders and the Kimberley Aboriginal Law and Culture Centre, instigated legal action to reduce alcohol-fuelled violence in Fitzroy Crossing. The restrictions were introduced in 2007.*

Alcohol has always been a big problem in the town. People drinking and alcohol-fuelled violence and those sort of things in the community. So people had started—the women in particular—started rallying about, 'Okay, we need to do something about this alcohol in this town.' Which is sad because both alcohol --- it's actually owned by Indigenous people and it was sad that the people that controlled those companies couldn't implement what was needed I suppose, without having to go to the outside world. So basically the women went to the Liquor Licensing Board to discuss options about how can we reduce the alcohol intake in town, which led to restrictions on takeaway alcohol, which led—at the time when I left—a lot of people started leaving town because they couldn't get alcohol. So they'd go to Derby, they'd go to Broome and stay there for couple of months. But the flip side of that was also, at the same time the recognition that there was an alcohol problem there also meant that a number of services started coming into town so a lot more services started getting based in Fitzroy. Prior to that it had been very much a fly-in fly-out type of service-based town. A lot of departments started actually locating staff into town so a lot of people that were service-based people could start living in town.

So it was basically, if you want to drink that's fine but you drink at the pub and when you've finished, you leave the pub and go home. What was happening was people going home, obviously they were drinking in the house around kids, the violence and everything else that was happening was happening in the house. Kids and grannies and that sort of stuff were witnessing it, being a part of it. So the idea was if you could restrict the alcohol going into the homes then hopefully you could restrict those negatives happening in the homes. So the restriction was put there basically—and it's still to this day—you can't buy any full-strength takeaway alcohol in Fitzroy Crossing.

ALISON FETTELL *(1952) outlines her role in a local political campaign in the coastal suburb of Bulli, north of Wollongong, in 2012.*

I had read this article about the local health district wanting to change what was happening at the Bulli [Hospital] Emergency Department. They wanted to talk to the community about their plans for this. I thought, 'Ooh', having known what the health department can do—very quickly—I thought, 'I might go to that meeting.' So I turned up to this meeting, took a couple of friends. I'd written a one page—five dot points—of what we need in this area because we're quite a long way from Wollongong. These five dot points ended up being the basis of our campaign. I had just thought before I went, going, 'This is what we have to have. We have to have 24/7. We have to have triage, treat and transport. We have to have that.' So I just went with a clear view of what I knew we needed and it was not what they wanted to do. The media happened to be there and because I seemed to know what I was talking about they asked me to have a say. Then people came up to me and said, 'Would you lead a campaign?' and next thing it was on. I just pulled a group together of friends and people who --- just a small group. I said, 'Look, before we say we're going to do this, we better find out what they're talking about. Like, what is this urgent care centre, what does that mean for Australia and is this an American model?' Which it *was*. Luckily I'd met this woman, she's a brilliant researcher. Between us we found out a lot of information. Then once we found the information out we got quite scared about what was happening. Not just at Bulli ED [Emergency Department] but for the whole health system. We *realised* that we were being Americanised.

So we were talking about privatisation then and now it's being talked about in a bigger picture. But we had discovered because of this little change in this Bulli ED, that this is where our health system was likely to head. We got really scared. So we ran it, we had a rally. I said, 'Look girls, if we'—and it was all women—'If we get a hundred people at this rally, I'll be rapt.' But it took a lot of work. We had the rally, 600 people turned up. *M'mm h'mm.* It was bigger than *Ben-Hur.*

***Milijana Stojadinovic** (1985) reflects on her communist roots and about politics in contemporary Australia.*

I feel very strong affiliation towards socialism. Again, going back to talking about what we were saying, that's because of my upbringing. My grandmother to this day believes in communism. She was a communist. Her brothers and sisters were a part of the partisans.

Susan Marsden: So what do you think of the political parties here then (laughs)?

I think it's positive that Julia Gillard is the prime minister. It's --- I guess it's a breath of fresh air to see a *woman* on the TV even though it's a *white* woman. It's nice to get that boys' club removed from the picture, from the physical picture. But I still think that at the end of the day, it's all the same crap.

Further Listening on Activism

Les Robinson, 1947, http://www.nla.gov.au/amad/nla.oh-vn6504265/1-2768
Donat Santowiak, 1950, http://nla.gov.au/nla.obj-220175608/listen/2-1863
Ouranita Karadimas, 1958, http://nla.gov.au/nla.obj-219918460/listen/2-3915
Phil May, 1962, http://www.nla.gov.au/amad/nla.oh-vn6569680/1-1812
Bronwyn Macdonald, 1964, http://www.nla.gov.au/amad/nla.oh-vn6390885/2-1238
James Mayol, 1974, http://www.nla.gov.au/amad/nla.oh-vn6449993/1-3675
Suzie Quartermain, 1975, http://nla.gov.au/nla.obj-220022403/listen/1-4563
Kirsty Wallett, 1982, http://www.nla.gov.au/amad/nla.oh-vn6290935/1-2496

Further Reading on Activism

Attwood, Bain, *Rights for Aborigines* (Sydney: Allen & Unwin, 2003).
Brett, Judith and Moran, Anthony, *Ordinary People's Politics: Australians Talk about Life, Politics and the Future of their Country* (North Melbourne: Pluto Press Australia, 2006).
Broome, Richard, *Aboriginal Australians: Black Responses to White Dominance, 1788–2001* (St Leonards: Allen & Unwin, 2001).
Burgmann, Verity and Lee, Jenny (eds), *Staining the Wattle: A People's History of Australia since 1788* (Melbourne: McPhee Gribble/Penguin, 1988).
Burgmann, Verity, *Power, Profit and Protest: Australian Social Movements and Globalisation* (Sydney: Allen & Unwin, 2003).

Doyle, Timothy, *Green Power: The Environment Movement in Australia* (Sydney: University of New South Wales Press, 2000).

Gerster, Robin and Bassett, Jan, *Seizures of Youth: "The Sixties" and Australia* (South Yarra: Hyland House, 1991).

Holden, Colin and Trembath, Richard, *Divine Discontent: The Brotherhood of St Laurence: A History* (North Melbourne: Australian Scholarly Publishing, 2008).

Hutton, Drew and Connors, Libby, *A History of the Australian Environment Movement* (Melbourne: Cambridge University Press, 1999).

Lake, Marilyn, *Getting Equal: The History of Australian Feminism* (St Leonards: Allen & Unwin, 1999).

Oppenheimer, Melanie, *Volunteering: Why We Can't Survive Without It* (Sydney: University of New South Wales Press, 2008).

Oppenheimer, Melanie, *All Work, No Pay: Australian Civilian Volunteers in War* (Walcha: Ohio Productions, 2002).

Pemberton, Gregory (ed.), *Vietnam Remembered* (Sydney: New Holland, revised edition, 2009).

Reynolds, Robert, *From Camp to Queer: Re-Making the Australian Homosexual* (Melbourne: Melbourne University Press, 2002).

Robinson, Shirleene and Ustinoff, Julie (eds), *The 1960s in Australia: People, Power and Politics* (Newcastle upon Tyne: Cambridge Scholars Publishing, 2012).

Willett, Graham and Smaal, Yorick (eds), *Intimacy, Violence and Activism: Gay and Lesbian Perspectives on Australasian History and Society* (Melbourne: Monash University Publishing, 2013).

Willett, Graham, *Living Out Loud: A History of Gay and Lesbian Activism in Australia* (Sydney: Allen & Unwin, 2000).

Wotherspoon, Garry, *Gay Sydney: A History* (Sydney: NewSouth Publishing, 2016).

CHAPTER 8

LATER LIFE

Like children, old people are often left out of history. They, too, may not be the movers and shakers of social and political change, though as life spans have lengthened across the past century the ageing population has become a topic of increasing concern and debate. With more Australians having many more years of life beyond retirement, and many of them healthy and active, 'old age' has expanded and become more rich and diverse. In this chapter our oldest narrators reflect on their experience of later life in recent decades and highlights both the vatality and challenges of old age.

Retirement, new kinds of voluntary and paid work, and the household economics of making do in old age are the focus of our opening section. Like many older adults, Ginette Matalon saw retirement from her public service job as an opportunity to spend more time with grandchildren and to enjoy a variety of voluntary work. She 'never looked back'. Clergyman Donald Grey-Smith was also tired of work and duty and wanted the 'freedom of not being available' to his parishioners at every moment. He also planned to do other things with his life, such as reading for leisure and learning the piano. The moment of his retirement, as he 'came down from the altar and took the chasuble off', was 'like a great weight was taken from me'. Veronica Schwarz enjoyed a similar sense of freedom when she took a redundancy package in her early fifties and set up a 'multipurpose business' of her own, running classes on things she loved and was good at. She has been living on her wits ever since, and she's 'loved it'.

Of course, as Ginette ruefully concludes, after retirement money no longer flows into the bank account every fortnight. Older Australians without substantial savings are financially vulnerable. Divorcee Fred Henskens describes the challenge of living on the old age pension and the importance of 'odd jobs' that supplement his income. Fred had lost his home but was fortunate to find a new life partner to share a new home and the bills. 'I'm not a millionaire anymore', laughs Fred, 'but I feel like a millionaire'. Fred's story highlights the ways in which the experience of old age has been affected not just by personal economic circumstances but also by changing types of financial support for older Australians, from the introduction of old age pensions in 1908 and the development after World War I of Repatriation benefits for war veterans and their families, through the development of compulsory superannuation schemes in the 1980s and 1990s. Many of the older Australians interviewed for this book, born between 1920 and 1950, were of a generation that benefitted from comparatively high rates of home ownership in middle-age.

Ageing often forces difficult decisions about housing, as frail bodies or minds need new types of accommodation or new forms of support. During her interview in 2012, Ruth Apps, a widow since 1976, contemplated the prospect of leaving the family home in western Sydney. Though Ruth has grown into the place after sixty-two years, the community of young families in which her children had been raised has gone, and the house is 'tired and I'm tired of it'. With the same positive attitude that characterised her earlier life, eighty-four-year-old Ruth is looking forward to moving to a smaller, more manageable home. While still in her sixties, Lynne Sanders-Braithwaite also reflected on new ways of living in later life with like-minded friends on north-coast New South Wales. She dreams of a different kind of nursing home, 'an old person's ageing place where we're all together with our music and our values'.

Sex and love don't stop when people reach their sixties and seventies. In 'Later love and loss', our narrators share the joy of love in later life and the grief of loss. For Ronnie Gauci, the death of his wife as they prepared for retirement is still raw. Ronnie recalls his terrible anger and grief and the reasons why, in the end, he did not take his own life. 'I'm not over it but it's a lot easier now—I can move on.' As a widow in her fifties, in 1988 Ginette Matalon fell in love again, with Victor, and they enjoyed seven 'fabulous, fabulous, fabulous' years before Victor's heart gave up. Grandmother Lynne Sanders-Braithwaite explains the pleasure of starting a new relationship in her sixties and finding the mix of security, care and adventure that had been missing from previous romances. Alison Fettell records the deepening of her sexual relationship as she and her female partner grow old together, but she is dismayed that they still don't feel safe holding hands in public despite changing attitudes to homosexuality.

In 'Pleasure and leisure in later life', Ruth Apps describes the value of lifelong friends and the creation of new friendships, but she also laments that her older friends are dying or moving into nursing homes as their minds falter and their bodies slow. Ruth herself still enjoys many pleasures, including a love of international travel that was initiated with her husband Bill in 1972 and continues with her daughter Julie. Other older Australians relish a variety of pastimes, from indoor cards and crosswords through the outdoor delights of place and nature. Michael Bicanic bought a shack on the north-east Tasmanian coast when his children were young and now, in his seventies, heads to the beach every weekend and relishes the 'shack life' of fishing and hunting. Kathleen Golder finds solace in her Hobart garden, where she grows an extraordinary crop of vegetables and 'the concentration, the bending, the stretching, the walking, the organising' helps her 'forget about a lot of other things'. Kathleen is less keen on the 'silly boxes' in her living room, the television and computer, and would rather walk and garden outside and write letters to friends because 'human contact is the way'. Not all older adults resist new technologies. Lynne Sanders-Braithwaite thanks 'all the gods in all the heavens' for sending her the 'great collective intelligence' of the Internet, which has eliminated isolation from her life and enabled communication with friends and family around the world.

Yet, inevitably, 'Ageing bodies' begin to limit life's activities and pleasures. Approaching his nineties, Bert Castellari tries to keep his 'faculties in condition', but the worsening of the deafness caused by war service has destroyed the joy of music and reduced his social life. Connie Shaw hopes that her disintegrating eyes will last her out so she can sustain her passion for computers, and she paid for private surgery when the public hospital said she was too old for a hip replacement. Connie accepts that she will probably end up in a wheelchair. Like many old people she worries about becoming dependent—'I don't really want to bother my kids'—and is grateful for support services that enable her to stay in her own home, for now. Alison Fettell recalls the almost total dependence of her own elderly mother—'showering her and wiping her bottom and doing all those things that you do, because there's very little control'—while pondering who will do the same for her a few years down the track. Ruth

Apps articulates many peoples' greatest fear—the loss of memory. Ruth exercises her own memory with puzzles and crosswords, because 'if you can't remember what you did as a child you've lost that joy, or sorrow, whichever it happens to be'.

Our older narrators imagine death in very different ways. At eighty-six, Ruth Apps is prepared for death but determined to 'go out swinging' and then have 'a really good send-off' with 'hymns and flowers, the whole lot'. While Ruth believes in heavenly immortality, Ginette Matalon refuses to go gently into the night. Having outlived two husbands she hates the separation of death but is not afraid of it because she has decided she is never going to die. 'So there's your answer, I'm eternal.' Kathleen Golder is well into her nineties and doesn't know if 'there is anything there'. Indeed, 'neither does anybody else'. 'If it's the end, when I've hit a brick wall and that's it, well that's it. I've been, come and gone.' As Kathleen concludes, with laughter in her determined voice, and with an accent that still betrays her northern English origins, 'there's billions, trillions before us have come and gone, so, so what. So I'm not going to think about it now. Not going to keep me awake tonight.'

Work, Retirement and Making Do

In the late 1990s, macular degeneration in her eyes was only one factor in ***GINETTE MATALON****'s (1936) decision to retire and to start a new life of voluntary work and grand-parenting.*

> I worked in employment for the government for seventeen years. I thought, 'They'd get me out of the office,' I would say, 'They'd get me out of here in a coffin.' In the meantime, since 1995, my sight was deteriorating. They've been very good. They

bought me enlargers to help me with the computer and they put the zoom text on to my computer—they really helped me a lot with my sight impairment.

In January one year, I went on holidays and I came back and I—I wasn't retirement age—I really didn't look forward to go back to the job. I wanted to stay at home to do more things with my grandchildren. So I went to see my supervisor with a date in mind and I said, 'I'd love to leave on the first of April.' She says, 'Why? Did somebody upset you or something?' I said, 'No, I don't want to work anymore.' I did it—I left. I didn't take a redundancy or anything—was the years where people took redundancies and thing—I just retired beautifully with a party and everything, and gifts and history of employment and everything. I gave them thirty-six weeks of sick leave. I never took sick leave. I thought that one day I'll really need it. I left it.

I never looked back. I'm very good also at closing doors. I never regretted my jobs and I settled in a whole series of honorary involvement in my life with secular and religious association, with family involvement and I never looked back on the jobs. Except that money didn't come into my account every fortnight.

In 1992, after her mother died, ***VERONICA SCHWARZ*** *(1939) left a senior role in the Victorian Education Department and set up in business by herself.*

When she died and then I got the redundancy package right in the middle of a year, I decided to form a little business of my own and start a multipurpose business in which I taught classes at the local neighbourhood houses and community centres and, you know, 'What can I teach?' I thought: 'Well, what am I reasonably good at and love? Painting and writing and meditation.' So I offered classes in those and taught them and they were quite popular and they went on for several years. That was good.

Katie Holmes: What are your memories of giving up formal work as a paid employee?

I loved it, absolutely loved it. I thought, 'God, I should have done this sooner. I never want to work for anyone else again.' It was such a sense of freedom, and of also responsibility. That didn't frighten me—it excited me.

So how old were you?

This is 1992, so I would have been fifty-two. And I haven't been employed since (laughs)! I've been—shall we say—living on my wits ever since but, yeah, I loved it.

DONALD GREY-SMITH *(1931) recalls his decision to retire from the Anglican church.*

I've taken my vocation as a priest seriously. I've always approached it as being a full-time occupation and by that I mean twenty-four hours a day, seven days a week. Not that I was doing churchy things all of that time, but I was available, and I was committed to the people that I was serving in—a full-time way is not a very good description, but it says what I'm trying to say, perhaps.

After all of that I was tired, and there were things which I had not been able to do in my life which I'd looked forward to doing, like playing the piano, having piano lessons and learning to get some enjoyment from playing the piano. Reading, not just reading things I needed to read associated with my ministry, but reading literature. And just the freedom of not being available.

I still remember, it was St Andrew's Day, 1996—I think that's right—when I celebrated the Eucharist for the last time and as I came down from the altar and took the chasuble off, it really was as if I—it was like a great weight—I really felt as if I was going to float up into the air, that the weight was taken from me. And I resisted all invitations to help out here or there or do a *locum tenens* for three months or something because I can't imagine being a part-time priest. It was a full-time commitment, and to just go and minister to people that you don't really know and you're never going to get to know, it didn't seem right to me, so retirement was the way to go.

FRED HENSKENS *(1929) had a successful drainage contract business, but lost his home and most of his money through divorce and a failed investment. For a time he lived on the pension in a shed at the back of his sister's property in Canberra, until he made a new home with his partner Evelyn.*

The biggest challenge is to try and live the way [you] possibly can. If you had a good super or a pension and all that it's alright, but if you start with nothing again, it's very hard to live just on a old age pension, you can't, if you haven't got your house and you haven't got friends or family you could live with first. I was lucky. When I lost everything I lived in a shed up at my sister's place you see. I got the pension and I did a bit of work here and there and I met a nice lady and I'm even happier now than anytime. I'd been married twice and this is the third time and I'm lucky that way. But I still do few odd jobs here now and then, for old pensioners. I do a bit of gardening here and there and they give me little bit. I'm allowed to earn sixty dollars a week.

I'm very happy now. My partner Evelyn, she's on the same pension as I am and we manage now. She doesn't get much but we get enough. We get by, and because I do a little job here and there so that helps. I'm not a millionaire anymore (laughs) but I feel like a millionaire.

*After retiring at the age of eighty-four, in 2012 widowed **RUTH APPS** (1926) reflects on the prospect of moving out of her Sydney family home and from the neighbourhood of Westmead near Parramatta.*

This house here? We came here in 1950 which is sixty-two years ago. We came to it as barely a shell. We didn't have much furniture or floor coverings or anything. It was a long way from Hurstville, a long ride from home. I wasn't really happy at first. I grew into the place.

Now it's about to be demolished—for high-rise—and I'm not at all worried about leaving. It's past its use-by date. I'm tired of it. The house is tired and I'm tired of it. I'm looking forward to moving to another place—a smaller villa type of thing—and so it's a circular thing in life. It's time at this age to move from something. I've had attachments to it. I don't have anymore.

Frank Heimans: What about the community around you? Is it still a factor?

Not anymore, because when we moved here we were all young families, young couples with young families. The children all walked to school together, it's about a ten-minute walk to their primary school. The children grew up together with the others who lived all around. They would play in that backyard—cricket and games—local kids all had a great time together.

Now I'm the only white Anglo-Saxon here. The rest are, oh, multicultural. Cambodians, Indians, Sri Lankans, Mauritians and such like. We get on well together but although they talk to me most of them haven't got young children. They mostly go to work. So it has changed radically. Probably it's one reason why I'm happy to move on.

*On north-coast New South Wales, **LYNNE SANDERS-BRAITHWAITE** (1949) draws upon indigenous and overseas inspiration about communities for older people.*

I think we need a nursing home for ourselves. There's a whole batch of us that are trying to work out which one, how much money we can get together to get a nursing home—not a nursing home but an old person's ageing place where we're all together with our music and our values. So there'll be tarot cards and astrology and political discussions and music. Down at Kempsey, the Aboriginal elders actually designed the Centre that they have down there and that's what we need to do, I reckon. I think sometimes with Findhorn [an ecovillage community] in Scotland—which I've always wanted to go to—and I was wondering how it is now. Not the bit that's the dot org stuff that I hate, but with the older people there. I had the good fortune to stumble across an article by someone who'd been there and they said you can feel the power of these people—who are now very old, older than us probably, with us coming through just on their tails—but she said basically, they don't leave the property and some of them are old enough not to even leave their residence very much, but the spiritual energy's really powerful.

Later Love and Loss

GINETTE MATALON *(1936) in Sydney was widowed for five years when she met Victor in 1988.*

The first day I went out with Victor, Victor met me at a bridge game in this building, in the hall downstairs. There was a poker table and a bridge table. I wasn't even included initially in the bridge game but my aunty, who was unwell and included in that bridge game, rang me and she said, 'I've got the flu. Can you replace me on bridge?'

I came and Victor realised that each of the other ladies at that bridge game had a husband at the poker table. I didn't have one. So he didn't introduce himself to me. He didn't do anything. And that night—no, the next night—when I came home from work, he rang me and he told me that he had noticed me—he asked for my name—at the bridge table, and that he was a fresh widower. He asked me whether I was broad-minded and I said, 'It depends.'

He says, 'I'm a fresh widower and I'd love to invite you out to go to the movies and a dinner at the Hakoah Club.' So I told him that I ate kosher (laughs) and he said, 'Well, we can do something around this.' We went out to see the film *Cousins* and we had dinner. Victor told me that night, 'I am taking you back to Egypt.' --- This meant a lot. It meant that he didn't want to have one outing with me and it meant that we would travel to Egypt. This was 1988 and in 1992 we went to Egypt.

I MET VICTOR IN 1988 and he died in October 1995. So all in all we were together for seven years but we had a fabulous relationship. Fabulous, fabulous, fabulous. He was sick from the time I met him but not sick in bed. I knew that he had a bad heart, but I fell in love and he fell in love with me—he had also lost his wife. I married him eventually.

Because he had a bad heart, because he had a history of his father dying relatively young, he wanted to live every minute of the day. He really, really wanted to live, so we travelled a lot, we did lots of things. And he was a very different to my first husband and he was fun to be with, very, very, very much fun to be with.

But there was a lot of adjustment because he came with baggage and I came with baggage. He was Sephardi, I was Ashkenazi. It was my opening to the Sephardi shul [synagogue]—we got married at a Sephardi shul. It was going there to a service totally alien to me. It was lots of things. Meeting up with friends, entering the world of playing cards—I had never touched a card in my life (laughs). We played card, he was a very strong gambler, at casinos. We never went on holidays to a place that didn't have a casino. First marriage: never went to a place that didn't have a ramp for the boat. Second marriage: had to have a casino. He would wake me up. He also thought that I brought him luck. The gamblers are very superstitious as far as luck, so he wanted me to sit next to him at every game.

In north Queensland, ***RONNIE GAUCI*** *(1947) recalls the loss of his wife soon after they had moved into a new home in preparation for retirement.*

It's amazing woman I married because she never cried. I was the softy. I might have a crusty, tough, outer appearance but when it comes to stuff like this I just break down. When the doctor told her I—'cause she actually started to slowly tell me it could be cancer—and I said, 'Don't be stupid.' I didn't want to believe it. But I think she knew. When the doctor told us the room went quiet. She just sat there. The doctor said no more and then I just couldn't hold it anymore. Tears came to my eyes—I started to cry. I got up, I paced around the room. I was so, so angry I actually punched the door—doctor's door. Still they sat there. He never turned to face me—he kept his back towards me. He never looked at us for one second.

My wife knew what I was going through—she just let me do it. I had to get out of there. I said, 'Look, do you need me here?' She said, 'No.' I said, 'You'll be all right?' She said, 'Yeah.' I said, 'I gotta get out of here.' I walked outside and tears coming down my eyes --- so I walked past all the people --- got outside—you're not supposed to smoke there but didn't care, just lit up smokes. Wandering round the yard and kicking things. I was so angry.

We come home and she stayed strong. She never cried --- she knew she had to stay strong for me (crying) --- and she stayed that way right till the day she died. It's the hardest part of my life. I remember when she passed away her sister said to me that she was so worried about me and I said, 'What do you mean worried about me?' She said, 'She was worried what you'd do.'

I remember the last two days before she died, I still—even though I could see she was getting worse, I could see the pain her face—my mind still didn't accept the fact that she was going to die. I don't know how to explain it. It's funny how I can sit here and see a couple and I can tell you what's going on between them but I couldn't see this. It's just like my mind wouldn't accept that I was going to lose her, even though I can see every day she was getting worse and worse.

My daughter come up from Brisbane because she was getting bad, and she was here with me and we decide to go and see her 'cause I was—all the time she was in hospital—I spend all day there with her. I didn't know of course at that time that she's going to be so close to death, and me daughter, I think she knew. Me daughter knew 'cause she wasn't part of this. Even though it was her mother, she could see because she was on the outside. To me, my wife and me were one, so I couldn't see it.

She knew how her mother loved her grandkids. So she said, 'Look, we got a photo here of all the five grandkids together, should get it blown up and we'll stick it up on the wall in her room.' I said, 'Oh yeah, that'd be nice.' So we did that. Went to the hospital and she was asleep 'cause by this time she's pretty well drugged up. So we stuck the photo up where she could see it.

I was pretty well concerned that she was going to die. Going by what this doctor told me. So I went in, held her hand, she looked me in the face again and then looked back at the photo of the grandkids and I sat with her for a while. Then she turned around to me and she tried to say something to me. I couldn't hear her so I got up and put my head close to her to try and see what she had to say. And she didn't say nothing, she just reached forward and kissed me on the cheek. I thought that was strange. It still didn't dawn on me.

I sat with her, she kept her eyes on that photo again. I stayed with her till she went to sleep and she never took her eyes off that photo. She fell asleep and I went home. Five-thirty that morning got a phone call that she'd passed away. --- I was devastated --- I was angry. Yet when I had the time to think about—which wasn't very long—I was happy she'd gone.

Hamish Sewell: End of her suffering.

Yes.

So come home, not a word was said. My daughter decides to stay for another week with me—even though she had a family down south. She didn't trust me on me own so she sat with me for a week. And the meantime the other son come back from Perth and he decides to spend two weeks with me—make sure I get over this a little bit. So they sat with me for three weeks all in all. I wouldn't go back to work—wasn't interested. Didn't care. I was still at the mill. This was a slack season, 'cause she'd died fourth of February. I took three weeks off. I rang my boss and they said, 'Look, take all the time you need.' So I looked at my roster and decided I'll go back to work on a midnight shift 'cause I didn't want to face anybody. I was still very raw.

So waiting till midnight shift—I mean, I was crying most of this time, most of these three weeks—about nine o'clock that night I thought, 'Oh, this is crazy,' you know, 'I may as well go in now—what's the point in me sitting here?' So I went in and the bloke I was relieving saw me. He said, 'Oh, what are you doing here?' I said, 'Look, don't ask any questions please.' I said, 'Can you go home?' He realised that it's 'no point in me staying here', so I needed to be at work. So he tapped me on the back, he said, 'Okay, well ---' So off he left.

That night I come close to suicide. --- My job as a watchman was to check things and make sure everything's secure. We used to do a round every three or four hours just driving round the car. I cried so much that night. I felt my heart was about to break and I was almost praying. I actually was praying that I have a heart attack and die there. I just couldn't --- didn't want to deal with it. I kept looking at the chimney stack. It's very high and there's a ladder going up the side of it. Kept looking at it, looking at it. I kept thinking what my wife wanted me to do after she'd gone and it kept interfering with my thoughts of jumping. Then I thought about the kids. I said, 'You can't do this. They've just lost their mother, their grandmother. You're gonna do this—it's selfish.'

So I fought it and I got through the night. I was supposed to knock off at seven o'clock and some people used to start at six a.m. and by six-thirty I had to leave, 'cause people were coming to me, 'Sorry' and so on. That just made things worse for me and I just told everybody, 'Look, the boss is looking for me, tell him I've gone home.' So I jump in the car and I cried all the way home.

That's how it was for twelve months. Come to the point where this was no good. I was actually going to work, I'd actually get to the car park and tears'd start, and I pick up me phone, ring the boss and say, 'Look, I'm in the car park.' He could hear I was crying, he said, 'Go home.' So I just come home. This went on too much and I realised it wasn't doing my boss or the company any good. I was ready to chuck it in to be honest but I asked him, 'Do you mind if I take three weeks off?' He said, 'Take it,' he said, 'with our blessing, take it.'

I took three weeks off—don't know why I did that—but I decided I needed to keep me mind working. So I decide to build a six-foot slasher that I can pull behind my mower so I can mow this place quicker. I immersed myself in that and I built this six-foot slasher that I can pull behind—a little ride on—and it almost got me sane again. Got me to the point where I went back to work and apart from the odd day where it hurt I got through the season. I got to the end of the season and now we're looking at the slack season. I turned sixty-four on eleventh of May. I thought, 'Well no, I can't do this anymore.' So I put in my notice and retired. My super was paid out into the whatever and everything so ---

So here I am on me own now, so I got through it. It's been four years now and, and it's good—it's okay—I got through the hard bits. It's easier as it goes, like they all say, but you never forget. There are *days* just like today talking about her, thinking about her, and I get emotional. Round her birthday, sorry, the day she died, the same thing happens—me daughter rings me up. Fourth of February. She didn't quite make sixty. And me daughter'd ring me up on the fourth and say, 'How you feel?' I said, 'Oh, not so bad now.' But in the years before that, we'd both sit there and cry over the phone. It's getting better. I have to say I'm --- I'm not over it but it's lot easier now—I can move on.

ALISON FETTELL *(1952), now living in Thirroul on the coast south of Sydney with her partner Jayne, describes the challenges, and the joys, of a same-sex relationship.*

I don't walk around with my partner holding her hand in public. I don't do that. I certainly wouldn't kiss her passionately in public because I don't feel I'm safe to do that or that it's accepted. We've had problems with youth, at times, in summer, coming past here and people know that we're the girls on the roundabout. I've been vilified.

Let me give you an example. There was this young man who came through, he was knocking over—a couple of them—knocking over rubbish bins and carrying on a treat, obviously drunk and they were only young. I called out to them because I won't let them get away with blue murder, and I said, 'Listen, young man, how about you pick that up?' He said, 'Oh,' he said, 'Why don't you go do something you old lesbian?' Right. I yelled back, 'Well, don't you call me old.'

What I'm saying is that people in the area know that I'm living in a same-sex relationship and I think we're somewhat of a—I don't know what the word is—a curiosity, to some degree. But there is still a level of I think discrimination, yes. So there's things I won't do. Jayne and I have attempted to walk hand in hand, and we *tried* it in Oxford Street *years* ago. There was a couple of young men, we really felt really unsafe.

They made some aggressive attempt to come close to us and it scared us both.

Roslyn Burge: IN THE TIME YOU'VE BEEN TOGETHER, how has your sexual relation changed?

Over time? I've probably quietened down somewhat over time (laughs), and *balanced* out I would say. I would say. But I have to say its intensity when it occurs has not changed and if anything probably more beautiful. There was a long time early in our relationship where we had a mismatch and that was very difficult. And I don't think that's different to any other relationship really. I think if a couple find themselves with exactly the same sexual energy at exactly the same time, always would be rather unusual.

But ours mismatched quite a lot and that did cause some problems. But it's interesting over time it's just—as I said—the whole thing has softened. Yes, as I said, it's quieter and softer as far as it not being *such* an issue in our relationship anymore. But it still exists and it's still wonderful.

At around the age of sixty in 2009, grandmother ***LYNNE SANDERS-BRAITHWAITE*** *(1949) started a new romantic relationship.*

Jo Kijas: What does a 'romantic' mean? I've never quite grasped it (laughs).

Well, I'll tell you what it's not for me. It's not—some of the other men that I had were 'romantic' in that inverted commas sort of thing with the flowers and the gifts. But the level of emotional interaction, intellectual interaction was—I can buy my own flowers and gifts if I want them, you know. But, with Izzy it's coming home to things done that I hadn't even said. He's noticed that they're the things I like, so there'll be a plant planted or something, some need met almost without it being asked for. That sort of thing I think's romantic. And being able to research and adventure back through similar things. I love that. Plus he also plays music. So he can sing John Sebastian songs to me. I go, 'Are you going to sing songs today?' 'Yes.' 'Oh that's good. I've never actually had a wandering minstrel of my own before.' So he sings. There's one song that I really like that he sings, and it's, 'I can't touch the sun for you'. It's a lovely song, 'cause I think *that* applies very much for this stage in my life. If I could touch the sun for you, I would. But it's hard. I like that sort of thing.

I suppose the romance to me is adding another dimension to life as I experience it. I always think that's romantic. You get led somewhere and, if I say, 'I've never been to that place'—I love to go places I've never been to before—I know that at some stage in the future we will get to that place. I've never had that certainty before. I don't know why it's romantic, but I know that if there's bills to be paid that are not my ones—well they're mine, but they're the ones that he's in charge of—they actually will be. The *romantic* men that I knew—which were many of them—didn't attend to details (laughs). I like my details attended to. I like, when you come to visit, you come almost exactly at the right time. I love that. I like that sort of thing. So to be fairly sure, it gives a frame of reference then, that you can be loose in.

The other one is that he's introduced a world to my children, a type of man that I don't think they've known before, and the grandkids just take him for granted as grandpa. He can also add like fear. We're driving along that road down here coming in one day. It was Christmas. My son's family had come and the little girl was six or seven. We didn't have a tree here. My daughter's birthday is Boxing Day, so it's always an issue to make that a special day for her. I went, 'Oh we still don't have a tree.' He just pulls the car up, jumps out of the car with a saw, chops a branch off a tree on the main road, and the girl's in the back, she's terrified because she's going to be a detective when she grows up. 'Come on quick, help me with this tree.'

We get home and Maddy [Lynne's granddaughter] just goes, 'Izzy's so terrifying.' It's good, it's sort of terrifying but safe. [Australian writer] Ross Fitzgerald talks about that, he doesn't say 'romantic' but something about, you can only be adventurous within a safe structure. Successfully adventurous within a safe structure. So there's a bit of that. But it doesn't come naturally to me.

Pleasure and Leisure in Later Life

In Hobart, ***KATHLEEN GOLDER*** *(1920) was well into her nineties in 2012 when interviewer Ben Ross asked about her enthusiasm for gardening.*

I can go out all day. I've always liked to be out and I used to do that on the vineyard. I used to take my lunch with me to go the pruning, because you're all day as you know pruning in the vineyard. I'd sit down there on the grass and eat my little sandwich, and a flask, and carry on pruning. I always liked to be out doing something out there.

You forget about a lot of other things, the concentration, the bending, the stretching, the walking, the organising, for the blood and bone and all this and that and all the nutrients, natural compost to turn, and to keep the family going with—and I do, I keep Jane going, I often give different members of the family whatever I grow. Plenty of spinach and, ah, let me think. There's leeks, there's fennel, there's lettuces, there's peas coming on, there's broad beans coming on, there's kale down there, there's turnips there, there's rocket. It's all up there. I can show you before you go.

Ben Ross: Just as a gardener myself, I'm interested, how do you keep the weeds down (laughs)?

Newspaper. The worms love a wad of newspaper, the worms love it underneath. I grow asparagus and globe artichokes and Jerusalem artichokes as well. It's all out there for you to see, before you go. Yes, I love the gardening. It's a great exercise—mentally and physically. I come in after perhaps four o'clock, feed the cat and dog and start to think about dinner in the evening.

Kathleen was less enthusiastic about electronic forms of entertainment.

THAT SILLY BOX THERE was given to me, the television. Somebody will put it on and say, 'You can watch this, it's all about Wales, or Scotland.' Then I might watch it, if it's something like that. Or it's all about food in France and then I would. But I'm not happy at all with it. No. I can well do without it.

And you know, the same with a computer. Saying now to one of my lads, 'I resent it sometimes because it's taking my ability, the ability away from me.' I love to write. I love to write. There's something there with my pen and my paper where I can sit down here and write a letter just any time. Pop an envelope, stamp, oh there's a couple there. It's a means of communication. But, how can you send a love letter on that damn thing? You can only send a love letter if you write it. You seal it and then it's opened the other end. You know, that expectation and that *feeling* that comes from deep inside you of opening this letter.

It's all new to me but I put up with it and I use it, but it's not going to use me. Same with the television. I won't let it use me. Watch this program, to watch this one, to watch the next one. Ha, ha, no. I'll go outside. I often walk out. Often walk out, away from it, because I don't want it. I can do without it. Yeah. Human contact's the way.

By contrast, for **LYNNE SANDERS-BRAITHWAITE** *(1949) on the north coast of New South Wales, the internet is a godsend for human contact.*

I think all the gods in all the heavens must have sent the Internet to us (laughs). Absolutely. It's like this giant collective intelligence that can be accessed, and it's the light of my life. Because I get sick, on occasions, it eliminates isolation from my life. Now I've got a son way down past Eden. Daily I'm in communication with one of his children, sometimes with him when he's in the mood, and we know what we all look like. Yeah, *marvellous* stuff. He's even been known to send messages from room to room (laughs).

No, but on a serious level, it's opened up my life in *many* ways. Love researching. Plus there's a whole lot of us now that, when it comes to the addiction side of my life—which now doesn't dominate like it did through that era of course 'cause that wouldn't be particularly healthy—but I have really good friends in New York State, you know, because I've never travelled myself overseas, I've got good friends in London, good friends in New York, Boston, and we match up on line. It's marvellous.

RUTH APPS *(1926) also reflects on the changing nature of friendships in later life.*

Friends are important. I have fewer friends now, and that's an age factor. They have died. They've gone into nursing homes. They've got dementia. I have a couple, say half a dozen very close friends much my own age. I also have younger friends. My daughters have had friends whose mothers have died and I've become a substitute mother. I have one in particular. I regard her as a *lovely* friend. She's in her forties and I'll open my front door and she'll be there and she'll say, 'I need a mum.' She'll have had trouble. She comes in and I chat. I regard her as a friend because I love her dearly.

My older friends, sadly, they're diminishing, and that's age. We're all in our eighties. Some have died in their seventies and that kind of thing. So I have fewer friends. I've one friend that I go out with every Thursday. Yes I love them dearly.

Ruth caught the 'travel bug' in her forties and still enjoys overseas travel in her eighties.

WHEN DID I BEGIN TO TRAVEL? 1972 we took our first trip to New Zealand. That was a three-week coach trip—Bill and I took that—that was our first trip out of Australia. We came back and we were bitten by the travel bug. In 1974, we took a cruise up to Tokyo—it was a six-week cruise on a cruise liner—and thoroughly enjoyed that. The next year we went to America and away we went, then the next year we went to Europe on a coach tour—a twenty-one-day coach tour—and that's the last coach tour I've taken. I mean Switzerland on Tuesday and Germany on Thursday was not funny. We thought it looked like a good idea. Since then we've travelled independently largely. You might go to a city and take a day trip out somewhere to see something in particular. But I've travelled widely.

Julie—my daughter—and I now travel together on our own. We use a Eurail pass. We travel to London and then spend some time in England, sometimes with a car, sometimes just around London. Then we get the Eurostar across to Paris and then travel by train all over Europe and we've pretty well covered it. There's always something else to see but we go about every eighteen months. So since about 1980 I've taken a trip away about—overseas that is—about every eighteen months. I love it. I'm spending my children's inheritance on it, and I'm not a bit apologetic.

***MICHAEL BICANIC** (1937) from north-east Tasmania relishes the 'shack life' on the east coast.*

I used to love a lot of trout fishing. I used to go up at lakes, Lake Pedder, I just like any lakes up in the highlands. Our car got a lot of use the way we were trout fishing. Now a friend of mine, he had a little shack at the east coast, Ansell's Bay, close to St Helens. He drive me one day, a few of us went to there and bream fishing, trevally, and the salmon. I thought, 'That's not bad. That's not far away.' Want to go from Scottsdale to Lake Pedder and back, that's a day's drive. Up here it's only one hour. Then I bought myself caravan. The kids was little. We used to go stay in a caravan. Put a little tent. Kids, they love it there, bit of sand and things. I built a shack. Put two rooms, a new bathroom, everything, because I own now land.

I go every weekend. This year I miss two weekends. After this interview—I'm packed up—I'm going to my shack. Put my boat in, do some fishing. Enjoy my time.

Ben Ross: So you spend your time there on your own mostly?

Mostly on my own because wife still teaching three days a week. She comes every third weekend. But I go every weekend. I love it. That's the country life, if you like it. Some will like city life. Not for me. Good day, you put a boat in. You see a few mates there and go fishing. Tomorrow night, tomorrow day maybe. 'Oh', he said. 'We take my boat'. Sunday we go through the channel out on the sea after tuna and things like that, where they're running, big fish. We just catch them for fun. I like eating the little fish. Nice and sweet.

Otherwise if you don't do fishing you maybe go with the boys, say a few drinks, barbecues. Go in the bush, cut a bit of wood. Sometimes I go a bit of hunting. Take the dogs, go in the bush. We take about three or four Cocker Spaniels. They're good for rough country because they don't jump, they go under bush. That's the type of dogs. Get the rabbits, wallabies, whatever you're allowed to hunt for. If you know the rules—the laws—well you never get in trouble. And well, that's the shack life. You know, just living the shack life.

Ageing Bodies

*Former journalist **BERT CASTELLARI**'s (1923) hearing was affected by his war service in a tank regiment.*

I look after myself. I eat a good diet. I'm a good, plain cook. I'm interested in food but I don't go in for anything fancy. Food is fuel. Food keeps you going, keeps your faculties in condition, so you can then do the things that matter.

There are a lot of things I'd like to participate in but then it comes back to hearing. You lose your hearing, you've lost a lot. It's cost me music. It cost me a lot of things like the Senate lectures. And I don't always hear them very well, but at least they put a transcript on the net. I go because I like to see the people, even if I have to read what they've said later. I would go to more of those things but I'm not going to be able to get a transcript or be able to hear participation. I'd like to be active but also—again—hearing is a real problem because I can't keep saying to people, 'I'm sorry, I didn't hear that.' I've got to surrender that.

***RUTH APPS** (1926) explains how she deals with her ageing mind and body.*

Memory is terribly important. At the moment I think my memory is fading a *little* bit but I work *very* hard on it. I do memory exercises. I do cryptic and ordinary crosswords and puzzles, which make you work hard at 'what was that word?' So I think you work on your memory. If you don't work on your memory it goes. Use it or lose it is perfectly true.

But if you can't remember what you did as a child you've lost that joy, or sorrow, whichever it happens to be. It's heartbreaking for me to visit my friends whose memory has gone and to see them look right through me, and have *no* memory of who I am. You ask them, 'What did you have for lunch?' and they can't remember. Sometimes they can remember back when they were children. I mean that's dementia, Alzheimer's and so on.

I *dread* that I might lose my memory—although they tell me I'm almost too old now, I'll only lose a little bit of memory—in any case I won't care, but I think I will care. I love my memory and when you think of people who've died—like a husband or whatever—if I couldn't remember the good times and the bad times and the argument times that we had, I'd be all the poorer for it.

Now I acknowledge I am eighty-six. I've got wrinkles. I can't walk as fast as you—I used to. I'll acknowledge that situation of age. All my heart and liver and kidneys, everything, have been working hard for a long time. So I pop the necessary pills, but then I go for a walk. Old age is what you make it. I know illness strikes and my husband died at seventy-six from cancer. He had no choice in that but right up till—he was diagnosed four months before he died—right up until that four months prior he was out and about and mowing lawns and doing things. In other words letting old age be there but not rule his life.

You can let old age rule your life or you can say, 'I'll go out swinging.' There's a joke in the family that says, 'As they carry my coffin out of the cathedral, I'll be knocking on the lid saying, "Doesn't anyone want something done?"' I think that's it, old age is what you make it. I'll die, and I accept that, and I have *no* worries about it because I've had a wow of a time. Dying doesn't worry me.

*A second car accident a few years before her interview in 2012, and then an assault by a burglar, significantly affected **CONNIE SHAW**'s (1937) mobility.*

The hip was just giving way because there was nothing to hold it. In hospital they said I had to put up with it because I was too old, too old to have the surgery, it wouldn't be guaranteed and that sort of things. But considering that most people in my family live a fairly long time, I just couldn't cope with that, so I ended up seeing a surgeon that specialises in hips. I went and saw him privately. I had it operated on privately in June and of course then I had to keep quiet for three months and now I have to learn to use the muscles again. Hopefully enough to get back to playing croquet (laughs).

I have concerns that I will probably end up in a wheelchair and that's going to be very awkward. I don't really want to bother my kids (laughs) when it's all boiled down. But I suppose, to a certain extent, I will probably at some time have to rely to a reasonable amount on them. I'm very lucky, I have the services from the Silver Chain [a not-for-profit which delivers home-based care] which are very helpful and that makes it possible for me to live here. They have done that for a long time, and it's very much appreciated. I've had times when I've been on the floor, not been able to get up, but I know somebody's coming in the morning and I'll be all right so there's no real reason to panic or anything like that.

I thought I was going to lose my sight and that's why you see me binding everything in bundles so nothing gets lost. I had one eye that wasn't very good. But the other one was fine. All of a sudden, everything started going out of shape. I panicked. There was a bit of shrapnel in the eye and it shifted and it went across the back of the eye. I needed surgery on that, and then after that cataracts. Really went downhill and for a while there it was quite a big worry that I would lose my eyesight, because what am I going to do with computers and things (laughs)? It's still a bit of a worry because I've still got a hole in the retina and one of the cataracts didn't work very well. I'm afraid he was a learner and it went wrong. But I think it's going to be all right. It should last me out (laughs).

ALISON FETTELL *(1952) learnt about the dependence of frail old age when she was caring for her dying mother.*

It was interesting when I was caring for mum—showering her and wiping her bottom and doing all those things that you do, because there's very little control—she was sitting on the edge of the bed and I was trying to get her knickers on and we were *laughing* our heads off about it, 'cause I couldn't get her foot in, right. So we were trying to do this and she said, 'Who'd have thought this was gonna happen?' I looked at her and I went, 'Yeah, who'd have dreamed it'd be me that'd be looking after you like this?' She said, 'So who do you reckon's going to do it for you?' We both looked at each other and we said, 'Probably Casey [Alison's youngest child].' So poor Case (laughs).

But I don't really have that expectation—not really. But Casey and I talk a lot. We bore the grandchildren to sleep—we talk so much. She'll talk to me about everything, I talk to her about everything. It's just one of those things.

Roslyn Burge: Have you talked about ageing with her—getting older?

Yes, I have. Both Jayne and I have got very clear wills and very clear direction and the two girls are our, I forget what you call it, like guardians.

Death

***KATHLEEN GOLDER** (1920) reflects on death.*

> They say grow old gracefully, well, that's a bit difficult at times. I feel fine about growing old and I say often, I am fine. I get my aches and I get my pains and I've had some problems—medical problems—but I've got over them all. Another day's another day tomorrow, and I'll eat and drink tonight and I'll be happy, and God knows what's happening tomorrow. I wouldn't have a clue. So I just choose to be myself and enjoy the necessary things to be happy. Cup of tea, whatever.

Ben Ross: Do you think about death?

> Oh yes, often. I say to myself, 'Well, if there's anything there, well I'll soon know.' In the meantime, I don't know. Neither does anybody else. If it's the end, when I've hit a brick wall and that's it, well that's it. I've been, come and gone. It's what is here now. My kids can sort all this out. Whatever. I think about it but I don't think about it in a morbid way. I don't dwell on it. It's not anything to be dour—Scottish word isn't that one—dour about. And what can you do about it? It's going to come to us all. And there's billions, trillions before us have come and gone, so, so what. So, I'm not going to think about it now. Not going to keep me awake tonight (laughs).

*At eighty-six, **RUTH APPS** (1926) knows that 'immortality is fast approaching'.*

> Up until, let's say about seventy, you're sure you're never going to die. You know in the back of your mind you're going to die.

What happens at around seventy is your peers and friends start to die and, obviously it accelerates. You know your immortality is fast approaching. At eighty-six, say I live to be a hundred—say—that's only fourteen years off. I look back fourteen years and it's gone nowhere, gone nowhere at all. So the time ahead of me is limited.

I am not the *least* bit worried. I would like to die comfortably. In other words I don't want to die in pain. I've told my doctor that, that I expect him to give me enough pills so that I'm not thrashing around on my deathbed. But as for closing my eyes and going to heaven it does not bother me one little bit. I accept that it is going to happen, and it'll happen sooner rather than later, and when it does, well, all I want is a really good send-off. I want hymns and flowers, the whole lot (laughs).

GINETTE MATALON *(1936) plans not to die.*

I'm never going to die. I've decided. To which my sons say, 'You'll be very bored, mum. You won't have anybody to talk to, to play cards.' But I've decided I'm not dying, so there's your answer, I'm eternal.

At this stage in my life, I'm not old. I'm not even a senior. So I'm --- at this stage in my life, I'm not old. I can't tell you how I'll be in ten years, fifteen years. I'm definitely not dying. My aim is to keep myself healthy. I'm not going to die. And I'll have to establish good relationship with younger generations.

I don't like death, the separation. Death creates separation. No, I don't like death at all. No, the people who tell you, 'I'm not afraid of death' and so on—it's their business. But I am not afraid of death because I know that I'm never going to die.

***LYNNE SANDERS-BRAITHWAITE** (1949) has a cinematic take on mortality.*

This year's been a bit of a rattler. I think my sister's death—'cause she was my younger sister—and now my ex-husband is critically ill, I *definitely* got scared somewhere in that, going, 'Oh what if I die suddenly?'

What I feel like—when I was a little girl we used to go to Campsie picture theatre, which is the next suburb to Belmore. I think it was the Odeon or one of those wonderful things with scrolls out the front. So in we'd go—this is as young teenagers—Elvis Presley was out and it was *Fun in Acapulco.* At the front near the screen was a clock, so you knew when the movie was going to end, and it was quarter past something and the movie was going to end at half past. Elvis was up there on the screen and I remember thinking, 'I have to get, someone has to stop the clock, I don't want this to end.' That's what I feel like with my life at the moment. It's like, 'Oh no, it's quarter past, I don't want it to reach half past. I still want to stay at *Fun at Aca*—I haven't seen him dive off the cliff yet.'

That's what I feel like my life is at the moment. It's like, I'm just getting the knack of this, you know, hang on.

Further Listening on Later Life

Kathleen Golder, 1920, http://nla.gov.au/nla.obj-219908851/listen/5-2633
Bert Castellari, 1923, http://www.nla.gov.au/amad/nla.oh-vn6252044/4-2088
Fred Henskens, 1929, http://nla.gov.au/nla.obj-219905240/listen/1-4826
Trish Barrkman, 1933, http://nla.gov.au/nla.obj-219822018/listen/0-7663
Ginette Matalon, 1936, http://nla.gov.au/nla.obj-219968733/listen/2-4919
James Box, 1946, http://nla.gov.au/nla.obj-219919883/listen/2-6360
Ronnie Gauci, 1947, http://nla.gov.au/nla.obj-219987144/listen/2-1607
Geraldine Box, 1949, http://nla.gov.au/nla.obj-219847431/listen/3-340
Peter Galvin, 1951, http://www.nla.gov.au/amad/nla.oh-vn6252046/2-3143
Alison Fettell, 1952, http://nla.gov.au/nla.obj-220185705/listen/2-5156

Further Reading on Later Life

Bornat, Joanna, 'Remembering and reworking emotions: the reanalysis of emotion in an interview', *Oral History* 38, no. 2 (2010), pp. 43–52.

Davison, Graeme, '"Our youth is spent and our backs are bent": the origins of Australian ageism', *Australian Cultural History* 14 (1995), pp. 40–62.

Feldman, Susan, Kamler, Barbara and Snyder, Ilana (eds), *Something that Happens to Other People: Stories of Women Growing Older* (Milsons Point: Vintage, 1996).

Hunter, Cecily, 'The concept of successful ageing: a contribution to a history of old age in modern Australia', *History Australia* 5, no. 2 (2008), pp. 42.1–42.15.

Jalland, Pat, *Old Age in Australia: A History* (Melbourne: Melbourne University Press, 2014).

Jalland, Pat, *Changing Ways of Death in Twentieth-Century Australia: War, Medicine and the Funeral Business* (Sydney: University of New South Wales Press, 2006).

Peel, Dawn, 'Towards a history of old age in Australia', *Australian Historical Studies* 32, no. 117 (2001), pp. 257–275.

Reiger, Kerreen and James, Margaret, 'Hatches, Matches and Despatches', in Verity Burgmann and Jenny Lee (eds), *Constructing a Culture: A People's History of Australia since 1788* (Melbourne: McPhee Gribble /Penguin, 1988), pp. 1–17.

Singer, Renata, *Older and Bolder: Life after 60* (Melbourne: Melbourne University Press, 2015).

Thane, Pat, *The Long History of Old Age* (London: Thames & Hudson, 2005).

CHAPTER 9

TELLING MY STORY

In this final chapter our narrators reflect on motivations for recording their life story (usually a brief response to a question at the start of the interview) and on the experience of remembering and recounting their life (often a longer response to a question at the end of the interview). The extracts in this book are just a fraction from the interviews produced by the Australian Generations Oral History Project. Australian Generations narrators were creating a historical record and they wanted that record to include the 'ordinary person's stories' that are often missing in history because, as Lynne Sanders-Braithwaite explains, 'they matter a lot'. Our older narrators want to set down their story for family and for the next generation of Australians. As Peter Galvin concludes, 'one generation should pass on their knowledge and skills to the next generation'. Ruth Apps believes that 'the voice of myself as an eighty-six-year-old should be heard. I think we did set up a lot of things here in this country.' Ruth wishes that life stories like hers had been recorded 'back when my grandparents or great-grandparents were around because you try to get historical facts and you can't always get them'.

Though the imperative to create an enduring record may be especially strong in later life, some young Australians also want to produce an archived account of their life and times. Adam Farrow-Palmer, born in 1988, likes 'the idea that in maybe a hundred years someone could listen and hear about my life to learn about what living in 2012, 2013 was like. That's really cool. They could go back and I would be contributing my experience to that historical account'.

Some narrators hope to convey social and political lessons from the past. Bronwyn Macdonald, for example, believes passionately that her son's experience of living with profound disability, and that of his family and other carers, 'needs to be examined' so that it will not 'always be like this'.

Aboriginal narrators are perhaps especially keen to record their history and culture. Lisa Jackson, born in 1972, notes that while the stories of the older Stolen Generations are becoming common knowledge, it is also '*important* for people to understand Aboriginal people of my generation' and 'the struggles that we've been through'. For one of our youngest narrators, Arthur Hunter from the Kimberley, 'talking about my culture and my history [makes me] *happy* cause I'm doing it because I'm getting my story out there for people to actually look at or listen to'.

Others trust that the stories of their own travails might help another person facing similar problems in their life. Donat Santowiak battled alcoholism for many years and his interview details the causes and consequences of addiction and his efforts to stay sober. Donat's story is awful *and* inspirational and, as he concludes, 'sometimes it can be just a very seemingly insignificant remark or something that might have a light-bulb moment for someone and be useful'. In the same spirit, Kim Bear reminds us that people connect and learn from each other through the stories we share. Stories are 'a great way to inform people about what it is to be human. Even if you say one thing that resonates with them, there's that connection made.'

Recording your life story may be a rewarding pleasure, but it is not always easy. For Donat Santowiak it was 'liberating' to tell the world 'this is who I am', but he also encountered a 'rollercoaster' of emotions triggered by difficult memories. Some narrators had sleepless nights between the first and second interview sessions. Rhonda King had 'trouble sleeping because I was remembering some really horrific events that happened in my life that we didn't speak about but it made it hard for me to sleep because I was remembering what happened'. David Cooper slept poorly after the first day of recording because 'I kept thinking about things that I hadn't thought about'. Yet David enjoyed the interview and appreciated the opportunity to 'think more deeply about things --- you verbalise something and it can put things back into perspective'. Through narrating our experiences we often make better sense of our life.

Narrators for the Australian Generations project appreciated how a skilled interviewer often helped them stretch and deepen their story, sometimes in unexpected ways. Rhonda King thanks Mary Hutchison for not 'injecting *your* judgment and your ideas and "Why didn't you do this, you *idiot*, what a stupid thought that was!"' Mary 'asked the questions and let the answers come out however they do come out', she let tangents flow and she asked 'hard questions' that 'awakened' Rhonda's memories and reflections. Lynne Sanders-Braithwaite knows that Jo Kijas' respectful presence, her questions, and the expectation of frankness and intimacy, made a difference to the story Lynne told. For Lynne 'the bit where ego wants to say a certain thing that sounds right instead of saying what is right or what really happened or how I feel' was 'fairly challenging. It's been delightful which is different from enjoyable.' Of course we can never be absolutely sure that any narrator is not misremembering or even fabricating an episode in their life. We all try to create a past we can live with, and sometimes we smooth over jagged edges and skip past difficult times. Our impression, however, is that the Australian Generations interviewees tried hard to be open and honest about their lives, warts and all.

It's probably easier to be frank about your life when it has turned out well. Donat Santowiak and Lynne Sanders-Braithwaite, for example, tell their excruciating stories about addiction from the standpoint of recovery and well-being. The many stories we recorded about mental ill-health were usually told when treatment was successful or the worst was over. People in the pits of despair were not likely to volunteer to be interviewed for our project (in a few cases we also decided against an interview when it seemed that professional care or counselling was more appropriate). Yet many people were determined—with great courage—to tell painful, embarrassing or even shameful stories from their lives. They wanted those stories on the record, though to protect themselves and others they sometimes decided to restrict access to the interview. Just under a third of the Australian Generations interviews are closed for a specified time period or are not available online. In due course, those interviews will become available and will add another layer of historical experience.

***RUTH APPS** (1926) considers the value of recording her experiences.*

> I think it's an interesting project in that I think the voice of myself as an eighty-six-year-old should be heard. I think we did set up a lot of things here in this country and I think it will be *useful*. I honestly wish that we had something like that back when my grandparents or great-grandparents were around because you try to resource, you try to get historical facts and you can't always get them.

Frank Heimans: **HAVE YOUR GRANDCHILDREN** *ever asked you for any advice, being an elder?*

They don't ask for general advice but they love to come and tell me --- see they're all university graduates or working, that type of thing. They always bring the partner—those who have—to see me. They say they love my stories. They'll sit there for hours. Some of those stories I've been telling you which are pretty trite really but they're things that they have never experienced. They have never walked to an orchard to get fruit to preserve, and they love my stories and whether that's advice or just something I don't know.

PETER GALVIN*'s (1951) family prompted his participation in this oral history project.*

The main reason was that I'd been pestered by my children, the three of them, into retelling or writing down the events that formed my life. Because I'd led, in their eyes I'd led a very interesting life. So when this came up, my wife read about it and she said, 'This is the sort of thing that you should do.' As a believer in that one generation should pass on their knowledge and their skills to the next generation, I thought 'Well okay, I'll give that a go.'

BRONWYN MACDONALD *(1964) considers what motivated* her *to share her story.*

When I first heard about the project I just thought it was an important way of recording my background and my current state. I just think that people should know firstly about my father's story because that's still held under the Secrecies

Act[1] and it worries me that the generations will die out before that information is shared. Secondly, I think that living with a disability in Australia is something that needs to be examined and I don't think that times will always be like this. I think that it's really going to change and it would be interesting to look back at how it was now.

LISA JACKSON*'s (1972) contribution was propelled by a desire to increase public understanding about Aboriginal lives.*

I became interested in this project because I think it's *important* for people to understand Aboriginal people of my generation. There's not a lot of stories out there about my generation and about the struggles that we've been through. I think it's important for people to know, to see that gap between --- well, the Stolen Generations and what happened with them but also future generations or the current generation which is what is happening now. So there's a bit of a *gap*, well in knowledge, from my perspective anyway. So I thought it was important for people to know that.

ADAM FARROW-PALMER *(1988) explains what drew him to the project.*

I saw an interview about it on the radio. They were calling out for people to join up and I really like the idea that in maybe a hundred years someone could listen and hear about my life to learn about what living in 2012 or 2013 was like. Think that's

1 Britain's Official Secrets Act protects state secrets. **BRONWYN'S FATHER** was one of the 'Dunera Boys'. He was a German Jew who came to Australia (via England) on the *Dunera* during World War II. He was interned at the Hay Internment Camp in southern New South Wales.

really cool. They could go back and I would be contributing my experience to that historical account.

GINETTE MATALON *(1936) recalls preparing for her interview.*

It's been very good. I enjoyed also the preparation for it, I must tell you. I worked a lot with my son Steve in finding all the documents because I thought if I couldn't remember a date or something, I had to find the --- exactly what had happened or I could neglect some vital part of my life. So we sorted out all the paperwork and it gave me pleasure to sort out and to look back into my past and so on. So it was good. It was a bit emotional looking for old photos, documents. Not many photos because amongst the things that we couldn't take out of Egypt were photos. So a few years later I wrote to my uncle—the one who stayed in Egypt—I said, 'Could you send me some photos?' He thought that this was a password for money. He says, 'We're not allowed (laughs) to send photos out of Egypt.' But I have very very little, very few photos of my childhood days in Egypt.

For ***GREER BLAND*** *(1944), this interview was a chance to begin documenting her memories.*

You don't go through your life in a few hours every day in your life so it's been fantastic. I've always wanted to do it and I guess this was, having someone record it for me was a good start if I ever decide to put these words down for my nieces and nephews who have been nagging me for quite some time. As a senior member of the family now and probably still with a fairly good memory of what went on over the generations, I'll be able to pass on to them. So, it's been very helpful to me in that regard. I'm glad I did it.

Catherine McLennan: Thank you so much, it's been really fantastic.

***LYNNE SANDERS-BRAITHWAITE** (1949) explains the challenges of narrating her story frankly to her interviewer Jo Kijas.*

I --- enjoyed is the wrong word. When I first saw it advertised, I thought it was a *really* important project, as I still do. I think that the ordinary person's stories matter a lot. So I sent in a little application which if it wasn't for the Internet I wouldn't have sent. What I didn't expect was when I knew it was actually coming up, to find it so intimidating. I didn't, *did not* expect that at all. I thought, 'Oh yeah, I can do that standing on one leg, that's easy.' I don't ask people into my home very often. 'Oh someone's actually going to come into my home space.' But it's proven to be really moving, challenging. I think—Jo and I were talking before—the bit where ego wants to say a certain thing that sounds right instead of saying what is right or what really happened or how I feel. I found that fairly challenging. It's been delightful which is different from enjoyable.

Lovely to get a chance to talk and to get a perspective on a generation. I think it's an exciting generation that I've lived through. I'm really grateful for the actual age group I lived through. I think I'll be grateful for the next phase too. It's nice being, not the centre of attention, but being really *heard*. I am actually accustomed to that, 'cause I have the good fortune to be in a situation where I often do that in smaller doses. But to sit there and chronologically do my life right through, I think this is the sort of thing that will assimilate over the next few months in me. I think I'll get a more sequential picture of my own life again and particularly in so far as where it fits into the generation and into my place and time and my people. Because I'm sixty-three next month, probably angrier and more radical politically than I've ever been because when I was a young woman I lacked the courage to act out on that. There's a couple of the young fellas on Facebook who say they're looking forward to meeting me and I said, 'I don't think we'll probably meet' because they live too far away. They said, 'At the rate we're going, we'll meet in the same gaol' (laughs).

DONAT SANTOWIAK *(1950) reflects on remembering and narrating his life story.*

What do they say? This is not a speech but they say there's always three speeches that we make. There's the one that we intend to make, there's the one we make, and then there's the one we wish we had made. That's just natural. So probably in reflection I might think, 'I wish I maybe said this or maybe didn't say that' but as we speak I'm contented and grateful for the opportunity to have shared this.

Alistair Thomson: M'mm. That segues neatly into what's often the last ***question I ask in an interview which is: really, what's it been like for you remembering and telling the story of your life?***

Well, internally there's been some rollercoaster moments in terms of some emotions surfacing that a memory might have been attached with. I think in some ways it's liberating 'cause again it's part of telling the world, 'Well this is who I am and, like it, great, don't like it, well then bad luck.' This is who I am. I don't know what anybody would get out of anything, we never know. But sometimes it can be just a very seemingly insignificant remark or something that might have a light-bulb moment for someone and be useful in some --- yeah.

KIM BEAR *(1959) reflects on interpreting and sharing her experiences through aural and written modes of storytelling.*

You can tell I like telling --- I enjoy stories. I like stories. I think stories are a great way to inform people about what it is to be human. Even if you say one thing that resonates with them, there's that connection made. I like hearing other people talk about, I'm very interested in how you can change your opinions based on somebody else's experience or 'Oh that had never occurred to me.' The way that it expands your thinking and in a way it makes you more human I think. Enjoying stories and listening to stories and telling stories is a good thing. So yes, writing is probably the *best* possible channel for me.

I've written for a very long time. I kept diaries and journals and at the New Guinea phase was particularly interesting because I can't *believe* how totally buttoned down I was at twenty-one. I found a diary from then not long ago where I'd set myself the task of making sure I wrote something every single day and discovered how much food I ate and how many things I tried to cook (laughs). But apart from that there wasn't a lot of other excitement going on. It just felt like this very strange reportage. But every now and again I'd make some comment about something that had happened. But I was an old woman in those books. It was amazing, and how astonishingly content I was within those boundaries. It really shocks me now when I look at it. I don't imagine that could've ever happened to me other than at that age. That was the funny thing, like I'd leapfrogged into middle age when I hadn't even been out of my teens.

I was also a *huge* letter writer. I had a number of people that I'd dash off these twenty-three page letters too. It was funny, one person—a very close girlfriend from school—and when I left school and then left the Gold Coast, I would sit down religiously every Saturday morning with my ashtray (laughs) and my cigarettes, and my very very to then times expensive writing paper because I love the act of writing and I love making beautiful letters. Every Saturday I would write pages and pages and pages to Louise. I think what I was trying to do was to take her on my new life with me because she was still at school and she was still on the Gold Coast and she still had the same boyfriend, and I felt like there was just this amazing other world out there that she and I'd certainly never talked and nor have we experienced it.

I wrote lots of letters to my grandmother, not so *long* because grandma wrote often but only little short amounts. She didn't always necessarily agree with things I would write to her about so I used to have to censor grandma's letters a fair bit. I wrote for a long time to my mum but didn't get a *reply* during that period.

Letters are you writing about your life. So this is probably why this [interview] doesn't feel like a very unusual thing for me to do because in the *writing* of it and the thinking on it you really begin to try and understand what you're making of it. I liked to make people laugh. I really enjoyed that side of writing. I know that in the writing time particularly to my girlfriend, there must've been *boxes* of letters. I'd seal them with wax seals, or I'd have special pens and I made such a to-do about stationary it wasn't funny. But I realised at one point in time, I was the only one who did that. Everyone's letters that came back to me were torn out of notepads and they would always start off the letter apologising for about their writing (laughs). I used to think, 'Boy I'm a hard taskmaster aren't I?' But I remember I've kept every letter I've ever received.

DAVID COOPER *(1959) considers how sharing* his *story prompted him to review his experiences.*

It makes you think. It's been good. It was good having the two days' gap in between, because that first night I just, I didn't sleep that well that night because I kept thinking about things that I hadn't thought about. Then it made me realise, no it wasn't the whole five years that I was at high school that I hated it, it was only the last three years. So it made me think more deeply about things. So in some ways it's like a bit of a counselling session too and you verbalise something and it can put things back into perspective. So it's been good from that point of view. Yeah so I've actually enjoyed it.

Of course everyone worries that they've said the wrong thing or they've made themselves look like an idiot but I'm a bit past that now. If people think I'm an idiot, they think I'm an idiot. So it's been good, I'm glad I've done it. The next stage will be interesting to see, where my wife and kids—'cause there will be things I would have told you that I've never said to them—so that will be interesting to see their reactions. That will be really interesting to see their reactions.

I have enjoyed it and I do like the idea of your ancestors at some stage in the future getting a bit of a window into what one of their grandfather or whatever was like. I like that concept of it. In fact, that concept's the most appealing bit, because you'd be dead by then, doesn't matter what they think (laughs). I think it's a good idea. I'll be interested to see what other people have said to you and have the things that I've said fit perfectly with everybody else or am I really weird and am I the only person that thinks those things that I've said. So from that point of view it's been good. But I definitely have enjoyed it.

RHONDA KING *(1965) contemplates the multi-faceted nature of her life story and how her interview has prompted reflection and family connection.*

Mary Hutchison: Is there anything that you think we've left out of this interview?

Oh my gosh there's so much but there's no way I'm going to (laughs) go into it otherwise we'll be here for another five days. There are lots of little bits and pieces that just --- I'm reminded of when we speak and I just think, 'Wow, that ---' Like I was saying to you last night, I had trouble sleeping because I was remembering some really horrific events that happened in my life that we didn't speak about but it made it hard for me to sleep because I was remembering what happened. There's a lot. Life is long. When you're forty-eight, there's been a lot of stuff that's happened (laughs).

I'd always thought my life would make an interesting book—maybe not the whole life—or a movie (laughs). But bits and pieces of it, I can see them being in movies and people going, 'Oh no, don't do it, don't do it! Oh she did it.' Like George off *Seinfeld*—'No, George, no! Oh George (laughs).' It's got elements of comedy and there are elements of heartache and drama and thriller and it's got so many things in it. A few times I've tried to write my own story but it's just so complex and so many angles and tangents everywhere that it became a task that I just didn't know if I could manage. I thought, 'Oh the opportunity to have someone interview me and have it recorded, and interview me that they're not a person who knows my life, they're just coming at it from a researcher perspective so ---' It becomes more --- it's easier to grasp it all in that way I think. So I thought, 'It'd be great to have that recording done and then I guess I can get a copy of it sometime and I can listen back to it. Maybe I can transcribe it and then I *can* write my own book.' I don't know (laughs).

So what's your experience of it then, having done this?

Oh it's been really good. I've really enjoyed the way that you've done the interview because you haven't decided that you're going to start injecting *your* judgment and your ideas and 'Why didn't you do this, you *idiot*, what a stupid thought that was!' So you've just asked the questions and let the answers come out however they do come out. You've allowed the tangents to happen as well. Sometimes I know you've asked me a question and I'm like, 'How am I on this subject (laughs)? Did you ask that question? I don't think so.' So you allowed the natural progression—if you want to call it that—to happen. You've asked some hard questions and I think I've been able to answer them okay. It's been good because like I said, it's awakened --- it's come at a good time because as I said to you, crossroads of faith, just receiving all my things home from America after that upheaval of my life seven years ago. It's like that seven-year mark—oh, what happens next? So it's almost been an opportunity to reflect on my life, where I've come from. It gave me a chance to talk to my mum, not that I don't talk to her, but to ask her those questions, '*When* did you actually get married? And *when* was Julie actually born? And *when* did she actually die?' So it's allowed that reconnection as well which has been really good, so I've really enjoyed it.

***SUZIE QUARTERMAIN** (1975) considers how she has dealt with challenges in what has been a good life punctuated with grief.*

I hope I haven't overloaded you with too much negativity.

Katie Holmes: No. For me it's a real privilege to talk with people about their lives. Obviously there's a huge amount of sadness in yours but I'm really thankful that you've felt able to talk about it and to share it.

Yeah. It's funny 'cause if people asked me what kind of life I've had I'd say it's been a good life. Which goes against everything I've just said and it goes against everything that I feel—'cause it hasn't been a bad life, just bad things have happened. In between those bad things there's been good stuff. I think having a good childhood makes it feel like a good life.

Well it gives you a good foundation doesn't it?

It certainly does. My mum and dad gave me coping skills, which I am big on giving Ava. Because you can't stop bad stuff happening to your kids but you can teach 'em how to cope. That's all you can do and that's what they did for me.

What a gift.

Absolutely. I've needed it (laughs).

*For **ARTHUR HUNTER** (1989), telling his story is an opportunity to share his Aboriginal culture and history.*

> I've been waiting for this interview but I didn't think it would be now or in this form. But I'm really glad I'm doing this. To get my word out there and save me saying it all the time to my mate—talking about my culture and my history. I'm talking about it, is actually a step forward for me so I can maybe do something later on. So it's been pretty good. I don't find a shame in doing it. I just feel, I feel *happy* 'cause I'm doing it because I'm getting my story out there for people to actually look at or listen to.

Further Listening on Telling My Story

Fred Henskens, 1929, http://nla.gov.au/nla.obj-219905240/listen/0-46
Veronica Schwarz, 1939, http://www.nla.gov.au/amad/nla.oh-vn6290927/3-2383
Geraldine Box, 1949, http://www.nla.gov.au/amad/nla.oh-vn6190857/3-4735
Russell Elliott, 1950, http://www.nla.gov.au/amad/nla.oh-vn6223258/6-1009~6-1044
Alison Fettell, 1952, http://nla.gov.au/nla.obj-220185705/listen/4-2080
Gina Polito, 1954, http://www.nla.gov.au/amad/nla.oh-vn6421369/3-5433
Ouranita Karadimas, 1958, http://www.nla.gov.au/amad/nla.oh-vn6252080/3-1781
Michelle Cripps, 1960, http://www.nla.gov.au/amad/nla.oh-vn6252075/0-52~0-88
Ian Reid, 1961, http://nla.gov.au/nla.obj-220066743/listen/0-56
James Finnegan, 1981, http://nla.gov.au/nla.obj-220176798/listen/3-1726
Gemma Nourse, 1989, http://nla.gov.au/nla.obj-220049717/listen/2-5225

Further Reading on Telling My Story

Abrams, Lynn, *Oral History Theory* (London and New York: Routledge, second edition, 2016, first published 2010).
Eakin, P. J., *Living Autobiographically: How We Create Identity in Narrative* (New York: Cornell University Press, 2008).
Linde, Charlotte, *Life Stories: The Creation of Coherence* (New York: Oxford University Press, 1993).
Portelli, Alessandro, 'What Makes Oral History Different', in Robert Perks and Alistair Thomson (eds), *The Oral History Reader* (London and New York: Routledge, third edition, 2016), pp. 48–58.

Radstone, Susannah, and Schwarz, Bill (eds), *Memory: Histories, Theories, Debates* (New York: Fordham University Press, 2010).

Roseman, Mark, 'Surviving Memory: Truth and Inaccuracy in Holocaust Testimony', in Robert Perks and Alistair Thomson (eds), *The Oral History Reader* (London and New York: Routledge, third edition, 2016), pp. 320–33.

Thomson, Alistair, 'Memory and Remembering in Oral History', in Donald A. Ritchie (ed.), *The Oxford Handbook to Oral History* (New York: Oxford University Press, 2011), pp. 77–95.

Thomson, Alistair, 'Memory Stories', in *Moving Stories: An Intimate History of Four Women Across Two Countries* (Sydney: University of New South Wales Press, 2011), pp. 295–327.

Yow, Valerie Raleigh, 'Oral history and memory', in *Recording Oral History: A Guide for the Humanities and Social Sciences* (Lanham: Rowman & Littlefield, 2015), pp. 41–76.

ACKNOWLEDGEMENTS

First and foremost, we acknowledge with gratitude the fifty narrators whose life stories are the heart of this book. It was a pleasure and a privilege to work with such rich interviews that were so generously contributed. Beyond the selected fifty, we are grateful to the other 250 people who recorded their life stories for the Australian Generations oral history project. Those life stories are no less valuable—we just didn't have room in the book for them all.

Oral history interviews are created in a relationship between interviewer and interviewee, and are shaped by the quality of that relationship and the skill of the interviewer. We acknowledge with thanks the expertise of all of the **AUSTRALIAN GENERATIONS INTERVIEWERS**: Atem Atem, Jeannine Baker, John Bannister, Roslyn Burge, Nicole Curby, Peter Donovan, Catherine Forge (nee McLennan), Karen George, Suzanne Gibson, Frank Heimans, Matthew Higgins, Katie Holmes, Mary Hutchison, Jo Kijas, Jill Kitson, Susan Marsden, Siobhan McHugh, Seamus O'Hanlon, Elaine Rabbitt, Kerreen Reiger, Sarah Rood, Ben Ross, Hamish Sewell, Matthew Stephen, Alistair Thomson, Elena Volkova and Rob Willis.

A large team, from several institutions, managed the Australian Generations project. We thank: members of the steering group from the National Library of Australia (Kevin Bradley), ABC Radio National (Michelle Rayner), Monash University (Seamus O'Hanlon, Alistair Thomson and Christina Twomey) and La Trobe University (Katie Holmes and Kerreen Reiger); the two project officers who administered the project (Kate James and Anisa Puri); our graduate students Nicole Curby and Cath Forge, who created excellent interviews and whose reflections on methodology were invaluable; and several research assistants including Johnny Bell (who drafted the further reading list), Jennifer Bowen (who produced many of the ABC radio programs), Aparna Ananthuni (who crafted interview summaries) and Justine Vincin (who created a Historypin map of interviews).

Behind the scenes, the project received support from several Monash administrative colleagues, including: Deepa Balakrishnan, Tom Bolton, Alice Davies, Tommy Fung, Silvie Luscombe and Lyndall Sargent. We were also guided by a national advisory team comprising oral history experts from several states: Jill Cassidy, Jan Gothard, June Edwards, Marsali Mackinnon and Janis Wilton; and an international advisory group: Joanna Bornat, Alexander Freund, Sean Field, Paula Hamilton, Alessandro Portelli, Rob Perks, Peter Spearritt and Lynette Russell. Monash University journalism academic Mia Lindgren offered expert advice about radio oral history. The Australian Generations project was funded by an Australian Research Council Linkage Grant (LP100200270), supplemented with financial and in-kind contributions from the National Library of Australia, ABC Radio National, Monash University and La Trobe University.

Staff in the National Library's wonderful Oral History and Folklore team archived the Australian Generations interviews, administered the transcription of the interviews featured in this book and offered trouble-shooting advice as we used the Library's pioneering audio delivery system. Many thanks to David Blanken, Hannah Gason, Shelly Grant, Rhys Kay and Simone Lark.

Friends and colleagues offered insightful comments on drafts of this book. Thanks to members of Alistair's Monash Research Group, the Melbourne Life Writers Group (Ian Britain, Susan Foley, Ruth Ford, Jim Hammerton, Katie Holmes, Jim Mitchell, John Rickard and Chips Sowerwine) and Sian Edwards, Bryn Thomson, Judy Thomson, and Lilli Thomson. Thanks also to Anjali Puri, Lalit Puri, Fatima Al Rayes, Thomas McAuley, Ajai Chopra and Elliot Livingston.

NARRATOR INDEX

The TRC number will locate the interview within the National Library of Australia's catalogue. Online readers can click on the url to listen to the interview.

GERALDINE BOX, born 1949 in Blackheath, New South Wales, interviewed by John Bannister in Perth on 17 January and 8 February 2012, TRC 6300/36, http://nla.gov.au/nla.obj-219847431/listen
16, 51, 85, 93, 95–6, 102–3, 125, 127, 128, 169, 186–7, 194, 265, 316–17, 323, 329, 379, 394

JAMES BOX, born 1946 in Corowa, New South Wales, interviewed by Frank Heimans in Sydney on 24 and 27 July 2012, TRC 6300/90, http://nla.gov.au/nla.obj-219919883/listen
85, 93, 238, 265, 290–1, 379

RACHEL BROWN (pseudonym), born 1985 in Cebu City, Philippines, interviewed by Elena Volkova in Brisbane on 26 and 28 September 2013 (interview closed at time of publication)
23, 73–4, 96–7, 114–15, 127–9, 177–8, 191–2

BRIAN CARTER, born 1931 in Hopetoun, Victoria, interviewed by Elaine Rabbitt in Ardyaloon (One Arm Point), Kimberley, Western Australia on 11 September 2012, TRC 6300/116, http://nla.gov.au/nla.obj-219958079/listen
93, 119, 125, 162–3, 249

BERTRAM (BERT) CASTELLARI, born 1923 in London, England, interviewed by Matthew Higgins in Canberra on 17 and 18 April 2012, TRC 6300/53, http://nla.gov.au/nla.obj-219871557/listen
51, 129, 137, 194, 196–7, 233, 236, 249–51, 298, 311, 322, 327–8, 353, 373, 379

DAVID COOPER, born 1959 in Bonbeach, Melbourne, interviewed by Alistair Thomson in Melbourne on 12 and 14 March 2013, TRC 6300/160, http://nla.gov.au/nla.obj-220009702/listen
2–3, 11, 24, 45–6, 74, 85, 89–90, 119, 122, 127, 133, 160, 173–4, 189, 204, 228–9, 235–6, 240, 246–7, 272, 286–7, 311, 320, 382, 390–1

LEO CRIPPS, born 1923 in Battery Point, Hobart, interviewed by Ben Ross in Hobart on 20 and 21 October 2012, TRC 6300/106, http://nla.gov.au/nla.obj-219947057/listen
19, 39–40, 160, 194, 200, 239, 273

MICHELLE CRIPPS, born 1960 in Hobart, interviewed by Karen George in Adelaide on 18 and 19 July 2012, TRC 6300/84, http://nla.gov.au/nla.obj-219910905/listen
2, 12, 20, 52, 64–5, 85, 93, 119, 137, 146, 155–6, 179, 233, 240, 265, 272, 291–3, 320, 322, 325, 341–2, 345, 394

RUSSELL ELLIOTT, born 1950 in Maryborough, Victoria, interviewed by Nicole Curby in Avoca, Victoria on 23 and 24 January 2012, TRC 6300/39, http://nla.gov.au/nla.obj-219850973/listen

DONALD GREY-SMITH, born 1931 in Rye, Victoria, interviewed by Peter Donovan in Adelaide on 9 and 10 December 2013, TRC 6300/241, http://nla.gov.au/nla.obj-220110052/listen
23, 27–8, 37, 74, 76–7, 95–6, 103–4, 125, 127, 163–4, 237, 251–2, 255–7, 351, 356–7

FRED HENSKENS, born 1929 in Batavia, Dutch East Indies, interviewed by Matthew Higgins in Canberra on 18 and 19 June 2012, TRC 6300/80, http://nla.gov.au/nla.obj-219905240/listen
19, 33–4, 126, 128, 162, 181, 202, 205–7, 239, 273–4, 311, 351–2, 357, 379, 394

ARTHUR HUNTER, born 1989 in Wyndham, Western Australia, interviewed by Elaine Rabbitt in Broome, Western Australia on 29 August 2012, TRC 6300/115, http://nla.gov.au/nla.obj-219957349/listen
3, 15–16, 20, 23, 25, 50–1, 92–3, 119, 123, 127, 137, 145–6, 160, 178–9, 192–3, 311, 382, 394

LISA JACKSON, born 1972 in Sydney, interviewed by Frank Heimans in Sydney on 22 June and 2 July 2012, TRC 6300/76, http://nla.gov.au/nla.obj-219901040/listen
1, 3, 12–14, 19–20, 23, 34–5, 47–8, 68–9, 74, 82–3, 93, 96, 110–12, 122, 135–6, 160, 179, 249, 311, 318–19, 325, 343–5, 382, 385

JASON JOHNSON, born 1981 in Cairns, Queensland, interviewed by Matthew Higgins in Canberra on 16 and 17 December 2013, TRC 6300/245, http://nla.gov.au/nla.obj-220115636/listen
17, 23, 48–9, 72–3, 83–4, 95, 112–13, 129, 146, 160, 198–200, 272, 296

OURANITA KARADIMAS, born 1958 in Albury, New South Wales, interviewed by Frank Heimans in Sydney on 21 and 28 July 2012, TRC 6300/89, http://nla.gov.au/nla.obj-219918460/listen
2, 9–10, 24–5, 44–5, 81–2, 87–8, 128, 160, 179, 188–9, 205, 225–6, 236, 244–6, 261–2, 284–5, 349, 394

RHONDA KING, born 1965 in Canberra, interviewed by Mary Hutchison in Canberra on 11 and 19 May 2013, TRC 6300/182, http://nla.gov.au/nla.obj-220035263/listen
x, 20–3, 46–7, 65–8, 93, 97, 116–17, 123–4, 126, 137, 140–1, 156, 171–3, 236, 240, 247, 265, 287–8, 311, 314–15, 382–3, 391–3

BARBARA KRICKL, born 1962 in Stuttgart, West Germany, interviewed by Frank Heimans in Sydney on 23 and 26 April 2012, TRC 6300/56, http://nla.gov.au/nla.obj-219875084/listen
37, 93, 119, 179, 204–5, 223–4, 298, 324, 338–40

JAY LOGAN, born 1981 in Nambour, Queensland, interviewed by Matthew Higgins in Canberra on 10 and 11 July 2014, TRC 6300/297, http://nla.gov.au/nla.obj-220182115/listen
22, 52, 71–2, 125, 137, 157–9, 200, 236, 263–4, 298, 311

IAN REID, born 1961 in Adelaide, interviewed by Peter Donovan in Adelaide on 12 and 13 September 2013, TRC 6300/208,
http://nla.gov.au/nla.obj-220066743/listen
16, 24, 52, 74, 82, 93, 96, 107–8, 190, 240, 293, 324, 337–8, 394

LESLIE (LES) ROBINSON, born 1947 in Oyster Bay, Sydney, interviewed by Hamish Sewell in Woodford, Queensland on 7 and 8 April 2014, TRC 6300/271,
http://nla.gov.au/nla.obj-220147383/listen
2, 8, 22, 24, 51, 55–6, 78, 93, 122–4, 127, 131–2, 148, 179, 183, 311, 349

LYNNE SANDERS-BRAITHWAITE, born 1949 in Summer Hill, Sydney, interviewed by Jo Kijas in Raleigh, New South Wales on 16 and 17 September 2012, TRC 6300/100,
http://nla.gov.au/nla.obj-219939572/listen
2, 9, 19–20, 34, 57–8, 85, 93, 125, 137, 152–3, 179, 185–6, 239, 249, 265, 278–80, 352–3, 358–9, 366–8, 370, 379, 381, 383, 387–8

DONAT SANTOWIAK, born 1950 in Katowice, Poland, interviewed by Alistair Thomson in Moe, Victoria on 19 and 20 June 2014, TRC 6300/292,
http://nla.gov.au/nla.obj-220175608/listen
22, 37, 51, 58–60, 124–5, 127–8, 137, 150–2, 179, 184–5, 203–5, 215–9, 239, 241, 265, 277–8, 303–5, 312–13, 349, 382–3, 388

VERONICA SCHWARZ, born 1939 in Darwin, interviewed by Katie Holmes in Brookfield, Victoria on 22 and 25 March 2013, TRC 6300/161,
http://nla.gov.au/nla.obj-220011117/listen
21–2, 28–9, 53–5, 93, 126, 137, 166–8, 194, 236, 241, 252–3, 298, 301–2, 313, 323–4, 333–6, 351, 355–6, 394

CONSTANCE (CONNIE) SHAW, born 1937 in Utrecht, Netherlands, interviewed by John Bannister in Perth on 21 and 23 November 2012, TRC 6300/146,
http://nla.gov.au/nla.obj-219992795/listen
19, 30–2, 93, 128, 182–3, 202–3, 205, 210–11, 241, 249, 298, 302–3, 324–5, 340–1, 353, 375–6

MILIJANA STOJADINOVIC, born 1985 in Stirling, Perth, interviewed by Susan Marsden in Adelaide on 5 November 2011 (interview closed at time of publication)
2, 14–15, 205, 226–8, 236, 247–8, 326, 348–9

KIRSTY WALLETT, born 1982 in Wagga Wagga, New South Wales, interviewed by Hamish Sewell in Brisbane on 17 and 18 April 2013, TRC 6300/170,
http://nla.gov.au/nla.obj-220023172/listen
17, 20, 49–50, 73, 97–8, 118–19, 123, 144–5, 237, 239, 242, 264–5, 297, 310–11, 349

GENERAL INDEX